The Hamlyn Concise Guide to
Military Aircraft
of the World

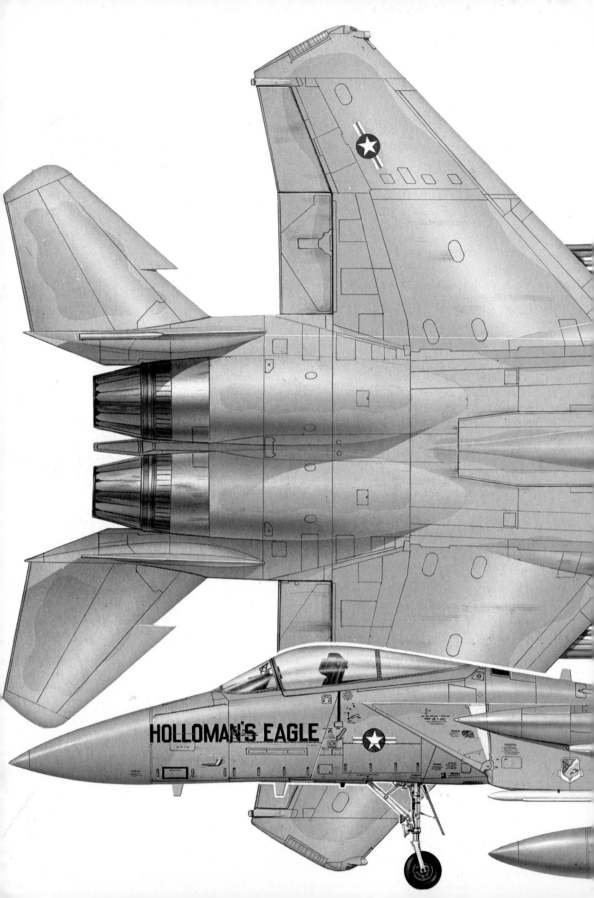

The Hamlyn Concise Guide to
Military Aircraft
of the World
Editor: Chris Chant

Hamlyn/Aerospace
London·New York·Sydney·Toronto

HO

AF
760 49

Published by
The Hamlyn Publishing Group Limited
London · New York · Sydney · Toronto
Astronaut House, Hounslow Road, Feltham,
Middlesex, England

Produced by Stan Morse
Aerospace Publishing Ltd
10, Barley Mow Passage
London W4

First published 1981

ISBN 0 600 34971 3 – Casebound
ISBN 0 600 34966 7 – Paperback

All correspondence concerning the content of
this volume should be addressed to Aerospace
Publishing Ltd. Trade enquiries should be addressed
to the Hamlyn Publishing Group Ltd.

Printed in England

Aeritalia G91R, G91T & G91Y

Aeronautica Militare Italiana G.91T/1 of the Scuola Volo Basico Avanzato Aviogetti at Amendola (Foggia), Italy, 1966.

History and notes

Designed to meet a 1953 NATO requirement for a light tactical support aircraft capable of operations from semi-prepared grass airstrips, the Fiat (later Aeritalia) G91 was based conceptually on the North American F-86K Sabre and first flew on 9 August 1956. The G91 was evaluated against three French contenders during 1957, and adjudged the clear winner. However, the notion that the type be adopted as standard by all NATO air forces failed to materialise, and it was only Italy and West Germany which placed the G91 in production.

Deliveries of the G91 ground-attack model to the Italian air force began in 1958. In the same year the new West German air force also opted for the type, licence production by the Flugzeug Union Süd (Messerschmitt-Dornier-Heinkel) being agreed in 1959.

Several variants of the numerically important G91R series were produced, all similar to the G91 in their ability to carry underwing offensive stores, but fitted with a variety of camera installations in a shortened nose. The G91R/1 first flew in 1959, and was adopted by the Italian air force: it had three 70-mm focal length cameras for front and oblique photography; the G91R/1A was similar, but fitted with improved navigational aids making the type independent of ground installations; and the G91R/1B introduced a reinforced structure, stronger wheel brakes and other equipment changes. The West German air force opted for a variant of the G91R/1B built to German specifications as the G91R/3: this has two 30-mm cannon in place of the four 0.50-in (12.7-mm) machine guns, doppler radar and Position and Homing Indicator equipment. The first West German G91R/3 unit became operational in 1962, and the first German-built G91R/3 flew in 1965. The final G91R variant was the G91R/4, in essence the G91R/3 with an armament fit derived from that of the G91R/1 and some equipment changes.

During 1958 there was developed the G91T, a two-seat advanced trainer with the combat capabilities of the G91. The only significant difference between the G91 and G91T was the latter's lengthened fuselage, necessary to accommodate the instructor's position just aft of and slightly above the pupil's position.

A more radical redesign led to the G91Y, which the Italian air force requested in 1965. The use of two General Electric J85-GE-13A turbojets in place

of the single Bristol Orpheus 803 turbojet boosted power by some 60%: the net result was great reliability extended range, greater payload and other benefits.

Specification (Aeritalia G91Y)

Type: single-seat tactical strike/reconnaissance fighter
Powerplant: two 2,725 lb (1236 kg) dry or 4,080 lb (1850 kg) with afterburning General Electric J85-GE-13A turbojets
Performance: (at maximum take-off weight) maximum speed at sea level Mach 0.93; maximum speed at 30,000 ft (9145 m) Mach 0.95; economical cruising speed at 35,000 ft (10670 m) Mach 0.75; maximum rate of climb at sea level (with afterburning) 17,000 ft (5180 m) per minute; service ceiling 41,000 ft (12500 m); take-off to 50 ft (15 m) 3,610 ft (1100 m); typical combat radius at sea level 372 miles (600 km); lo-lo-lo mission with 2,910 lb (1320 kg) load 240 miles (385 km); ferry range with maximum fuel 2,175 miles (3500 km)
Weights: basic empty 8,117 lb (3682 kg); normal take-off 17,196 lb (7800 kg); maximum overload 19,180 lb (8700 kg)
Dimensions: span 29 ft 6½ in (9.01 m); length 38 ft 3½ in (11.67 m); height 14 ft 6½ in (4.43 m); wing area 195.15 sq ft (18.13 m²)
Armament: two 30-mm DEFA cannon; four underwing pylons for 1,000-lb (454-kg) bombs, 750-lb (340-kg) napalm containers, rocket packs each containing seven or twenty-eight 2-in (50-mm) rockets, or 4 5-in (127-mm) rocket containers.
Operator: Italy

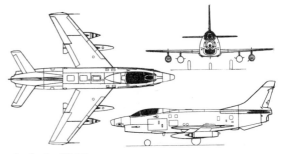

Aeritalia G91Y

5

Aeritalia G222

History and notes

The initial Aeritalia G222 originated with NBMR-4 (NATO Basic Military Requirement Four) formulated in 1962, resulting in several V/STOL tactical transport projects (using combined cruise turboprops and lift jets), none of which were realised. However, the research project contract for the G222 V/STOL transport awarded to Fiat by the Italian air force in 1963 was extended to cover the type's subsequent development in more conventional form. An official contract for two military transport prototypes, originally designated G222TCM, and a static test airframe, was finally signed in 1968, the aircraft being considered a successor to the ageing Fairchild C-119 transports then in Italian service. Delays caused by changes in official policy, take-over of the parent company, and funding problems held up the completion of the first prototype, and it was not flown until 18 July 1970. The second prototype joined the flight-test programme on 21 July 1971. These aircraft have 3,060/2,870-shp (2283/2141-kW) CT64-820 turboshaft engines and are unpressurized; the production model is pressurized, and fully air-conditioned and able to operate from semi-prepared airstrips in all weathers.

The highly successful trials resulted in a firm Italian order for 44 production G222s in August 1972; by that time arrangements had been made to involve most of the Italian aircraft industry in the G222 programme.

The G222 airframe was redesigned once more to take the more powerful General Electric T64-P4D turboprop engines and incorporate other detail improvements. The production prototype was flown on 23 December 1975, by which time Aeritalia had also obtained its first export order from Argentina.

The fuselage of the basic G222 transport version is an all-metal fail-safe structure, the underside of which forms a loading ramp. In standard troop-transport configuration the G222 carries 44 fully equipped troops (32 sidewall seats and 12 folding seats), as a paratroop transport 32 (in sidewall seats). As an ambulance, the G222 has space for 36 stretcher cases and two seated casualties, plus four medical attendants, while converted for cargo transport the aircraft has provision for a 3,305-lb (1500-kg) capacity cargo hoist and 135 tie-down points.

Specification

Type: twin-turboprop general-purpose transport
Powerplant: two 3,400-shp (2536-kW) Fiat-built General Electric T64-GE-P4D turboprops driving Hamilton Standard 63E60 three-blade variable-pitch propellers; provision in fuselage for eight Aerojet General jet-assisted take-off rockets, delivering a total additional thrust of 7,937 lb (3600 kg) for take-off in overload condition
Performance: (standard transport at maximum take-off weight) maximum speed at 15,000 ft (4575 m) 336 mph (540 km/h); cruising speed at 14,750 ft (4500 m) 224 mph (360 km/h); maximum rate of climb at sea-level 1,705 ft (520 m) per minute; time to 14,750 ft (4500 m) 8 minutes 35 seconds; service ceiling 25,000 ft (7620 m); take-off run 2756 ft (840 m); range with maximum payload at optimum cruising speed at 19,685 ft (6000 m) 435 miles (700 km); range with 44 fully-equipped troops 1,380 miles (2220 km); ferry range with maximum fuel 3,075 miles (4950 km)
Weights: (standard transport) empty 32,165 lb (14590 kg); maximum payload 18,740 lb (8500 kg); normal take-off 54,013 lb (24500 kg); maximum take-off and landing 58,422 lb (26500 kg)
Dimensions: span 94 ft 2 in (28.70 m); length 74 ft 5½ in (22.70 m); height 32 ft 1¾ in (9.80 m); wing area 882.6 sq ft (82.00 m²)
Operators: (operational or on order) Argentina, Italy, Libya, United Arab Emirates (Dubai), Somalia

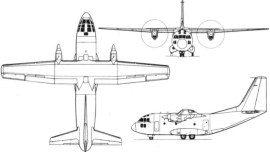

Aeritalia G222 (T64 engines)

Based at Dubai and shown in the markings of the Dubai Air Force is this Aeritalia G222 tactical transport, delivered November '76.

Aermacchi MB326 & MB326K/Impala Mk2

One of the eight Aermacchi M.B.326B advanced trainers purchased in 1965 by the Tunisian Republican Air Force.

History and notes

A classic example of the modern genre of jet trainer/light attack aircraft, the Aermacchi MB326 series has been in production for over 20 years, and accounts for over 10% of the 7,000 or more Macchi-designed aircraft built by the parent company since before World War I.

Dr-Ing Ermanno Bazzocchi began design of the MB326 in 1954, and the prototype first flew on 10 December 1957 on the power of a 1,750-lb (794-kg) Viper 8 turbojet. Flight tests and service evaluation soon confirmed the MB326's eminent suitability for all stages of pilot training, and the type was ordered into production for the Italian air force. The type began to enter service in 1962, and has since then been produced in three basic two-seat variants and one single-seat model.

The first basic model was powered by the 2,500-lb (1134-kg) Viper 11, and comprised the 100 MB326s for the Italian air force, eight armed MB326Bs for Tunisia, four unarmed MB326Ds for the Italian airline Alitalia, nine armed MB326Fs for Ghana (like the Tunisian aircraft these have six underwing hardpoints), 97 armed MB326Hs assembled or licence-built by the Commonwealth Aircraft Corporation for Australia, 40 unarmed MB326M trainers for South Africa, and 125 basically similar but armed aircraft for South Africa assembled or licence-built by the Atlas Aircraft Corporation under the designation Impala Mk 1.

The second basic model was powered by the 3,410-lb (1547-kg) Viper 20 Mark 540. The prototype of this variant was the MB326G, which first flew in 1967. Production in Italy centred on the MB326GB armed model for Argentina, Zaïre and Zambia, while in Brazil EMBRAER has built the similar MB326GC under the designation AT-26 Xavante for Brazil.

The final two-seat model is powered by the 4,000-lb (1814-kg) Viper 632-43, and comprises the MB326L variant with an airframe based on that of the single-seat MB326K combined with two-seat accommodation. It combines full attack capability with training potential.

The MB326's viceless handling, excellent manoeuvrability and good weapon-carrying capability made it an obvious candidate for development into a single-seat light close-support aircraft, but it was not until 1970 that Aermacchi flew the prototype MB326K with the instructor's space used to house ammunition for the inbuilt 30-mm cannon, avionics and extra fuel. It was not until 1974 that production of the Viper 600-engined MB326K got

under way with an order from the Dubai Police Air Wing and another from South Africa.

Specification (Aermacchi MB326/Atlas Impala Mk 2)

Type: single-seat close air support or tactical reconnaissance aircraft, and limited air-to-air interceptor

Powerplant: one 4,000-lb (1814-kg) static thrust Rolls-Royce Viper 632-43 turbojet (MB326K); 3,360-lb (1524-kg) static thrust Viper 540 (Impala Mk 2)

Performance: (MB326K) maximum speed, clean, at 5,000 ft (1525 m) 553 mph (890 km/h); maximum speed with armament at 30,000 ft (9150 m) 426 mph (686 km/h); typical combat radius, according to altitude and external load 167-644 miles (268 1036 km); ferry range with two drop-tanks more than 1,323 miles (2130 km);

Weights: empty equipped 6,885 lb (3123 kg); take-off, clean, 10,240 lb (4645 kg); maximum take-off, with armament 13,000 lb (5897 kg)

Dimensions: span over tip-tanks 35 ft 7 in (10.85 m); length 35 ft 0¼ in (10.67 m); height 12 ft 2 in (3.72 m); wing area 208.3 sq ft (19.35 m²)

Armament: two 30-mm DEFA 553 cannon in lower fuselage, each with 125 rounds; and up to 4,000 lb (1814 kg) of external stores on six underwing stations, typical loads including four 1,000-lb (454-kg) bombs, or two 750-lb (340-kg) and four 500-lb (227-kg) bombs, or six 7.62-mm (0.3-in) Minigun pods, or two AS.11 or AS.12 air-to-surface missiles, or two Matra 550 Magic air-to-air missiles, or various launchers for 37-mm, 68-mm, 100-mm, 2.75-in or 5-in rockets, or (on innermost port station) a four camera reconnaissance pod

Operators: Dubai, Ghana, South Africa (Impala 2), Tunisia

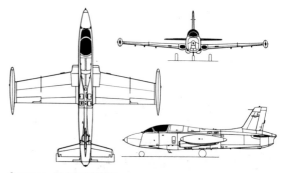

Aermacchi M.B.326E

Aermacchi M.B.339

History and notes

Following the receipt of a study contract from the Italian air force in 1972, Aeronautica Macchi undertook no fewer than nine separate design studies in its efforts to evolve a second-generation jet trainer to succeed the M.B.326 and Aeritalia (Fiat) G91T during the 1980s. Seven of these were variants of a design known as the M.B.338, with numerous permutations of single or twin Viper, Larzac, Adour, RB.401 and TFE 731 turbojets or turbofans. Not surprisingly, the single-Viper versions would have offered little advance in performance over the later models of the M.B.326; neither, as it turned out, did the intermediately-powered models, which also would have been more expensive to produce than the M.B.326; while the two most powerful versions, with a single Adour and twin Larzacs respectively, offered a marked increase in performance only at a considerably higher cost.

The most encouraging studies were the two proposed models of the M.B.339, powered by either a single Larzac turbofan (M.B.339L) or a single Viper 600 series turbojet (M.B.339V). Moreover, a major part of the M.B.339 airframe was common with that of the M.B. 326K, only the forward fuselage, with its modified cockpit and much superior all-round view, plus the enlarged vertical tail, being essentially different. In February 1975 the Italian air force decided to adopt the Viper-powered version to meet its requirements, and the first of two prototypes made its initial flight at Venegono airfield on 12 August of the following year. Only comparatively minor modifications, to provide an anti-skid braking system for the main landing gear and a steerable nosewheel, plus improved air-conditioning in the cockpit, were introduced on the second prototype, which flew for the first time on 20 May 1977. (An amusing subliminal

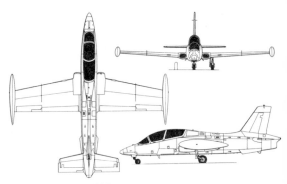

Aermacchi M.B.339

touch is Aermacchi's use of the word 'nine' in various languages in the registration of the development aircraft: I-NOVE for the first prototype, I-NINE for the second, and I-NEUF for the first production machine.)

Redesign of the forward fuselage permits the rear (instructor's) seat to be elevated above that of his pupil in the now-fashionable manner, the elongated tandem canopy providing an all-round view much improved over that from the M.B.326. Both occupants have Martin-Baker zero-zero ejection seats, fitted only in the E, K, and L models of the earlier M.B.326. The avionics are suitably increased and updated to include Tacan, navigation computer, blind landing instrumentation, IFF (identification friend or foe), and both VHF and UHF radio. Fuselage and permanent wingtip tanks give a total 311 Imperial gallons (1413 litres) of usable fuel as standard, with a 75-Imperial gallon (340-litre) drop-tank able to be carried on the middle pylon under each wing.

Following the two prototypes (the second of which

First (on the right) and second of the Aermacchi M.B.339, the improved and updated successor to the M.B.326. The first of an initial batch of 15 production aircraft for the Aeronautica Militare flew in 1978, and 100 in all are on order.

Aermacchi M.B.339

represents the production standard), the Italian air ministry ordered an initial batch of 15 M.B.339s, of an expected total of about 100. Although developed initially as an Italian air force trainer, the 339 retains the six wing hardpoints of its predecessor. Thus, Aermacchi has achieved a successor to the M.B.326 with a compromise design. It may lack some sophistication and the performance 'edge' of the British Aerospace Hawk or Dassault-Breguet/Dornier Alpha Jet. However, these factors may be more than offset by the lower unit cost, plus the commonality with an already well-proven airframe.

Specification

Type: tandem two-seat basic/advanced jet trainer and close-support aircraft
Powerplant: one 4,000-lb (1814-kg) Piaggio-built Rolls-Royce Viper 632-43 turbojet
Performance: maximum limiting Mach number 0.86 (603 mph/971 km/h equivalent airspeed); maximum speed at sea level 558 mph (898 km/h); maximum speed at 30,000 ft (9150 m) 508 mph

(817 km/h) or Mach 0.77; maximum range on internal fuel 1,093 miles (1760 km); maximum range with two underwing drop-tanks 1,310 miles (2110 km); maximum rate of climb at sea level 6,600 ft (2012 m) per minute; service ceiling 48,000 ft (14630 m)
Weights: empty equipped 6,889 lb (3125 kg); take-off, clean 9,700 lb (4400 kg); maximum take-off, with underwing stores 13,000 lb (5895 kg)
Dimensions: span over tip-tanks 35 ft 7½ in (10.86 m); length 36 ft 0 in (10.97 m); height 13 ft 1¼ in (3.99 m); wing area 207.74 sq ft (19.30 m²)
Armament: six underwing hardpoints, the outer pair each able to carry a 750-lb (340-kg) store and the others 1,000 lb (454 kg) each, subject to a maximum load of 4,000 lb (1814 kg). The two inboard points can carry 30-mm or multi-barrel 7.62-mm guns in a Macchi pod, and the two centre points are 'wet' for the carriage of drop-tanks. Wide variety of weapon loads including bombs, napalm, AS.11/AS.12 or Magic missiles, launchers for 50-mm, 68-mm or 2.75-in rockets, or a single four-camera reconnaissance pod
Operator: Italy

Aero L-29 Delfin

Serving in the basic and advanced training roles with the Egyptian Arab Air Force is the Czechoslovak L-29 Delfin.

History and notes

Even among the air forces of the Warsaw Pact nations, where large production contracts are common, manufacturing figures of over 3,000 of a single type of jet trainer indicate a successful design. The first studies leading to the Aero L-29 were made in 1955 by a team under K. Tomas and Z. Rublic. Known as the XL-29, the prototype flew for the first time on 5 April 1959, powered by a Bristol Siddeley Viper turbojet. The second prototype, which made its initial flight in July 1960, and a small pre-production batch of L-29s for service evaluation, had the nationally-designed M 701 turbojet.

A year later the Delfin (dolphin) was subjected to competitive evaluation against the Yakovlev Yak-30 and PZL-Mielec TS-11 Iskra. As a result, all Warsaw Pact countries (except Poland, which decided to continue supporting its own TS-11) decided to adopt the Delfin as their standard basic and advanced jet trainer. The first production Delfin was completed in April 1963, and approximately 3,500 had been built

before the run ended some 12 years later. More than 2,000 of these were supplied to the Soviet air force, whose L-29s were assigned the reporting name 'Maya' by the NATO Air Standards Co-ordinating Committee, and about 400 to the Czech air force. Others were supplied to the air forces of Bulgaria, the German Democratic Republic, Hungary and Romania. From its introduction the Delfin enabled these services to inaugurate 'all-through' training on jet aircraft, by replacing earlier piston-engined types. It was designed not only for basic pilot training but also for advanced and combat weapon training.

The L-29's concept is based upon a straightforward, easy-to-build design, simple to fly and uncomplicated to operate. Flight controls are manual, with generous wing flaps and a perforated airbrake on each side of the rear fuselage. The Delfin does not readily stall or spin, and its safety and reliability are said to be high. There is a manual backup for the

Aero L-29 Delfin

landing gear, and both occupants are provided with ejection seats though, unlike modern trainers, the instructor's (rear) seat is no higher than the pupil's. Runway requirements are modest, and it can operate from grass, sand or waterlogged airstrips.

Aero also built a small batch of the single-seat L-29A Delfin Akrobat, for aerobatic displays, but this did not go into large-scale production. Neither did an attack version, the L-29R, but the standard L-29 was supplied to a number of countries (including Egypt) equipped for this role, with a modest weapon load on two underwing pylons. The L-29 was superseded in production at the Aero factory in the mid-1970s by the L-39.

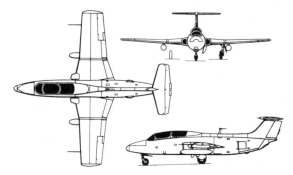

Aero L-29 Delfin

Specification

Type: tandem two-seat basic and advanced jet trainer
Powerplant: one 1,960-lb (890-kg) Motorlet M 701 VC-150 or S-50 turbojet
Performance: maximum speed at 16,400 ft (5000 m) 407 mph (655 km/h); maximum speed at sea level 379 mph (610 km/h); maximum range on internal fuel 397 miles (640 km); maximum range with two underwing drop-tanks 555 miles (895 km); maximum rate of climb at sea level 2,755 ft (840 m) per minute; service ceiling 36,100 ft (11000 m)

Weights: empty 5,027 lb (2280 kg); maximum take-off 7,231 lb (3280 kg)
Dimensions: span 33 ft 9 in (10.29 m); length 35 ft 5½ in (10.81 m); height 10 ft 3 in (3.13 m); wing area 213.1 sq ft (19.80 m²)
Armament: provision for two 7.62-mm gun pods, two 220-lb (100-kg) bombs, eight air-to-surface rockets or two drop-tanks, on pylon under each wing
Operators: Bulgaria, China, Czechoslovakia, Egypt, East Germany, Guinea, Hungary, Indonesia, Iraq, Nigeria, Romania, Syria, Uganda, USSR, Vietnam

Aero L-39 Albatros

A desert-camouflaged Aero L-39 Albatros flown by the Iraqi Air Force College at Rashid.

History and notes

Designed before the Soviet armed intervention in Czechoslovakia in 1968, the L-39 is now well on the road to emulating its predecessor, the L-29 Delfin, as the standard jet trainer for Warsaw Pact (except Poland) and other air forces. Aero began with three prototypes, the middle one of which flew for the first time on 4 November 1968; the other two were subjected to structural and fatigue tests. Pilot for the first flight was Rudolf Duchon, who had also been responsible for the early test programme of the L-29 nine years before. The powerplant selected for the L-39 is the Soviet-designed Ivchenko AI-25 turbofan, and most of the early delays in the aircraft's development are thought to be the result of problems encountered in relating this to the L-39's airframe, so rendering it acceptable for licence produc-

tion in Czechoslovakia. One of the chief problems seems to have been the supply of air to the engine: by late 1970, at which time five flying prototypes had been completed, modified intakes of greater length and increased area were noticed on these development aircraft. During the following year, a pre-production batch of 10 L-39s was built to the modified configuration, and series production began in late 1972. By 1979, more than 1,000 had been ordered, of which more than half had been completed.

These are of three main versions. The basic L-39, for elementary and advanced jet training, has been supplied in quantity to the Czech and Soviet air forces, plus those of other Warsaw Pact nations, as a successor to the L-29; it began to enter service in

Aero L-39 Albatros

1974. When equipped for weapons training, the two-seater is known as the L-39Z. A single-seat armed variant, for use in the light close-support and ground-attack roles, is designated L-39D; Iraq is known to be among the operators of this version.

Specification
Type: tandem two-seat basic and advanced jet trainer (L-39), weapons trainer (L-39Z) and single-seat light ground-attack aircraft (L-39D)
Powerplant: one 3,792-lb (1720-kg) Walter Titan turbofan (Ivchenko AI-25-TL built under Czech licence by Motorlet)
Performance: maximum speed at sea level 435 mph (700 km/h); maximum speed (trainer, clean) at 19,685 ft (6000 m) 485 mph (780 km/h), (L-39D) at same altitude with four rocket pods 391 mph (630 km/h); range on internal fuel (trainer) 528 miles (850 km), (L-39D with rocket pods) 485 miles (780 km); maximum range with two drop-tanks and no weapons 994 miles (1600 km); maximum rate of climb at sea level (trainer) 4,330 ft (1320 m) per minute, (L-39D) 3,150 ft (960 m) per minute; service ceiling (trainer) 37,730 ft (11500 m), (L-39D) 29,525 ft (9000 m)
Weights: empty 7,341 lb (3330 kg); take-off (trainer, clean and with tip-tanks empty) 10,075 lb (4570 kg); maximum take-off (L-39D with four

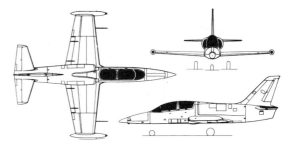

Aero L-39 Albatros

rocket pods) 11,618 lb (5270 kg)
Dimensions: span 31 ft 0½ in (9.46 m); length 40 ft 5 in (12.32 m); height 15 ft 5½ in (4.72 m); wing area 202.4 sq ft (18.80 m²)
Armament: (L-39D) up to 2,425 lb (1100 kg) of weapons on four underwing points, including bombs of up to 1,102-lb (500-kg) size, pods of 57-mm or 130-mm rockets, gun pods, a single five-camera reconnaissance pack, or two drop-tanks; centreline point under fuselage for podded gun, believed to be a twin-barrel Soviet GSh-23 of 23-mm calibre with about 180 rounds
Operators: Afghanistan, Bulgaria, Czechoslovakia, East Germany, Hungary, Iraq, Libya, Romania, USSR

Aérospatiale SA.316B/SA.319B Alouette III

History and notes
The Aérospatiale Alouette III is an enlarged and most successful development of the Alouette II, with increased cabin capacity, improved equipment, more powerful turbine engine and generally enhanced performance. The prototype, designated SE.3160, was first flown on 28 February 1959, followed by the first production series known as SA.316A. In June 1960 an Alouette III with seven people aboard demonstrated its extraordinary performance by making landings and take-offs at an altitude of 15,780 ft (4810 m) on Mont Blanc in the French Alps. Five months later the same Alouette III with two

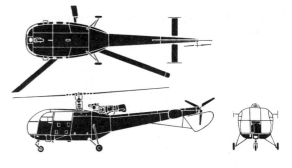

Aérospatiale SA.316C Alouette III

Aérospatiale Alouette III of 3 Sqn, Royal Malaysian Air Force, based at Kuala Lumpur and used for liaison and forward air control duties.

Aérospatiale SA.316B/SA.319B Alouette III

Aérospatiale Alouette III of the Força Aerea Portuguesa, operated in Portuguese Guinea in 1971 and based at Bissau Airport.

crew and a 550-lb (250-kg) payload made landings and take-offs at an altitude of 19,698 ft (6004 m) in the Himalayas — both hitherto unprecedented achievements for a helicopter. The SA.316A was built for domestic and export market and, in June 1962, became subject to a licence-production agreement with HAL in India. The first Indian-assembled Alouette III was flown on 11 June 1965.

Various experimental developments followed, including an all-weather variant which made its initial flight on 27 April 1964. The subsequent SA.316B, first flown on 27 June 1968, featured strengthened main and tail rotor transmissions and was generally slightly heavier, but could carry more payload. It became the principal production version, with first deliveries made in 1970, and was an immediate export success. The Alouette III prototypes and the first two production series were powered by Turboméca Artouste IIIB turboshaft engines, replaced by the Artouste IIID on the SA.316C, built in limited numbers only.

The Alouette III cabin is more enclosed than that of the Alouette II, and can accommodate up to seven persons (or pilot and six fully equipped troops). All passenger seats are easily removable to provide an unobstructed cargo space. There is provision for an external sling for hauling loads up to 1,650 lb (750 kg) or, for the air/sea rescue role, a hoist of 380-lb (175-kg) capacity. Like most other light general-purpose helicopters, the Alouette III can also be used for casualty evacuation, carrying two stretcher cases and two seated persons behind the pilot. But the most popular military modifications became the two-seat light attack version armed with a selection of anti-personnel and anti-armour weapons, and the naval version, used principally in anti-submarine role.

Experiments with the thermically more efficient and more economical Astazou turboshaft engine led to the SA.319B, which is a direct development of the SA.316B. The first experimental SA.319B prototype was completed and flown in 1967, but full production did not start until 1973.

The Alouette III variants were even more successful on the international market than those of its predecessor, and by 1 April 1978 no less than 1,382 machines had been sold (with 1,370 delivered) to 190 civil and military operators in 72 countries. In addition to licence-production by HAL at Bangalore in India (200), similar agreements were signed with ICA-Brassov in Romania (for 130) and Switzerland (for 60). In Indian service the Alouette III has proved so successful that a special armed version known as Chetak is now under development by HAL.

Specification

Type: (SA 316B Alouette III) general-purpose helicopter

Powerplant: one 870-shp (649-kW) Turboméca Artouste IIIB turboshaft, derated to 570 shp (425 kW)

Performance: (standard version, at maximum take-off weight) maximum speed at sea level 130 mph (210 km/h); maximum cruising speed at sea level 115 mph (185 km/h); maximum rate of climb at sea level 850 ft (260 m) per minute; service ceiling 10,500 ft (3200 m); hovering ceiling in ground effect 9,450 ft (2880 m); hovering ceiling out of ground effect 5,000 ft (1520 m); range with maximum fuel at sea level 298 miles (480 km); range at optimum altitude 335 miles (540 km)

Weights: empty 2,520 lb (1143 kg); maximum take-off 4,850 lb (2200 kg)

Dimensions: diameter of main rotor 36 ft 1¾ in (11.02 m); diameter of tail rotor 6 ft 3¼ in (1.91 m); length (rotor blades folded) 32 ft 10¾ in (10.03 m); width (rotor blades folded) 8 ft 6¼ in (2.60 m); height 9 ft 10 in (3.00 m); main rotor disc area 1,026 sq ft (95.38 m²)

Operational equipment: (assault role with reduced crew) choice of one 7.62-mm (0.3-in) AA52 machine-gun on tripod behind the pilot's seat, firing to starboard through door space, or one 20-mm MG 151/20 cannon in open turret-type mounting port side of cabin, or four AS.11 or two AS.12 wire-guided anti-tank missiles on external launching rails, or 68-mm rocket pods.

Operators: (military) Abu Dhabi, Argentina, Austria, Bangladesh, Belgium, Burma, Denmark, Dominican Republic, Ecuador, Ethiopia, France, Ghana, Hong Kong, India, Indonesia, Iraq, Ireland, Israel, Ivory Coast, Jordan, Laos, Lebanon, Libya, Malagasy, Malaysia, Mexico, Morocco, Nepal, Netherlands, Pakistan, Peru, Portugal, Rhodesia, Romania, Saudi Arabia, Singapore, South Africa, Switzerland, Tunisia, Venezuela, Yugoslavia, Zaire, Zambia

Aérospatiale (Fouga) CM.170 Magister/ CM.175 Zèphyr

IAI-built CM 170 (No 207) of the Heyl Ha'Avir aerobatic team. These aircraft were often used in the ground-attack role during the Arab-Israeli wars of 1967 and 1973.

History and notes

One of the most-widely used trainer/light attack aircraft, the Air Fouga (later Potez and now Aérospatiale) CM.170 Magister was produced to méet an *Armée de l'Air* requirement for a jet trainer (the first in the world). The prototype made its first flight on 23 July 1952, and a pre-production batch of 10 was ordered the following year. An initial order of 95 for the *Armée de l'Air* was placed in 1954 and the first production aircraft made its maiden flight on 13 January 1954.

A specially-equipped naval version was produced for the *Aéronavale*, designated CM.175 Zéphyr. Two prototypes and 30 production aircraft were built to this standard, and the Zéphyr provides naval pilots with their initial experience of operating from an aircraft-carrier.

In addition to French-manufactured Magisters offered for export, the trainer was manufactured under licence in West Germany by Flugzeug-Union-Sud for *Luftwaffe* training school. However, with the transfer of most German flying training to the United States by the end of the 1960s, the Magister was phased out of service. Valmet OY in Finland built 62 Magisters under licence (in addition to 18 purchased from France) and Israel Aircraft Industries also acquired manufacturing rights for the type, building many for light tactical use as well as training. Total production was 916 aircraft.

The tandem cockpits are pressurized and air-conditioned, with individually-regulated oxygen supplies. Ejection seats are not fitted. VHF, blind flying equipment and radio compass are standard in the trainer, while UHF, Tacan and IFF may be fitted to armed Magisters.

Armament combinations include two 7.5-mm (0.295-in) or 7.62-mm (0.3-in) machine-guns mounted in the nose, with 200 rounds of ammunition per gun. A gyro gunsight is fitted in both cockpits, the rear one having periscopic sighting. Underwing ordnance loads include two Matra Type 181 pods each with eighteen 37-mm rockets, two launchers each mounting seven 68-mm rockets, four 55-lb (25-kg) air-to-ground rockets, eight 88-mm rockets, two 110-lb (50-kg) bombs, or two Nord AS.11 air-to-ground guided missiles.

Israel is the foremost operator of the Magister as a light attack aircraft, some 80 remaining in service as both trainers and operational aircraft. The Magister

Aérospatiale (Fouga) CM.170 Magister

was particularly successful during the Six-Day War of June 1967, flying ground attack sorties on both the Egyptian and Jordanian fronts. The Irish Army Air Corps also operates the Magister in the dual light attack/training role, six Super Magisters being based at Baldonnel near Dublin.

Specification

Type: Jet trainer and light attack aircraft
Powerplant: (Magister) two 880-lb (400-kg) Turboméca Marboré IIA turbojets; (Super Magister) two 1,058-lb (480-kg) Turboméca Marboré VI.
Performance: (Magister) maximum speed at 30,000 ft (9144 m) 444 mph (715 km/h), (Super Magister) 463 mph (745 km/h); (Magister) service ceiling 36,090 ft (11000 m), (Super Magister) 44,300 ft (13500 m); (Magister) range 575 miles (925 km), (Super Magister) 585 miles (940 km)
Weights: empty equipped 4,740 lb (2150 kg); take-off with external tanks 6,835 lb (3100 kg); maximum take-off 7,055 lb (3200 kg)
Dimensions: span over tip tanks 39 ft 10 in (12.15 m); length 33 ft (10.06 m); height 9 ft 2 in (2.80 m); wing area 186.1 sq ft (17.30 m²)
Armament: two 7.5-mm (0.295-in) or 7.62-mm (0.3-in) machine-guns in the nose, and underwing rockets, bombs or Nord AS.11 missiles
Operators: Algeria, Bangladesh, Belgium, Cameroon, Finland, France, Ireland, Israel, Lebanon, Libya, Morocco, Rwanda, Salvador, Senegal, Togo, Uganda

Aérospatiale/Westland SA.341/342 Gazelle

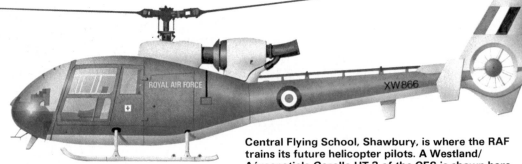

Central Flying School, Shawbury, is where the RAF trains its future helicopter pilots. A Westland/Aérospatiale Gazelle HT.3 of the CFS is shown here.

History and notes

The SA.341 Gazelle all-purpose lightweight helicopter originated as Aérospatiale project X 300 to meet a French army requirement for a light observation helicopter. The designation was changed to SA.340 soon afterwards. The finished design showed close affinity to the SA.318C Alouette II, and eventually used the same Astazou II powerplant and transmission system. Unlike Alouette II, however, the new helicopter features a fully enclosed fuselage structure and has two pilots side-by-side, with full dual controls. It also introduced two innovations: the fenestron, or shrouded tail rotor, and a rigid modified Bölkow-type main rotor. And it shows every sign of sharing its predecessor's sales success and popularity.

While still in the final design stages the SA.340 attracted British interest leading to a joint development and production share-out agreement signed on 22 February 1967 and officially confirmed on 2 April 1968. The first prototype, designated SA.340.001 was flown on 7 April 1967, and the second on 12 April 1968. These were followed by four pre-production SA.341 Gazelles (first flown on 2 August 1968), of which the third was equipped to British army requirements, assembled in France, and then re-assembled by Westland in the UK as the prototype Gazelle AH.1. It was first flown on 28 April 1970.

The first French production Gazelle, SA.341.1001, was cleared for its initial test flight on 6 August 1971; it had a longer cabin than its predecessors, an enlarged tail unit and an uprated Astazou IIIA engine. The initial Westland-assembled Gazelles followed early in 1972 (first flown on 31 January 1972). These comprised the first AH.1 for the British army, HT.2 for the Fleet Air Arm, and HT.3 for the RAF. The Gazelle entered service in the UK in May 1973, successfully passing the personnel familiarisation/training stage, and was then released for operational deployment, primarily to the Army Air Corps. The Gazelles procured by the Fleet Air Arm and RAF are used mainly for training purposes.

In the meantime, Gazelles in France had begun replacing Alouette IIs in service in increasing numbers, and the much faster light helicopter was

acclaimed an unqualified success. No special modification is necessary to convert the Gazelle into an ambulance: two stretchers can be carried, one above the other, in the left side of the cabin, leaving space for the pilot and one seated medical attendant. There is also provision for a variety of operational equipment that can be fitted according to role, including a 1,540 lb (700 kg) cargo sling, a 300 lb (135 kg) rescue hoist, photographic or survey equipment, and armament. Military loads can comprise two rocket pods, wire-guided missiles or fixed forward-firing machine-guns, as well as reconnaissance flares and smoke markers.

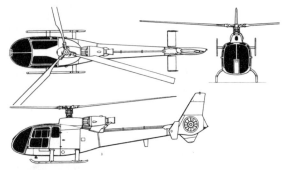

Aérospatiale/Westland SA.341 Gazelle

Specification

Type: (SA.341/342) five-seat utility helicopter
Powerplant: (SA.341): one 590-shp (440-kW) Turboméca Astazou IIIA turboshaft
Performance: (SA.341 at maximum take-off weight) maximum permissible speed at sea level 193 mph (310 km/h); maximum cruising speed at sea level 164 mph (264 km/h); economical cruising speed at sea level 144 mph (233 km/h); maximum rate of climb at sea level 1,770 ft (540 m) per minute; service ceiling 16,400 ft (5000 m); hovering ceiling in ground effect 9,350 ft (2850 m); hovering ceiling out of ground effect 6,560 ft (2000 m); range at sea level with maximum fuel 416 miles (670 km); range with pilot and 1,102 lb (500 kg) payload 223 miles (360 km)
Weights: (SA.341G) empty 2,002 lb (908 kg); maximum take-off 3,970 lb (1800 kg)

Aérospatiale/Westland SA.341/342 Gazelle

Dimensions: diameter of main rotor 34 ft 5½ in (10.50 m); diameter of tail rotor 2 ft 3⅜ in (0.695 m); length 39 ft 3⁵/₁₆ in (11.97 m); width (rotor blades folded) 6 ft 7⁵/₁₆ in (2.015 m); height 10 ft 2⅝ in (3.15 m); main rotor disc area 931 sq ft (86.5 m²)

Armament: provision for two pods of Matra or Brandt 2.75-in (68-mm) rockets, four AS.11 or two AS.12 wire-guided anti-tank missiles, four or six HOT wire-guided missiles, two forward-firing 7.62-mm (0.3-in) machine-guns, reconnaissance flares or smoke markers

Operators: by 1 April 1978 total of 745 sold (670 delivered) to 115 civil and military operators in 29 countries. In military service in Egypt, France, India, Iraq, Kuwait, Libya, Syria, UK; single examples in Senegal and Trinidad-Tobago; licence-built by Westland Helicopters in the UK and SOKO in Yugoslavia

Aérospatiale SA.342 Gazelle with 'Fenestron' shrouded fan anti-torque tail rotor.

Aérospatiale/Westland SA.330 Puma

Westland/Aérospatiale SA.330 Puma HC.1 of 230 Sqn, Royal Air Force, operated from Odiham, Hants.

History and notes

The Puma was originally developed by Sud-Aviation to meet a French army requirement for an all-weather/all-climate medium tactical transport helicopter capable of day and night operations. The design was finalised as a twin-engined aircraft with a large four-blade main rotor, semi-retractable tricycle landing gear (with provision for emergency pop-out flotation units), two independent hydraulic systems and dual flight controls as standard.

The first of two SA.330 prototypes was flown on 15 April 1968, powered by Turmo IIIC-4 engines, the last of six pre-production aircraft on 30 July 1968, and the first SA.330B production aircraft in September 1968. Deliveries to the French army (ALAT) began in March 1969, and the helicopter became operational in June 1970.

In 1967, while still under construction, the SA.330 was selected for the RAF Tactical Transport Programme and became subject to a joint production agreement between Aérospatiale and Westland in the UK. The last pre-production SA.330 was modified to RAF specifications and extensively tested during 1969. The first Westland-built SA.330E Puma HC.1 was flown on 25 November 1970, and the first RAF Puma squadron formed in 1971. All RAF Pumas feature a rescue hoist of 606-lb (275-kg) capacity and an internally-mounted cargo sling of 5,511-lb (2500-kg) capacity as standard. In 1979 40 additional Pumas are to be received by the RAF, probably in order to replace the ageing Wessex assault helicopters.

The initial military export version of the Puma, designated SA.330C, was first flown in September 1968 and options were soon taken up by several foreign air arms. The parallel civil passenger and cargo development, the SA.330F, made its first flight on 26 September 1969 and received its French certificate of airworthiness in October 1970.

Operational experience with the first civil and military series led to the introduction of more powerful Turmo IVA engines. The re-engined civil version, the SA.330G, and its military counterpart, the SA.330H, were initially produced with the Turmo IVA, later replaced by the Turmo IVC with air intake de-icing. First deliveries took place in 1973.

Aérospatiale/Westland SA.330 Puma

A subsequently more detailed redesign resulted in the SA.330J civil version and its military counterpart, the SA.330L, introduced in 1976. Apart from increased take-off weight these current production versions are notable as the first helicopters outside the USSR to be certified for all-weather operations including flights in icing conditions.

The SA.330L (and earlier military versions) can be used as tactical transports (16–20 troops), cargo transports, air ambulances (six stretchers and six seated casualties), or assault/fire support helicopters, with a wide range of armament available for this role.

Specification

Type: (SA.330L) medium transport helicopter
Powerplant: two 1,575-shp (1175-kW) Turboméca Turmo IVC turboshafts
Performance: (SA.330L at 13,230 lb/6000 kg) maximum permissible speed 182 mph (294 km/h); maximum cruising speed 168 mph (271 km/h); maximum rate of climb at sea level 1,810 ft (552 m) per minute service ceiling 19,680 ft (6000 m); hovering ceiling in ground effect 14,435 ft (4400 m); hovering ceiling out of ground effect 13,940 ft (4250 m); maximum range at normal cruising speed (no reserves) 355 miles (572 km)
Weights: (SA.330L) empty 7,970 lb (3615 kg); maximum take-off and landing 16,315 lb (7400 kg)

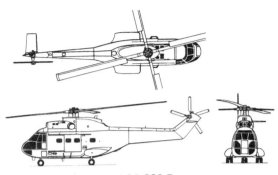

Aérospatiale/Westland SA.330 Puma

Dimensions: diameter of main rotor 49 ft 2½ in (15.00 m); diameter of tail rotor 9 ft 11½ in (3.04 m); length 59 ft 6½ in (18.15 m); width (rotor blades folded), 11 ft 5¾ in (3.50 m); height 16 ft 10½ in (5.14 m); main rotor disc area 1,905 sq ft (176.7 m²)
Armament: (optional) provision for various combinations of weapons, including side-firing 20-mm cannon, axial-firing 7.62-mm (0.3-in) machine-guns and/or rockets and missiles
Operators: (in service or on order) Abu Dhabi, Algeria, Argentina, Cameroun, Chile, Ecuador, France, Indonesia, Ivory Coast, Kuwait, Mexico, Nigeria, Pakistan, Portugal, Romania, South Africa, Spain, UK, West Germany, Zaire, Zambia, others

Aérospatiale SA.321 Super Frelon

One of eight Aérospatiale SA.321K Super Frelon assault helicopters used by the Heyl Ha'Avir, in service since 1966.

History and notes

Evolved from the smaller Sud-Aviation SA.3200 Frelon (Hornet) medium transport helicopter first flown on 10 June 1959, the Super Frelon was designed with technical assistance from Sikorsky Aircraft in the USA and built in cooperation with Fiat in Italy. As a result the SA.321 series embodies some typical Sikorsky characteristics such as watertight hull for amphibious operations, float-type sponsons housing the main landing gear, and a Sikorsky-designed rotor system. The first Super Frelon prototype, originally designated SA.3210-01, was flown on 7 December 1962, powered by three 1,320-shp

(985-kW) Turboméca Turmo IIIC-2 engines, representing the tróop transport version. In July 1963 this aircraft set up serveral international helicopter records, including a speed of 212 mph (341 km/h) over a 3-km course, and a speed of 217.77 mph (350.47 km/h) over a 15/25-km course. The second prototype, flown on 28 May 1963, was representative of the maritime version and featured stabilizing floats on the main landing gear supports. This was followed by four SA.321 pre-production aircraft, and an *Aéronavale* order for 17 aircraft designated SA.321G. This version was designed

Aérospatiale Super Frelon

specifically for maritime patrol/anti-submarine role and became the first Super Frelon series to go into production. The SA.321G prototype was flown on 30 November 1965, and production deliveries started early in 1966.

The Super Frelon had attracted foreign interest even before it had entered French service and the first export orders were soon in hand. The Super Frelons built for Israel were designated SA.321K and were fitted out as military transports, but after delivery in 1967 often proved their value in the airborne assault role.

The latest versions in production and service are the SA.321Ja passenger/cargo transport, a heavier version of the SA.321J and the SA.321H, a simplified universal military helicopter without stabilizing floats, external fairings or de-icing equipment.

Specification
Type: (SA.321) heavy duty helicopter
Powerplant: (SA.321G) three 1,550-shp (1156-kW) Turboméca Turmo IIIC-6 turboshafts (Turmo IIIE-6 in SA.321H)
Performance: (at maximum take-off weight) maximum permissible speed at sea level 171 mph (275 km/h); cruising speed at sea level 155 mph (250 km/h); maximum rate of climb at sea level 1,312 ft (400 m) per minute; service ceiling 10,325 ft (3150 m); hovering ceiling in ground

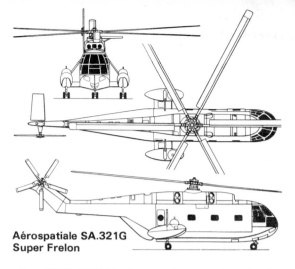

Aérospatiale SA.321G Super Frelon

effect 7,120 ft (2170 m); normal range at sea level 509 miles (820 km); range at sea level with 7,716 lb (3500 kg) payload 633 miles (920 km); endurance in ASW role 4 hours
Weights: empty (SA.321G) 15,130 lb (6863 kg); empty (SA.321H) 14,775 lb (6702 kg) maximum take-off (both versions) 28,660 lb (13000 kg)
Dimensions: diameter of main rotor 62 ft 0 in (18.90 m); diameter of tail rotor 13 ft 1½ in (4.00 m); length of fuselage 63 ft 7¾ in (19.40 m); width (SA.321G) 17 ft 0¾ in (5.20 m); height (SA.321G, rotor blades and tail folded) 16 ft 2½ in (4.94 m); height at tail rotor 21 ft 10¼ in (6.66 m); main rotor disc area 3,019 sq ft (280.55 m²)
Operators: France, Iran, Israel, Libya, South Africa

Agusta A 109A

History and notes
The basic A 109A is notable as the first Agusta-designed helicopter to be built in large series, and is the end product of a special market analysis initiated in 1965. Initially envisaged for commercial use only, the A 109 was designed around a single 690-shp (515-kW) Turboméca Astazou XII engine, but mainly for additional safety considerations redesigned in 1967 to take two 370-shp (276-kW) Allison 250-C14 turboshafts. The projected A 109B military utility model was abandoned in 1969 in favour of the eight-seat A 109C Hirundo (Swallow) civil version, the first of three prototypes flying on 4 August 1971. Protracted trials, minor alterations and other factors caused unforeseen delays and the first A 109 pre-production aircraft was not completed until April 1975. Delivery of production machines, designated A 109A, commenced in 1976.

In addition to its designed role as a light passenger transport, the A 109A can be adapted for freight carrying, as an air ambulance, or for search-and-rescue tasks. It proved a great commercial success and by early 1978 the A 109A was subject to some 250 orders and options.

The obvious military potential of the A 109A was

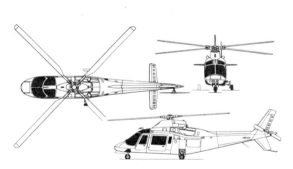

Agusta A 109C

soon recognised and in 1975 Agusta SpA concluded a co-operation agreement with Hughes Aircraft, manufacturers of the TOW (Tube-launched Optically-tracked Wire-guided) missile. Subsequent trials carried out by the Italian army in 1976-77 with five A 109A helicopters armed with various TOW missiles were extraordinarily successful and resulted in two military derivatives, for light attack/anti-armour/close support tasks, and naval operations.

The first military version is available in several variants: as a light attack helicopter (two or three crew, two machine-guns, HOT or TOW missiles, or rocket-launchers), equipped for battlefield reconnaissance, artillery observation or electronic warfare, or as a radio relay post. It can also be converted into a light troop/personnel transport (pilot plus seven troops) or as an air ambulance (two stretchers and two medical attendants). Optional additional equipment includes armoured seats for the crew and emergency flotation gear. All variants can also be fitted with infra-red suppression systems.

The A 109A maritime derivative, currently under development, also retains the same general configuration, structure and powerplant but has been specially designed for shipboard service. Variants include ASW, anti-ship, electronic warfare, armed and coast guard patrol surveillance, air ambulance, search-and-rescue, and utility.

Specification

Type: light general-purpose helicopter
Powerplant: two Allison 250-C20B turboshaft engines, each developing 420 shp (313 kW) for take-off, 385 shp (287 kW) continuous power, derated to 346 shp (258 kW) for twin-engine operation
Performance: (at 5,400 lb/2450 kg) maximum permissible level speed 193 mph (311 km/h); maximum cruising speed at maximum continuous power 165 mph (266 km/h); optimum cruising speed at sea level 143 mph (231 km/h); maximum rate of climb at sea level 1,620 ft (493 m) per minute; service ceiling 16,300 ft (4968 m); hovering ceiling in ground effect 9,800 ft (2987 m); hovering ceiling out of ground effect 6700 ft (2042 m); maximum range at sea level 351 miles (565 km); maximum endurance at sea level 3 hours 18 minutes
Weights: empty 3,120 lb (1415 kg); maximum take-off 5,402 lb (2450 kg)
Dimensions: diameter of main rotor 36 ft 1 in (11.00 m); diameter of tail rotor 6 ft 8 in (2.03 m); length of fuselage 35 ft 1¾ in (10.71 m); height 10 ft 10 in (3.30 m); main rotor disc area 1,022.6 sq ft (95.0m²)
Armament: two 7.62-mm (0.3-in) flexibly-mounted machine-guns and two XM-157 rocket-launchers (each with seven 2.75-in/70-mm rockets) basic; alternative weapons include HOT or TOW missiles and an electrically-operated 7.62-mm (0.3-in) Minigun on a flexible mount; a fully automatic 7.62-mm (0.3-in) MG 3 machine-gun; an XM-159C launcher for nineteen 2.75-in (70-mm) rockets, an Agusta launcher for seven 81-mm (3.2-in) rockets, or a 200A-1 launcher for nineteen 2.75-in (70-mm) rockets.
Naval version (ASW role): two homing torpedoes, six marine markers; MAD gear optional
Naval version (ASV role): high-performance long-range radar plus AS.12 or other wire-guided missiles; other naval equipment fitted according to mission
Operators: (in service or ordered/on option) Argentina, Belgium, France, Mexico, the Philippines, Switzerland, UK, USA, Yugoslavia, other countries

Antonov An-12 Cub

History and notes

The Soviet equivalent of the Lockheed C-130 Hercules, the Antonov An-12 'Cub' was the result of a chain of development which started in the mid-1950s. By that time it was recognised that the turboprop engine, offering far higher power/weight ratios than the piston engines, as well as power outputs considerably greater than most piston engines, would revolutionize the design of military transport aircraft. Such aircraft generally operate over short distances; the fact that the fuel consumption of the turboprop was at the time higher than that of the piston engine was thus of secondary importance compared with the prospect of a military freighter with sufficient power to lift a large payload from a short and unprepared field.

The first Antonov aircraft designed around this formula was the twin-engined An-8, which was designed in 1953–54 and made its first flight in the autumn of 1955. Like the contemporary C-130, it adopted what has become the classic layout for a military freighter, with high wing, landing gear in

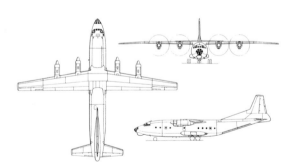

Antonov An-12 Cub

side fairings on a fuselage with a flat, low-level floor, and a rear loading door with integral ramp under the unswept rear fuselage.

The An-8 was tested with turboprops from the Kuznetsov and Ivchenko bureaux, both these Soviet design teams including many German engineers captured in 1945. Invchenko's AI-20 was chosen as the powerplant for the An-8, about 100 of which were built for the VTA (the Soviet military air transport force). Some remain in service.

An Aeroflot requirement for an airliner designed for rough-field operations led to the development of the four-engined An-10 airliner from the An-8, and it was this type which formed the basis for the An-12.

The military An-12PB, differing from the airliner in having a more upswept rear fuselage and an integral rear loading ramp, flew in 1958 and from the early 1960s became the standard Soviet military transport. A peculiarly Soviet feature of the military versions is the rear gun turret, although this lacks radar guidance and can be only a token defence. (Indian An-12s were, however, used as bombers in the 1965 Indo-Pakistan war, escaping without loss.) Later in their service life, Russian air force An-12s were fitted with improved radar equipment.

Although the type does not seem to have been pressed into service in as many roles as the C-130, the An-12 has since 1970 been seen in the electronic counter measures (ECM) and electronic intelligence (Elint) role, joining the increasing number of Russian aircraft loitering in the vicinity of war zones and NATO exercises.

Specification
Type: heavy tactical freighter, (Cub-B) ECM aircraft and (Cub-C) electronic intelligence (Elint) platform
Powerplant: four 4,000-shp (2984-kW) Ivchenko AI-20K turboprops
Performance: maximum cruising speed 400 mph (640 km/h); economic crusing speed 360 mph (580 km/h); service ceiling 33,500 ft (10200 m); range with 22,000-lb (10000-kg) payload 2,100 miles (3400 km)
Weights: empty (estimated) 75,000 lb (35000 kg); maximum payload 44,000 lb (20000 kg); maximum take-off 134,500 lb (61000 kg)
Dimension: span 124 ft 7 in (38.0 m); length 108 ft 6 in (33.1 m); height 32 ft 3 in (9.83 m); wing area 1,309 sq ft (121.73 m²)
Armament: two 23-mm NR-23 cannon in tail turret
Operators: Algeria, Bangladesh, Egypt, India, Indonesia, Iraq, Poland, Sudan, USSR, Yugoslavia

Among its transport aircraft the Iraqi air force numbers some six Antonov An-12s, very useful for the medium logistics and trooping roles.

Antonov An-22 Cock

History and notes
One of the most technically impressive of Soviet aircraft designs, the mighty Antonov An-22 'Cock' strategic freighter took the world by surprise when it arrived at the Paris air show in June 1965. It has since become a symbol of Soviet imperialism, spearheading the shipment of arms to client states in Africa and elsewhere, using its vast range and payload to fly long diversions and so avoid hostile territory. Its combination of range with field performance is outstanding, and in many respects it outshines the later Ilyushin Il-76 'Candid' by a large margin.

Following the development of the twin-engined An-8 into the An-10 and An-12, and the design and testing of the An-24, the Antonov bureau turned its

attention to a very large strategic freighter closely based on the successful An-12. The An-22 is very unusual, in fact, in being a successful example of a direct scaling-up process. The wing of the An-22 is an almost exact 1.7:1 linear scale of the An-12 wing, and is typically Antonov with its anhedralled outer panels. The major difference in shape between the two aircraft is in the rear fuselage and tail. Rear fuselage aerodynamics and structure are probably the most demanding area in the design of a large military transport, with the linked problems of drag around a rear ramp and aerodynamic tail loads on an open-ended fuselage. The An-22's twin-fin layout was chosen to overcome predicted problems with flexing of the rear fuselage, the original design hav-

Antonov An-22 Cock

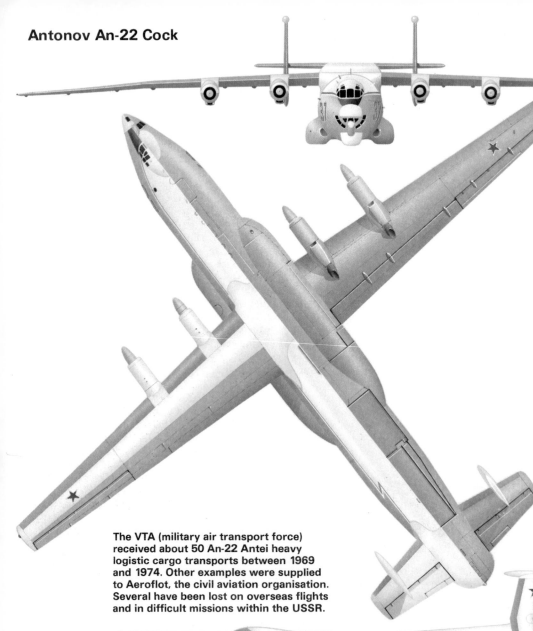

The VTA (military air transport force) received about 50 An-22 Antei heavy logistic cargo transports between 1969 and 1974. Other examples were supplied to Aeroflot, the civil aviation organisation. Several have been lost on overseas flights and in difficult missions within the USSR.

ing included a single fin.

The key to the An-22's efficiency is its high wing-loading, comparable with that of the Boeing 747. This is an almost inevitable effect of the square/cube law when the design of a smaller aircraft is scaled up so dramatically. Despite the high loading, however, the An-22 has an excellent field performance as a result of the fact that much of the wing is 'blown' by the slipstream of the four contra-rotating propeller units. Like those of the An-12, the flaps are double-slotted. Early An-22s had propellers with a diameter of 18 ft 6 in (5.6 m), similar to those of the Tu-95; production aircraft have propellers of 20 ft 4 in (6.4 m), presumably because the An-22 cruises at a lower speed than the swept-wing Tupolev, and propeller tip speeds are less critical.

The An-22 carries a crew of five or six, and there is a cabin in the forward fuselage for about 28 passengers, possibly including a relief crew on long flights. The main hold can accommodate a twin SA-4 'Ganef'

Antonov An-22 Cock

missile launcher on its tracked carrier, as well as any of the Soviet Union's armoured fighting vehicles, including main battle tanks. The hold is fitted with mechanical handling, including electric roof cranes and winches.

Design of the An-22 started in early 1962 to meet civil and military requirements, following the Soviet government's decision to support the exploitation of natural resources in Siberia by air. The civil and military requirements were compatible, because the new aircraft was intended to carry heavy construction equipment and machinery as well as armoured vehicles. The first aircraft flew on 27 February, 1965, and was demonstrated at a day's notice at the Paris air show in June of that year. It was the world's largest and heaviest aircraft until the first flight of the Lockheed C-5 in June 1968. The first production An-22 entered service with Aeroflot in 1967 — a short gestation period, particularly by Soviet standards, for so large an aircraft.

Only about 100 of these giant freighters have been built, and production is generally thought to have been ended in 1974. Deliveries are believed to have been shared about equally between the Soviet VTA (air transport force) and Aeroflot, but the civil aircraft are equipped to the same standard as military variants and are always available for military use. Aeroflot aircraft have been used for military airlifts where the presence of a red-starred VTA aircraft might have been provocative.

Despite its spectacular weight-lifting capability and field performance, the An-22 is probably of only limited use to the Soviet Union. Perhaps its most important role in the future will be to sustain an internal airlift capability linking the European and Chinese fronts. It is also useful in its role of supporting client states, but so large a freighter is probably out of place at a short frontal airstrip. As the US Air Force has found with the Lockheed C-5A, it is hard to justify a large force of super-heavy freighters

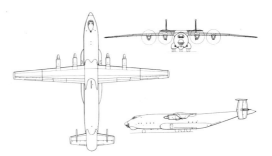

Antonov An-22 Cock

when most items of military equipment can be carried in smaller aircraft such as the Il-76 or Lockheed C-141; the only item which really demands C-5 or An-22 capacity is the main battle tank, and tanks cannot be airlifted in significant numbers except by a force of freighters that even the Soviet Union could scarcely contemplate acquiring.

Specification

Type: heavy strategic freighter
Powerplant: four 15,000-shp (11190-kW) Kuznetsov NK-12MV turboprops
Performance: maximum speed 460 mph (740 km/h); cruising speed 320 mph (520 km/h); service ceiling 25,000 ft (7500 m); range with 100,000-lb (45000-kg) payload 6,800 miles (11000 km); ground roll at maximum weight 5,000 ft (1500 m)
Weights: empty 250,250 lb (113500 kg); maximum payload about 175,000 lb (80000 kg); maximum take-off 550,000 lb (250000 kg); wing loading 148 lb/sq ft (725 kg/m^2)
Dimensions: span 211 ft 4 in (64.42 m); length (prototype) 189 ft 7 in (57.8 m); height 41 ft 2 in (12.55 m); wing area 3,713 sq ft (345 m^2)
Operator: USSR

Antonov An-26 Curl/An-30 Clank/An-32 Cline

History and notes

Development of a military freighter from the Antonov An-24 'Coke' airliner was logical, especially in view of the increased performance available with the addition of an auxiliary engine in the An-24RV.

The first rear-loading variant of the An-24 was the An-24TV, demonstrated in 1967. The aerodynamic shape of the rear fuselage was largely unchanged, but a loading hatch suitable for air-dropping was added beneath the rear fuselage, together with an internal winch and conveyor system. The original An-24TV had only two engines, but the first aircraft was modified in 1967-69 as the An-24RT with a booster engine as fitted to the An-24RV. The An-24RT could not accept large loads through the rear

door, and does not appear to have gone into large-scale production. However, it forms the basis for the An-30 'Clank' photographic survey transport aircraft, first displayed in 1974. This aircraft features an extensively glazed nose and ventral ports for cameras or other survey equipment.

Before the development of the An-30, however, a new version of the basic aircraft appeared. Displayed in 1969, the An-26 'Curl' introduced a redesigned rear fuselage, including a door large enough to admit any load which can be accommodated in the cabin and a rear-loading ramp. Small vehicles can be driven into the hold, while other cargoes can be handled by built-in powered con-

Antonov An-26 Curl/An-30 Clank/An-32 Cline

A Yugoslav Air Force Antonov An-26 Curl transport, one of a number in service with this air arm.

veyors and winches. A large bulged observation window is fitted to the left side of the fuselage, just aft of the flight-deck, presumably for increased accuracy in paradropping operations. The An-26 appears to be the standard light tactical transport of the Warsaw Pact air forces, and considerable efforts to export the type have been made.

The latest development of the An-26 appears to be intended to overcome the hot-and-high performance problems which afflict the earlier aircraft, even with the auxiliary engine in operation. First revealed in 1977, the An-32 is powered by completely different engines from those fitted to the earlier aircraft: 5,180-shp (3864-kW) Ivchenko AI-20Ms, yielding almost twice as much power as the AI-24s of the An-26. The AI-20M is an uprated version of the An-12 powerplant. The greater power demands propellers of greater diameter than those fitted to the An-26; in order to avoid total redesign of the wing, the engines have had to be mounted well above the wing, so that the propeller axes are above the widest point of the fuselage.

The An-32 was ordered by India in 1979; 95 of the aircraft are to be acquired, with a steady move from direct purchase to licence manufacture.

Specification
Type: (An-26 and An-32) light tactical transport; (An-30) photographic survey aircraft (specifications for An-26)
Powerplant: two 2,820-shp (2104-kW) Ivchenko

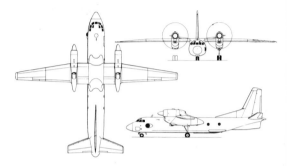

Antonov An-32 Cline

AI-24T turboprops and one 1,980-lb (900 kg) Tumansky RU-19-300 turbojet
Performance: maximum cruising speed 270 mph (435 km/h) at 20,000 ft (6100 m); range with 12,130-lb (5500-kg) payload 560 miles (900 km); range with 6,800-lb (3100-kg) payload 1,370 miles (2200 km); take-off field length 4,200 ft (1240 m); landing field length 5,700 ft (1740 m)
Weights: empty 33,120 lb (15020 kg); maximum take-off and landing 53,000 lb (24000 kg)
Dimensions: span 95 ft 9 in (29.2 m); length 78 ft 1 in (23.8 m); height 28 ft 6 in (8.575 m); wing area 807 sq ft (75 m²)
Operators: Angola, Bangladesh, Cuba, Hungary, Peru, Poland, Romania, (An-30) Somalia, USSR, Yugoslavia.

Beech Model 45/T-34C Mentor

History and notes
In 1948 Beech built as a private venture a two-seat trainer evolved from the V-tail civil Bonanza. The trainer differed primarily in having tandem seating for pupil and instructor, and by the substitution of a conventional tail unit. This aircraft was designated the Beech Model 45 Mentor, and flew for the first time on 2 December 1948.

At about this same period the USAF, in common with many other air forces, was trying to make up its mind about the trend of future primary training. The problem facing them all was whether or not, as a result of the introduction into service of turbine

engines, all training should be on jet-powered aircraft. At the time it was a difficult question to answer. It meant not only that the most ham-fisted of student pilots would have to cope from the outset with aircraft of much higher performance, but that at the same time they would be faced with the problem of handling a power unit which had not then been developed to a point of great reliability. On the plus side they would work throughout their training with turbine engines and a constant handling technique: retention of piston-engine power for primary trainers would bring the need for a transition phase

Beech Model 45/T-34C Mentor

To modernise the Fuerza Aerea Ecuatoriana's training elements, 20 Beech T-34Cs have been delivered.

from piston to turbine engines at some stage. USAF planners chose the latter as the most prudent course at that time.

Among the various types which were evaluated were three examples of the Beech Model 45, two powered by the 205-hp (153-kW) Continental E-185-8 engine, one by a 225-hp (168-kW) Continental E-225-8, and all three were designated YT-34 by the USAF. These three aircraft made their first flights in May, June and July 1950, and were tested extensively during the competition period, being flown not only by evaluation pilots, but also in the primary training role with pupils and instructors. Almost three years later, on 4 March 1953, the USAF selected the Model 45 as its new primary trainer, under the designation T-34A Mentor, and ultimately 450 were built for that service, 350 by Beech and 100 by the Canadian Car & Foundry Company in Montreal, Canada. US Navy evaluation of the Model 45 began soon after the USAF had placed its initial contract with Beech, and on 17 June 1954 the US Navy ordered 290 of these trainers, under the designation T-34B. A total of 423 were acquired eventually.

The US Navy decided in 1973 to investigate the possibility of retaining the tried and trusted Mentor

Beech T-34C, two-seat turboprop-powered primary trainer, for service with the US Navy. Developed in 1948 from the civil Bonanza, it was used extensively as a piston-engined trainer until conversion to turboprop power in 1973 brought new orders.

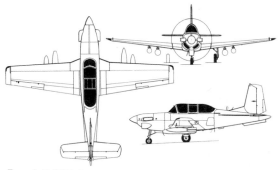

Beech T-34C-1

in service, and gave Beech a contract to convert two T-34Bs to turboprop power. The first of these flew for the first time on 21 September 1973, and following a satisfactory evaluation programme Beech has received contracts for some 170 new production aircraft under the designation T-34C Mentor. In addition to the new turboprop engine, these aircraft have air-conditioned accommodation for pupil and instructor, and advanced avionics.

Specification

Type: two-seat turboprop-powered primary trainer
Powerplant: one 715-shp (533-kW), torque-limited output 400-shp (298-kW), Pratt & Whitney Aircraft of Canada PT6A-25 turboprop
Performance: (T-34C) maximum speed 257 mph (414 km/h); maximum cruising speed 247 mph (398 km/h); range at 20,000 ft (6100 m) 749 miles (1205 km)
Weights: empty 2,630 lb (1193 kg); maximum take-off (T-34C) 4,274 lb (1938 kg), (T-34C-1) 5,500 lb (2495 kg)
Dimensions: span 33 ft 3 7/8 in (10.16 m); length 28 ft 8½ in (8.75 m); height 9 ft 10 7/8 in (3.02 m); wing area 179.9 sq ft (16.71 m²)
Armament: (T-34C-1) four underwing hardpoints with a maximum total capacity of 1,200 lb (544 kg), which can include practice bombs or flares, BLU-10/B incendiary bombs, Mk-81 bombs, SUU-11 Minigun pods, LAU-32 or -59 rocket pods, AGM-22A anti-tank missiles, or towed target equipment
Operators: (T-34C) Algeria, US Navy; (T-34C-1) Argentina, Ecuador, Indonesia, Morocco, Peru

Bell Model 204 UH-1 Iroquois/Agusta-Bell AB204

Bell Model 204 (actually Agusta-built AB 204B) of the Austrian Luftstreitkräfte HG III based at Linz.

History and notes

In 1955 the US Army initiated a design competition to speed the procurement of a new helicopter suitable for casualty evacuation, instrument training, and general utility duties. In June 1955 the US Army selected the Bell Helicopter Company's proposal, this having the company designation Model 204, and which became known to the US Army, initially, as the H-40, changed to HU-1 when it entered service, and given the name Iroquois. It was also the first of the 'Hueys', a nickname evolved from the HU-1 designation which, in 1962 became redesignated UH-1 under the tri-service rationalisation scheme.

The US Army's first order was for three prototypes, under the designation XH-40. The first made its first flight on 22 October 1956, and these were used by Bell for test and development. Just prior to that first flight, six pre-production YH-40s were ordered and all were delivered by August 1958. One remained with Bell, but the others were distributed one each to Eglin AFB and Edwards AFB, and three to Fort Rucker, for trials. Duly ordered into production, nine pre-production HU-1As were delivered on 30 June 1959, and were followed into service by 74 production examples.

The HU-1A was followed into service by an improved HU-1B, of which more than 700 were built, early production having 960-shp (716-kW) Lycoming T53-L-5 engines, and late production models 1,100-shp (820-kW) T53-L-11 engines. Other improvements in the HU-1Bs included redesigned main rotor blades, and an enlarged cabin to accommodate a crew of two, and seven passengers or three stretchers. In the autumn of 1965 the UH-1B was superseded in production by the UH-1C which had an improved 'door-hinge' rotor with wide-chord blades, this new main rotor conferring some increase in speed and improved manoeuvrability.

The model 204B was built in small numbers by Bell for civil use and military export. Generally similar to the UH-1B, these were of 10-seat capacity, had the larger-diameter rotors of the UH-1F, and T53-L-11 engine. Model 204Bs and UH-1s have been built by Fuji in Japan, under sub-licence from Mitsubishi, and continue in production in 1979. Agusta in Italy

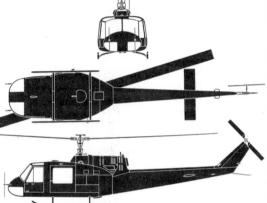

Bell Model 204/UH-1 Iroquois

has also built the Model 204B in large numbers under licence for both armed services and commercial users, many powered by Rolls-Royce Gnome turboshafts.

Specification

Type: general utility helicopter

Powerplant: (late production UH-1C) one 1,400-shp (1044-kW) Lycoming T53-L-13 turboshaft

Performance: (UH-1C) maximum speed at sea level 148 mph (238 km/h); cruising speed at 5,000 ft (1525 m) 143 mph (230 km/h); range with maximum fuel (no allowances) 382 miles (615 km)

Weights: (UH-1F) operating, empty 4,902 lbs (2224 kg); maximum gross 9,000 lbs (4082 kg)

Dimensions: (UH-1C) diameter of main rotor 44 ft 0 in (13.41 m); diameter of tail rotor 8 ft 6 in (2.59 m); length (rotor fore and aft) 42 ft 7 in (12.98 m); height 12 ft 8½ in (3.87 m); main rotor disc area 1,520 sq ft (141.21 m²)

Armament: 0.30-in (7.62-mm) machine-guns, rocket packs, homing torpedoes, or air-to-surface missiles, according to version

Operators: Austria, Canada, Ethiopia, Greece, Iran, Italy, JGSDF (Japan), Kuwait, Lebanon, Morocco, Norway, Oman, RAAF, RAN, RNZAF, Spain, Sweden, Switzerland, Turkey, USAF, US Army, USMC, USN Zambia

Bell Model 205/UH-1D/UH-1H Iroquois/

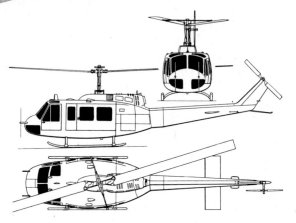

Royal Moroccan Air Force Agusta-Bell 205A. Two squadrons operate 24 of these helicopters.

History and notes

The undoubted success of the Bell UH-1A/B Iroquois gave convincing proof that there was little wrong with the basic design of this utility helicopter. As detailed in the Model 204 entry, the UH-1A/B was developed continuously for differing roles and with progressively more powerful engines.

In early 1960 Bell proposed an improved version of the Model 204 design with a longer fuselage, plus additional cabin space resulting from relocation of the fuel cells, thus providing accommodation for a pilot and 14 troops, or space for six stretchers, or up to 4,000 lb (1814 kg) of freight. In July 1960, therefore, the US Army awarded Bell a contract for the supply of seven of these new helicopters for service test, these having the US Army designation YUH-1D and being identified by Bell as their Model 205. The first of these flew on 16 August 1961, and following successful flight trials was ordered into production for the US Army, the first of these UH-1Ds being delivered to the 11th Air Assault Division at Fort Benning, Georgia, on 9 August 1963. The powerplant of these aircraft was the 1,100-shp (820-kW) Lycoming T53-L-11 turboshaft, and the standard fuel storage of 220 US gallons (832 litres) could be supplemented by two internal auxiliary fuel tanks to give a maximum overload capacity of 520 US gallons (1968 litres) of fuel. Large scale production of the UH-1D followed for the US Army, as well as for the armed forces of other nations, and 352 were built under licence by Dornier in Germany for service with the German army and air force.

The UH-1D was followed into production by the more or less identical UH-1H which differed, however, in the use of the more powerful 1,400-shp (1044-kW) Lycoming T53-L-13 turboshaft engine. Delivery of this version to the US army began in September 1967, and the type was still in production in early 1979. Built extensively for the US Army, nine were supplied to the RNZAF, and under the terms of a licence agreement which was negotiated in 1969, the Republic of China (Taiwan) produced a total of 118 of these aircraft for service with the Nationalist Chinese Army. Variants of the UH-1H include the CH-118 (originally CUH-1H) built by Bell for the Canadian Armed Force's Mobile Command, with the first of 10 being delivered on 6 March 1968; and the HH-1H local base rescue helicopter of which 30 were ordered for the USAF on 4 November 1970,

Bell UH-1H Iroquois

and of which deliveries were completed during 1973.

The UH-1D/H was employed extensively on a very wide range of duties in south-east Asia and was regarded by many as *the* workhorse helicopter in Vietnam. In particular, the type played a major role in special warfare operations in Laos, Cambodia, and in some of the remote areas of South Vietnam, and USAF historians have commented that in this latter theatre of operations nearly all battlefield casualties were evacuated by UH-1 helicopters.

Specification

Type: civil and military utility helicopter
Powerplant: (UH-1H) one 1,400-shp (1044-kW) Lycoming T53-L-13 turboshaft
Performance: (UH-1H) maximum and cruising speed 127 mph (204 km/h); range with maximum fuel (no allowances or reserves) 318 miles (512 km)
Weights: (UH-1H) empty 5,210 lb (2363 kg); basic operating (troop carrier) 5,557 lb (2521 kg); mission weight 9,039 lb (4100 kg); maximum take-off 9,500 lb (4309 kg)
Dimensions: (UH-1H) diameter of main rotor 48 ft 0 in (14.63 m); diameter of tail rotor 8 ft 6 in (2.59 m); length (rotor fore and aft) 57 ft 9⅝ in (17.62 m); height 14 ft 6 in (4.45 m); main rotor disc area 1,809 sq ft (168.06 m²)
Armament: none
Operators: Iran, Italy, Kuwait, Morocco, New Zealand, Saudi Arabia, Spain, Taiwan, Turkey, United Arab Emirates, US Army, West Germany, Zambia, Zimbabwe

Bell Model 206 JetRanger/OH-58 Kiowa/ TH-57 SeaRanger

History and notes

In 1960 the US Army launched a design competition for a new aircraft which it identified as a Light Observation Helicopter (LOH). Perhaps, more truthfully, it was seeking two or three helicopters in just one all-purpose design, for the LOH was required to fulfil casualty evacuation, close support, observation, photo-reconnaissance and light transport missions. Prior to that time no one aircraft had been able to embrace such a wide range of duties, and the specification called for four seats, a 400-lb (181-kg) payload, and cruising speed of around 120 mph (193 km/h). Twelve US helicopter manufacturers put forward design proposals, from which Bell, Hiller and Hughes were each contracted to build five prototypes for competitive evaluation. From the tests which followed, the Hughes HO-6 (later OH-6A) was selected for production as the US Army's LOH.

If the US Army had some doubts of the capabilities of Bell's HO-4 submission, the company did not share them, and after losing the competition built a new prototype which it designated as the Model 206A JetRanger. This flew for the first time on 10 January 1966, and on 20 October 1966 this aircraft received FAA certification, after which it entered production for commercial customers, and was built also by Agusta in Italy. The JetRanger was fundamentally the same as the OH-4A (formerly HO-4) prototypes, except for fuselage modifications to provide seating for five. It has been built in large numbers since 1966, and continues in production in 1979 under the designation Model 206B JetRanger III, having been the subject of progressive development and improvement programmes.

Bell Model 206B JetRanger

Specification

Type: light observation helicopter
Powerplant: (OH-58A) one 317-shp (236-kW) Allison T63-A-700 turboshaft
Performance: (OH-58A) maximum speed at sea level 138 mph (222 km/h); cruising speed 117 mph (188 km/h); maximum range at sea level with 10% reserves 299 miles (481 km)
Weights: (OH-58A) empty 1,464 lb (664 kg); operating 2,313 lb (1049 kg); maximum take-off 3,000 lb (1361 kg)
Dimensions: (OH-58A) main rotor diameter 35 ft 4 in (10.77 m); length (rotor turning) 40 ft 11¾ in (12.49 m); height 9 ft 6½ in (2.91 m); main rotor disc area 978.8 sq ft (90.93 m²)
Armament: (Agusta-built HKP 6 for Swedish Navy) depth bombs, mines, and torpedoes can be carried on under-fuselage mountings; (OH-58) a variety of gun, rocket and other armament options.
Operators: Australia, Austria, Brazil, Canada, Iran, Italy, Saudi Arabia, Spain, Sweden, Turkey, US Army, US Navy

OH-58C development version of the Bell OH-58A Kiowa. This has an uprated 420-shp (313-kW) Allison T63-A-720 turboshaft engine, and a flat glass canopy to eliminate reflections.

Bell Model 209/AH-1 HueyCobra

History and notes

The Korean War, which started on 25 June 1950, showed very quickly how the helicopter had important contributions to offer in that style of land warfare.

With their unique capability of taking off from and landing on virtually any surface which could support their laden weight, they were able to infiltrate behind enemy lines to rescue aircrew, many of whom were injured, and to pick up wounded infantrymen from 'no man's land' situations. It was clear too that if helicopters could infiltrate enemy territory for rescue operations, they could carry out similar sorties to put men, weapons and supplies behind an enemy's lines. Soon transport helicopters were designed to perform this task, but it was necessary to evolve well armed aircraft to provide escort and fire support for them, a role which could be fulfilled most effectively only by other helicopters.

One of the first of the aircraft to be developed for deployment in this latter category was Bell's Model 209. This company had begun investigation of the armed-helicopter concept in 1963 with the OH-13X Sioux Scout, a tandem-seat derivative of the Model 47, and when aircraft within this category were required urgently for operational use in Vietnam, an interim step to meet the requirement was taken by arming examples of the Model 204 Iroquois, a single-rotor turbine-powered helicopter. The Model 204 had originally the US Army designation H-40, later changed to HU-1, and it was this designation which gave rise to the popular nickname of Huey for these aircraft, tending to make the official name Iroquois superfluous. HU-1As were among the first US Army helicopters to serve in Vietnam. Thirteen of these were modified to carry two machine-guns and 16 air-to-surface rockets, and were flown by the Army Utility Tactical Transport Helicopter Company. HU-1Bs were equipped more specifically for an armed escort role, with a pair of electrically-operated machine-guns mounted on each side of the fuselage, or with up to 48 air-to-surface rockets, 24 on each side. In 1962, under a new US tri-service designation scheme, these two aircraft became redesignated UH-1A and UH-1B respectively, but despite this the 'Huey' nickname was to persist.

While these Model 204 types were exploring, and proving, the escort helicopter concept, Bell were busy pushing through a crash programme to meet the US Army's AAFSS (Advanced Aerial Fire Support System) requirement (to replace the costly Lockheed AH-56 Cheyenne) this taking the form of a redesign of the well-proven Model 204. Thus, the privately-funded prototype retained the wide-chord rotor of the UH-1C, as well as its transmission systems and Lycoming T53-L-13 turboshaft engine. The fuselage, however, was entirely new, its most notable features being the narrow frontal area (3 ft 2 in (0.97) m at its widest point), short stub wings and a machine-gun turret mounted beneath the fuselage nose. This flew for the first time on 7 September 1965, and was transferred to Edwards AFB in December 1965 for service trials to be carried out. Little time was needed for the US Army to satisfy itself that Bell's Model 209 was suitable for the AAFSS requirements, it being announced on 11 March 1966 that it was intended to order the aircraft into production. Designated originally AH-1G and named HueyCobra, the first two pre-production prototypes were ordered on 4 April 1966, and nine days later a first batch of 110 were contracted for the earliest possible delivery, this proving to be June 1977, with initial deployment to Vietnam starting in the autumn of that year. Of the total of 1,178 ordered by mid-1971, 38 were assigned to the US Marine Corps pending delivery of a twin-turbine version, designated AH-1J, treated in a separate entry.

See page 28 for three view.

Specification

Type: armed escort and close-support helicopter
Power Plant: (AH-1G) one Lycoming T53-L-13 turboshaft engine derated to 1,100 shp (820 kW); (AH-1R/S) one 1800-shp (1,342-kW) Lycoming T53-L-703 turboshaft engine.
Performance: (AH-1G) maximum speed at maximum take-off weight 172 mph (277 km/h); maximum range at S/L with maximum fuel and 8% reserves 357 miles (573 km): (AH-1S) maximum speed at maximum take-off weight with TOW missiles 141 mph (227 km/h); maximum range at S/L with maximum fuel and 8% reserves 315 miles (507 km)
Weights: (AH-1G) empty 6,073 lb (2754 kg); mission 9,407 lb (4266 kg); maximum take-off 9,500 lb (4309 kg); empty 6,479 lb (2939 kg); mission 9,975 lb (4525 kg); maximum take-off 10,000 lb (4535 kg)
Dimensions: diameter (main rotor) 44 ft 0 in (13.41 m); diameter (tail rotor) 8 ft 6 in (2.59 m); length (rotors fore and aft) 52 ft 11½ in (16.14 m); height 13 ft 6¼ in (4.12 m); main rotor disc area 1,520.4 sq ft (141.20 m²)
Armament: (AH-1G/R) XM-28 subsystem with two 7.62-mm Miniguns and 4,000 rounds of ammunition for each gun; or two SM-129 40-mm grenade launchers, each with 300 rounds; or one of each of the above; XM-35 subsystem with one 20-mm six-barrel cannon and 1,000 rounds of ammunition; four XM-159 packs each containing seven air-to-surface rockets; or two XM-18E1 Minigun pods: (AH-1Q/S) eight BGM-71A TOW air-to-surface missiles; plus rockets on stub-wings; M-197 turret cannon with 750 rounds of ammunition.
Operators: Israel, Spain, US Army, US Marine Corps

Bell Model 209/AH-1 Huey Cobra

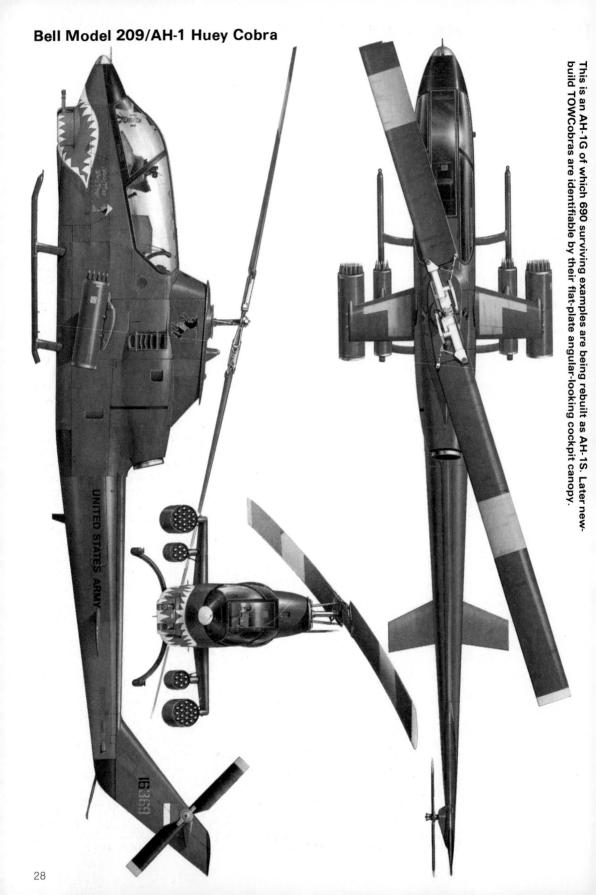

This is an AH-1G of which 690 surviving examples are being rebuilt as AH-1S. Later new-build TOWCobras are identifiable by their flat-plate angular-looking cockpit canopy.

Bell Model 209/AH-1T TOWCobra/AH-1J SeaCobra

History and notes

Somewhat confusingly, the Bell Model 209 appears in two basic families: the single-engine Model 209/AH-1, and the twin-engine version which is described here. This latter variation of the original Model 209, which was ordered into production to meet the US Army's AAFSS (Advanced Aerial Fire Support System) requirement, was produced originally for service with the US Marine Corps, who required that their version of this attack helicopter should have the extra reliability offered by a twin-engine powerplant. The USMC had shown early interest in the potential of a well armed close-support helicopter, for it seemed an ideal aircraft for deployment in support of the type of operations which are typically and traditionally those of the US Marines. Their evaluation of the US Army's AH-1G led to the initial order to Bell in May 1968 for 49 aircraft under the designation AH-1J SeaCobra. Pending delivery of these, the USMC acquired 38 single-engine AH-1G HueyCobras for training and initial deployment, and these entered service in 1969.

The AH-1J SeaCobra is dimensionally basically similar to the US Army's AH-1G. The major difference is in the powerplant, the SeaCobra having a 1,800-shp (1342-kW) Pratt & Whitney Aircraft of Canada T400-CP-400 turboshaft, the militarised version of the same company's PT6T-3 Turbo Twin Pac unit, with two PT6 power sections. In this particular installation the engine and transmission are flat-rated for a normal continuous power output of 1,100 shp (820 kW), but there is a take-off and five-minute emergency power rating of 1,250 shp (932-kW). Reference to the AH-1G will show that this take-off rating represents a power increase of 13.6%, and as a result the tail rotor pylon of the AH-1J has been strengthened and the blade chord of the tail rotor increased to cope with the additional loading and torque.

Armament differs from that of the HueyCobra,

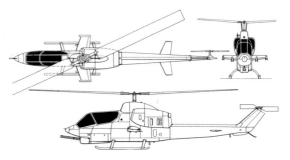

Bell AH-1T (improved SeaCobra)

with the chin-mounted turret housing a three-barrel 20-mm XM197 cannon developed by the General Electric Company. A lightweight version of that company's M61 cannon, this weapon has a firing rate of 750 rounds per minute, but as the total ammunition carried in the magazine is 750 rounds, a 16-round burst limiter is included in the firing mechanism. As with the AH-1G/H, various stores can be carried on the four hardpoints beneath the small stub wings.

On 22 December 1972 Bell announced receipt of an order from the US Army for 202 AH-1Js and these, generally similar to those for the USMC, were acquired by Iran, via the US government, deliveries to that country beginning in 1974. The initial batch of 49 SeaCobras for the USMC was followed, in 1973, by an order for 20 more, for delivery during 1974–75, and on 5 June 1974 Bell received an order to modify the last two aircraft from this production run so that they could carry an increased payload and also have improved performance.

This version of the Model 209 was known initially as the Improved SeaCobra, but has since acquired the USMC designation AH-1T. It differs from the AH-1J in having a more powerful 1,970-shp (1469-kW) Pratt & Whitney Aircraft of Canada

Bell AH-1T SeaCobra, known also as the Model 209 Improved SeaCobra, which has been developed from the twin-engine AH-1J SeaCobra. Ordered for the US Marine Corps, these helicopters have an uprated power-plant, a new dynamic system and advanced technology features.

Bell Model 209/AH-1T TOWCobra/AH-1J Sea Cobra

T400-WV-402 turboshaft. Resulting from the use of this engine, the AH-1T has an improved rotor and tail rotor related to the type developed for the Bell Model 214, an uprated transmission system, a slightly lengthened fuselage to accommodate more fuel, and a lengthened tail boom. The USMC has ordered 57 production aircraft, the first of these being delivered to the USMC on 15 October 1977. Since that time it has been decided to modify 23 of these to launch eight Hughes BGM-71A TOW air-to-surface wire-guided missiles. These are carried in double two-round pods mounted on the stub-wings, and are guided to the target via the crew's helmet sights and a stabilized TOW sight. This version of the Model 209 is known as the TOWCobra.

Specification

Type: close-support armed helicopter
Powerplant: (AH-1J) one 1,800-shp (1342-kW) Pratt & Whitney Aircraft of Canada T400-CP-400 turboshaft; (AH-1T) one 1,970-shp (1469-kW) Pratt & Whitney Aircraft of Canada T400-WV-402 turboshaft
Performance: (AH-1J) maximum speed 207 mph (333 km/h); maximum range (no reserves) 359 miles (578 km)

Weights: (AH-1J) operating 7,261 lb (3294 kg); basic combat 9,972 lb (4523 kg); maximum take-off 10,000 lb (4536 kg);
(AH-1T) empty 8,014 lb (3635 kg); operating 8,608 lb (3905 kg); maximum take-off 14,000 lb (6350 kg)
Dimensions: (AH-1J) main rotor diameter 44 ft 0 in (13.41 m), tail rotor diameter 8 ft 6 in (2.59 m), length (rotor turning) 52 ft 11½ in (16.14 m), height 13 ft 6¼ in (4.12 m), main rotor disc area 1,520.4 sq ft (141.25 m²); (AH-1T) main rotor diameter 48 ft 0 in (14.63 m), tail rotor diameter 9 ft 8½ in (2.96 m), length (rotor turning) 58 ft 0 in (17.68 m), main rotor disc area 1,809.5 sq ft (168.11 m²)
Armament: (AH-1J) XM197 20-mm gun in chin turret, and two underwing hardpoints on each stub wing can accommodate weapons which include XM-18E1 0.3 in (7.62 mm) Minigun pods, and XM-157 (seven-tube) or XM-159 (19-tube) folding-fin rocket pods; (AH-1T) eight TOW missiles in four two-round launchers on outboard stub wing hardpoints, plus other weapons on vacant hardpoints and XM197 gun in chin turret
Operators: (AH-1J) Iran, US Marine Corps; (AH-1T) US Marine Corps

Bell Model 212/UH-1N Twin Two-Twelve

Italian Navy (Marinavia) Agusta-Bell AB.212ASW anti-submarine helicopter.

History and notes

First intimation of a twin-engined version of the Bell Model 205 came on 1 May 1968, when Bell Helicopter Company announced that the Canadian government had approved development of a new general-purpose helicopter. This was to use the basic UH-1 airframe, combined with the PT6T Turbo Twin Pac powerplant produced by Pratt & Whitney Aircraft of Canada. The Canadian authorities later ordered 50, with options on 20 more. The Canadian helicopters were designated initially as CUH-1N, but the official Canadian military designation is CH-135. At the same time the United States armed services announced orders for this aircraft which Bell had designated the Model 212, and which was allocated the tri-service designation UH-1N.

These initial orders comprised 79 for the USAF, 40 for the US Navy and 22 for the US Marine Corps; later orders totalled 159 for the US Navy and

Marine Corps.

Despite Canadian origins, the first production examples of the UH-1N were delivered to the USAF in 1970, but it was not until 3 May 1971 that the first CH-135 for the Canadian Armed Forces was handed over officially with the balance of the order being completed within a year. Other air forces which ordered military versions of this helicopter include those of Argentina and Bangladesh.

Simultaneously with the production of military helicopters, Bell began to manufacture a commercial version which is known as the Twin Two-Twelve and this first received FAA certification in October 1970.

The PT6T (T400) powerplant of the Model 212 was developed initially for this aircraft, financed jointly by Bell, the Canadian government, and Pratt & Whitney Aircraft of Canada. It not only provides 1,800 shp (1342 kW) at its take-off rating, but offers true engine-out capability, plus improved performance in hot day/high altitude operations. This is due to its unique construction, comprising two Pratt & Whitney PT6 turboshaft engines mounted together and each driving into a combining gearbox with a single output shaft.

The Bell Model 212 is built under licence by Agusta in Italy with the designation AB 212, and the first deliveries of these aircraft were made in late 1971. They are generally similar to the Bell production aircraft, but Agusta has developed an anti-submarine variant which has the designation AB 212ASW.

Specification

Type: general-purpose/ASW/ASV helicopter
Powerplant: (UH-1N) 1,800-shp (1342-kW) Pratt & Whitney Aircraft of Canada PT6T-3 Turbo Twin-Pac turboshaft engine, flat rated to 1,290 shp

(962 kW) for take-off
Performance: (UH-1N) maximum cruising speed at sea level 115 mph (185 km/h); maximum range with standard fuel at sea level (no reserves) 248 miles (399 km)
Weights: (UH-1N) maximum take-off and mission 10,500 lb (4763 kg); (Twin Two-Twelve) maximum take-off 11,200 lb (5080 kg)
Dimensions: diameter of main rotor 48 ft 2¼ in (14.69 m); diameter of tail rotor 8 ft 6 in (2.59 m); length (rotors fore and aft) 57 ft 3¼ in (17.46 m); height 14 ft 10¼ in (4.53 m); main rotor disc area 1,809 sq ft (168.06 m²)
Armament: (AB 212ASW) homing torpedoes, depth charges, and air-to-surface missiles
Operators: Argentina, Bangladesh, Canada, Italy, Japan, Norway, Peru, US Air Force, US Marine Corps, US Navy

Bell Model 214 Huey Plus

Iranian Army Aviation
Bell 214A transport helicopter.

History and notes

On 12 October 1970, Bell announced that it had developed as a company-funded project an improved version of the military Model 205/UH-1H, to which it had given the designation Model 214 Huey Plus. The prototype was powered by a 1,900-shp (1417-kW) Lycoming T53-L-702 turboshaft engine, driving a newly-developed main rotor of increased diameter to derive the maximum efficiency from the high-powered turboshaft engine. The airframe was basically that of the Model 205, but had been modified to increase the strength of areas and components which would be put under stress by the increased engine torque and new rotor. Minor internal rearrangement made possible the provision of accommodation for a crew of two and up to 12 passengers. Maximum speed at max take-off weight was 190 mph (306 km/h), but despite this 49.6% increase in speed by comparison with the Model 205, the Model 214 failed to attract the US Army.

However, on 22 December 1972 Bell announced that it had received an order from the US Army for the supply of 287 of these aircraft, to be acquired by Iran through the US government under the designation Model 214A, and six more were ordered in March 1977. These Model 214As were to be powered by the 2,930-shp (2185-kW) Lycoming LTC4B-8D

Agusta-Bell AB214

turboshaft engine, enabling this aircraft, with a strengthened transmission, to carry an increased payload. In February 1976, the government of Iran ordered 39 more aircraft, designated Model 214Cs, which were to be equipped especially for search and rescue missions. These orders were increased by a total of 400 Model 214 aircraft when Bell and the Iranian government agreed in 1975 to establish a helicopter manufacturing industry in Iran. This plan was changed in March 1978 to cover the manufacture in Iran of 50 Model 214As, and 350 of a new version designated Model 214ST with 19-seat capacity and powered by two 1,625-shp (1212-kW) General

Bell Model 214 Huey Plus

Electric T700-GE-TIC turboshaft engines.

In early January 1979 it was reported that the post-Shah Iranian government had terminated this project, but it is believed that Bell will continue with development of the 214ST in the US as a company-funded project. Delivery of Model 214As for Iran began on 26 April 1975, and Bell have also developed a civil version known as the Model 214B BigLifter, which received FAA certification on 27 January 1976.

Specification

Type: single-engine utility helicopter

Powerplant: (214A) one 2,930-shp (2185-kW) Lycoming LTC4B-8D turboshaft
Performance: (214A) cruising speed 161 mph (259 km/h); maximum range at maximum take-off weight 283 miles (455 km)
Weights: (214A) maximum take-off 13,800 lb (6260 kg); maximum take-off with external load 15,000 lb (6804 kg)
Dimensions: (214A) main rotor diameter 50 ft 0 in (15.24 m); tail rotor diameter 9 ft 8 in (2.95 m); main rotor disc area 1,963.5 sq ft (182.4 m²)
Armament: none
Operators: Iran

Beriev Be-12 Tchaika

The Soviet Naval Air Force or AV-MF still operates a number of Beriev Be-12 Mail medium-range maritime patrol amphibians.

History and notes

Together with the Japanese Maritime Self-Defence Force, the AVMF (Soviet Naval Aviation) is the last major service to operate fleets of combat flying-boats and amphibians. Elsewhere, the role of the patrol flying-boat was taken over by long-range landplanes in the 1950s. This process may continue, as no amphibious replacement for the Beriev Be-12 *Tchaika* (seagull), codenamed 'Mail' by NATO, has been reported, and the AVMF has now introduced its first specialized landplane for the maritime reconnaissance role, the Ilyushin Il-38 'May'.

The Beriev design bureau, based at Taganrog on the Sea of Azov, has been the main supplier of marine aircraft to the Soviet navy since 1945, most of its aircraft going to the Northern and Black Sea Fleets. The origins of the Be-12 go back to the LL-143 prototype of 1945, which led in 1949 to the Be-6 'Madge'. This latter twin-engined flying-boat served with success until 1967.

Following the Be-6, the Beriev team carried out a considerable amount of research into jet-powered flying boats, producing the straight-winged Be-R-1 of 1952 and the swept-wing Be-10 of 1960-61. The latter, powered by two Lyulka AL-7RVs (unreheated versions of the Su-7 powerplant), established a number of seaplane records in 1961, but only three or four are believed to have been built.

The lessons learned in the design of the Be-R-1 and Be-10, however, were incorporated in the design

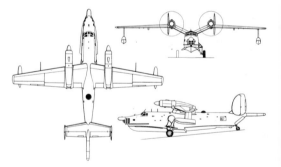

Beriev Be-12 (M-12) Mail

of a much improved flying-boat based loosely on the Be-6 and originally identified by NATO as a re-engined version of the older type. In fact, the Be-12, designated M-12 in AVMF service, bears little more than a general resemblance to the Be-6, sharing only the gull-wing layout and twin tail of its predecessor.

The considerable weight-lifting capability of the Be-12 was demonstrated in a series of class records for amphibians set up in 1964, 1968 and 1970, suggesting a normal weapons load as high as 11,000 lb (5000 kg). The Be-12 can load on the water through large side hatches in the rear fuselage, and stores can be dropped through a watertight hatch in the hull aft of the step. Unlike land-based ASW plat-

Beriev BE-12 Tchaika

forms, a marine aircraft can, in reasonably calm conditions, settle on the water and search with its own sonar equipment, rather than relying exclusively on sonobuoys. It is assumed that the Be-12 has this capability.

With the increasing use of the Mil Mi-14 'Haze' ASW helicopter and the Ilyushin Il 38 'May', there would seem to be a diminishing ASW role for the Be-12, although the type will certainly remain in service as a high-speed search-and-rescue (SAR) vehicle. It is also believed to have been used for mapping, geophysical survey and utility transport. By Soviet standards the type was not built in large numbers, only 75 being reported in service in the late 1970s.

Specification
Type: maritime patrol and reserve amphibian
Powerplant: two 4,190-shp (3126-kW) Ivchenko AI-20D turboprops
Performance: maximum speed 380 mph (610 km/h); economical patrol speed 200 mph (320 km/h); maximum range 2,500 miles (4000 km)
Weights: estimated empty 47,840 lb (21700 kg); maximum take-off about 66,140 lb (3000 kg)
Dimensions: span 97 ft 6 in (29.7 m); length 99 ft (30.2 m); height on land 23 ft (7.0 m)
Armament: bombs, rockets or guided ASMs on underwing pylons; depth charges and sonobuoys in fuselage bays
Operators: USSR

Boeing B-52 Stratofortress

USAF Strategic Air Command Boeing B-52G fitted with latest electro-optical viewing system blisters beneath the nose.

History and notes
By normal standards long since rendered obsolete as a result of its unacceptable vulnerability to anti-aircraft missiles, the mighty Boeing B-52 Stratofortress has seen two would-be successors fall by the wayside, and remains one of the three US strategic deterrents (the other two being the land and sea-launched missiles). More than a billion dollars has been spent on the 315 or so aircraft remaining in the front-line fleet to improve their safety, reliability, performance and weapon-delivery accuracy.

What was to become SAC's 'long rifle' began life in 1948 as a turboprop successor to the piston-engined Boeing B-50, itself a development of the B-29 Superfortress, whose nuclear missions against Japan brought World War II to a close in 1945. Designers were faced with a quandary: the B-50's successor was clearly going to have turbine engines, but how to use them? Ordinary jet engines of the period were so thirsty that a huge airframe would be needed to carry all the fuel. The answer was to harness them to large propellers, as the Soviet Union was to do later with its Tupolev Tu-95 'Bear'. Deciding on the right propulsion system was perhaps the biggest headache facing the early jet-bomber designers. Turboprops were the obvious answer, because they were more economical than pure jets, but on the other hand they were more complicated and less reliable.

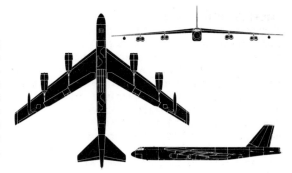

Boeing B-52H Stratofortress

Then, in 1949, Pratt & Whitney brought out the J57 engine. Far and away superior to any other US powerplant, it was to become over the next 30 years one of aviation's really great engines. Originally giving 7,500-lb (3402-kg) thrust, it helped to change the philosophy of both Boeing and the USAF.

The prototype B-52 took to the air for the first time on 15 April 1952. Its technology was based on the medium-range B-47 that had flown five years previously. Thus it had an extremely thin, shoulder-mounted wing, with engines clustered in podded pairs, and a tandem mainwheel arrangement with wing-mounted outrigger wheels to keep the wings level on the ground.

The first three production aircraft were designated B-52As, though they spent their lives at Boeing as test and development aircraft, beginning an improvement programme that has gone on to this day. The first version to join the USAF was the B-52B, virtually identical to the -A but with a navigation/bombing system. Of the 50 built, 27 were converted as RB-52B reconnaissance versions.

The B-52C was substantially improved in performance and equipment, and was the first model to have the white anti-radiation under-surface finish. It was succeeded by the B-52D, with an improved fire-control system for the tail armament of four 0.5-in (12.7-mm) machine-guns. As the B-52Ds were being turned out by Boeing's Wichita plant (the production line was progressively transferred there because of the huge build-up of KC-135 tanker construction at the Seattle factory), the USAF was thinking about the giant bomber's successor. This was to be the WS-110, later the North American B-70.

But the B-70 was years in the future, and B-52 improvement continued with the B-52E, having a more advanced navigation and weapons system, and with a new flight-deck layout to house the equipment displays. Continuing weight increases called for more power, especially at take-off, and the B-52F had a later version of the J57 engine, fitted like earlier versions with water injection to boost take-off power.

The B-52G, which was initially planned to be the final version pending arrival of the B-70, brought along a host of major improvements, and was the biggest single advance of any model. The airframe was substantially redesigned to save weight and to make it safer; integral wing-tanks greatly increased fuel capacity; the tail gunner was relocated in the crew compartment, this saving considerable weight; the fin was shortened; and provision was made for launching ECM decoys and stand-off missiles. The decoy was a small jet aeroplane known as the Quail, designed to have a radar signature similar to that of the bomber to confuse missile radars. One hundred and ninety-three B-52Gs were built, the last in 1960. The missile to go with it was the AGM-28 Hound Dog, which had a range of 750 miles (1207 km). The B-52G in fact was to be less a bomber than the first stage of a missile.

Meanwhile, Boeing and the USAF were planning between them yet another version, the B-52H, to which the specification applies. This really was the final model. It was characterized by two major changes: the introduction of the new Pratt & Whitney TF33 turbofan engine, which at once gave a much greater thrust increase and a considerably lower specific fuel consumption, and structural changes which permitted the aircraft to fly at low altitudes without excessive fatigue problems. It also exchanged the four 0.5-in (12.7-mm) tail guns for a single fast-firing 'Gatling' type gun. It was built to carry Skybolt ballistic missiles under the wings and Quail decoys in the bomb-bay.

The final B-52H, the last of 744 B-52s, rolled out of Wichita in June 1962. The Skybolt missile, which had also been ordered by the RAF, was cancelled in December of that year, while the B-70 project had already been terminated. The B-52s were clearly going to have to soldier on for a long time while the USAF made up its mind what to do about a replacement.

In 1963 the B-52D was studied as a CBC (conventional bomb carrier) and the following year rebuilding of B-52Ds began at Wichita to permit the type to carry 105 'iron' bombs of 750-lb (340-kg) nominal weight, but actually weighing 825 lb (374 kg). In 1965 rebuilt CBC aircraft started to hammer suspected Communist hideouts in South Vietnam and the supply route from North Vietnam known as the Ho Chi Minh trail. The B-52s operated from Andersen AFB on Guam island, 2,600 miles (4185 km) away in the Pacific. Each mission lasted some 10 to 12 hours, with air-refuelling by means of Boeing KC-135 tankers. The B-52s were more feared than any other US weapon.

Since then the USAF launched a new B-52 successor, initially called AMSA (Advanced Manned Strategic Aircraft), later becoming the Rockwell B-1. This also has been cancelled, and there is nothing on the horizon to follow the B-52. Meanwhile a new generation of weapons has come along, such as the SRAM (Short-Range Attack Missile) and the ALCM (Air-Launched Cruise Missile). The SRAM entered service with the B-52G and H versions, and in 1977 the Hound Dog stand-off missile was withdrawn. Apart from a training wing of B-52Ds at Guam, SAC strength is made up of G and H versions. These have been structurally rebuilt and fitted with 14 to 18 new sensor and avionic systems including the ASQ-151 Electro-optical Viewing System. The B-52 is now designated as a carrier for the AGM-86B air-launched cruise missile, and the first B-52G fitted with the relevant Offensive Avionics System was completed in mid-1980.

Specification

Data for B52H only:

Type: long-range strategic bomber

Powerplants: eight 17,000-lb (7711-kg) Pratt & Whitney TF33-P-3 turbofans

Performance: maximum speed Mach 0.95 or 630 mph (1014 km/h) at 40,000 ft (12192 m); typical cruising speed 565 mph (909 km/h) at 36,000 ft (10973 m); service ceiling 55,000 ft (16764 m)

Weight: maximum take-off 505,000 lb (229066 kg)

Dimensions: span 185 ft (56.39 m); length 157 ft (47.85 m); height 40 ft 8 in (12.4 m)

Armament: one T-171 20-mm gun in General Electric rear gun position, 20 SRAM missiles (ALCM due to become operational in the 1980s) and Quail decoys

Operator: US Air Force

Boeing C-135 Series

Boeing KC-135 Stratotanker of the United States Air Force.

History and notes

In August 1954 the USAF announced that it intended to procure a number of tanker/transports developed from the prototype Boeing 367-80 which had first flown a few weeks earlier. These were allocated the designation KC-135A and the first of these made its initial flight on 21 August 1956. Ten months later, on 28 June 1957, the first was delivered to Castle AFB, California. Since that time a family of variants have been built in large numbers for service with the USAF, primarily as tankers (Stratotankers) or cargo transports (Stratolifters), but many have been built or converted for special purposes.

Designated Model 717 by Boeing, these aircraft differ primarily from the later Model 707 by having a smaller-diameter fuselage, deletion of cabin windows, reduced size and weight, and the capability of carrying 80 passengers or an equivalent weight in cargo on the main deck. All equipment for the tanker role is accommodated on the lower deck, or normal cargo area, this including the pivoted 'flying boom' refuelling gear. Subsequently this was modified for probe-and-drogue refuelling of Tactical Air Command or US Navy Marine Corps aircraft. Two modified KC-135As are used by the US Federal Aviation Agency (FAA) to check navigation aids throughout the United States.

Other variants of the Model 717 tanker/transport include the KC-135B, generally similar to KC-135As but powered by turbofan engines. Seventeen were built to serve as Airborne Command Posts for the Strategic Air Command. These aircraft, subsequently redesignated EC-135C, have TF33 turbofan engines, a flight-refuelling receptacle as well as a boom, suitable avionics to act as a control centre, and a crew of 16. EC-135A is the designation of turbojet-powered aircraft equipped to act as backups to the EC-135Cs. The EC-135G/H/K are turbojet-powered command posts with more advanced equipment, and the EC-135J is a turbofan-powered variant of the EC-135H. EC-135L aircraft are turbojet-powered KC-135As equipped for a dual role of command posts and airborne communications relay stations.

Special-purpose test aircraft for use by USAF Systems Command carry the designations C-135A, JKC-135A, KC-135A, and NKC-135A. RC-135Ds with turbojet engines and RC-135Cs and RC-135Es with turbofan engines all have the boom deleted and are equipped instead with sophisticated avionics and

Boeing C-135

a crop of radar antennae for various reconnaissance, Elint and other missions. C-135F is the designation applied to 12 dual-purpose tanker/transports (with booms terminating in a drogue) supplied to the French air force. Last of the Stratotanker variants are three NC-135As equipped initially to monitor the blast of nuclear weapons during tests, and used also during 1965 with special equipment to study a total solar eclipse.

The Model 717 Stratolifter family differs from the foregoing by being equipped specifically to serve as long-range transports, with the refuelling boom deleted. There is a structural similarity between these two basic 'tanker/lifter' types, but interior changes in the latter provide accommodation for up to 126 troops, or 44 stretchers plus 54 sitting casualties. Galley and toilet facilities are provided at the rear of the cabin, and provision is made for an alternative all-freight role. The initial version is the C-135A with turbojet engines, first flown on 19 May 1961, and delivered to MATS on 8 June 1961 to become the service's first strategic jet transport.

Other versions include C-135Bs, similar to the above but with turbofan engines; four RC-135A (Boeing Model 739) reconnaissance aircraft for the 1,370th Photo Mapping Wing of the MAC; 10 similar RC-135Bs with turbofan engines; VC-135B is the designation of 11 C-135Bs modified to serve as VIP transports; and 10 WC-135Bs, similar to C-135Bs, are equipped for long-range weather reconnaissance duties.

The life of the USAF's fleet will be extended into the next century by powerplant and structural modifications. Between 1982 and 1991 the fleet of

KC-135s will be re-engined with General Electric/SNECMA CFM-56 turbofans, complementing a current wing reskinning programme. The lower fuel consumption of the CFM-56s almost doubles the fuel available for refuelling operations. Re-engined aircraft will be designated KC-135REs.

Specification
Type: turbine-powered tanker/transport
Powerplant: (KC-135A derivatives) four 13,500-lb (6124-kg) Pratt & Whitney J57-P-59W turbojets; (C-135B) four 18,000-lb (8165-kg) thrust Pratt &

Whitney TF33-P-5 turbofans
Performance: /C-135B) maximum speed 600 mph (966 km/h); average cruising at 35,000 ft (10670 m) 530 mph (853 km/h)
Weights: (C-135B) operating empty 102,300 lb (46403 kg); maximum take-off 275,500 lb (124965 kg)
Dimensions: (KC-135A) span 130 ft 10 in (39.88 m); length 136 ft 3 in (41.53 m); height 38 ft 4 in (11.68 m); wing area 2,433 sq ft (226.03 m²)
Armament: none
Operators: France, US Air Force

Boeing E-3 Sentry

Boeing E-3A Sentry AWACS of the United States Air Force. The first of 34 aircraft on order was delivered in March 1977.

History and notes
The requirement for an Airborne Warning And Control System (AWACS) aircraft was first proposed by the USAF in 1963, at which time it was planned for up to 64 specially-equipped aircraft to be provided. They were then considered essential to alert US air defence of approaching Soviet bomber attacks, and to act as mobile control centres in no fixed geographical position, able to control all national air activities in both nuclear or conventional combat operations. Since the origination of the concept, economic considerations have made it necessary to reduce considerably the number of aircraft to be acquired initially.

Though an AWACS is a development of the traditional Airborne Early-Warning (AEW) aircraft, the entire concept is far more all-embracing. It also fulfils the roles of the Airborne Command Post (ACP), typified by the EC-135 variants which have served with the USAF's Strategic Air Command. AWACS is a combination of both families, with advanced on-board avionics that make possible the simultaneous co-ordination of many differing air operations, so that these aircraft could command and control the entire air effort of a nation, embracing strike, interception, reconnaissance and interdiction, plus the backup roles of support and airlift.

Two main areas of use have been planned by the USAF, with the Tactical Air Command (TAC) using its AWACS aircraft for airborne surveillance, and as a command centre for the rapid development of TAC forces. A differing role is envisaged for the same aircraft by Aerospace Defense Command (ADC), who

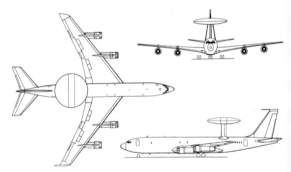

Boeing E-3A Sentry

regard the AWACS aircraft as 'hard to find' command and control posts.

Boeing was the successful one of two contenders for the supply of an AWACS aircraft, being awarded a contract on 23 July 1970 to provide two prototypes under the designation EC-137D. The company's proposed AWACS was based on the airframe of the Boeing Model 707-320B commercial transport, and the prototypes were modified in the first place to carry out comparative trials between the prototype downward-looking surveillance radars designed by the Hughes Aircraft Company and Westinghouse Electric Corporation. These tests continued into the autumn of 1972, and on 5 October the USAF announced that Westinghouse had been selected as prime contractor for the advanced radar that was to be the essential core of the AWACS. This has the difficult task of seeking and identifying low-flying

Boeing E-3 Sentry

The easily identifiable Boeing E-3A Sentry Airborne Warning and Control System (AWACS) aircraft for service with the USAF. The 30-ft (9.14-m) diameter rotodome houses a 24-ft (7-32m) diameter antenna.

targets at ranges as great as 230 miles (370 km), and in the case of high altitude attack at even greater ranges.

The USAF has acquired an extensive knowledge of the operation and capabilities of the Boeing Model 707, especially in the form of the smaller EC-135 variants which have served well and long. It was clear that with far more advanced equipment the same aircraft could provide the desired potential, thus ensuring that equipment acquired for and experience derived from the EC-135 would offer an important and reliable contribution to the AWACS concept.

Very little modification of the basic 707-320B airframe was required to make it suitable for the new role. Most important, and an external identification feature *par excellence,* is the large rotodome assembly carried on two wide-chord streamlined struts, which are secured to the rear upper fuselage. New engine pylon fairings are provided for the more powerful turbofan engines which power the pre-production EC-137Cs and production aircraft, the latter having the designation E-3A (the original choice of eight General Electric TF34 engines was abandoned to save money). The remainder of the essential avionics aerials (antennae) are housed within the wings, fuselage, fin and tailplane. Internal modifications include the provision of floor rein-

forcement, and new cooling and wiring installations. The normal crew consists of four flight crew and 13 AWACS specialists. The main operating area above the floor is equipped with nine MPCs (Multi-Purpose Consoles) for the specialist mission crew. Other crew manage systems and radar maintenance.

Not surprisingly, the mass of avionics equipment necessary for the E-3A to fulfil its appointed role needs considerable electrical power, and this is supplied by generators with a combined capacity of 600 kVA. Complex cooling and air-conditioning systems ensure dissipation of excessive heat and the creation of an ideal working environment for crew and equipment. Thus, a liquid cooling system protects the radar transmitter, which is housed in the aft cargo hold, while a conventional air-cycle and ram-air environmental control system is responsible for crew comfort and the safe operation of other avionics equipment.

The overfuselage rotodome is 30 ft 0 in (9.14 m) in diameter and has a maximum depth of 6 ft 0 in (1.83 m). It incorporates the AN/APY-1 surveillance radar and IFF/TADIL C antennae. During operational use the rotodome is driven hydraulically at 6 rpm, but in non-operational flight it is rotated at ¼ rpm to ensure that low temperatures do not cause the bearing lubricant to congeal and prevent emergency operation. The initial Westinghouse radar operates on

Boeing E-3 Sentry

pulse Doppler technology, providing long-range, accuracy and downlook capability: it scans mechanically in azimuth and electronically from ground level up into the stratosphere. Westinghouse was awarded a contract in 1976 to develop maritime surveillance capability which could be an add-on feature to the existing radar and this, if adopted, would be retrofitted to in-service E-3As.

Heart of the AWACS is an IBM 4-Pi CC-1 high-speed computer, with a processing speed of some 740,000 operations per second, main memory capacity of 114,688 words, and mass memory size of 802,816 words. Navigation is provided by duplicated Carousel IV INS (Inertial Navigation System), AN/ARN-120 Omega and AN/APN-213 Doppler. Installed communications equipment provides HF, VHF and UHF for transmission/reception of information in clear/secure mode, in either vocal or digital form.

The first production E-3A was delivered to the USAF's 552nd Airborne Warning and Control Wing at Tinker AFB, Oklahoma, on 24 March 1977. A total of 10 were scheduled for delivery by the end of 1978, and production funding for a total of 22 aircraft had been approved by mid-1978. NATO plans to acquire 18 E-3As for basing in West Germany, and the total USAF procurement is to reach 34 Sentries.

Specification

Type: airborne early-warning and command post aircraft
Power Plant: four 21,000-lb (9525-kg) Pratt & Whitney TF33-PW-100/100A turbofans
Performance: maximum speed 530 mph (853 km/h) at altitude; endurance 6 hours at a distance of 1,000 miles (1609 km) from base; service ceiling 40,000 ft (12192 m)
Weights: empty 172,000 lb (78019 kg); maximum take-off 325,000 lb (147419 kg)
Dimensions: span 145 ft 9 in (44.42 m); length 152 ft 11 in (46.61 m); height 42 ft 5 in (12.93 m); wing area 2,890 sq ft (268.5 m²)
Aramament: none
Operators: NATO (from 1982), USAF

Boeing E-4/747

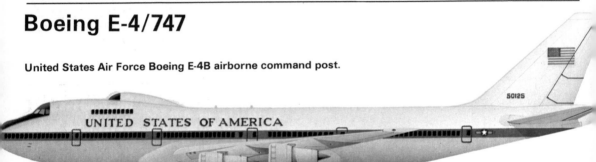

United States Air Force Boeing E-4B airborne command post.

History and notes

No matter how good they may be, a country's strategic forces are of little use in war unless it is possible to maintain reliable and coherent command and control of these forces. To ensure that it retains just such a capability, even in the aftermath of a nuclear attack, the United States Department of Defense has made plans to cope with all foreseen eventualities. It has created a National Military Command System, through which National Command Authorities are able to issue orders, and receive a feedback of information to show whether the orders were effective or not.

Currently there are three major command sources, the first two being the National Military Command Center, and the Alternate National Military Command Center. The latter is underground, for obvious reasons, but both of these have fixed geographical positions, and it has been appreciated for some number of years that an airborne command post would represent something approaching the ideal, its mobility in three dimensions making it a far more difficult target for an enemy to locate, especially in sufficient time to prevent massive retaliation to a surprise attack. This thinking led to procurement of the Boeing EC-135 Airborne Command Post (ABNCP), and these special versions of the Boeing C-135 family have been operational in this role since the early 1960s.

That the retention of a viable ABNCP is critical

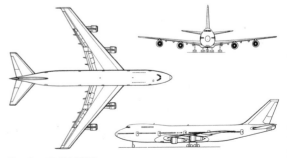

Boeing E-4B/747

can be appreciated by considering that just one of these aircraft can control America's force of ICBMs, its manned bombers, and its nuclear-powered missile-carrying submarines. Confidence in the created National Military System depends upon a survivable ABNCP, and DoD planners are in the process of replacing the ageing EC-135 by a new Boeing E-4 Advanced Airborne Command Post (AABNCP) which it is believed will have much increased survivability. This new and vital aircraft relies upon utilisation of the Boeing 747 airframe, and the announcement of an initial contract for two 747Bs to be converted to serve as AABNCP aircraft was first released on 28 February 1973. Follow-up contracts for two more aircraft were awarded in July and September 1973. It was announced subsequently that the total planned force is six aircraft, and it was anticipated that these would be fully operational in 1983.

Three aircraft of the initial four which were contracted became operational as E-4As in an ABNCP role. They were built with Pratt & Whitney F105 engines, and had avionics and equipment removed from EC-135 aircraft. The first of these E-4As, which represents an interim development stage, was handed over in December 1974. The second and third followed in May and September 1975, all three delivered initially to Andrews AFB, Maryland.

The remaining three aircraft have more advanced avionics and equipment, and different engines, under the designation E-4B. The first was delivered to the USAF in August 1975, and the installation of its advanced command, control and communications equipment was completed on schedule towards the end of 1979.

The three E-4As are being updated to E-4B standard, and in addition to advanced avionics will have a high-capacity air-conditioning system to maintain an equitable temperature for their operation, a large capacity electrical generating system, SHF and LF/VLF communications, and nuclear thermal shielding.

Boeing 747s are used in transport, air refuelling and electronics roles by Iran.

Specification
Type: special-purpose airborne command post
Powerplant: four 52,500-lb (23814-kg) thrust General Electric F103-GE-100 turbofans
Performance: maximum speed 655 mph (1054 km/h) at 36,000 ft (10973 m); endurance more than 12 hours
Weights: maximum weight 775,000 lb (351538 kg)
Dimensions: span 195 ft 8 in (59.64 m); length 231 ft 4 in (70.51 m); height 63 ft 5 in (19.33 m); wing area 5,500 sq ft (510.95 m²)
Armament: none
Operators: Iran, US Air Force

Boeing Vertol Model 107/CH-46/UH-46 Sea Knight

History and notes
Shortly after the formation of Vertol Aircraft Corporation in March 1956 the company initiated a design study for a twin-turbine commercial transport helicopter. In formulating the design, special attention was given to ensuring that it would be suitable also for military use if the armed forces showed an interest in its procurement. As a result, the tandem rotor layout which had been developed fully by Vertol, and the Piasecki Helicopter Corporation before it, was chosen because of its known performance and reliability. Twin turbines were chosen

to power this new helicopter, for despite the fact that they had not then acquired a long history of reliability and economy, there was no doubt that these engines offered a superior power/weight ratio, and were improving progressively all the time.

Construction of a prototype (company designation Model 107) began in May 1957, and the first flight was recorded on 22 April 1958. Company testing and development progressed well, and an extensive

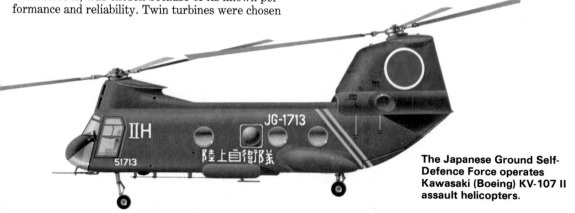

The Japanese Ground Self-Defence Force operates Kawasaki (Boeing) KV-107 II assault helicopters.

Boeing Vertol Model 107/CH-46/UH-46 Sea Knight

demonstration tour aroused considerable interest. First of the armed forces wishing to evaluate this new helicopter was the US Army which, in July 1958, ordered 10 slightly modified aircraft under the designation YHC-1A. and the first of these flew on 27 August 1959 for the first time. By that time the US Army had become more interested in a larger, more powerful helicopter which Vertol had developed from the Model 107 and, in consequence, reduced its order to only three YHC-1As.

When the US Marine Corps showed an interest in this aircraft one was modified as the Boeing Vertol Model 107M, with GE-8B engines (see data), and this was successful in winning the USMC's design competition in February 1961, and was ordered into production under the designation HRB-1 (changed to CH-46A in 1962), and given the name Sea Knight.

The first CH-46A flew on 16 October 1962, and testing continued into late 1964, with the first US Marine squadrons taking these aircraft into service in early 1965. Since then a number of versions have been built, including the CH-46D for the USMC, generally similar to the CH-46A, but with 1,400-shp (1044-kW) T58-GE-10 turboshaft engines; the CH-46F for the USMC, generally similar to the CH-46D, but with additional avionics; the UH-46A Sea Knight, similar to CH-46A, procured by the US Navy with first deliveries to Utility Helicopter Squadron 1 in July 1964; and the UH-46D for the US Navy, virtually the same as the CH-46D. The US Marine Corps plans to update 273 of its Sea Knights to CH-46Es, with 1,870-shp (1394-kW) General Electric T58-GE-16 turboshafts and other improvements.

Kawasaki in Japan acquired from Boeing Vertol

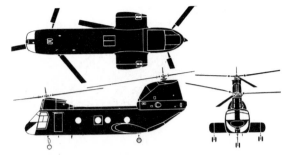

Boeing Vertol CH-46 Sea Knight

worldwide sales rights for the Model 107-II, and continues to produce these helicopters in 1979 under the designation KV-107/II.

Specification
Type: tandem-rotor utility transport helicopter
Powerplant: (CH-46A) two 1,250-shp (932-kW) General Electric T58-GE-8B turboshafts
Performance: (CH-46D) maximum speed 166 mph (267 km/h); maximum cruising speed 165 mph (266 km/h); range at AUW of 20,800 lb (9435 kg) with 4,550-lb (2064-kg) payload and 10% reserves 238 miles (383 km)
Weights: (CH-46D) empty equipped 13,067 lb (5927 kg); maximum take-off 23,000 lb (10433 kg)
Dimensions: (CH-46D) rotor diameter (each) 51 ft 0 in (15.54 m); length (rotors turning) 84 ft 4 in (25.70 m); height 16 ft 8½ in (5.09 m); main rotor disc area (total) 4,086 sq ft (379.6m²)
Armament: none
Operators: Canada, Japan, Sweden, Thailand, US Marine Corps, US Navy

Boeing Vertol 114/234/CH-47-Chinook

History and notes
Following the evaluation of submissions by five US helicopter manufacturers, the US Army selected Boeing Vertol's Model 114 as most nearly meeting its requirements for a 'battlefield mobility' helicopter. This was expected to be suitably equipped for all-weather operations, to lift a load of 2 US tons (4,000 lb/1814 kg) internally or of 8 US tons (16,000 lb/7258 kg) suspended from an external sling, carry a maximum of 40 troops with full equipment, to have straight-in rear loading, be suitable for casualty evacuation roles, and be able to airlift any component of the Martin Marietta Pershing missile system. An initial contract for five YHC-1Bs was placed in June 1959, but soon after entering service these were redesignated YCH-47A and given the name Chinook.

Boeing Vertol's Model 114 was, in effect, a larger and more powerful version of the CH-46 Sea Knight. The non-retractable landing gear is of quadricycle

Boeing Vertol CH-47C Chinook

configuration, and the fuselage has sealed and compartmented fairing pods on each side of the lower fuselage and extending for almost three-quarters of the fuselage length, to supplement the buoyancy of

Boeing Vertol 114/234/CH-47 Chinook

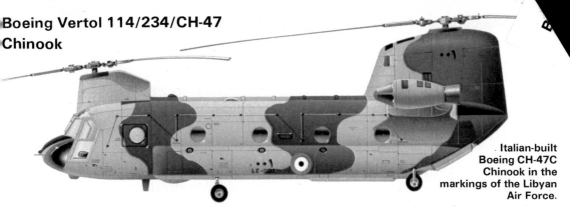

Italian-built Boeing CH-47C Chinook in the markings of the Libyan Air Force.

the sealed lower fuselage for water operations. The first YHC-1B made its first flight on 21 September 1961, by which time the first production contract for CH-47A aircraft had been placed. These were powered initially by 2,200-shp (1641-kW) Lycoming T55-L-5 turboshaft engines, subsequently by 2,650-shp (1976-kW) T55-L-7 turboshafts, and deliveries of CH-47As began in December 1972.

Since that time a number of versions have been built, including the CH-47B, a development with more powerful 2,850-shp (2125-kW) T55-L-7C turboshafts, redesigned rotor blades and other detail refinements, the first of two prototypes making its first flight during October 1966, with deliveries beginning on 10 May 1967. The current production version has the designation CH-47C/Model 234 and is powered by two 3,750-shp (2796-kW) T55-L-11C turboshafts, has a strengthened transmission system, and increased fuel capacity. The first of these aircraft made its initial flight on 14 October 1967, and deliveries of production aircraft began in early 1968.

Chinooks operated in South-east Asia proved most valuable, not only for the transport of troops and supplies, and for casualty evacuation, but also for the recovery of disabled aircraft and the airlift of refugees. Chinooks are still considered an important component of the US Army's helicopter air logistic forces, and all surviving CH-47A/B aircraft are being modernised, this being initially to CH-47C standard.

Chinooks are built in Italy for European and Middle East customers, with manufacture beginning in 1970. Elicotteri Meridionali acquired from Boeing Vertol co-production and marketing rights in 1968, and construction of the airframe to CH-47C standard is carried out by SIAI-Marchetti. Boeing Vertol is also developing in America a Model 234LR Commercial Chinook for civil transport and offshore oilfield support.

Specification
Type: tandem-rotor medium transport helicopter
Powerplant: (CH-47C) two 3,750-shp (2796-kW) Lycoming T55-L-11C turboshafts
Performance: (CH-47C) average cruising speed 153 mph (246 km/h); ferry range with maximum intergral and internal auxiliary fuel (at optimum altitude, 10% reserves) 1,331 miles (2142 km)
Weights: empty 21,162 lb (9599 kg); maximum take-off 46,000 lb (20865 kg)
Dimensions: rotor diameter (each) 60 ft 0 in (18.29 m); length (rotors turning) 99 ft 0 in (30.18m); height 18 ft 7¾ in (5.68 m); main rotor disc area (total) 5,655 sq ft (525.35 m²)
Armament: none, except as detailed above for ACH-47A
Operators: Australia, Austria, Canada, Germany, Iran, Italy, Korea, Libya, Morocco, Spain, Thailand, Turkey, UK, US Army, US National Guard, Vietnam

British Aerospace (Hawker Siddeley) 748/Andover C.2/Coastguarder

History and notes
Better known as an airliner, the BAe (HS) 748 has sold in large numbers as a military transport. Fifty per cent (including the Andover CC.1) of the 350 sold earn their keep by hauling cargo and personnel for armed services. The type's large-span wing and powerful turboprops give good field performance, and carriage of bulky and outsize loads is facilitated by an optional cargo door on the left behind the wing. Military specialization extends to a strengthened floor, fittings according to role, and

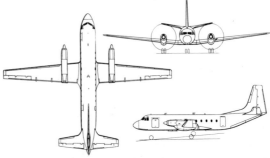

British Aerospace 748 Srs 2A/Andover C.2

British Aerospace (Hawker Siddeley) 748/Andover C.2/ Coastguarder

Queen's Flight HS Andover CC.2 maintained by the Royal Air Force at Benson, Oxfordshire.

overload take-off and landing weights, which produce a corresponding improvement in payload/range performance.

The 748 evolved from an Avro design for a short/medium-range twin-turboprop airliner embarked on in January 1959. The first prototype flew on 24 June 1960 and was produced as the Series 1 for seven years. Included in this batch were two Andover CC.2s for the Queen's Flight. The Series 2A, the principal military variant, differs from the Series 2 (in production from 1967) in having more powerful Rolls-Royce Dart 534-2 or 535-2 engines. The latter powerplant is now standard. Subsequent development produced the Series 2B, with improvements designed to better 'hot and high' performance: an increase in span of 4 ft (1.22m) and the fitting of Dart 536-2 turboprops. All flight regimes are improved, and payload is increased by 2,000 lb (907 kg).

The latest in this line is the Coastguarder, British Aerospace's bid to gain a foothold in the overcrowded maritime patrol and protection market. The prototype was converted from a Series 2A and flew on 18 February 1977. Changes have since been extended to fitting a wet wing. Although basically still a 748, the Coastguarder has undergone a number of modifications, revolving primarily around the electronics. A standard crew comprises two pilots, two beam observers and a tactical navigator. An important part of the Coastguarder's duties will be search and rescue, and to this end a 1-ft (0.3-m)-diameter chute is fitted in the rear fuselage, through which can be ejected five-man dinghies and

marker flares. The tactical navigator, seated over the wing, has an MEL Marec radar display and plotting table, Decca 72 Doppler and a Decca 9447 tactical air navigation system computer and display. The radar provides 360° coverage over 230 miles (370 km) for the tactical navigator, and 285 miles (460 km) for the pilot. A 'zoom' effect allows selective magnification of any part of the display. As with the other military variants, the Coastguarder can be converted to carry seats on full-length rails. For airdropping of survival equipment to accident victims, the wide rear door is optional.

Specification
Type: transport
Powerplant: two 2,280-ehp (1687-kW) Rolls-Royce Dart 534-2 or 535-2 single-shaft turboprops
Performance: cruising speed 281 mph (452 km/h); maximum rate of climb at sea level 1,420 ft (433 m) per minute; range with maximum payload 1,066 miles (1714 km); range with maximum fuel 1,624 miles (2613 km)
Weights: empty equipped 25,453 lb (11545 kg); maximum take-off 46,500 lb (21092 kg); optional overload maximum take-off 51,000 lb (23133 kg)
Dimensions: span 98 ft 6 in (30.02 m); length 67 ft 0 in (20.42 m); height 24 ft 10 in (7.57 m); wing area 810.75 sq ft (75.35 m²)
Armament: none
Operators: Argentina, Australia, Belgium, Brazil, Brunei, Colombia, Ecuador, India, Nepal, New Zealand, Thailand, UK, Zambia

---

British Aerospace (Hawker Siddeley) Buccaneer

Used for low-level strike and reconnaissance duties, the HS Buccaneer S.2B equips three Royal Air Force squadrons in Germany.

History and notes
Designed by a team under B.P. Laight of Blackburn Aircraft Ltd in the days before most pioneer British aircraft companies lost their separate identities in the mergers of the 1960s and 1970s, the Buccaneer was itself something of a pioneer. It has consistently

proved to be a far better aeroplane than many have given it credit for, and is still giving valuable service more than 25 years after its conception. Developed to Royal Navy requirement NA.39 (issued in the early 1950s) as a two-seat carrier-based low-level strike

British Aerospace (Hawker Siddeley) Buccaneer

Buccaneer S.2Bs of No 15 Sqn, RAF, with two more about half a mile away, streak across the North Sea on a simulated low-level attack mission from their German base at Laarbruch. The Buccaneer is unusual in being able to attack in the clean configuration.

aircraft, it was the first such type in the world actually to be built for this high-speed under-the-radar means of penetrating enemy airspace. The airframe design incorporated a number of then-novel features, such as a full wings-and-tail boundary layer control system for maximum lift; area-ruling of the bulky fuselage; and the fuselage tail-cone was split vertically and hinged so that the two halves could be deployed as airbrakes.

Blackburn's B.103 design was chosen in 1955 to meet the NA.39 requirement, an order being placed in July of that year for an evaluation batch of 20 aircraft; the first nine of these were allocated primarily for manufacturer's trials (initial flight being made on 30 April 1958), and the next five to the Ministry of Aviation for further development. Powerplant of the pre-production models was a pair of 7,000-lb (3175-kg) static thrust de Havilland Gyron Junior DGJ.1 turbojets; the full naval 'kit' of folding wings and nose, arrester hook, plus catapult points, was introduced on the fourth example, which carried out the first carrier compatibility trials. The fifth NA.39 was used for weapon testing, and numbers 15 to 20 were used to equip No 700Z Flight at RNAS Lossiemouth, an Intensive Flying Trials Unit formed in 1961 to prepare the aircraft for entry into Fleet Air Arm service.

An initial production order, for 40 aircraft, had been placed in October 1959, these being designated Buccaneer S.1. The first example made its maiden flight on 23 January 1962, and on 17 July of the same year No 801 Squadron of the Fleet Air Arm was commissioned as the first operational Buccaneer squadron. The squadron embarked in HMS Ark Royal in the following January. Two additional squadrons, Nos 800 and 809, were later formed with the S.1, replacing Supermarine Scimitars in the strike role. Production of this model ended in December 1963, powerplant being the Gyron Junior

British Aerospace Buccaneer S.2B

101 of 7,100 lb (3220 kg) static thrust.

The S.1 was decidedly underpowered, and the Rolls-Royce Spey turbofan was therefore selected to power the major Buccaneer production variant, the S.2. Two of the pre-production NA.39s served as Mk 2 prototypes in 1963, the first of 84 production S.2s making its initial flight on 5 June 1964. With lower fuel consumption, plus some 30 per cent more power, the S.2 (identifiable by its larger, oval-shaped intakes) had a considerably better range than the S.1, a factor further enhanced by the provision in this variant for in-flight refuelling. This model began entering FAA service in October 1965, eventually equipping Nos 800, 801, 803 and 809 Squadrons, operating from the aircraft-carriers Ark Royal, Eagle and Victorious. Last to retire was No 809 from HMS Ark Royal, in 1979. A fully 'navalised' version of the Buccaneer, although scheduled for operation from shore bases, was the Mk 50 supplied in 1965 to the South African air force. These 16 aircraft, to aid their potential use from 'hot and high' airfields, were fitted with a Bristol Siddeley BS.605 twin-chamber rocket motor in the rear of the fuselage, enabling a 30-second boost of 8,000 lb (3628 kg) static thrust to be added to that of the basic powerplant to provide increased power for take-off.

British Aerospace (Hawker Siddeley) Buccaneer

The Royal Navy Buccaneer S.2s were not, however, retired when the progressive depletion of Britain's carrier force caused their withdrawal from Fleet Air Arm service. From 1969 onwards they were instead transferred to the Royal Air Force, whose first Buccaneer squadron (No 12) became operational with the type in July 1970, followed shortly afterwards by No 208 Squadron. With some changes to the internal systems and equipment to meet their new operator's requirements, they were then redesignated S.2A, about 70 aircraft being converted in this manner. Subsequently they underwent a further updating/modification programme, from which they emerged as Buccaneer S.2Bs, the primary difference being a capability to deliver the Martel anti-radar TV-guided missile. Other changes involved a new, bulged weapons bay door (accommodating an additional fuel tank) and detail improvements to the airframe. Apart from those converted to the new S.2B standard, 43 more were ordered as new-production aircraft, the first of these making its initial flight on 8 January 1970. The S.2B equips Nos 15 and 16 Squadrons, based at RAF Laarbruch in Germany. Two other RAF Buccaneers acted as systems trials aircraft for the Panavia Tornado multi-role combat aircraft. Before their retirement, the remaining Royal Navy Buccaneers also underwent comparable modifications, receiving the new designation S.2C (without Martel capability) and S.2D (with Martels).

It is the Buccaneer's high subsonic speed, plus an ability to accept continually updated systems and weapons throughout its career, that have kept it a viable front-line combat aircraft for nearly two decades. Aside from the usual capacity for underwing-mounted weapons, it has the novel feature of a rotary bomb door, on the inside of which conventional or nuclear weapons can be carried. By rotating to expose these for delivery, it avoids the drag penalty of the more orthodox type of door which opens into the surrounding airstream, so avoiding adverse effects upon its performance at the crucial moment of weapon release. The tough airframe is ideal for the high-g weaving flight paths demanded by the terrain-following nature of its primary low-level attack role. On-board systems provide night and all-weather attack capability; Doppler-type navigation, moving-map display linked to a computer, and radar acquisition of the target are standard.

Specification

Type: tandem two-seat low-level strike and reconnaissance aircraft
Powerplant: two 11,255-lb (5105-kg) Rolls-Royce Spey 101 turbofans
Performance: (except Mk 1) maximum speed at 200 ft (61 m) 645 mph (1038 km/h); typical hi-lo-hi range with weapons 2,300 miles (3700 km); endurance with two in-flight refuellings 9 hours; maximum rate of climb at sea level 7,000 ft (2134 m) per minute; service ceiling over 40,000 ft (12200 m)
Weights: (except Mk 1) empty about 30,000 lb (13610 kg); typical take-off 46,000 lb (20865 kg) to 56,000 lb (25400 kg); maximum take-off 62,000 lb (28123 kg); typical landing 35,000 lb (15876 kg)
Dimensions: (except Mk 1) span 44 ft 0 in (13.41 m); span folded 19 ft 11 in (6.07 m); length 63 ft 5 in (19.33 m); length folded 51 ft 10 in (15.79 m); height 16 ft 3 in (4.95 m); height folded 16 ft 8 in (5.08 m); wing area 514.7 sq ft (47.82 m^2)
Armament: (S.2B) four 1,000-lb (454-kg) bombs, multi-sensor reconnaissance pack, or 440-Imperial gallon (2000-litre) fuel tank, on inside of rotary bomb door; up to 3,000 lb (1360 kg) of bombs and/or missiles on each of four underwing attachments; making total possible weapons load of 16,000 lb (7257 kg)
Operators: South Africa, UK

British Aerospace (BAC) Canberra

History and notes

A total of 27 marks of BAe (BAC) Canberra were built, including seven variants of the Martin B-57 for the US Air Force, during a production run of more than 10 years. Britain manufactured 901 aircraft, Australia made 48 for the Royal Australian Air Force, and the USAF flew 403 built under licence by Martin in Baltimore, Maryland, for a total of 1,352.

Some of the more important British-built marks included the PR.3 reconnaissance version with stretched fuselage to house more fuel, the T.4 side-by-side trainer, the B.6 with wet wings and more power, the reconnaissance PR.7 and, later, Shorts' high-altitude PR.9 with enlarged span, extended chord, offset canopy and much more powerful Avon

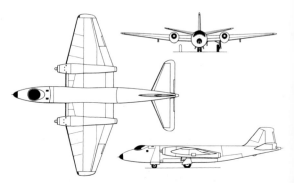

British Aerospace Canberra B.6

British Aerospace (BAC) Canberra

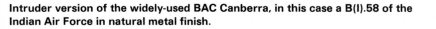

Indian Air Force BAC Canberra B Mk 66, one of ten purchased by the service for strike duties.

Intruder version of the widely-used BAC Canberra, in this case a B(I).58 of the Indian Air Force in natural metal finish.

206 engines. The PR.9's fighter-style offset cockpit was pioneered by the most versatile of all the marks, the B(I).8. This was a two-seat long-range night interdictor, high-altitude bomber and target marker, whose armament is listed below. The U.10 was an unmanned target modified from the B.2 by Shorts.

Specification

Type: two/three-seat bomber, reconnaissance aircraft and trainer

Powerplant: two 7,500-lb (3357-kg) Rolls-Royce Avon 109 turbojets; (PR.9) two 11,000-lb (4990-kg) Avon 206

Performance: maximum speed at sea level 517 mph (827 km/h) or Mach 0.68; maximum speed at 40,000 ft (14630 m) 541 mph (871 km/h); range with maximum fuel (no reserves) 3,630 miles (5840 km); range with maximum load (no reserves) at 2,000 ft (600 m) and 10 minutes over target at full power 805 miles (1295 km); maximum rate of climb at sea level 3,400 ft (1035 m) per minute

Weights: empty equipped 27,950 lb (12678 kg); maximum take-off 54,950 lb (24925 kg); maximum zero-fuel 33,180 lb (15050 kg); maximum landing 40,000 lb (18145 kg)

Dimensions: span 64 ft 0 in (19.51 m), (PR.9) 67 ft 10 in (20.67 m); length 65 ft 6 in (19.96 m), (PR.9) 66 ft 8 in (20.32 m); height 15 ft 8 in (4.77 m); wing area 960 sq ft (89.19 m²), (PR.9) 1,045 sq ft (97.08 m²)

Armament: six 1,000-lb (454-kg) or one 4,000-lb (1814-kg) and two 1,000-lb (454-kg) or eight 500-lb (226-kg) bombs internally, plus up to 2,000 lb (907 kg) of stores on underwing pylons; four Hispano 20-mm cannon; sixteen 4.5-in flares internally; two AS.30 missiles; two packs of 37 rockets externally

Operators: Argentina, Australia, Ecuador, Ethiopia, India, Peru, Rhodesia, South Africa, UK, Venezuela

British Aerospace (Hawker Siddeley) Harrier

History and notes

A decade after its entry into service the BAe (HS) Harrier is still, with the sole exception of the USSR's later but far less sophisticated Yakovlev Yak-36 'Forger', unique as the world's only operational V/STOL (vertical/short take-off and landing) combat aircraft. The origins of its design go back 12 years further still, to 1957, when Sir Sydney Camm of Hawker Aircraft and Dr Stanley Hooker of Bristol Siddeley Engines got together to design a tactical aircraft around Bristol's radical new turbofan engine, then known as the BS.53. Evolved specifically to give jet-lift to vertical take-off fixed-wing aircraft, the BS.53's exhaust airflow was discharged through four nozzles, in fore-and-aft pairs, each of which could be pivoted through more than 90° to vector (direct) the exhaust thrust rearward, vertically downward, or to any intermediate angle. Around the Pegasus, as the engine was eventually christened, Camm designed an essentially conventional all-metal shoulder-wing monoplane of compact dimensions, with anhedral on the wings and tailplane, a single-seat cockpit in the nose, and a large semi-circular fixed-geometry air intake on each side of the fuselage. The landing gear was less orthodox, comprising a single nosewheel and twin main wheels, mounted in tandem on the centreline, plus a small balancer wheel on a retractable outrigger leg at each wingtip.

Known in its original form as the Hawker P.1127, the first of six prototypes made its initial hovering flight on 21 October 1960. Less than a year later, on 12 September 1961, the first complete transitions were made to and from vertical and horizontal flight. Vertical take-off was accomplished by vectoring the thrust from the engine downward; after a

This Harrier GR.3 of RAF No 4 Sqn at Gutersloh would probably be one of the NATO machines to escape an attack.

safe height was reached, the four nozzles were rotated slowly rearward to provide forward thrust for the transition to horizontal flight. As soon as forward speed increased sufficiently for wing lift to support the aircraft, the nozzles were rotated fully aft. This sequence was reversed for vertical landings. To stabilize the aircraft during hovering and low-speed manoeuvres, small reaction control jets mounted in the nose, tail and each wingtip were activated; operated by the control column and rudder pedals, these utilized compressed air bled from the engine.

In-flight transitions soon became commonplace, and Hawker Siddeley was awarded a contract for nine more advanced pre-production aircraft to undergo evaluation in the fighter/ground-attack role. These were known as the Kestrel F(GA).1, the first example making its maiden flight on 7 March 1964. Subsequently, a special three-nation squadron was formed in the UK, with pilots from the Royal Air Force, the Federal German *Luftwaffe* and all three US services. Between April and November 1965 this unit tested the Kestrel under various simulated operational conditions.

Before this, however, the British government had already ordered, in February 1965, another six development aircraft. These were the first to be given the name Harrier, and the first made its initial flight on 31 August 1966. By that time the Mach 2 Hawker Siddeley P.1154 multi-role V/STOL aircraft intended for the RAF and Royal Navy had been replaced by production Harriers for the RAF only. The single-seat Harrier GR.1 was developed for ground-attack/reconnaissance, and the tandem two-seat T.2 for combat readiness training. Total orders for the RAF subsequently rose to 132 single-seaters and 19 of the two-seat version, the first production examples of each model making their maiden flights on 28 December 1967 and 24 April 1969 respectively.

The Harrier officially entered service with the Royal Air Force on 1 April 1969 — the service's 51st birthday — the first aircraft being used to equip an Operational Conversion Unit at RAF Wittering, Northants. In the following year the first T.2s entered service, and both initial models were powered by Pegasus 101 turbofans of 19,000-lb (8618-kg) static thrust. They were later upgraded, being redesignated GR.1A and T.2A after refitting with 20,000-lb (9072-kg) Pegasus 102s; currently, they are designated GR.3 and T.4, powered by Pegasus 103s, and equip one RAF squadron in the UK and three in Germany. The RAF generally operates the Harrier GR.3 as a STOVL (short take-off and vertical landing) aircraft, since with a short take-off run it can carry a greater load of weapons than when taking off vertically. Equipment includes an inertial system, flight-refuelling probe, head-up display and laser rangefinder. Both the two-seater and the single-seater have the same nominal weapon-carrying capability, though the two-seater has a greater empty weight.

At about the time the Harrier entered RAF service, an initial buy of 12 was made by the US Marine Corps. This service, one of the first in the world to exploit the helicopter for tactical warfare in Korea and Vietnam, well appreciated the operational flexibility offered by VTOL. The prospect of allying this to the performance of a fixed-wing jet combat aircraft was too strong to resist, and the initial order was soon raised to 110, including eight two-seaters. USMC Harriers, designated AV-8A and TAV-8A respectively, have Pegasus 103 engines, but lack several of the navigation/attack systems of the RAF's GR.3. Instead they carry AIM-9 Sidewinder missiles for air-to-air combat, in which role the US Marine Corps pilots have added a remarkable new trick to the Harrier's repertoire. Known as VIFF (Vectoring In Forward Flight), this makes use of the thrust-vectoring facility in dogfighting situations, where it gives the aircraft an unprecedented manoeuvrability that no other warplane can match.

British Aerospace (Hawker Siddeley) Harrier

This drawing shows a Harrier GR.3 of No 4 Sqn, RAF Gutersloh, the airbase nearest to the Warsaw Pact forces. This aircraft is fitted with ARI-18228 analog-controlled rear warning radar receivers, with front/rear aerials (yellow) on the fin and at the rear of the tail-nozzle fairing. Ajax and other ECM equipment is said to be carried, together with MB Associates MFCD (multiple flare and chaff dispenser). Not fitted to XZ 131 in this drawing are the bolt-on ferry wingtips, which add more than 4 ft to the span, or the clip-on FR probe.

British Aerospace (Hawker Siddeley) Harrier

The USMC has one training and three operational squadrons equipped with the Harrier, and is campaigning strongly for the Advanced Harrier, the AV-8B developed by McDonnell Douglas. Another development is the Sea Harrier.

To date, the only other operator of the standard Harrier, equivalent to the USMC versions, is the Spanish navy, by whom the aircraft is known as the Matador. Eleven AV-8Ss and two TAV-8Ss equip one Spanish squadron. In early 1979, controversy, promoted by the USSR, surrounded the British government's decision, in principle, to supply Harriers to the People's Republic of China, which is reported to require a large number of these unique aircraft.

Specification

Type: V/STOL close-support/reconnaissance aircraft (single-seat models) and combat readiness trainer (two-seaters)
Powerplant: one 21,500-lb (9752-kg) Rolls-Royce Pegasus 103 vectored-thrust turbofan
Performance: maximum speed at low altitude more than 737 mph (1186 km/h); maximum Mach number in dive 1.3; combat radius with 3,000-lb (1360-kg) external load (AV-8A) after vertical take-off 57 miles (92 km), with short take-off 414 miles (667 km); range with one in-flight refuelling (GR.3) 3,455 miles (5560 km); time to climb to 40,000 ft (12200 m) from vertical take-off 2 minutes 22.7 seconds; service ceiling more than 55,000 ft (15240 m)
Weights: basic operating weight empty, including crew (GR.3) 12,300 lb (5580 kg); (AV-8A) 12,200 lb (5533 kg); (two-seaters) 13,750 lb (6237 kg); maximum take-off (single-seat, short take-off) over 25,000 lb (11340 kg)
Dimensions: span 25 ft 3 in (7.70 m); length (AV-8A) 45 ft 6 in (13.87 m); length (GR.3 with laser nose) 45 ft 7¾ in (13.91 m); length (two-seater) 55 ft 9½ in (17.00 m); height (single-seater) 11 ft 4 in (3.45 m); height (two-seater) 13 ft 8 in (4.17 m); wing area 201.1 sq ft (18.68 m²)
Armament: centreline and four wing attachments for external stores, maximum demonstrated load being 8,000 lb (3630 kg); RAF aircraft cleared for operations with more than 5,000 lb (2268 kg); ventral strakes can be replaced by two 30-mm Aden gun/ammunition pods in lieu of centreline store; wing points able to carry various combinations of bombs, gun pods, rockets and flares; provision in AV-8A for two 30-mm Aden guns and Sidewinder air-to-air missiles
Operators: Spain, UK, US Marine Corps

British Aerospace (Hawker Siddeley) Hawk

A British Aerospace Hawk T Mk 1 in the markings of No 4 Flying Training School, Royal Air Force, based at RAF Valley.

History and notes

The British Aerospace Hawk, originally known as the Hawker Siddeley HS.1182, is replacing the Royal Air Force's Gnat, Jet Provost and Hunter trainers. By early 1980 the aircraft had additionally been ordered by three export customers, and British Aerospace sees a market for up to 3,000 Hawk-type machines by the mid-1980s.

The HS.1182 was selected for the RAF in 1971 in preference to a BAC design; five months later the Adour turbofan was chosen in place of the Rolls-Royce Viper turbojet. In March 1972 an order was placed for 176 Hawks. There was no prototype and only one pre-production aircraft, the first 10 production Hawks being allocated to the test programme. This saved considerable time, and the first two operational aircraft were handed over to the RAF in November 1976.

The Hawk is a tandem-seat transonic ground-attack and training aircraft of conventional layout, with a low-mounted wing. Its primary structure is designed for a safe fatigue life of 6,000 hours in the exacting conditions demanded by the RAF. Simplicity of design and manufacture are emphasized to ensure that the aircraft has a high utilization rate and is inexpensive to operate. One man can prepare the aircraft for its next flight in less than 20 minutes between sorties, and in the weapon-training role it can be re-armed by four men in less than 15 minutes.

Low operating costs are contributed to by the efficient Adour turbofan, which is an unaugmented version of that employed in the SEPECAT Jaguar. The Adour is of modular construction, so the spares holding is reduced. Any module can be changed without the need to rebalance the rotating assemblies, and large doors beneath the engine bay permit easy access and removal. An integral gas-turbine starter running off the aircraft's fuel supply makes the Hawk independent of external aids.

A British Aerospace Hawk T.1 trainer of the RAF's Tactical Weapons Unit is seen on a rocket exercise off the Welsh coast. The RAF currently requires a total of 193 Hawks for training and point defence.

The Hawk had a remarkably trouble-free development programme, entering service only 27 months after its maiden flight. All performance objectives were met, and the top speed proved to be higher than expected. The aircraft has reached Mach 1.15 in a dive and has a maximum level speed of Mach 0.88, allowing student pilots to experience transonic handling before they progress to true supersonic types. Even better figures could be achieved by fitting a more powerful engine, and possibilities which have been examined by the manufacturer include the uprated -56 version of the Adour and an unaugmented version of the Turbo-Union RB.199 turbofan. A single-seat Hawk, with additional fuel and/or avionics, has been studied by British Aerospace.

The RAF operates the aircraft for weapon instruction as well as flying training, with three pylons. The centreline pylon is normally occupied by an Aden cannon pod, with Matra rocket launchers or practice bombs beneath the wings. Potential export customers often demand heavier armament, however, and British Aerospace has tested the Hawk with about 40 combinations of air-to-surface and air-to-air weaponry. Two stations can be fitted beneath each wing, giving a total of five, and the use of multiple racks allows the aircraft to carry an exceptional 6,500 lb (2954 kg) of stores in the form of six 1,000-lb (454-kg) bombs plus the Aden gunpack. Wingtip air-to-air missiles can also be fitted.

By the end of 1978, deliveries to the RAF were running at six aircraft a month, with 100 delivered. British Aerospace has also been awarded a contract by the US Navy to study the modifications necessary to make the aircraft suitable for its VTX-TS requirement, aimed at replacing the fleet of Rockwell T-2 Buckeyes and McDonnell Douglas TA-4 Skyhawks. Changes would include altering the landing gear for operations from aircraft-carriers, and fitting an arrester hook.

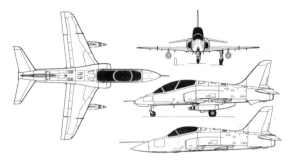

British Aerospace Hawk T.1 (lower side view of proposed single-seat attack variant)

Specification

Type: multi-role trainer and light attack aircraft
Powerplant: one 5,340-lb (2427-kg) Rolls-Royce/Turboméca Adour turbofan
Performance: maximum level speed at sea level 625 mph (1000 km/h); maximum speed 662 mph (1060 km/h); ceiling 50,000 ft (15240 m); time to 30,000 ft (9145 m) 6 minutes 20 seconds; ferry range (clean) 1,520 miles (2433 km); ferry range with two 100-Imperial gallon (455-litre) auxiliary fuel tanks 1,933 miles (3093 km)
Weights: take-off (trainer role) 11,100 lb (5030 kg); maximum take-off 17,097 lb (7755 kg); maximum landing at 13-ft (3.96-m) per second descent 10,250 lb (4650 kg)
Dimensions: span 30 ft 9½ in (9.39 m); length 38 ft 11 in (11.85 m); height 13 ft 1 in (4.0 m); wing area 179.64 sq ft (16.69 m^2)
Armament: up to 6,500 lb (2954 kg) of stores, including Aden 30-mm cannon pod and six 1,000-lb (454-kg) bombs; also Matra 155 rocket launchers, practice bombs and a wide range of other stores
Operators: ordered by Finland (50), Indonesia (8), Kenya (12), and used by UK

British Aerospace (Hawker) Hunter

History and notes

Another design by Sydney Camm, continuing the tradition of the Hurricane, Typhoon, Tempest, Fury and Sea Fury, the Hunter has been Britain's most successful post-war fighter. A total of 1,985 were built, including 445 built under licence in Belgium and Holland. Not only an extremely capable warplane, the Hunter will always be remembered by its pilots as a sheer delight to fly. It has served with 19 air arms around the world, and is still operational with 14 of them. All surviving variants are powered by the Rolls-Royce Avon turbojet, though the Armstrong Siddeley Sapphire powered the Mks 2 and 5. The prototype, P.1067, flew on 20 June 1951, and was followed exactly one month later by the first prototype Hunter F.1. The first production F.1 flew on 16 May 1953, and the first two-seater approximately two years later. Deliveries of brand-new aircraft continued until 1966, during which time the breed was continually improved. All versions of the aircraft were supersonic in a shallow dive, and power, armament and fuel capacity were progressively increased to reach a peak in the Mk 9. This variant, embodying all the lessons to come out of the earlier marks, is powered by the 10,150-lb (4604-kg) Rolls-Royce Avon 207; it packs a greater punch, in the form of heavier underwing capacity, and is generally beefed up to capitalise on its improved potency in the ground-attack role. So great an improvement was this mark that the manufacturer has had a steady flow of refurbishing and remanufacturing work over the years, more than 700 aircraft having undergone the treatment.

The United Emirate air force has a ground-attack squadron formed in 1970, operating eight FGA.76s and two T.77 trainers from Sharjah. Chile, with 37 Hunters (33 FGA.71s and four T.77s), was faced with a grave problem as the Labour government, which opposed the government of this South American country, for a time prohibited any arms dealing. In mid-1978 only 20 of the Hunters were flying, the remainder being grounded for lack of spares and service support. Five ground-attack squadrons of the Indian air force fly some 130 F.56/T.66s. Iraq, with a variety of Russian and Western machines on strength, still operates 30 FGA.9/FR.10s (46 delivered) in three strike squadrons. Kenya's one fighter-bomber squadron flies five FGA.9s received in 1974. A ground-attack squadron of the Kuwait air force has retired its four single-seat FGA.57s but five two-seat T.67s continue to operate alongside Mk 83 Strikemasters. Lebanon's *Force Aérienne Libanaise* is spearheaded by 17 F.70s (including six bought in 1975 to make up for attrition) and two T.66 two-seaters. The Sultan of Oman's air force, now equipped with SEPECAT Jaguars, continues to fly some 15 FGA.6s from Thumrayt. Oman bought 31 Hunters from Jordan in 1975, and those not operational are kept in storage. A fighter wing of the *Fuerza Aérea del Peru* flies F.52s (16 delivered).

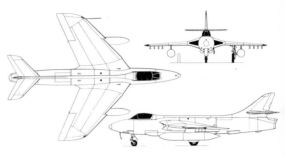

British Aerospace Hunter FGA.9

The Qatar air force has two FGA.78s (a third was destroyed in 1977) and one T.79, all based at Doha, mainly for use on coastal patrol duties. Rhodesia, heavily involved in anti-guerilla operations, flew nine FGA.9s with two squadrons (Nos 1 and 2) based at Thornhill. The Republic of Singapore air force flies about 30 single-seaters (Mk 74s) with Nos 140 and 141 Sqns, in addition to seven T.75s and four reconnaissance FR.74As. Fiercely neutral Switzerland operates nearly 150 Hunters, the fleet having been bolstered in 1974 by an order for 60 to tide the air force over until a new air-superiority fighter was chosen (the Northrop F-5E was eventually selected). The Swiss aircraft are particularly capable: they carry Sidewinder missiles and Saab bombing computers, and equip nine squadrons for ground-attack and two for surveillance. Two forces of the United Kingdom use the Hunter: an RAF tactical weapons unit based at Brawdy has 80-odd Mk 6As in Nos 63, 79 and 234 Sqns, and 30 aircraft equip a second unit at Lossiemouth. Hunters are also occasionally detached to Gibraltar on training missions. Some 20 are based at Valley for training. The Fleet Air Arm flies GA.11s.

Specification

Type: single-seat fighter, fighter-bomber and fighter-reconnaissance; or two-seat training aircraft

Powerplant: one 10,150-lb (4604-kg) Rolls-Royce Avon 207 single-shaft turbojet

Performance: Maximum speed 710 mph (1144 km/h) at sea level; 620 mph (978 km/h) or Mach 0.94 at height; range (internal fuel) 490 miles (689 km); range (with 230-Imperial gallon/1046-litre drop-tanks) 1,840 miles (2965 km); initial rate of climb 8,000 ft (2438 m) per minute

Weights: empty equipped 13,270 lb (6020 kg); clean 17,750 (8051 kg); maximum take-off 24,000 lb (10885 kg)

Dimensions: span 33 ft 8 in (10.26 m); length (single-seaters) 45 ft 10½ in (13.98 m); length (two-seaters) 48 ft 10½ in (14.9 m); height 13 ft 2 in (4.26 m); wing area 349 sq ft (32.4 m²)

Armament: four 30-mm Aden cannon in self-contained, removable package beneath cockpit

British Aerospace (Hawker) Hunter

floor; external stores include two 1,000-lb (454-kg) bombs, two clusters of six 3-in (76.2-m) rockets, two 100-Imperial gallon (456-litre) or 230-Imperial gallon (1046-litre) drop-tanks, two Sidewinder or (exceptionally) Firestreak air-to-air missiles
Operators: Abu Dhabi, Chile, India, Iraq, Kenya, Kuwait, Lebanon, Oman, Peru, Qatar, Zimbabwe, Singapore, Switzerland, UK

Swiss Air Force or Flugwaffe Hawker Siddeley Hunter Mk 58 fighter-bomber of the Surveillance Wing, circa 1968.

Indian Air Force HS Hunter Mk 56. In 1979 the type equipped four squadrons.

HS Hunter T Mk 7 two-seat advanced trainer of No 4 Flying Training School, RAF Valley.

Force Aérienne Libanaise HS Hunter F.70, one of 17 in service and the principal Lebanese AF combat type.

Part of the United Emirates Air Force, Abu Dhabi has a squadron of eight HS Hunter FGA.76 fighter-bombers based at Sharjah.

British Aerospace (Hunting) Jet Provost

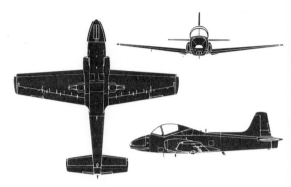

BAC Jet Provost
T.5 basic trainer
on the strength of
the Royal Air
Force College,
Cranwell, Lincs.

History and notes

For 20 years the Royal Air Force's standard basic
trainer, the BAe (formerly Hunting, then BAC) Jet
Provost replaced the piston-engined Hunting Provost between 1959 and 1961. The concept of *ab initio* jet training had been tested using the Jet Provost T.1 in 1955.

The production Jet Provost T.3 flew on 22 June,
1958 and deliveries commenced a year later. In 1961
the more powerful T.4 entered service and enabled
the RAF's basic flying syllabus to be extended, thus
reducing usage of more expensive advanced
trainers. Export versions, designated T.51 and T.52,
were developed with armament, enabling them also
to be employed in the light attack role.

The Jet Provost is all-metal. Side-by-side Martin-
Baker lightweight ejection seats are fitted.

Internal fuel totals 182 Imperial gallons (827
litres) in six wing tanks. Tip tanks each carry an additional 48 Imperial gallons (827 litres). The wings
incorporate slotted flaps and airbrakes. RAF aircraft were delivered with Rebecca and UHF navigation and radio, with VHF and radio compass
available on export models. Armed export versions
carry two machine-guns in the intake walls, with 600
rounds of ammunition per gun. An underfuselage
gunpack, housing two 0.5-in (12.7-mm) machine-
guns with 100 rounds per gun, can also be fitted.
Alternative underwing ordnance loads include: 24
Sura rockets, twelve 25-lb (11.3-kg) or 8-cm (3.15-in)
Oerlikon rockets, six 60-lb (27.2-kg) rockets, eight
25-lb (11.3-kg) bombs, or two 100-lb (45.4-kg) bombs.

In 1967 the T.5 (export version BAC.145) introduced a pressurized cabin with better view and a
lengthened nose housing avionics. A new wing has
greater fatigue life, and increased capacity for fuel
and underwing weapons.

In mid-1967 BAC completed refurbishing 157 T.3
and 5, fitting DME and VOR to produce the T.3A
and 5A.

Foreign users of the Jet Provost include Iraq,
which flies 16 T.52 in the light-attack role; Sri
Lanka, which has eight T.51s with a training unit;
the Sudan, with three BAC.145s used for light attack; and Venezuela, which is replacing its T.52
weapons trainers with Rockwell T-2D Buckeyes.

Specification

Type: basic jet trainer and light attack aircraft
Powerplant: one 1,750-lb (795-kg) Rolls-Royce
Viper 102 (T.3); one 2,500-lb (1135-kg) Rolls-Royce

British Aerospace Jet Provost T.5

Viper 202 (T.52 and T.5)
Performance: maximum speed at 20,000 ft (6100
m) 410 mph (660 km/h) (T.52); maximum speed at
25,000 ft (7600 m) 440 mph (708 km/h) (T.5);
service ceiling 21,700 ft
(6600 m) (T.3); service ceiling 34,500 ft (10500 m)
(T.5); range with maximum fuel 700 miles (1130
km) (T.52); range with maximum fuel (tip tanks
fitted) 900 miles (1450 km) (T.5)
Weights: normal take-off 7,400 lb (3365 kg) (T.52);
normal take-off 7,630 lb (3460 kg) (T.5); maximum
landing 7,250 lb (3288 kg) (T.52); maximum
overload 9,200 lb (4173 kg) (T.5)
Dimensions: span (over tanks) 36 ft 11 in (11.25
m); length 32 ft 5 in (9.88 m) (T.3 and 52); length
33 ft 7½ in (10.25 m) (T.5); height 10 ft 2 in (3.10
m); wing area 213.7 sq ft (19.80 m²)
Armament: two 0.303-in (7.7-mm) machine-guns
and twin 0.5-in (12.7-mm) machine-gun pack,
rockets, or 200-lb (91-kg) bomb load (T.52)
Operators: Iraq, Sri Lanka, Sudan, UK,
Venezuela

This British Aerospace Jet Provost T.3 is on a dual
exercise making a circuit of the city of York.

British Aerospace (BAC) Lightning

Royal Saudi Air Force BAC Lightning F.53 interceptor of 2 Sqn, RSAF, based at Tabuk.

History and notes

When the BAC (now part of BAe) Lightning finally entered service in 1960 it heralded a new era for the Royal Air Force.

The Lightning F.1 had a Ferranti Airpass Mk 1 interception and fire-control radar in the central nose cone, guided missiles (heat-seeking Firestreaks) and truly supersonic performance. The first production model of this operational version, designated F.1, flew on 29 October 1959, and deliveries to RAF No 74 Sqn began the following summer. F.1s were also supplied to Nos 56 and 111 Sqns. The final production aircraft of this mark, the F.1A, had provision for flight refuelling and UHF radio. Next development was the F.2, with better range, ceiling and speed, more advanced electronics, Hawker Siddeley Red Top air-to-air missiles in place of Firestreaks, liquid-oxygen breathing system and a steerable nosewheel. The first F.2 flew on 11 July 1961, and the type later equipped Nos 19 and 92 Sqns in Germany. A total of seven T.2 and T.4 trainers were delivered to Saudi Arabia in 1966–67. The F.3, a further development, was powered by 16,360-lb (7420-kg) Avon 300-series reheat turbojets. It had no guns, and for long-range ferrying two large over-wing jettisonable fuel tanks could be fitted, along with a flight-refuelling probe under the port wing. The first F.3, incorporating a larger, square-tip fin, flew on 16 June 1962, and the type entered service with No 74 Sqn in mid-1964, subsequently re-equipping also Nos 23, 29, 56 and 111 Sqns. The F.6 was the result of a long-overdue decision in 1965 to follow BAC's advice and nearly double the fuel capacity and fit the cambered, kinked wing leading-edge which had first been flown nine years earlier. This latter modification allowed operation at greater weights. Increased fuel capacity (in the form of a much enlarged ventral tank), coupled with the low subsonic drag of the new leading edge, gave the F.6 a tremendous improvement in effectiveness. Both Saudi Arabia and Kuwait bought a developed version of the F.6, designated F.53. Saudi Arabia still operates 31 F.53s (32 delivered), two F.54s, three F.52s and five two-seat T.55s. Twenty of the F.53s fly with No 2 Sqn at Tabuk in the north on interception duties, and the remaining aircraft operate from the OCU (Operational Conversion Unit) at Dharan.

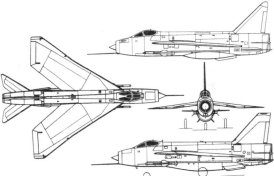

British Aerospace Lightning F.6
(upper side view of F.1)

Specification

Type: (F.6) single-seat supersonic all-weather interceptor, strike and reconnaissance aircraft
Powerplant: two 15,680-lb (7112-kg) Rolls-Royce Avon 302 turbojets
Performance: maximum speed Mach 2.3 or 1,500 mph (2415 km/h) at 40,000 ft (12190 m); range (internal fuel only) 800 miles (1288 km); initial rate of climb 50,000 ft (15240 m) per minute; time to operational height (around 40,000 ft/12190 m) and speed of Mach 0.9 (clean) 2 minutes 30 seconds; acceleration from Mach 1 to Mach 2+ (clean) 3 minutes 30 seconds.
Weights: empty equipped about 28,000 lb (12700 kg); loaded 50,000 lb (22680 kg)
Dimensions: span 34 ft 10 in (10.61 m); length 55 ft 3 in (16.84 m); height 19 ft 7 in (5.97 m); wing area 380.1 sq ft (35.31 m²)
Armament: large, two-portion ventral pack contains fuel tank (rear) and (forward) either more fuel or a pack housing two 30-mm Aden guns (120 rounds each); operational packs mounted ahead of ventral bay include two Firestreak or Red Top air-to-air missiles, or 44 2-in (50.8-mm) spin-stabilized rockets, or five Vinten 360 70-mm cameras, or (night reconnaissance) cameras and linescan equipment and underwing flares; underwing/overwing hardpoints can carry up to 144 rockets or six 1,000-lb (454-kg) HE, retarded or fire bombs.
Operators: Saudi Arabia, UK

British Aerospace (Hawker Siddeley) Nimrod MR

Royal Air Force HS Nimrod MR.1 long-range maritime patrol aircraft of 203 Sqn, Kinloss, Scotland.

History and notes

The name Nimrod, after the 'mighty hunter' of the Book of Genesis, was a most suitable choice for this aircraft. Its own genesis lies in the world's first jet airliner, the de Havilland Comet, which was adopted as a military transport by the Royal Air Force in 1955. Some 10 years later, in early 1965, when the RAF was seeking a new maritime patrol aircraft, the British government decided not to authorize the development of an entirely new aeroplane, but to see what could be done by adapting the basic airframe of the Comet 4. The outcome of that programme is now acknowledged as one of the finest overwater patrol and anti-submarine aircraft in service in the world today.

Nimrod development began with the allocation of two ex-airline Comet 4Cs, which in 1965-66 were modified as Hawker Siddeley 801 prototypes for the new design. Principal modifications were the substitution of four Rolls-Royce Spey turbofan engines for the Avon turbojets of the Comet, and the addition of a new, unpressurized lower compartment beneath the basic pressure shell of the original airliner. The new lower fuselage was used to house a search radar, much of the specialized avionics, and the 48 ft 6 in (14.78 m) weapons bay. The first HS.801 was flown on 23 May 1967; the second, which retained its original Avon engines and was used primarily as a maritime avionics testbed, followed it into the air on 31 July 1967. Wings and horizontal tail surfaces remained essentially those of the Comet 4C, as did the landing gear, apart from being strengthened for the higher operating weights. Additional new structural features were a large dorsal fin, a fat ECM (electronic countermeasures) pod on top of the main fin, a magnetic anomaly detector (MAD) boom behind the rear fuselage, a searchlight in the right leading-edge fuel tank, and underwing pylons for air-to-surface missiles.

An initial contract was placed for 38 production aircraft, to be known as the Nimrod MR.1; the first of these flew on 28 June 1968, and deliveries began to No 201 Squadron of RAF Strike Command in October of the following year. A further batch of eight MR.1s was ordered in 1972, to permit the equipping of six RAF squadrons (Nos 42, 120, 201, 203, 206 and one other) with this version of the Nimrod. In the previous year, however, three examples of a different version, known as the R.1, were received by

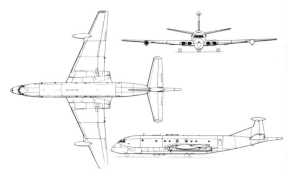

British Aerospace Nimord MR.2

No 51 Squadron. These have a shorter, blunt tailcone and the wing leading-edge pods are of a modified size and shape. It is obvious that these three aircraft are employed for electronic reconnaissance and the monitoring of foreign emissions, although they are described officially as 'calibration' aircraft.

Primary Nimrod roles, for which it carries a standard crew of 12, are those of anti-submarine warfare, maritime surveillance of the United Kingdom defence area (including the North Sea and the eastern Atlantic) and anti-shipping strike. The large weapons bay can accommodate a wide variety of ordnance, in addition to which there is ample storage space in the rear of the pressurized fuselage compartment for sonobuoys, marine markers and other detection gear. Twelve hours is a typical patrol endurance, and an on-station patrol of more than six hours can be maintained at a distance of 1,150 miles (1850 km) from its shore base. This capability is made possible by cruising on only two engines, with the other pair shut down, and the Nimrod can, if necessary, cruise and climb on only one engine. Range can be extended still further by installing up to six auxiliary fuel tanks in the weapons bay. Search radar in the nose is an ASV-21D by EMI, and a Marconi computer-based system provides integrated navigation/weapon selection and delivery with appropriate operator displays in the tactical compartment. If required, the Nimrod can be used in a secondary transport role, with seats for up to 45 troops.

Since 1975 the RAF's fleet of MR.1 Nimrods has been undergoing a modernization programme, being

British Aerospace (Hawker Siddeley) Nimrod MR

The watcher watched, as BAe Nimrod MR.1 XV246 is photographed (in colour) whilst itself photographing the Soviet ASW helicopter cruiser *Leningrad* (in black and white).

re-delivered from 1978 in updated form as MR.2s. In consequence, only five of the eight additional Nimrods ordered in 1972 were actually delivered as MR.1s: one of the others was utilized as a Mk 2 development aircraft, while the seventh and eighth have been allocated to a similar role in the evolution of the early-warning Nimrod AEW.3. Though the MR.2 is a major rebuild, the essence of the conversion is to modernize and improve the operational equipment. A new Marconi digital computer, able to store much more information than that in the MR.1, is integrated with a Ferranti inertial navigation system; the new EMI radar, appropriately known as Searchwater, has its own sub-system, based on a Ferranti digital computer, for data processing. The Searchwater system, designed to function in spite of hostile ECM, can detect submarines or surface vessels over long ranges, track several different targets simultaneously, and present a clutter-free display to the operators in the tactical compartment. The AQS-901 acoustics processing and display systems (also computer-based) are believed to be the most advanced in the world, and are compatible not only with all NATO sensors but also the new Australian Barra buoy. Communications include twin HF transceivers and teletype/encryption system. The crew complement remains unchanged, comprising two pilots, two navigators, flight engineer, radio operator, radar operator, two sonics systems operators, another for the ECM/MAD installations, plus two observers whose job also includes loading the sonobuoy and marker launchers. A galley, eating and rest areas are provided in the centre fuselage. Nimrods are expected to serve well into the 1990s, and in many respects the MR.2 is superior to all other similar platforms.

Specification

Type: anti-submarine patrol, anti-shipping strike and electronic reconnaissance aircraft

Powerplant: four 12,140-lb (5507-kg) Rolls-Royce Spey 250 turbofans

Performance: maximum speed 575 mph (926 km/h); maximum transit speed 547 mph (880 km/h); economical transit speed 490 mph (787 km/h); typical patrol speed at low level (on two engines) 230 mph (370 km/h); typical mission endurance 12 hours; typical ferry range 5,755 miles (9265 km); normal operational ceiling 42,000 ft (12800 m)

Weights: typical empty 86,000 lb (39010 kg); normal maximum take-off 177,500 lb (80510 kg); maximum overload take-off 192,000 lb (87090 kg); typical landing 120,000 lb (54430 kg)

Dimensions: span 114 ft 10 in (35.00 m); length (except R.1) 126 ft 9 in (38.63 m); length (R.1) 118 ft 0 in (35.97 m); height 29 ft 8½ in (9.08 m); wing area 2,121 sq ft (197.05 m²)

Armament: wide variety of ASW weapons, in six lateral rows, in 48 ft 6 in (14.78 m) long ventral bay; these may include up to nine torpedoes plus depth charges, or combinations of mines, bombs, depth charges or nuclear weapons of various sizes; alternatively, weapons bay can be occupied by up to 15,100 lb (6849 kg) of auxiliary fuel in six supplementary tanks, or by a combination of weapons and fuel. Bay for sonobuoys and launchers in rear of pressurized fuselage. Hardpoint under each wing for mine, gun pod or rocket pod, or (if required, though currently deleted from RAF aircraft) an air-to-surface missile

Operator: UK

British Aerospace (Avro) Shackleton AEW.2

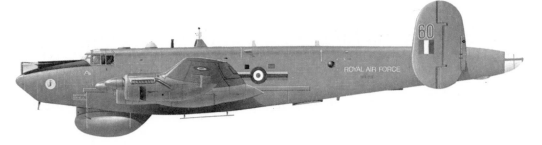

Avro Shackleton AEW Mk 2 of 8 Sqn, Royal Air Force, at Lossiemouth.

History and notes

The airborne early-warning version of the veteran Avro Shackleton was developed in 1971 to provide the Royal Air Force with warning of low-level intruders in the UK air-defence region. It replaced the Westland (Fairey) Gannet AEW.3 which, with the rundown of aircraft-carrier operations, was left no seaborne base. The AEW Shackleton's APS-20F radar in the forward fuselage, with scanner in the chin position, was even older than the airframe, having served first in Douglas AD-4W Skyraiders and then in Gannet AEW.3s. Other changes included Orange Harvest electronic countermeasures and increased fuel capacity.

The first Shackleton AEW.2 flew from Woodford on 30 September 1971, and the 12 aircraft converted to the role entered service with No 8 Sqn in 1972, this unit having been formed in January of that year at Kinloss. Its aircraft named after characters in *The Magic Roundabout* television series, are the last survivors of this ageing design still in service with the RAF. The aircraft are now based at Lossiemouth and will be replaced by 11 British Aerospace AEW.3 Nimrods from 1982.

The AEW.2 normally carries a crew of nine, comprising captain, co-pilot, radio navigator, navigating navigator, engineer and four radar operators. There are three radar displays, so having a fourth operator allows a little flexibility and rest-time, no small consideration on a 12-hour mission. The Gannet, which the Shackleton replaced, had a normal mission endurance of about three hours, some two of which would have been on task, so two operators for its two scopes were adequate. The senior radar operator is the Tactical Co-ordinator (Tacco), who is responsible for seeing that the other operators, the equipment and the aircraft are used to the best effect tactically. Unlike its pioneer predecessors (used by the Americans from 1946), the updated APS-20F radar is ground-stabilized from the aircraft's Doppler. It also differs in being north-stabilized. Lack of height finding equipment makes interception direction a somewhat harder task than it need be: the McDonnell Douglas Phantom, with more powerful radar than its RAF partner, the BAe (BAC) Lightning, is for this reason easier to direct. Apart from the Orange Harvest electronic countermeasures,

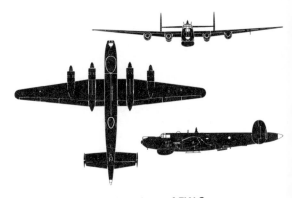

British Aerospace Shackleton AEW.2

limited in range and more suited to the maritime patrol role, the AEW Shackleton carries an APX-7 IFF (identification friend or foe) interrogator and both active and passive SIF (selective identification facility) operating through a coded pulse within the IFF signal. With the SIF in the active mode the operator can place a 'window' over a particular target; in the passive mode a particular interceptor liaising with a Shackleton would be the only aircraft tallying with all IFF returns. Radio includes two PTR 175 VHF/UHF, two R52 UHF and a pair of Collins 618T single-sideband HF sets. An airborne moving-target indicator fitted to the aircraft in 1974 cuts out returns from surface vessels when necessary.

Specification

Type: nine-seat airborne early-warning aircraft
Powerplant: four 2,455-hp (1816-kW) Rolls-Royce Griffon 57A liquid-cooled piston engines
Performance: maximum speed 272 mph (439 km/h); typical operating ceiling 20,000 ft (6100 m); rate of climb (initial) 850 ft (260 m) per minute; endurance 14 hours; range about 4,000 miles (6437 km)
Weights: empty 57,000 lb (25855 kg); gross 98,000 lb (44450 kg)
Dimensions: span 120 ft 0 in (36.58 m); length 87 ft 3 in (26.59 m); height 16 ft 9 in (5.1 m)
Armament: electronic countermeasures only
Operator: UK

British Aerospace (BAC) Strikemaster

Royal Saudi Air Force BAC Strikemaster Mk 80 based at Riyadh; No 9 and No 11 Sqns operate the fleet of 46.

History and notes

Although based on a 1950s design, the BAe (BAC) Strikemaster offers a number of air forces relatively cheap, effective firepower. It is derived from the Hunting (later BAC/British Aerospace) Jet Provost, which in turn was a radical development of the Percival Provost piston-engined basic trainer. The Jet Provost proved to be a highly successful trainer, selling in large numbers to the RAF and overseas air arms, and was progressively upgraded. The final versions are pressurized and more powerful. The next step was to give the aircraft teeth, and the BAC 145 was the first multi-role attack version. This was in turn refined to produce the relatively more sophisticated Strikemaster, a private-venture project which has side-by-side ejection seats and eight underwing hardpoints capable of carrying up to 3,000 lb (1360 kg) of stores. This ordnance capacity, coupled with the more powerful Viper Mk 535 turbojet engine, makes the Strikemaster particularly suitable for counter-insurgency combat operations, reconnaissance, and pilot and weapons training.

The first Strikemaster flew on 26 October 1967, and a total of 145 have since been sold. Ten more were built in 1978 against the possibility of new or repeat orders. The Strikemaster did, in fact, set a world record for repeat orders by export customers, so effective has it proved. Of the 16 Strikemaster Mk 89s bought by Ecuador, 14 survivors equip a strike/trainer unit. Ecuador is a good example of a re-order customer: its initial order covered eight aircraft but this was later increased to 12, delivery of which began in early 1973. Delivery of a further four was completed in July 1976. The Strikemaster is one of 29 types operated by the *Fuerza Aerea Ecuatoriana* and works alongside Cessna A-37s and Lockheed T-33As in the training and strike role. It is, probably more than any other factor, the Strikemaster's versatility and value for money which have made it so successful. It can operate from rough strips, lifting as much as a specialised bomber would have been carrying in the 1930s and delivering it at 400+ mph (640+ km/h). Until the announcement in 1977 of a $75 million order for Northrop F-5E/Fs, the Strikemaster, along with five BAe (HS) Hunter FGA.9s, was the Kenyan Air Force's most potent warplane.

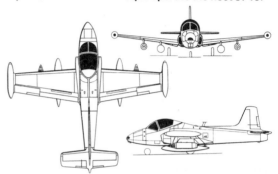

British Aerospace 167 Strikemaster

Specification

Type: (BAC 167) two-seat light tactical support aircraft and trainer

Powerplant: one 3,410-lb (1547-kg) dry Rolls-Royce Viper 535 turbojet

Performance: maximum design speed 518 mph (834 km/h); maximum level speed at 18,000 ft (5485 m) (clean) 450 mph (724 km/h); combat radius with 3,000-lb (1360-kg) weapon load (lo-lo-lo, 5 minutes over target, 10% reserves) 145 miles (233 km); ferry range 1,615 miles (2600 km); initial climb (max fuel, clean) 5,250 ft (1600 m) per minute

Weights: empty equipped 6,195 lb (2810 kg); with two crew, full internal fuel and practice bombs and racks 10,600 lb (4808 kg); maximum allowed 11,500 lb (5215 kg)

Dimensions: span 36 ft 10 in (11.23 m); length 33 ft 8½ in (10.27 m); height 10 ft 11½ in (3.34 m); wing area 213.7 sq ft (19.85 m²)

Armament: Two 7.62-mm (0.3-in) FN machine-guns (fixed forward-firing, with 550 rounds each); underwing stores (maximum 3,000 lb/1361 kg) include two 75- and 50-Imperial gallon (341- and 227-litre) drop-tanks, four Matra launchers each containing 18 68-mm SNEB rockets, four LAU-68 seven-round rocket-launchers, four 540-lb (245-kg) ballistic or retarded bombs, four 551-lb (250-kg) or 1,102-lb (500-kg) bombs, 24 practice bombs, BAe/Vinten five-camera reconnaissance pod, or Sura 80-mm rockets.

Operators: Ecuador, Kenya, Kuwait, New Zealand, Oman, Saudi Arabia, Singapore, Sudan

British Aerospace (BAC) VC10 C.1

Royal Air Force BAC VC10 of 10 Sqn at Brize Norton, Oxon, used for long-range transport flight.

History and notes

The Royal Air Force's BAe VC10 C.1 is a specially modified variant of the VC10 civil transport. The first VC10 C.1 (Model 1106), 14 of which had been ordered for RAF Transport Command (now No 38 Group, RAF Strike Command), flew in November 1965. Deliveries to No 10 Sqn at RAF Brize Norton, Oxfordshire, began the following year.

The C.1 version is based on the standard (not Super) civil model, but incorporates a number of the improvements featured on the Super VC10. These include more powerful Conway engines, increased gross weight, and a 'wet' fin. Reversers are fitted on the outer engines, the leading edge is extended, the nose has a flight-refuelling probe, and an APU (Artouste 526) is fitted in the tailcone to provide ground power at remote locations.

The VC10 C.1 has a large cargo door on the left of the forward fuselage, and the strengthened floor has a 20-in (50-cm) grid of 10,000-lb (4500-kg) lashing points. In the trooping role, rearward-facing seats can accommodate up to 150, though a 125-seat layout is usual on scheduled flights. In the casevac role, up to 78 stretcher patients can be carried, but an alternative layout, more appropriate to peacetime needs, provides for nine stretcher cases and 61 seated patients. Cargo capacity is 54,000 lb (24495 kg).

The wing has a 32° 30' sweepback at quarter chord. Fowler flaps are fitted, and slats extend over the major part of the leading edge. Spoilers on the upper surface also serve as airbrakes.

When the VC10 began to operate with No 10 Sqn, British defence commitments were worldwide, with significant forces stationed in the Far East and Persian Gulf. However, in January 1968 a Defence White Paper announced drastic cuts in the resources of all three services and the withdrawal of most forces stationed outside Europe. Consequently the importance of the strategic transport role diminished. RAF Transport Command became Air Support Command in 1967, and five years later the formation was reduced to Group status within RAF Strike Command.

Nevertheless, a strategic airlift capability has been found vital. Relief operations and the evacuation of British citizens from trouble spots highlight the need

British Aerospace VC10 C.1

for an intercontinental air transport force. Among recent such operations in which RAF VC10s have participated are the evacuation of over 13,000 civilians from war-torn Cyprus in July 1974, the evacuation of 5,700 people from Angola in October the following year, the reinforcement of the British garrison in Belize when that country was threatened by invasion from neighbouring Guatemala in 1977, and the evacuation of British citizens from Iran in early 1979.

Currently 11 VC10 C.1s are on the strength of No 10 Sqn, each named in honour of a British airman awarded the Victoria Cross.

Specification

Type: long-range strategic transport
Powerplant: four 21,800-lb (9890-kg) Rolls-Royce Conway Mk 250 turbofans
Performance: cruising speed at 38,000 ft (11600 m) 550 mph (886 km/h); rate of climb at sea level 3,050 ft (930 m) per minute; range with maximum fuel 7,128 miles (11470 km); range with maximum payload 4,720 miles (7600 km)
Weights: maximum take-off 323,000 lb (146500 kg); maximum landing 225,000 lb (102100 kg)
Dimensions: span 146 ft 2 in (44.55 m); length 158 ft 8 in (48.36 m); height 39 ft 6 in (12.04 m); wing area 2,932 sq ft (272.4 m^2)
Operator: UK

British Aerospace (Handley Page) Victor K.2

Royal Air Force Handly Page Victor K. Mk 2 tanker aircraft of 55 Sqn, RAF Marham, Norfolk.

History and notes

One of two bombers designed around Specification B.35/46, the Handley Page HP.80 Victor was the last of the V-bombers to enter service with the Royal Air Force. The Avro Vulcan, to the same requirements, had become operational in mid-1956. Technically highly advanced for its time, the Victor was designed to operate fast and high, above virtually all known defences. As it turned out, when the aircraft did finally enter service in 1956 after a lengthy development phase, it had been overtaken by fighters and missiles capable of interception at its designed operating altitudes.

In 1964 Handley Page was contracted to convert the remaining B.1/1As into probe-and-drogue flight refuelling tankers for the RAF. Operational aircraft were fitted with Flight Refuelling Mk 20b pod under each wing to replenish high-speed tactical aircraft and fighters. A Flight Refuelling Mk 17 hose drum in the rear of the bomb bay supplied bombers and transport aircraft. To raise capacity, two extra fuel tanks were fitted in the remainder of the bomb bay, which could be modified quickly to retain bombing capability as necessary. The first six tankers, designated K.1/1A, carried only the underwing refuelling points, and these aircraft entered service with No 55 Sqn at Marham in August 1965. In 18 months of trials the six K.1s transferred 6,718,700 lb (3044914 kg) of fuel in 10,646 real and practice

British Aerospace Victor K.2

refuelling contacts and participated in nearly 40 overseas exercises. Two BAC Lightning fighters could be supplied simultaneously at the rate of 150 Imperial gallons (680 litres) per minute. Nos 57 and 214 Sqns were equipped with three-point K.1As, and No 55 Sqn received its first improved models in the spring of 1967.

By 1954 design was in hand on the Victor Mark 2, and the first B.2 flew on 20 February 1959. This larger version was much heavier and more powerful, the engines being 20,600-lb (9344-kg) Rolls-Royce Conway 201 turbofans. Changes compared with the Mk 1 included greater span, larger air intakes, a dorsal fillet forward of the fin and a retractable scoop on each fuselage side to supply two turbo-

The BAe (Handley Page) Victor K.2 is the RAF's standard air-refuelling tanker, seen here serving with No 55 Sqn from Marham and refuelling a Jaguar GR.1 of No 54 Sqn in March 1978. Ex-civil VC10 and Super VC10 transports are being rebuilt for the tanker role.

alternators for the totally new electrical system. A Turboméca Artouste turbine in the starboard wing root drove the APU (Auxiliary Power Unit) which also supplied ground power. Armament was the Hawker Siddeley Blue Steel Stand-off bomb (air-to-surface missile), which became operational in February 1964 with No 139 Sqn at Wittering. Two years earlier this squadron had been also the first unit to receive the updated Victor. Although considerably improved, the Victor B.2 was no less vulnerable at height, and the aircraft's role was changed to include low-level attack, and only 34 were built, 22 being cancelled.

The Victor SR.2, a strategic reconnaissance version of the Victor B.2, had the primary role of high-altitude maritime reconnaissance. A single aircraft could radar-map the entire Mediterranean in one seven-hour sortie, and four could map the North Atlantic in six hours. Photoflash bombs allowed night operations. Despite its bulk, a production Victor B.1 exceeded its Mach 1 in a shallow dive in 1957, and routine high-speed flights included England to Malta in two hours (655 mph/1050 km/h), and an Atlantic crossing in three hours eight minutes (644 mph/1030 km/h). A number of Victor B.2s were converted to the strategic reconnaissance role, but 24 K.2 tanker conversions of the B.2 are now serving with Nos 55 and 57 Sqns and 232 OCU at Marham. The K.2 is a complete rebuild, by British Aerospace at Woodford, with three hose-reels and reduced span.

Specification

Type: five-seat strategic bomber (B.1/1A, B2.); four-seat flight-refuelling tanker (K.1A, K.2); strategic reconnaissance aircraft (SR.2)
Powerplant: four 11,000-lb (4990 kg) Armstrong Siddeley Sapphire 202 turbojets (Mk 1/1A); four 20,600-lb (6344-kg) Conway 201 turbofans (B.2, SR.2, K.2)
Performance: maximum speed (both marks) 640 mph (1030 km/h) or Mach 0.92 at 40,000 ft (12192 m); maximum cruising height 45,000 ft (13700 m) (Mk 1), 55,000 ft (16750 m) (Mk 2); combat radius (Mk 2) 1,725 miles (2780 km) at high/low level, 2,300 miles (3700 km) at high level, 4,600 miles (7400 km) with flight refuelling
Weights: empty 79,000 lb (35834 kg) (Mk 1), 91,000 (41,277 kg) (Mk 2); maximum take-off 180,000 lb (81650 kg) (Mk 1), 233,000 lb (101150 kg) (Mk 2)
Dimensions: span 110 ft 0 in (33.53 m) (B.1), 120 ft 0 in (36.58 m) (B.2), 117 ft 0 in (35.7 m) (K.2); length 114 ft 11 in (35.05 m); height 28 ft 1½ in (8.59 m) (Mk 1), 30 ft 1½ in (9.2 m) (Mk 2); wing area 2,406 sq ft (223.5 m²) (Mk 1) 2,597 sq ft (241.3 m²) (Mk 2)
Armament: internal bay for various nuclear or conventional weapons, including up to 35 1,000-lb (454-kg) bombs; one Blue Steel Mk 1 air-to-surface missile semi-recessed beneath fuselage (B.2); electronic countermeasures; no armament on tankers
Operator: UK

British Aerospace (Hawker Siddeley/Avro) Vulcan

Royal Air Force Hawker Siddeley Vulcan B.2 long-range strategic bomber, in low-visibility markings, from the Waddington Wing.

History and notes

To carry out the strategic bombing of Germany during World War II, Britain developed a trio of four-engined bombers, of which the Handley Page Halifax and Avro Lancaster were the star performers. When, in 1946, the air staff issued its requirements for a post-war jet-driven generation of strategic bombers, it was to be the same two companies that were responsible for the aircraft that fulfilled the need: Handley Page with the crescent-winged Victor and Avro with the delta-winged Vulcan. In both cases the configuration was new and untried, yet each survived early teething troubles to become highly successful in their chosen role and adaptable to a number of others; they have also enjoyed a period of Royal Air Force service far in excess of that of their illustrious forebears.

Delta wings were to undergo a considerable vogue in the 1950s, but at the time the RAF issued its Specification B.35/46, a year after the end of World War II, no powered delta-wing aircraft had been flown, and A.V. Roe's brilliant technical director, Roy Chadwick, decided to air-test the configuration initially by building a series of smaller research aircraft with a generally similar shape. The first of these was the single-seat Avro 707, flown for the first time on 4 September 1949 and powered by a 3,500-lb (1588-kg) static thrust Rolls-Royce Derwent 5 turbojet. Twenty-six days later it crashed, killing test pilot S.E.Esler. This was hardly an auspicious beginning, but the modified 707B, flown by R.J. (Ro-

The British Aerospace Vulcan V.2 is another long-serving type which has been continually updated, some of the electronics changes showing externally. The RAF also has four rebuilt as SR.2 strategic reconnaissance platforms, serving with No 27 Sqn at Scampton.

ly) Falk, took to the air on 6 September 1950 and quickly displayed extremely docile handling qualities. One major modification was made on the third aircraft, the 'high speed' Avro 707A, when the dorsal intakes for the engine were relocated in the wing roots; the 707A flew for the first time on 14 June 1951, and was followed by a second 707A on 20 February 1953. Last of the research prototypes, the Avro 707C, flew on 1 July the same year and was completed as a side-by-side two-seater, to provide training in the particular techniques necessary in flying a tailless delta.

Long before this, in January 1948, Avro had received the go-ahead for two prototypes of the full-size B.35/46 design, the Avro 698, some 20 times the weight of the little 707s. However, the British government remained wary of the unorthodox design; a production contract did not follow until June 1952, and in the meantime the more conventional Vickers Valiant was ordered as a back-up in the event of a possible failure of the Handley Page and Avro types. When the Avro 698 prototype first flew on 30 August 1952, it was powered by four 6,500-lb (2948-kg) static thrust Rolls-Royce Avon RA.3 turbojets, substituting for the planned installation of Bristol B.E.10 (Olympus) engines which were not then ready. In the following year it was refitted with 8,000-lb (3629-kg) static thrust Armstrong Siddeley Sapphires; Olympus Series 100 engines, of 9,750-lb (4423-kg) static thrust, were installed in the second prototype, which made its maiden flight on 3 September 1953.

A little less than 18 months later, on 4 February 1955, Falk flew the first production Vulcan B.1 (four 10,000-lb/4536-kg static thrust Olympus Mk 101s),

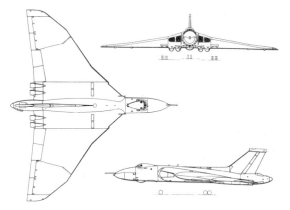

British Aerospace Vulcan B.2

and at the SBAC Display at Farnborough in the following September eclipsed even his own outstanding earlier performances by slow-rolling the second production example of this 99-ft (30.18-m) span bomber. Any remaining doubts — and there were not many — about the control and stability of such a large aeroplane, with no separate tailplane or elevators, were quickly dispelled. The only noteworthy problem was a slight buffeting when pulling g at high altitude, and this was remedied by decreasing the angle of sweepback on the centre panels of each wing, giving a kinked and cambered leading edge instead of the former straight line. This was applied to existing Vulcan 1s, successive batches of which introduced more powerful models of the Olympus engine; the eventual standard for all Vulcan 1s was the 13,500-lb (6123-kg) static thrust Olympus 104. Deliveries of 45 B.1s began in

British Aerospace (Hawker Siddeley Avro) Vulcan

February 1957, to No 230 Operational Conversion Unit; first operational squadron, from July 1957, was No 83, followed by Nos 101 and 617. The internal bomb bay was large enough to carry twenty-one 1,000-lb (454-kg) bombs or mines, and pressurized accommodation was provided for a five-man crew: pilot and co-pilot (on ejection seats), navigator, radar operator and an air electronics officer. All B.1s still in service in 1961 were upgraded to B.1As with a new tailcone containing ECM (electronic countermeasures) equipment.

Major production version, however, was the B.2, with more powerful engines, much larger wings and capability for carrying the Hawker Siddeley Blue Steel thermonuclear stand-off missile. The new wings, of markedly thinner section and fitted with elevons, began flight testing on the second Vulcan prototype on 31 August 1957, and the first production Vulcan 2 (17,000-lb/7711-kg static thrust Olympus 201s) flew on 30 August 1958. On receipt of the new version, Nos 83 and 617 Squadrons passed on their Mk 1As to Nos 44 and 50 Squadrons; No 617 was the first, in February 1963, to become operational with the Blue Steel. Additional Vulcan squadrons included Nos 9, 12 and 35, production of approximately 50 of this version ending in 1964.

As the B.1/1As were phased out, all of the squadrons listed came to fly the B.2, and after the Skybolt fiasco of 1961–62, followed by the adoption of the submarine-launched Polaris missile as Britain's primary nuclear deterrent, it became necessary to adapt the Vulcan for low-level operation, to maintain its capability to penetrate enemy airspace against improved-quality Soviet detection radars and surface-to-air missiles. To this new requirement the Vulcan adapted very successfully, carrying conventional HE bombs and adopting a two-tone camouflage of green and grey for its new role instead of the all-white finish employed previously. Continuing improvement in power was maintained, Vulcans being re-engined in 1962–64 with 20,000-lb (9072-kg) static thrust Olympus 301 engines. The Vulcan's third role, that of strategic reconnaissance, began in 1973 when a number of bombers were converted to SR.2s for this purpose; since 1974, these have been operated by No 27 Squadron.

Specification
The following data are for the B.2.
Type: low-level tactical bomber and strategic reconnaissance aircraft
Powerplant: four 20,000-lb (9072-kg) static thrust Rolls-Royce Olympus 301 turbojets
Performance: maximum speed at high altitude 645 mph (1038 km/h); cruising speed at high altitude about 625 mph (1006 km/h); combat radius without refuelling 1,725 miles (2776 km); combat radius with one in-flight refuelling 2,875 miles (4627 km); range with normal bomb load about 4,600 miles (7403 km); service ceiling about 65,000 ft (19810 m)
Weights: maximum take-off about 250,000 lb (113400 kg)
Dimensions: span 111 ft 0 in (33.38 m); length (including refuelling probe) 105 ft 6 in (32.16 m); length (without probe) 99 ft 11 in (30.45 m); height 27 ft 2 in (8.28 m); wing area 3,964 sq ft (368.27 m²)
Armament: no defensive armament; up to twenty-one 1,000-lb (454-kg) bombs in internal weapons bay
Operator: UK

Canadair CL-41 Tutor

History and notes
The Canadair CL-41's development programme was privately funded by the company, because of the Canadian government's early lack of interest in this basic jet trainer. Two prototypes were built, powered by a 2,400-lb (1088-kg) Pratt and Whitney JT12A-5 turbojet, the first flying on 13 January 1960. In September 1961 the Canadian government ordered 190 CL-41As for the Royal Canadian Air Force (now the Canadian Armed Forces) with the designation CT-114 Tutor. These were powered by the General Electric J85-CAN-40 turbojet of 2,850-lb (1290-kg) thrust. Delivery took place in 1963-6.

Further development resulted in the CL-41G armament trainer and light attack aircraft. This has uprated engines and six underwing hardpoints; the landing gear is modified for soft field operation, and 'zero level' automatic ejection seats are fitted. In March 1966 the Royal Malaysian Air Force ordered 20, named Tebuan (wasp) in Malaysian service.

Features include side-by-side seats, upward-opening canopy, lateral door-type airbrakes, 'T' tail, and steerable nosewheel. Internal fuel totals 258 Imperial gallons (1170 litres), in five cells in the fuselage.

Main user of the CT-114 Tutor in the Canadian Armed Forces is Training Command's No 2 Flying Training School at Moose Jaw, Saskatchewan. After primary training on the Beech CT-134 Musketeer, pupils do some 200 hours on the CT-114 to reach 'wings' standard, and proceed to specialized training for combat jets, multi-engined types or helicopters.

Ten Tutors were modified for the Golden Hawks (later Snowbirds) aerobatic team and the type also

Canadair CL-41 Tutor

Canadair CL-41G Tebuan armed jet trainer of the Royal Malaysian Air Force. Two squadrons, Nos 6 and 9, operate the 16 surviving Tebuans of 20 originally supplied. This machine was on the strength of 9 Sqn at Kuantan.

serves with the Flying Instructors' School. These units share the Moose Jaw base with No 2 FTS.

In 1976 the Canadian Armed Forces began a 113-aircraft modification programme which includes provision of external fuel tanks, upgrading of avionics, changes to the canopy electrical system and relocation of the engine ice-detector probe.

Deliveries to Malaysia began in 1967 and a new base was constructed to accommodate the Tebuans at Kuantan on the peninsula's east coast. Two squadrons fly the type: No 9 Sqn is an advanced training unit, while No 6 operates in the light strike role.

Canadair CL-41 Tutor

Specification

Type: two-seat training and tactical support aircraft

Powerplant: (CL-41G) one 2,950-lb (1340-kg) General Electric J85-J4 turbojet

Performance: maximum level speed at 28,500 ft (8700 m) 480 mph (774 km/h); service ceiling 42,200 ft (12800 m); maximum range 1,430 miles (2300 km)

Weights: empty 5,296 lb (2400 kg); maximum

take-off 11,288 lb (5130 kg); maximum landing 8,900 lb (4040 kg)

Dimensions: span 36 ft 5.9 in (11.13 m); length 32 ft (9.75 m); height 9 ft ¾ in (2.84 in); wing area 220 sq ft (20.44 m²)

Armament: six wing hardpoints can carry up to 4,000 lb (1815 kg) of bombs, rockets, gun pods or air-to-air missiles

Operators: Canada, Malaysia

CASA C-212 Aviocar

History and notes

The Spanish air force's requirement to replace several of its elderly transport aircraft such as the Douglas DC-3, the licence-built Junkers Ju 52/3m and the CASA Azor led to CASA drawing up a specification for a twin-turboprop transport which would be a general-purpose aircraft capable of adaptation for a number of roles. The possibility also of civil orders was not overlooked.

The result is the C-212 Aviocar, designed for a crew of two and up to 18 troops or, in a civil configuration, 19 passengers. The first prototype flew on 26 March 1971 and was demonstrated with verve at the Paris air show only 10 weeks later; its STOL performance was well demonstrated although the main spar suffered some damage apparently as a result of reverse pitch being applied while the aircraft was still several feet above the runway.

The second prototype flew in October 1971 and the

test programme continued, being rewarded by an order from the Spanish air ministry for an initial batch of eight pre-production aircraft, which made their maiden flights between November 1972 and February 1974. The type was given the Spanish air force designation T.12. The C-212A (T.12B) is a utility transport, and the first of 45 was delivered on 20 May 1974; the first squadron to be equipped with the new type was No 461 at Gando in the Canary Islands.

Five examples of the C-212AV were ordered as VIP transports and the first arrived in May 1976. Of the eight pre-production Aviocars, six were completed as C-212B (TR.12A) photographic and survey versions with two Wild RC-10 cameras and a darkroom, and the other two became C-212E navigation trainers. Following the delivery of these two aircraft, the Spanish air force ordered three

CASA C-212 Aviocar

more of the same type to bring its total Aviocar orders to 61.

Other military export customers have included Indonesia (28), Jordan (3) and Portugal (20) for the C-212A, Jordan (1) C-212AV and Portugal (4) C-212B. The most recent military customer has been Chile, which has ordered eight Aviocars, four each for the army and navy. For civil use the government of Nicaragua bought five C-212As, but the basic commercial version is the C-212C of which three were ordered by Pertamina in Indonesia for operation by Pelita Air Service and Merpati Nusantara Air Lines, and the Turkish operator Bursa Hava Yollari has two.

As a result of considerable sales interest in the Far East, CASA concluded a licence agreement with Nurtanio Aircraft Industries in Indonesia; production began in mid-1976 and 18 had been completed by 1979. Production rate was established at one per month increasing to two a month by 1982. At present it is envisaged that around 80 aircraft will come from the Nurtanio line.

CASA has received orders for about 150 Aviocars and more than 120 had been delivered by 1979; the production rate is about 48 aircraft a year.

In April 1978 CASA flew the prototype of a higher-powered and heavier Aviocar, the C-212-10. This was a conversion of the 138th production aircraft, featuring a strengthened airframe and two 865-shp (645-kW) Garrett-AiResearch TPE331-10 turboprops. The more powerful engines enable the maximum take-off weight to be increased by 2,205 lb (1000 kg) to 16,534 lb (7500 kg) and the maximum payload from 4,410 lb (2000 kg) to 7,054 lb (3200 kg)

In its troop-transport configuration the standard Aviocar can carry light vehicles or up to 18 fully-equipped troops; the rear loading ramp can be used for paratroop and cargo drops. In the ambulance role 12 stretcher (litter) patients and two attendants can be carried. As a navigation trainer desks for five pupils and an instructor can be fitted.

The VIP versions supplied to the Spanish and Jordanian air forces have 12 passenger seats and folding tables.

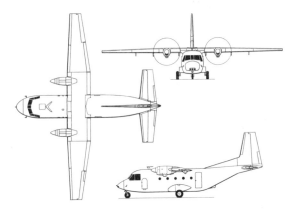

CASA 212 Aviocar

Specification

Type: utility transport
Powerplant: two 750-shp (560-kW) Garrett-AiResearch TPE331-5-251C turboprops
Performance: maximum speed at 12,000 ft (3660 m) 223 mph (359 km/h); cruising speed at 12,000 ft (3660 m) 171 mph (275 km/h); rate of climb at sea level 1,800 ft (548 m) per minute; service ceiling 26,700 ft (8140 m); take-off run to 50 ft (15 m) 1,588 ft (484 m); landing run from 50 ft (15 m) 1,263 ft (385 m); range with maximum fuel and 2,303-lb (1045-kg) payload 1,093 miles (1760 km)
Weights: empty 8,609 lb (3905 kg); maximum take-off (14,330 lb (6500 kg)
Dimensions: span 62 ft 4 in (19.00 m); length 49 ft 10 in (15.20 m); height 20 ft 8 in (6.30 m); wing area 430.56 sq ft (40.0 m²)
Operators: Chile, Indonesia, Jordan, Portugal, Spain, Thailand

One of four CASA C-212 Aviocars operated by the Royal Jordanian Air Force from Amman.

CASA C-101 Aviojet

Striking splinter camouflage on the fourth prototype of the new Spanish CASA C.101 Aviojet.

History and notes

Spain's aircraft industry is quite small, but a number of indigenous designs have emerged in recent years following licence production of designs from Germany and other countries. CASA (Construcciones Aeronauticas SA) is one of the oldest European aircraft companies and was founded in 1923. Since then it has been busily engaged in aircraft production and is also a large sub-contractor, being involved in such programmes as the Airbus A300 and the HFB 320 Hansa, together with licence production of the Northrop F-5 for the Spanish air force, and considerable overhaul work for both the Spanish and US air forces.

In 1972 Hispano Aviación SA merged with CASA and by mid-1978 the two companies had built some 3,500 aircraft, including the HA-200 jet trainer. Work on this aircraft, the F-5 and the Hansa stood CASA in good stead when it was asked to design a replacement for the HA-200, and in September 1975 the company was awarded a development contract for a basic and advanced jet trainer. Six prototypes were covered, four for flight test and two for fatigue testing. The first prototype, by then wearing the company designation C-101, flew on June 27, 1977, followed in September by the second. The third and fourth followed on 26 January and 17 April 1978 respectively and, following manufacturer's trials, were handed over to the Spanish air force for service testing in late 1978, by which time the name Aviojet had been chosen. The military designation will be E.25.

Assistance in the design stage came from MBB in West Germany, while the US Northrop company helped with the jet inlet and wing design. Imported components include Dowty landing gear, tandem Martin-Baker ejection seats, US-built air-conditioning and pressurization system, Garrett-AiResearch engine and Sperry STARS integrated flight control system.

Production of the initial batch of 10 Aviojets began in early 1978 to meet orders for 60 for the Spanish air force as a replacement for the Hispano HA-200 and HA-220s, of which 80 or more are still in service. All these will eventually need to be replaced and further orders for Aviojets up to a total of around 120 are expected. Deliveries were due to begin in October 1979 and the Aviojet is to enter service with

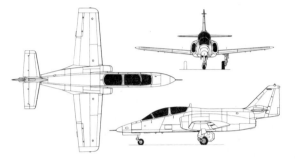

CASA 101 Aviojet

the training units in 1980.

As in the case of the HA-200/220 it seems likely that a strike variant will be developed to replace the 20 or so HA-220s still in service.

Specification

Type: basic and advanced jet trainer and light strike aircraft

Powerplant: one 3,500-lb (1587-kg) thrust Garrett-AiResearch TFE731-2-25 turbofan

Performance: maximum speed at sea level 420 mph (676 km/h); maximum speed at 25,000 ft (7620 m) Mach 0.69; cruising speed at 35,000 ft (10675 m) Mach 0.61; rate of climb at sea level 3,350 ft (1021 m) per minute; service ceiling 41,000 ft (12495 m); take-off run to 50 ft (15 m) 2,950 ft (900 m); landing run from 50 ft (15 m) 2,165 ft (660 m); ferry range 2,485 miles (4000 km)

Weights: basic operating 6,519 lb (2957 kg); maximum take-off (trainer) 10,361 lb (4700 kg); maximum take-off (ground-attack) 12,345 lb (5600 kg)

Dimensions: span 34 ft 9 in (10.60 m); length 40 ft 2 in (12.25 m); height 13 ft 11 in (4.25 m); wing area 215.3 sq ft (20.00 m²)

Armament: underfuselage attachment for a 30-mm cannon, a 12.7 mm (0.5-in) gun, reconnaissance camera or laser designator; three hardpoints under each wing can carry up to 4,410 lb (2000 kg) of stores consisting of rocket pods, missiles, bombs or napalm canisters; a tow target can also be carried beneath each wing

Operator: Spain

Cessna Model 318E/A-37 Dragonfly

Cessna A-37B Dragonfly flown by the 104th Tactical Fighter Squadron, Maryland Air National Guard, US Air Force.

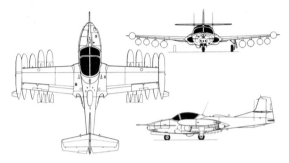

History and notes

During 1962 two Cessna T-37 trainers were evaluated by the USAF's Special Air Warfare Center to consider their suitability for deployment in the counter-insurgency (COIN) role. The aircraft chosen for this evaluation were two T-37Bs, and these were first tested with their original power-plant of two 1,025-lb (465-kg) thrust Continental J69-T-25 turbojets, at a take-off weight of 8,700 lb (3946 kg), which was almost 33% above the normal maximum take-off weight. After a first test period, the airframes were modified to accept two 2,400-lb (1089-kg) thrust General Electric J85-GE-5 turbojets. This vast increase in power made it possible for the aircraft, then designated YAT-37D, to be flown at steadily increasing maximum take-off weights until a safe upper limit of 14,000 lb (6350 kg) was reached. There was, clearly, plenty of scope for the carriage of a worthwhile load of weapons.

This exercise had been more academic than essential, until the need of the war in Vietnam made the USAF take a closer look at this armed version of what had proved to be an excellent trainer. Accordingly, Cessna were requested to convert 39 T-37B trainers to a light-strike configuration, a contract being awarded in 1966: this related to the conversion of new T-37B aircraft taken from the production line. The new model was based on the earlier experiments with the two YAT-37Ds, and equipped with eight underwing hardpoints, provided with wingtip tanks to increase fuel capacity, and was powered by derated General Electric J85-GE-5 turbojets.

Delivery of these aircraft to the USAF began on 2 May 1967, and during the latter half of that year a squadron numbering 25 of these aircraft, designated A-37A and named Dragonfly, underwent a four-month operational evaluation in South Vietnam. Following this period of investigation, they were transferred for operational duty with the 604th Air Commando Squadron at Bien Hoa; in 1970 they were assigned to the South Vietnamese air force.

During this period, Cessna had been busy building the prototype of a purpose-designed light-strike aircraft based on the T-37 airframe, and this flew for the first time in September 1967.

The A-37B differed in its construction from the prototype YAT-37D which had been evaluated in 1963–64. The airframe had been stressed for 6-g loading, maximum internal fuel capacity was increased to 507 US gallons (1920 litres), with the

Cessna A-37B Dragonfly

ability to carry four auxiliary tanks with a combined capacity of 400 US gallons (1516 litres), and there was also provision for flight-refuelling. Powerplant was changed to two General Electric J85-GE-17A turbojets. A GAU-2B/A 7.62-mm Minigun was installed, and the eight underwing hardpoints were able to carry in excess of 5,000 lb (2268 kg) of mixed stores. For the assessment of results both gun and strike cameras were carried, and while the provision of armour would have added a significant weight penalty which could not be afforded, some measure of protection for the crew of two was provided by the inclusion of layered nylon flak-curtains installed around the cockpit.

Specification

Type: two-seat light strike aircraft
Powerplant: two 2,850-lb (1293-kg) thrust General Electric J85-GE-17A turbojets
Performance: maximum speed at 16,000 ft (4875 m) 524 mph (843 km/h); maximum cruising speed at 25,000 ft (7620 m) 489 mph (787 km/h); range with maximum fuel at 25,000 ft (7620 m) with reserves 1,012 miles (1629 km); range with maximum payload, including 4,100 lb (1860 kg) external weapons 460 miles (740 km)
Weights: empty equipped 6,211 lb (2817 kg); maximum take-off 14,000 lb (6350 kg)
Dimensions: span 35 ft 10½ in (10.93 m); length 28 ft 3¼ in (8.62 m); height 8 ft 10½ in (2.71 m); wing area 183.9 sq ft (17.08 m²)
Armament: can include bombs, incendiary bombs, cluster bombs, rocket pods and gun pods
Operators: Chile, Ecuador, Guatemala, Thailand, US Air Force, US Air National Guard, South Vietnam

Dassault Mirage III/5

Mirage IIICJ interceptor in Heyl Ha'Avir markings, operational at the time of the 1967 war.

725

Dassault Mirage IIIR reconnaissance aircraft of 33 Escadre de Reconnaissance I CATac, l'Armee de l'Air, at Strasbourg.

33-TA

History and notes

The Dassault Mirage III holds the distinction of being the first European aircraft to fly at twice the speed of sound, which it achieved in October 1958, and it has since gone on to become one of the world's most successful military aircraft. Dassault was one of three companies which built prototypes to meet a requirement formulated by the French air staff in the early 1950s. The specification called for a small supersonic interceptor with good armament and a fast rate of climb, and capable of acting independently of ground control.

Sud-Ouest's answer was the Trident, which was powered by a large rocket motor and two small turbojets. Sud-Est adopted the opposite combination, its Durandal having a large turbojet and a small rocket. Dassault's MD.550 had two small Viper turbojets plus a rocket. The type was named Mirage, because Dassault intended it to be 'like a desert vision, so that enemy pilots should see it but never catch up with it'.

The Mirage III-001 took to the air in November 1956 and quickly provided valuable information about the aerodynamics, flight controls and variable supersonic intakes which would be required of a production fighter. By this time the French air force was showing marked interest in the project, and a pre-production batch of 10 Mirage IIIs was ordered only six months after the type's maiden flight. The first of these flew in May 1958, and the initial production contract was awarded in October of that year. Two years later the first Mirage IIIC made its maiden flight, and the next month it was handed over to the French air force.

Despite its thin flapless wing, inefficient at low speeds, the Mirage III can take off from and land on a 2,600 ft (800 m) runway while carrying its standard air-to-air armament. The Mirage IIIC is a single-seat interceptor powered by a SNECMA Atar 9B of 13,228-lb (6000-kg) static thrust. Its rate of climb and ceiling can be increased by fitting an SEP 844 rocket motor rated at 3,307 lb (1500 kg) thrust,

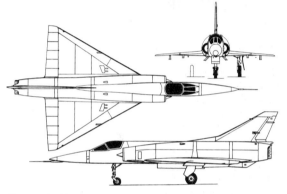

Dassault Mirage 5

which can be jettisoned after use if desired. Alternatively, an extra fuel tank can be fitted in the same space if the rocket is not installed. So far as is known, no export customers use the rocket installation. The Mirage IIIC carries a Thomson-CSF Cyrano Ibis fire-control radar; its normal armament comprises Matra R.530 and AIM-9 Sidewinder air-to-air missiles in addition to the two built-in cannon carried as an alternative to rocket fuel.

The next major version was the Mirage IIIE, a long-range fighter-bomber. Its fuselage is slightly longer, and an Atar 9C is installed. The use of Cyrano II radar, together with a doppler radar and navigation computer, allows the IIIE to fly at low level in all weathers and to carry out blind attacks, though it cannot hug the ground or strike point targets as can the General Dynamics FIII and Panavia Tornado. Other major variants in the series include the Mirage IIIB and IIID two-seat trainers; the IIIO built under licence in Australia; and the IIIR reconnaissance version with five OMERA Type 31 cameras or the SAT Cyclope infra-red package. The Mirage IIIS was built under licence in Switzerland and carries a Hughes Taran fire-control system, with the same company's Falcon missiles replacing French types.

Israel asked for a simplified ground-attack version, the Mirage 5. This retains the basic airframe of its predecessor, but has miniaturized electronics tailored to its new role. The smaller electronics volume has allowed the fuel capacity to be increased by 110 gallons (500 litres), and the weapon load has also been improved by the use of up to seven attachment points. The Mirage 5, which made its maiden flight in May 1969, does not carry the Cyrano fire-control radar but can be fitted with an Aida II ranging radar in its place. Two-seat and reconnaissance versions have been built and the Mirage 5, like the III, is designed for a service life of 5,000 hours flying over a period of 25 years. The Israeli batch of 50 was paid for, but were then embargoed by General de Gaulle and finally used by France.

Specification

Type: single-seat interceptor (IIIC), all-weather fighter-bomber (IIIE), reconnaissance aircraft (IIIR), two-seat trainer (IIIB and IIID), or ground-attack aircraft and day fighter (5 and 50)
Powerplant: (IIIE and 5) Mach 2.2 or 1,460 mph (2336 km/h) at 40,000 ft (12190 m); cruising speed Mach 0.9 at 36,090 ft (11000 m); maximum level speed at sea level 863 mph (1390 km/h); ground-attack combat radius (5) 760 miles (1220 km); time to Mach 1.8 at 60,040 ft (18300 m) with SEP rocket and one AAM (IIIE) 7 minutes 40 seconds; time to Mach 1.8 at 49,870 ft (15200 m) (5) 6 minutes 48 seconds
Weights: empty (IIIE) 15,875 lb (7200 kg); empty (5) 15,210 lb (6900 kg); mission take-off, clean (IIIE), 21,605 lb (9800 kg); mission take-off, clean (5) 20,500 lb (9300 kg); maximum take-off (IIIE and 5) 29,760 lb (13500 kg)
Dimensions: span (IIIE and 5) 27 ft (8.22 m); length (IIIE) 49 ft 3 in (15.03 m); length (5) 50 ft 10 in (15.50 m); height (IIIE) 13 ft 11 in (4.25 m); height (5) 14 ft 9 in (4.50 m); wing area (IIIE and 5) 375 sq ft (35 m²)
Armament: (IIIE) two 30-mm DEFA cannon and (ground-attack mission) one AS.30 air-to-surface missile or two 1,000-lb (454-kg) bombs under the fuselage and two 1,000-lb (454-kg) bombs beneath the wings; (intercept mission) one or two R.530 air-to-air missiles and guns or Sidewinder air-to-air missile; (5) two 30-mm DEFA cannon and up to 8,818 lb (4000 kg) of stores including 1,000-lb (454-kg) bombs, JL-100 rocket pods with eighteen 68-mm projectiles each, napalm, AS.30 air-to-surface missile, etc
Operators: (III) Argentina, Australia, Brazil, Egypt, France, Israel, Lebanon, Libya, Pakistan, South Africa, Spain, Switzerland, Venezuela; (5) Abu Dhabi, Belgium, Colombia, Egypt, France, Gabon, Libya, Pakistan, Peru, Venezuela, Zaire; (50) Sudan

Dassault Mirage F1

History and notes
The Dassault Mirage F1 is effectively a successor to the extremely successful Dassault Mirage III/5 series, although it differs substantially from the design which was originally planned to replace this family. In 1964 Dassault was awarded a French government contract to build a prototype of the F2 two-seat fighter, with a conventional wing and tail-plane, and powered by a SNECMA/Pratt & Whitney TF306 turbofan. This aircraft made its maiden flight in June 1966, and in December of that year it was followed into the air by the first F1, a smaller single-seat fighter which Dassault had designed as a private venture and sized to the smaller Atar turbo-jet.

The F1 crashed, but still proved a more attractive proposition than its larger brother, and in September 1967 the French government ordered three pre-production F1s together with a structural test airframe. The first of these new aircraft made its maiden flight in March 1969 and completed its initial series of flight trials some three months later. Despite being powered by a SNECMA Atar 9K31, which produced less thrust than the 9K50 adopted later, the first pre-production F1 notched up a series of impressive performances during this early period. These included a speed of Mach 2.12 or 1,405 mph (2260 km/h) at 36,090 ft (11000 m), and 808 mph (1300 km/h) at low level.

The F1 has proved to be more than an adequate successor to the Mirage III as a multi-role aircraft, with emphasis on a large payload, easy handling at low altitude and a high rate of climb. Compared with its predecessor, the F1 has a higher maximum speed (Mach 2.2 rather than Mach 2), three times the endurance at high Mach numbers, three times the patrol time before and after an interception, twice the tactical range at sea level, a 30% shorter take-off run at greater maximum weight, 25% lower approach speed, and improved manoeuvrability at both subsonic and supersonic speeds.

The short take-off and landing performance results from the high-lift system, comprising leading-edge droops and large flaps, fitted to the sharply swept wing. At its average mission weight the F1 can take off and land within 1,700 ft to 2,600 ft (500 to 800 m). Although the Mirage III and F1 have practically identical external dimensions — and in particular the same wetted area — the internal

Dassault Mirage F1

This Dassault-Breguet Mirage F1C fighter is serving with EC 1/12 based at Cambrai. The 68th production aircraft, it has the standard CATac grey/white finish; wing-walkers keep within yellow lines.

2-YN

fuel capacity of the later aircraft is 40% more than that of its forebear. This has been achieved by eliminating bladder-type tanks and replacing them with integral fuel space.

The variant in service with the French air force is the F1 C interceptor, the first production example of which made its maiden flight in February 1973. The initial batch comprised 105 aircraft, and a further 109 are expected to be acquired eventually. The F1A is a ground-attack and VFR (visual flight rules) fighter version, with only a ranging radar instead of the Cyrano IV, and simpler avionics. The deletion of some of this equipment allows extra fuel to be carried. The F1A is built under licence by Atlas Aircraft in South Africa as well as being supplied directly by Dassault. The F1E was planned in two versions: one with the Atar 9K50 and the other with the SNEC-MA M53. The latter version made its maiden flight in December 1974 and was offered to Belgium, Holland, Denmark and Norway in competition with the Saab Viggen and General Dynamics F-16. This contest was won by the US aircraft and the M53-powered aircraft was discontinued. The F1E has more advanced avionics suiting the aircraft to the all-weather role.

The F1B, which took to the air for the first time in May 1976, is a dual trainer. Changes from the single-seat variants are minimal, although no internal guns are carried. This can be remedied by fitting external pods containing the weapons. The radar screen and head-up display are repeated in the rear cockpit, allowing the F1B to act as a fully operational trainer.

Specification

Type: single-seat interceptor and ground-attack fighter

Powerplant: one 15,870-lb (7214-kg) SNECMA Atar 9K50 afterburning turbojet

Performance: maximum speed Mach 2.2 or 1,450 mph (2320 km/h) at 39,990 ft (12190 m); maximum speed at sea level Mach 1.2 or 920 mph (1472 km/h); maximum combat radius 400 miles (640 km) with 3,520-lb (1600-kg) load at low level; endurance 3 hours 45 minutes; time to climb to Mach 2 at 39,990 ft (12190 m) 7 minutes 30 seconds; stabilized supersonic ceiling 60,695 ft (18500 m).

Weights: empty 16,315 lb (7400 kg); operational (pilot, guns, internal fuel) 24,030 lb (10900 kg); operational (with air-to-air missiles) 25,350 lb (11500 kg)

Dimensions: span 27 ft 8 in (8.44 m); length 50 ft (15.25 m); height 13 ft 9 in (4.50 m); wing area 269 sq ft (25 m²)

Armament: two 30-mm DEFA 553 cannon with 125 rounds per gun and (intercept mission) two R.550 Magic air-to-air missiles, or two AIM-9 Sidewinder air-to-air missiles, or two R.530 or Super 530 air to air missiles with option of two Magic; or (attack mission) up to 8,818 lb (4000 kg) on seven hardpoints, with combinations such as eight 1,000-lb (454-kg) bombs, or four 36-round rocket launchers, or gun pods, or one AS.30 or AS.37 Martel air-to-surface missile, or other payloads such as napalm

Operators: Ecuador, Egypt, France, Greece, Iraq, Kuwait, Libya, Morocco, South Africa, Spain.

Dassault-Breguet Atlantic

History and notes

The Breguet Atlantic has the distinction of being the first combat aircraft to be designed and built as a completely multi-national project. In January 1958, NATO issued an NBMR (NATO Basic Military Requirement) for a long-range maritime-patrol aircraft. Breguet submitted its Br.1150 project, which was studied along with 24 other designs from a total of nine countries, and in November of that year the alliance's group of experts selected the French company's submission.

The first prototype Atlantic made its maiden flight at Toulouse in October 1961 and was followed by two other aircraft before the initial production machine took to the air in September 1964. The French navy began to receive the type in July 1965, eventually accepting two-thirds of the 60 aircraft in the first batch; the other 20 were put into service by the German navy. The first Atlantic in the second production batch made its initial flight in January 1971 and was later supplied, along with eight others to the Netherlands navy. The Italian air force received the

remaining 18 aircraft in this batch, deliveries ending in July 1974. Production thus totalled 87, of which three have since been transferred from the French navy to Pakistan.

The Atlantic's main mission is to hunt and attack submarines, but the aircraft can fulfil a wide variety of secondary roles including anti-ship missions, minelaying, coastal reconnaissance, fleet escort and the direction of air-sea rescue missions.

The Atlantic's Thomson-CSF search radar can detect a submarine's schnorkel at ranges of up to 46 miles (75 km) even in rough seas. Sonobuoys are jettisoned through chutes in the rear fuselage, and the 'sting' for a magnetic-anomaly detector (MAD) is mounted behind the tail section. Information from the sensors is fed to individual displays in the Plotac display and control system.

Various improved versions of the Atlantic have been studied under a number of designations, including Mk II and M4, and in March 1977 the French government finally decided to launch preliminary

Dassault-Breguet Atlantic

Aéronautique Navale Breguet Atlantic anti-submarine patrol aircraft. Four units are equipped with 35 aircraft.

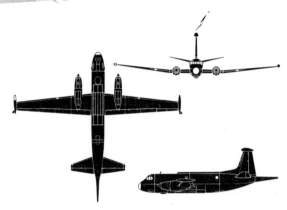

design work on this project, now known as ANG (Atlantic *Nouvelle Génération*). This was followed in February 1978 by a go-ahead for the programme, with the French navy to receive 42 ANGs. The schedule laid down in 1978 calls for the first ANG prototype, converted from a Mk 1 Atlantic, to make its maiden flight in the second half of 1980, with the second following in the first half of 1981. Production ANGs would be delivered from mid-1984.

Specification

Type: anti-submarine and maritime-patrol aircraft
Powerplant: four 6,100-ehp (4551-kW) Rolls-Royce Tyne 21 turboprops, built by a multi-national consortium
Performance: maximum design speed 408 mph (658 km/h); maximum sea-level speed 368 mph (593 km/h); cruising speed 345 mph (556 km/h) or Mach 0.5 at 24,935 ft (7600 m); typical patrol speed 196 mph (315 km/h); ceiling 30,020 ft (9150 m); maximum endurance 18 hours; maximum range 5,180 miles (8340 km); sea-level take-off run at maximum gross weight 5,750 ft (1750 m)
Weights: empty equipped 55,115 lb (25000 kg); maximum take-off 98,105 lb (44500 kg); maximum fuel weight 40,740 lb (18500 kg); maximum ordnance load 6,614 lb (3000 kg)

Dassault-Breguet Br. 1150 Atlantic

Dimensions: span 119 ft 1 in (36.30 m); length 104 ft 2½ in (31.75 m); height 37 ft 4 in (11.33 m); wing area 1,293 sq ft (120.0 m²)
Armament: bombs, 385-lb (175-kg) depth charges, air-to-surface rockets, Mk 44 or LX.4 homing torpedoes, AM.39 Exocet anti-ship missiles, AS.37 Martel anti-radiation missiles, AS.12 air-to-surface missiles
Operators: France, Italy, Netherlands, Pakistan, West Germany

---

Dassault-Breguet Mirage 2000

History and notes

Although called Mirage, and having a plan form similar to that of the well-known Mirage III, the Dassault-Breguet Mirage 2000 is a completely new aircraft. Dassault was building the French air force *Avion de Combat Futur* (ACF) when the project was cancelled in 1975, only six months before the prototype was due to fly. The French air force had decided that the ACF, a twin-engined aircraft based on SNECMA M53-5 bleed-turbojets was too big. It wanted a smaller aircraft, with approximately the performance of the General Dynamics F-16 lightweight fighter.

On 18 December 1975 the French government gave a go-ahead on this new programme, which was styled the Mirage 2000. Four prototypes were ordered and Dassault decided to build a fifth example to aid the development of export versions.

In the Mirage 2000, for which the 19,840 lb (9000 kg) SNECMA M53-5 bleed-turbojet engine had to provide a thrust:weight ratio of 1:1 at combat weights, the aircraft has been made as small and as light as possible. To enhance manoeuvrability, the aircraft has an electronic fly-by-wire flight control system which allows the aircraft centre of gravity range to be extended further aft than on a conventional aircraft.

The delta wing is large compared with Dassault's previous designs, reduced wing-loading providing better low-speed performance, and permitting higher turn-rates at high altitude. The wing has almost no camber, but leading-edge flaps (very rare on deltas) and large trailing-edge elevons, which droop as flaps during manoeuvres, can produce more lift per unit area than the inefficient conven-

Dassault-Breguet Mirage 2000

France's newest air superiority interceptor, the delta-winged Dassault Mirage 2000, seen in initial prototype form.

tional delta wing.

Nine hardpoints, five under the fuselage and four under the wings, can carry up to 11,025 lb (5000 kg) of ordnance. Normal air-interception duties will be carried out with two Matra Super 530 and two Matra 550 Magic air-to-air missiles. Two 30-mm DEFA cannon are mounted in the fuselage. Sidewinder missiles can be carried instead of Magic on export versions.

Dassault test pilot Jean Coureau made the first flight of the Mirage 2000 on 10 March 1978, reaching Mach 1.3. The aircraft was flown from Istre, although it had been built at St Cloud. The second Mirage 2000 flew on 18 September 1978 and three more are due to fly before 1981, including a two-seater. The French air force is reported to want up to 400 examples, but only 130 are expected to be ordered for the air-interceptor role. The remainder are probably to be strike and reconnaissance aircraft. Mirage 2000 deliveries will begin in 1982, and production should reach four aircraft per month by 1984.

Specification
Type: single-seat multi-role fighter
Powerplant: one 19,840-lb (9000-kg) SNECMA M53-5 continuous-bleed after burning turbojet
Performance: estimated maximum speed Mach 2.3 or 1,520 mph (2445 km/h) above 36,090 ft (11000 m); estimated tactical radius with two Matra Super 530 and two Matra 550 Magic air-to-air missiles and two 374-gallon (1700-litre) drop

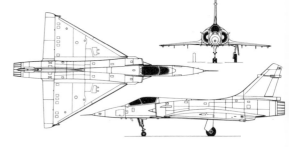

Dassault-Breguet Mirage 2000

tanks 435 miles (700 km); time to Mach 2 at 49,210 ft (15000 m) from brake release with four air-to-air missiles 4 minutes; range (with drop tanks) 932 miles (1500 km); service ceiling 65,600 ft (20,000 m)
Weights: estimated empty 14,080 lb (6400 kg); normal take-off (with internal fuel and four air-to-air missiles) 21,825 lb (9900 kg); maximum take-off weight (maximum external ordnance) 33,070 lb (15000 kg)
Dimensions: (estimated) span 29 ft 6 in (9.00 m); length 50 ft 3½ in (15.33 m); height 17 ft 6 in (5.30 m); wing area 430.5 sq ft (40.00 m^2)
Armament: two 30-mm DEFA cannon and (air-superiority) two Matra 550 Magic plus two Matra Super 530 air-to-air missiles or (strike) up to 11,025 lb (5000 kg) of ordnance on nine external points (five under fuselage, four under wing)
Operator: France (on order)

Dassault-Breguet Super Etendard

History and notes
As its name implies, the Dassault-Breguet Super Etendard is an updated version of Dassault's Etendard IVM carrier-based attack aircraft. The need for a replacement for the original aircraft had been recognised in the mid-1960s, and the maritime variant of the SEPECAT Jaguar, designated model M, was intended to fill this role. This version differed from the land-based Jaguar in having single main wheels, extended undercarriage stroke, all the modifications required for carrier operations and equipment tailored to the naval strike role. Despite its completion of flight and carrier trials, the Jaguar M was cancelled, primarily on grounds of cost and

politics. Having evaluated the McDonnell Douglas A-4 Skyhawk and LTV A-7 Corsair II (France already operates the same company's F-8 Crusader), the *Aéronavale* decided to adopt an improved Etendard. Dassault converted two standard Etendard IVM airframes, and the first of three Super Etendard prototypes flew on 28 October 1974.

The Super Etendard contains many improvements over the earlier aircraft, not the least of which are 10% more thrust (at a lower specific fuel consumption) and new high-lift devices on the wing, which together permit a heavier gross weight on the catapult strop and, consequently, greater fuel capacity and armament.

Dassault-Breguet Super Etendard

Seventh production Super Etendard carrier-based attack aircraft of the Aéronautique Navale. A total of 71 are on order.

The first prototype was used to prove the engine installation, testing the external load-carrying capabilities and performing firing trials of the AM.39 Exocet air-to-surface anti-ship missile, of which the Super Etendard carries one under the starboard wing. The second prototype flew on 25 March 1975, and was involved in navigation-system and bombing trials.

The third prototype was the first example with the new wing to fly. The first production aircraft flew on 27 November 1977, and deliveries began on 28 June 1978, when the third production aircraft was handed over to the *Aéronavale*.

Specification

Type: single-seat transonic carrier-based attack aircraft
Powerplant: one 11,265-lb (5110-kg) SNECMA Atar 8K-50 single-shaft turbojet
Performance: maximum speed 745 mph (1200 km/h) at sea level, Mach 1 at altitude; range at altitude (clean) more than 1,243 miles (2000 km); initial rate of climb 24,600 ft (7500 m) per minute; service ceiling 45,000 ft (13700 m)
Weights: empty equipped 14,220 lb (6450 kg); maximum take-off 26,455 lb (12000 kg)

Dassault-Breguet Super Etendard

Dimensions: span 31 ft 6 in (9.6 m); span folded 25 ft 7 in (7.8 m); length overall 46 ft 11½ in (14.31 m); height overall 12 ft 8 in (3.86 m); wing area 305.7 sq ft (28.4 m^2)
Armament: two 30-mm DEFA cannon (125 rounds each) in bottom of engine air-intake trunks; underfuselage hardpoints for 551-lb (250-kg) bombs; four underwing hardpoints for 882-lb (400-kg) bombs; Magic air-to-air missiles or rocket pods; optional, one AM.39 Exocet air-to-surface missile under starboard wing and one external fuel tank under port wing
Operators: France (Aéronavale)

Dassault-Breguet Mirage IV

History and notes

The French, renowned for their highly nationalistic policies, decided in 1954 to create their own nuclear deterrent force. One of the first priorities was to develop a launch platform for the weapons. The project was headed by Dassault in association with a number of other companies, including Sud-Aviation (responsible for the wing and rear fuselage) and Breguet (tail surfaces). In the face of a requirement calling for a long, high-speed mission (likely to the Soviet Union), Dassault looked initially at developments of the Vautour but later directed its attention at a 1956 design for a twin-engined night fighter.

The original prototype Mirage IV flew on 17 June 1959, and was powered by two 13,225-lb (6000-kg) SNECMA Atar 09 augmented turbojets. Take-off weight was approximately 55,100 lb (25000 kg). On its 14th test flight (in July 1959) it reached Mach 1.9, and it attained Mach 2 on its 33rd flight. Three pre-production prototypes, the first of which flew on 12 October 1961, followed the prototype. Powered by a

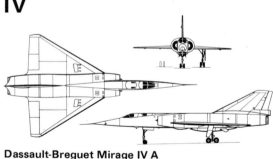

Dassault-Breguet Mirage IV A

pair of 14,110-lb (6400-kg) Atar 09Cs, this aircraft was larger and more representative of the production Mirage IVA, incorporating a large circular radome under the centre fuselage forward of the semi-recessed nuclear free-fall bomb. The first pre-production aircraft underwent bombing trials and development at Colomb-Béchar; the second aircraft, a similar machine, was used to develop the navigation and flight-refuelling systems; and the third aircraft, a completely operational model with Atar 09Ks, full equipment including nose-probe for

Dassault-Breguet Mirage IV

Dassault Mirage IVA of l'Armée de l'Air's "Force de Frappe", with a crew of two.

refuelling, and armament, flew on 23 January 1963. Satisfied with the trials, the French air force ordered 50 production Mirage IVAs for delivery in 1964–65. A repeat order for a further 12 was placed later. Fifty of the 62 delivered are expected to remain in service in the nuclear strike role until 1985, when silo-based S-3 strategic missiles (first operational in 1976) will maintain the country's deterrent until the year 2000. A total of 33 aircraft on call for service equip six squadrons in two wings (91 and 94 *Escadres*) dispersed among six bases. Twelve have been converted for long-range, high/low-level reconnaissance, which will be the type's main role from 1985. Although a heavy machine and fairly 'hot' to operate, the Mirage IVAs of the French air force are on extremely quick alert. They can take off straight out of the hardened shelters in which they are housed, with their engines running at full power, and have even operated off short, unpaved strips with the aid of auxiliary take-off rockets and fast-drying chemicals sprayed onto the surface to harden the ground run.

Specification

Type: two-seat supersonic strategic bomber
Powerplant: two 15,432-lb (7000-kg) reheat SNECMA Atar 9K turbojets.
Performance: maximum dash speed at 40,060 ft (13125 m) 1,454 mph (2340 km/h or Mach 2.2); maximum sustained speed 1,222 mph (1966 km/h or Mach 1.7) at 60,000 ft (19685 m); tactical radius (dash to target, high-subsonic return) 770 miles (1240 km); ferry range 2,485 miles (4000 km); time to 36,090 ft (11000 m) 4 minutes 15 seconds
Weights: empty equipped 31,967 lb (14500 kg); maximum loaded 73,800 lb (33475 kg)
Dimensions: span 38 ft 10½ in (11.85 m); length 77 ft 1 in (23.5 m); height 17 ft 8½ in (5.4 m); wing area 840 sq ft (78 m²)
Armament: electronic countermeasures; one 60-kiloton freefall bomb recessed in belly; or, alternatively, up to 16,000 lb (7257 kg) of ordnance on wing and fuselage hardpoints
Operator: France (Armée de l'Air Commandement des forces Aériennes Stratégique)

Dassault-Breguet/Dornier Alpha Jet

History and notes

An international project between France and West Germany, the Dassault-Breguet/Dornier Alpha Jet will serve with *l'Armée de l'Air* in the advanced training role, and with the *Luftwaffe* with the additional tasks of light strike and reconnaissance. On 22 July 1969 the governments of France and West Germany announced that they had a requirement for a new subsonic basic and advanced training aircraft. A total of around 200 each was envisaged, to replace the Lockheed T-33s and Fouga Magisters then in service and beginning to show their age. France had originally hoped to fill this role with the two-seat SEPECAT Jaguar, but it was eventually realised that so powerful a supersonic trainer was foolish, so an alternative had to be found. On 24 July 1970 it was announced that the Alpha Jet had been selected to equip the two forces not only in the training role but also for battlefield-reconnaissance duties and light strike, following a change in *Luftwaffe* requirements.

The whole programme has suffered a slippage of more than two years, causing a corresponding delay to production deliveries. The go-ahead decision was taken on 26 March 1975, nearly 18 months after the first prototype flew on 26 October 1973. The first *Luftwaffe* aircraft flew on 12 April 1978, nearly six months after the first series aircraft. The first of 33

Dassault-Breguet/Dornier Alpha Jet

aircraft for Belgium took to the air on 20 June 1978. Production is centred in France, along with flight testing, as Dassault Breguet is prime contractor and Dornier industrial collaborator. The assembly line in Belgium will be closed down in 1980, by which time all the country's aircraft are due to have been delivered. In 1978 the Alpha Jet cost in the region of $4.5 million, making it the most expensive of the new generation of trainers. It is also, however, one of the most capable at the cost of seven maintenance man-hours per flying hour, and a limited fatigue life of 10,000 hours. Aspect ratio may be increased to improve single-engine performance. France's Alpha

Dassault-Breguet/Dornier Alpha Jet

Dassault-Breguet/Dorner Alpha Jet shown in the operational camouflage planned for the 200 aircraft on order for the Luftwaffe.

Jets will replace T-33s and Mystère IVs, which have been used for advanced and weapons training respectively. For some reason France does not fit zero-zero ejection seats, though the West Germans do. Students will spend some 70 hours on a new basic trainer and then a similar period on Magisters before moving up to the more complex Alpha Jet. Belgian students will move straight from SIAI -Marchetti SF.260 primary trainers to the new jet. Weapon-training and light strike variants for the *Luftwaffe* will be able to carry nearly 5,000 lb (2268 kg) of stores on one centre-fuselage and four underwing hardpoints.

Specification

Type: two-seat advanced trainer and light strike/ reconnaissance aircraft
Powerplant: two 2,976-lb (1350-kg) SNECMA/ Turboméca Larzac 04 two-shaft turbofans
Performance: maximum speed at sea level 622 mph (1000 km/h); maximum speed at 30,000 ft (9144 m) or Mach 0.85; combat radius (including 5 minutes combat) with maximum external load 254 miles (410 km); combat radius (ground-attack, lo-lo-lo), 391 miles (630 km); ferry range (internal fuel and two 68.2-Imperial Gallon (310-litre) drop-tanks) 1,725 miles (2780 km); time to 30,000 ft (9145 m) under 7 minutes
Weights: empty equipped (trainer) 7,374 lb (3345 kg); empty equipped (strike) 7,716 lb (3500 kg); normal take-off (trainer, clean) 11,023 lb (5000 kg); normal take-off (strike) 13,448 lb (6100 kg); maximum take-off (strike, external stores) 15,983 lb (7250 kg)
Dimensions: span 29 ft 10¾ in (9.11 m); length 40 ft 3¾ in (12.29 m); height 13 ft 9 in (4.19 m); wing area 188.4 sq ft (17.5 m²)
Armament: underfuselage pod containing a 30-mm DEFA or 27-mm Mauser cannon (150 rounds each) or 7.62-mm (0.3-in) machine-gun (250 rounds); four underwing hardpoints each carrying up to thirty-six 68-mm (2.68-in) rockets or high-explosive/ retarded bombs up to 882 lb (400 kg) in weight, or cluster dispensers, or drop tanks etc; provision also for air-to-air (Magic) or air-to-surface (Maverick) missiles
Operators: Belgium, France, Ivory Coast, Morocco, Qatar, Togo, West Germany

De Havilland Canada DHC-4 Caribou

History and notes
DHC took the decision to build the DHC-4 in 1956 and the aim was to develop an aircraft with the load carrying capability of the DC-3 and the STOL performance of the Beaver and Otter. The Canadian army placed an order for two and the US Army followed with five. The US Secretary of Defense waived a restriction which limited the US Army to fixed-wing aircraft with empty weight less than 5,000 lb (2268 kg).

The prototype flew in July 1958. The high wing had a characteristic centre section with marked anhedral. The rear door was designed as a ramp for items weighing up to 6,720 lb (3048 kg). In the trooping role up to 32 soldiers could be carried. The Caribou served with the RCAF as the CC-108 and with the US Army as the AC-1 (1962 designation, CV-2A). As a result of its evaluation of the first five aircraft the US Army adopted the Caribou as standard equipment and placed orders for 159.

The second batch were uprated and designated CU-2B. Following tension on the border between

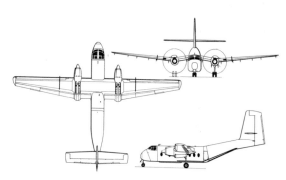

De Havilland Canada DHC-4 Caribou

China and India, the US Army handed over two Caribous to the Indian air force in early-1963. In January 1967 the 134 Caribous still in service with the US Army were transferred to US Air Force charge as C-7As or C-7Bs. The aircraft was a general sales success and examples flew with air forces throughout the world. In Canadian service

De Havilland Canada DHC-4 Caribou

the Caribou was replaced by the DHC-5 Buffalo and surplus examples were sold to a number of nations including Columbia, Oman and Tanzania. Many of the Canadian aircraft had been loaned to the United Nations and seen extensive international service. Production ceased in 1973.

Royal Malaysian Air Force de Havilland Canada DHC-4 Caribou shown in 1970 when flown by 5 Sqn, RMAF.

Specification
Type: STOL tactical transport
Powerplant: two 1,450-hp (1080-kW) Pratt & Whitney R-2000-7M2 air-cooled radial piston engines
Performance: (at maximum take-off weight) maximum speed at 6,500 ft (1980 m) 216 mph (347 km/h); maximum cruising speed at 7,500 ft (2285 m) 182 mph (293 km/h); range with maximum payload and full reserves 242 miles (390 km)
Weights: empty 18,260 lb (8283 kg); maximum

take-off and landing 28,500 lb (12930 kg); maximum zero fuel 27,000 lb (12250 kg)
Dimensions: span 95 ft 7½ in (29.15 m); length 72 ft 7 in (22.13 m); height 31 ft 9 in (9.70 m); wing area 912 sq ft (84.73 m²)
Armament: none
Operators: Abu Dhabi, Australia, Cameroon, Canada, Ghana, India, Kenya, Kuwait, Malaysia, Oman, Spain, Taiwan, Tanzania, Thailand, Uganda, US Air Force, Zambia

De Havilland Canada DHC-5 Buffalo

History and notes
De Havilland Canada began work on the Caribou II in May 1962 in response to a US Army request for proposals for a new 41-seat STOL tactical transport. DHC was selected from 25 candidates to build four evaluation aircraft and the first made its maiden flight in April 1964. It was designed to be compatible with the Boeing-Vertol Chinook helicopter and to carry loads such as the Pershing missile, 105-mm howitzer or a ¾-ton truck. These four aircraft were delivered to the Army as YAC-2s, since redesignated C-8A. Although no further US orders followed, the Canadian Armed Forces took delivery of 15 DHC-5As designated CC-115s; six have since been converted to the maritime patrol role. Following delivery of 24 to the Brazilian air force and 16 aircraft to the Peruvian air force in 1972 the production line closed.

In 1974 DHC proposed two developed versions to the Indian air force. Designated DHC-5B and DHC-5C respectively, they were powered by General Electric CT64-P4C and Rolls-Royce Dart RDa.12 engines. Although no Indian order was forthcoming, the company judged that there was a continuing demand and invested $4 million in Buffalo improvements. The line was re-opened in 1974 to produce initially 19 of the improved D-model. A further 24 followed.

Because of the interest of the Canadian Depart-

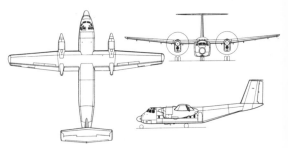

De Havilland Canada DHC-5D Buffalo

ment of Industry, Trade and Commerce, DHC and NASA in STOL capability and the suitability of the C-8A Buffalo as a test bed, an agreement was signed in 1970 between the Canadian and American governments covering the development of a jet research aircraft. Based on the Buffalo, it was designated NASA/DITC XC-8A. This much-modified aircraft, with clipped wings, fixed undercarriage and powered by two Rolls-Royce Spey engines, made its first flight in May 1972. Apart from its unique augmentor wing, the engines make use of vectored nozzles.

The Buffalo has also spawned two other interesting research aircraft. The first to fly was the XC-8A ACLS fitted with an air-cushion landing

De Havilland Canada DHC-5 Buffalo

The Force Aérienne Togolaise is one user of the de Havilland Canada DHC-5D Buffalo, with its short take-off and landing properties.

system. This derivative can take off and land on an air cushion which, when inflated, looks like an elongated tyre inner tube. The first ACLS take-off by the Buffalo was on 31 March, 1975 and the first ACLS landing 11 days later. Aircraft fitted with the ACLS would be able to operate from rough fields, soft soil, swamps, water, ice or snow. The NASA/Boeing QSRA quiet short-haul research aircraft is the third Buffalo development, with four turbofans blowing over a new wing.

Specification
Type: STOL tactical transport
Powerplant: (DHC-5A) two 2,650-shp (1976-kW) General Electric T64/P2 turboprops; (DHC-5D) two 3,133-shp (2336-kW) General Electric T64-415 turboprops
Performance: (DHC-5A at maximum take-off weight) maximum cruising speed 271 mph (435 km/h); economical cruising speed 208 mph (335 km/h); range with maximum payload and full reserves 507 miles (815 km); (DHC-5D at maximum take-off weight) maximum cruising speed 288 mph (463 km/h); range with maximum payload and full reserves 691 miles (1112 km)
Weights: (DHC-5A) empty 23,157 lb (10505 kg); maximum take-off 41,000 lb (18598 kg); maximum landing 39,000 lb (17690 kg); maximum zero fuel 37,000 lb (16783 kg); (DHC-5D) empty 25,160 lb (11412 kg); maximum take-off 49,2000 lb (22316 kg); maximum landing 46,900 lb (21273 kg); maximum zero fuel 43,500 lb (19730 kg)
Dimensions: span 96 ft 0 in (29.26 m); length 79 ft 0 in (24.08 m); height 28 ft 8 in (8.73 m); wing area 945 sq ft (87.8 m²)
Armament: none
Operators: Brazil, Canada, Ecuador, Kenya, Mauritania, Oman, Peru, Sudan, Tanzania, Togo, United Arab Emirates, Zaïre, Zambia

Dornier Do 28D Skyservant

Kenya Air Force Dornier Do28D Skyservant light transport, believed to be based at Eastleigh.

History and notes
In the early 1950s Dipl-Ing Claudius Dornier established design offices in Madrid. Under the auspices of the Spanish aircraft manufacturer CASA, prototypes of the Do 25 and Do 27 STOL transports were flown in 1954 and 1955 respectively.

When the postwar embargo on aircraft manufacture in Germany was lifted, production of the Do 27 was transferred there, deliveries commencing in late 1956. Some 30 months later came the first flight of the twin-engined Do 28. To retain the STOL

qualities of an aerodynamically clean high wing, the 225-hp (190-kW) Lycoming engines were mounted on stub-wings, flanking the six-seat cabin. Some 120 examples of the Do 28A and B were built.

The prototype Do 28D Skyservant flew on 23 February 1966. Its box-like fuselage seated 12 passengers, and 380-hp (283-kW) engines were installed.

The production Do 28D-1 was later fitted with wheel spats, wing fences and a large dorsal spine. These first four were the first to be delivered to the

Dornier Do 28D Skyservant

Luftwaffe, as VIP transports, in 1970.

By this time 101 had been allocated to the *Luftwaffe* as communications transports, a further 20 going to the *Marineflieger.* Skyservant roles include photographic survey, ambulance and para-dropping duties. Its robust construction and a take-off run of the order of 920 ft (280 m) has made it suitable for operation in Africa and other harsh environments. Most Skyservants exported are Do 28D-2s, lengthened by 6 in (15 cm), with larger fuel tanks in the engine nacelles and aerodynamic improvements to wing and tailplane. Dual controls became standard, and new landing lights were installed in the detachable fibreglass wingtips, which have anhedral. Freight doors may be replaced by a sliding door for supply-dropping. Additional stores or 55-gallon (250-litre) fuel tanks may be attached to underwing hardpoints.

A Skyservant with turboprops flew in April 1978. Dubbed the TurboSky, the Do 28D-6 has two 400-shp (298-kW) Pratt & Whitney Aircraft of Canada PT6A-110s.Turboprop power and reliability, combined with a near aerobatic manoeuvrability and STOL capability, may attract orders from several air arms.

Specification
Type: light passenger, freight and liaison transport

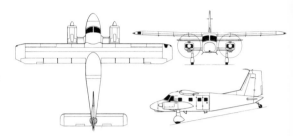

Dornier Do 28D Skyservant

Powerplant: two 380-hp (283-kW) Lycoming IGSO-540 piston engines
Performance: maximum speed at 10,000 ft (3050 m) 201 mph (323 km/h); cruising speed 143 mph (230 km/h); range with 12 passengers 497 miles (800 km); range with 3,000-lb (1360-kg) payload 125 miles (200 km); service ceiling 24,000 ft (7300 m)
Weights: empty 4,615 lb (2095 kg); maximum loaded 8,040 lb (3647 kg)
Dimensions: span 49 ft 2½ in (15.0 m); length 37 ft 4¾ in (11.4 m); height 12 ft 9½ in (3.9 m); wing area 302 sq ft (28.06 m²)
Armament: none
Operators: Cameroon, Ethiopia, Israel, Kenya, Malawi, Morocco, Nigeria, Somalia, Thailand, West Germany, Zambia

Embraer EMB-111

History and notes
A significant newcomer to the ranks of maritime patrol aircraft, the EMBRAER EMB-111 is a development of the EMB-110 Bandeirante to meet the needs of the Brazilian air force (FAB). As the P-95, at least 16 were ordered for the Coastal Command of the FAB and initial deliveries were made in 1978. The Chilean navy also ordered six of the similar EMB-111(N).

The EMB-111 is similar in most respects to the short fuselage C-95 Bandeirante (EMB-110) but it has PT6A-34 engines and a ventral fin. Wingtip fuel tanks bring fuel capacity up to 560 Imperial gallons (2545 litres). Maximum endurance exceeds 8 hours, which allows the type to be used on search and rescue, inspection of civilian and military surface craft, protection of oil rigs, pollution control and other tasks. Five crew are normally carried, comprising a pilot, co-pilot, two observers and a radar operator. Equipment includes a galley, toilet, eight-man liferaft, Motorola locator beacon, and survival stores which are dropped via the rear door.

A prominent nose radome houses the aerial for a Cutler-Hammer APS-128 SPAR-1 search radar. This can identify low-profile targets at 60 miles (96 km) in disturbed sea conditions. The display is

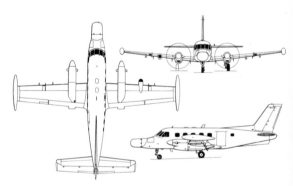

**EMBRAER EMB-110P Bandeirante
(Brazilian Air Force C-95)**

repeated on a cockpit monitor. A Litton LN-33 inertial navigation system is interfaced with the radar. Three underwing pylons can carry depth charges, bombs or three rocket pairs, and a 50-million candlepower searchlight is carried on the right wing.

Specification
Type: maritime patrol aircraft
Powerplant: two 750-shp (560-kW) Pratt & Whitney Aircraft of Canada PT6A-34 turboprops

Embraer EMB-111

Brazil's air arm, Forca Aerea Brasileira, operates 12 EMBRAER EMB-111 maritime patrol aircraft from Salvador.

Performance: maximum speed at 10,000 ft (3050 m) 251 mph (404 km/h); long-range cruising speed at 10,000 ft (3050 m) 216 mph (347 km/h); stalling speed (flaps down) 82 mph (132 km/h); rate of climb at sea level 1,320 ft (403 m) per minute; service ceiling at 12,000 lb (5443 kg) 23,720 ft (7230 m); maximum range with 45-minute reserves 1,695 miles (2725 km)

Weights: empty equipped 7,502 lb (3403 kg); maximum take-off 15,432 lb (7000 kg)
Dimensions: span 52 ft 4½ in (15.96 m); length 48 ft 8 in (14.83 m); height 15 ft 6½ in (4.74 m); wing area 312 sq ft (29.00 m²)
Armament: assorted underwing stores
Operators: Brazil, Chile

Fairchild A-10 Thunderbolt II

History and notes

Considering that the close support role figures prominently among the normal commitments of most air forces, it is at first sight surprising that so few aircraft have actually been designed for the job. The answer is, of course, that the task has traditionally been done by superannuated air combat aircraft, whose performance is no longer up to the mark. Close support is an obligation to ground forces, and air forces are much keener to spend their budgets on air combat or strategic aircraft.

A few aeroplanes have been specially adapted for ground attack, and especially for anti-tank work, by the addition of special weapons, mainly large-calibre guns. The Hawker Hurricane IID, for example, had twin Vickers 40-mm cannon under the wings and was notably effective against Axis tanks in the Western Desert during 1942.

But now a unique aeroplane has appeared, which may well tip the balance of power between NATO forces and the massed might of the Warsaw Pact armoured forces in Central Europe — and the ability of this force to move fast and far under cover of darkness was shown by the overnight invasion of Czechoslovakia in 1968. The Fairchild A-10 Thunderbolt II was born of the recognition that the adaptation of air combat aircraft would no longer suffice to produce adequate ground attack/anti-tank capability. They were actually too fast, lacked the manoeuvrability needed for battlefield warfare, and their weapons were unsuitable against the growing resistance to damage of tanks.

In 1967 the USAF solicited proposals from no fewer than 21 companies. Most of the entries came up with turboprop propulsion, and the USAF, dissatisfied, went back to its studies; it was not clear that any of the designs put up for consideration would be a significant advance on the already existing types.

But by 1970 the USAF felt it could issue a realistic specification, and two companies, Northrop and Fairchild, were chosen to build competitive aeroplanes under the new 'Fly before Buy' policy adopted by the US Defense Department. The USAF planners defined four principal aims: combat effectiveness, survivability, simplicity, and responsiveness. Broadly translated, these equated in order to (a) a warload of 16,000 lb (7258 kg) with partial fuel, or 12,000 lb (5443 kg) with full tanks, (b) sufficient armour or, failing that, enough redundancy of equipment to withstand considerable punishment and still get home, (c) a modest financial outlay, consistent with another newly announced policy called 'Design to Cost', and (d) the ability to operate from primitive or unprepared areas (meadows, for example) sufficiently close to the front line that little time be lost getting there in response to calls from the local ground force commander.

The competitive A-X (Attack, Experimental) programme ran for two years, with the Fairchild A-10 in January 1973 being judged the winner over its Northrop A-9 rival. Development went ahead smoothly, production beginning in 1975, the first squadrons forming in 1976 and 1977. The first units were in 1978 deployed to Europe, the arena for which the A-10 was designed.

From the beginning, the primary armament was to be a special anti-tank gun with seven barrels rotating round a common axis, after the manner of the Gatling-type guns used in the Lockheed F-104G Starfighter and the McDonnell Douglas F-4E Phantom, but firing 30-mm rather than 20-mm rounds. These shells, weighing 1.6 lb (0.73 kg)

Fairchild A-10 Thunderbolt II

This A-10A was photographed while firing its extremely powerful tank-killing gun. One of the 11 pylons is carrying a laser-guided 'smart bomb'.

travelling at two-thirds of a mile a second, and containing lethal warheads, were to have sufficient energy to penetrate the heaviest armour existing or projected.

For all its conventional, even clumsy, appearance, the A-10 is as cleverly thought out as, say the Grumman F-14 or McDonnell Douglas F-15 fighters. Its large wing provides the lift to keep it turning tightly over the battlefield at 300 kt (345 mph/556 km/h), carrying more than seven tons (7.11 tonnes) of bombs or rockets; it also supplies the space needed for these stores, which take up a considerable amount of room. The maximum speed is startlingly low: only 450 kt (518 mph/834 km/h). A fully retracting undercarriage is not therefore essential. The two General Electric TF34 turbofan engines are mounted over the rear fuselage, where they do not get in the way of the pilot's field of view and where their relatively cool exhaust tends to be hidden by the wing during an attack, further reducing the A-10's vulnerability to heat-seaking missiles.

The pilot sits in a thick titanium 'bath', resistant to all but the heaviest-calibre shells. The most important areas of the aeroplane are also armoured, or are designed so that, if they are hit, the aeroplane can still fly back to base.

The main criticism of the type, not shared by the USAF, is that it is limited to fair weather operations. Fairchild has therefore developed with private funding a two-seat model, the Night/Adverse Weather A-10 demonstrator. This has extra equipment such as radar, low-light TV, forward-looking infra-red (FLIR), radar altimeter and laser rangefinder. The inputs from these are displayed to the weapons system officer in the rear seat, who keeps the pilot informed by means of the latter's head-up display (HUD). The N/AW A-10 clearly has great potential for European operations, but the USAF has yet to be convinced.

Specification

Type: single-seat close support/anti-tank bomber

Powerplant: two General Electric TF34-GE-100 high-bypass turbofans, each of 9,065 lb (4112 kg) thrust

Performance: nominal cruise speed (no external stores) 345 kt (397mph/640km/h); design maximum speed, 450 kt (518 mph/722 km/h); take-off roll (maximum weight) 3,800 ft (1158 m); loiter endurance (250 nautical miles from base, 18 Mk82 bombs and 750 rounds of GAU-8 ammunition), 2 hours

Weights: operating weight (aircraft ready to fly, less fuel, ammunition and pilot) 24,000 lb (10886 kg); maximum external payload (full internal fuel) 11,980 lb (5434 kg); maximum payload (with partial fuel) 16,000 lb (7258 kg); empty weight 20,700 lb (9389 kg)

Dimensions: span 57 ft 6 in (17.53 m); length 54 ft 4 in (16.26 m); height 14 ft 8 in (4.47 m); wing area 506 sq ft (47.01 m^2)

Armament: one 30-mm rotating-barrel gun plus various combinations of external stores

Operator: US Air Force

Unique among modern combat aircraft, the A-10A is a jet counterpart of the World War II Stormovik or Hs 129, being modest in performance but well protected and capable of delivering knock-out blows. This example is depicted in the TAC camouflage scheme now becoming standard.

FMA IA-58 Pucará

Argentinian FMA IA-58 Pucará attack aircraft of II Escuadron de Exploration y Ataque based at Reconquista AFB, Argentina.

History and notes

The IA-58 Pucará, originally known as Delfin, is a twin-turboprop counter-insurgency aircraft developed by FMA *(Fábrica Militar de Aviones)*, part of the Argentine air force's *Aérea de Material Córdoba* division, to meet an air force requirement. Following testing of an unpowered aerodynamic prototype, the first powered Pucará made its maiden flight in August 1969. The second prototype, which took to the air in September 1970, was fitted with Turboméca Astazou XVIG turboprops in place of the AiResearch TPE 331s used in the initial aircraft, and the French powerplant has been the standard for all subsequent Pucarás. The first production machine made its initial flight in November 1974, and 20 had been delivered by the autumn of 1978.

The Pucará is named after the stone strongholds built on mountain tops by the Incas and Aimaras to protect themselves from attack, and the aircraft is likewise designed to withstand a determined onslaught. Its main mission is armed reconnaissance over land and sea, together with fire support; counter-insurgency roles can also be carried out. The two-man crew sit in tandem, with the co-pilot's seat 10 in (25 cm) higher than that of the pilot so that both have the best all-round view. The windscreen and cabin floor are designed to stop machine-gun bullets.

The IA-58 is an all-metal aircraft with a T-tail and rough-field landing gear. It can dive at maximum speed from cruising height to bring its armament to bear on targets of opportunity, and its tight turning radius allows the crew to keep their target in sight even in difficult mountain terrain. The IA-58 can operate from small grass fields 'no larger than a football pitch', and the take-off run can be reduced to only 262 ft (80 m) by fitting three rockets to the centreline pylon.

The Pucará packs a powerful punch in the form of two Hispano-Suiza HS-804 20-mm cannon each with 270 rounds and four Browning 7.62-mm machine-guns each with 900 rounds. Studies have been made of an alternative installation comprising a pair of 30-mm cannon and only two Brownings. The Matra 83-A 3 illuminated reflex sight with adjustable depression angle gives great flexibility in weapon delivery. Both the guns and the external stores, carried on four wing pylons and one on the centreline, are operated by buttons on the control column. A programmer allows stores to be released in any quantity from two to 40, with two firing modes available.

Specification

Type: reconnaissance, close-support and counter-insurgency aircraft
Powerplant: two 988-hp (735-kW) Turboméca Astazou XVIG turboprops
Performance: maximum level speed at 9,840 ft (3000 m) 312.5 mph (500 km/h); maximum diving speed 469 mph (750 km/h); service ceiling 32,810 ft (10000 m); stalling speed (gear and flaps up) 78 mph (125 km/h); take-off run over a 50-ft (15-m) obstacle 984 ft (300 m); initial sea-level rate of climb 3,547 ft (1080 m) per minute; radius of action — outward flight at 19,680 ft (6000 m), penetration and 5 minutes over target at height of 492 ft (150 m), return at 26,240 ft (8000 m), with 10% reserves — 250 miles (400 km) with 3,306-lb (1500-kg) payload, and aircraft weighing 14,300 lb (6500 kg)
Weights: empty 8,810 lb (4000 kg); maximum take-off 14,960 lb (6800 kg); maximum payload 5,984 lb (2720 kg)
Dimensions: span 47 ft 6¾ in (14.50 m); length 46 ft 9 in (14.25 m); height 17 ft 10½ in (5.36 m); wing area 326.1 sq ft (30.30 m²)
Armament: two Hispano-Suiza HS-804 20-mm cannon and four Browning 7.62-mm (0.3-in) machine guns plus up to 3,564 lb (1620 kg) of external ordnance on five stations: typical weapons include general-purpose, fragmentation and incendiary bombs; mines; one or two torpedoes; and up to three AGM-12B Bullpup air-to-surface missiles
Operator: Argentina

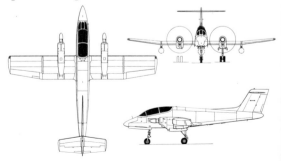

FMA IA 58 Pucará

Fokker F27 Friendship/Maritime

Peru's naval air arm, Servicio Aeronavale, operates two Fokker F.27M Maritimes, the first being illustrated.

History and notes

In March 1976, some 21 years after the maiden flight of the F27 Friendship prototype, Fokker-VFW flew the first F27 Maritime. In the 1950s and 1960s the Friendship was sold mainly to civil operators, but most recent orders have been from government agencies or the military.

The F27 Maritime is a major new development, equipped with a Litton search radar in a belly radome, inertial navigation system, radar altimeter, new autopilot and uprated communications. Although the Maritime does not carry offensive stores, two racks each holding 16 flares can be installed in the engine nacelles. Fuel capacity is increased to give an endurance of 10 to 12 hours. Designed as a medium-range patrol aircraft, its roles include fishery patrol, surveillance of offshore oil platforms and coastal shipping lanes, search and rescue, and environmental control. The rear fuselage has bulged observation windows.

The original 32-seat F27 Mk 100 sold well and 83 were built before it was supplemented by the more powerful Mk 200 (first flight 1959), the freight-door equipped Mk 400 Combiplane (first flight 1961), the Mk 500 with a 5-ft (1.5-m) fuselage stretch (first flight 1967) and the current Mk 600 (first flight 1968).

Fairchild built and sold 205 F-27s and FH-227s between 1958 and 1973, these differing only in details. Although the FH-27 is the same length as the F27, the stretched FH-227 is about 12 in (30.5 cm) longer than the F27 500. Total sales of Dutch-built examples have now passed 500, making it the top-selling European airliner.

The basic military versions are the 400M, capable of carrying 45 parachute troops or 13,550 lb (6145 kg) of freight or 24 stretchers and nine attendants, and the 500 M with accommodation for 50 paratroopers, 14,590 lb (6620 kg) of freight or 30 stretchers and attendants.

The F27 Maritime is aimed at customers who cannot afford expensive patrol aircraft such as the Lockheed Orion. Three examples have been ordered by Spain and two are in service with the Peruvian navy. Although Fokker-VFW remains confident of orders, competition is fierce.

Specification

Type: (Mk 400M/500M) medium-range military transport; (Maritime) medium-range maritime patrol and fishery protection aircraft
Powerplant: two 2,140-shp (1596-kW) plus 525-lb (238-kg) thrust Rolls-Royce Dart Mk 532-7R turboprops
Performance: (Mk 400M/500M at maximum take-off weight) normal cruising speed 298 mph (480 km/h); range with full payload and reserves 1,375 miles (2213 km); (Maritime at maximum take-off weight with pylon tanks) normal cruising speed 265 mph (427 km/h); search speed 168 mph (270 km/h); endurance 10 to 12 hours
Weights: (400m) empty 23,360 lb (10596 kg); maximum take-off 45,000 lb (20410 kg); maximum landing 41,000 lb (18600 kg); maximum zero fuel 37,500 lb (17010 kg); (500M) empty 24,325 lb (11034 kg); maximum take-off 45,000 lb (20410 kg); maximum landing 42,000 lb (19050 kg); maximum zero fuel 39,500 lb (17900 kg); (Maritime with typical equipment fit) empty 27,400 lb (12430 kg); maximum take-off 45,000 lb (20410 kg); maximum landing 43,500 lb (19730 kg); maximum zero fuel 39,500 lb (17920 kg)
Dimensions: span 95 ft 2 in (29.00 m); length (Mk 400M/Maritime) 77 ft 3½ in (35.56 m); height (Mk 400M/Maritime) 27 ft 11 in (8.50 m); length (Mk 500M) 82 ft 2½ in (25.06 m); height (Mk 500M) 28 ft 7¼ in (8.71 m); wing area 753.5 sq ft (70.0 m²)
Armament: normally unarmed apart from racks for flares installed in the rear of the engine nacelles
Operators: Algeria, Argentina, Burma, Ghana, Indonesia, Iran, Italy, Ivory Coast, Netherlands, Nigeria, Pakistan, Peru, Philippines, Senegal, Spain, Uruguay

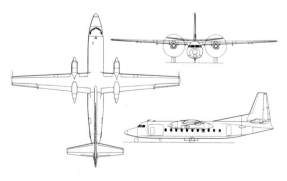

Fokker-VFW F27 Friendship 500

General Dynamics F-16 Fighting Falcon

History and notes

Small, lightweight, agile, hard to see and hard to hit, the General Dynamics F-16 is one of the most promising fighter designs to emerge in recent years. Its origins go back to February 1972, when General Dynamics, Boeing, LTV, Lockheed and Northrop all submitted proposals to the US Air Force for a new lightweight fighter (LWF) with exceptional manoeuvrability. Two months later General Dynamics and Northrop were each given contracts for two prototypes, to be flown against one another (and other contemporary USAF fighters) in a competitive fly-off to decide the winner. The choice was not an easy one, for both General Dynamics' YF-16 and Northrop's twin-engined YF-17 gave equally excellent performances, neither really deserving to lose.

Originally there was no intention of building an LWF in quantity, but this was overturned by the emergence of a large export market, initially in Europe. Selection of the F-16 for the USAF was announced in January 1975, and five months later came the news that four European air forces (those of Belgium, the Netherlands, Norway and Denmark) had chosen the F-16 to replace Lockheed Starfighters and other types in their respective modernization programmes. Another substantial contract followed in October 1976, when the Imperial Iranian air force ordered 160, to carry total orders beyond the 1,000 mark. The USAF now plans to have nearly 1,400 eventually, and the four NATO countries have ordered 348. The latter will be divided 116 to Belgium, 102 to the Netherlands, 72 to Norway and 58 to Denmark; there are assembly lines in Belgium and the Netherlands in addition to that in the USA. In all cases the totals include a proportion of tandem two-seat F-16B fighter/trainers.

The first YF-16 prototype made its maiden flight on 20 January 1974. An exhaustive fly-off against the YF-17 occupied almost the whole of that year, and after the F-16's acceptance a further eight modified development aircraft were built; six single-seat F-16As and two two-seat F-16Bs. The first of these flew on 8 December 1976 and the last in June 1978. The production go-ahead was announced in the spring of 1978, when General Dynamics was authorized to start building the first 105 aircraft for the USAF, the first 192 for Europe, and the first 55 for Iran. August 1978 saw the initial flight of a series-built F-16A, and in the winter of 1978-79 the 388th Tactical Fighter Wing at Hill AFB, Utah, became the first USAF unit to receive the new fighter; European deliveries began shortly afterwards.

Some of the latest technology can be seen in the aerodynamic structure, and in the avionics and fire-control systems of the F-16. For example, the way that the wings are blended into the body, instead of being 'stuck on', not only helps to save weight but increases the overall lift at high angles of attack and reduces drag in the transonic speed range. Moveable flaps on the wing leading- and trailing-edges, controlled automatically by the aircraft's speed and altitude, enable the wing to assume an optimum configuration for lift under all conditions of flight. The highly-swept strakes that lead forward alongside the nose provide further lift; they also prevent wing-root stall, reduce buffeting, and improve directional stability and roll control. A lot of thought has gone into cockpit design to get the canopy shape, seat angle and instrument layout just right, so that the pilot has the maximum field of view and maximum efficiency with a minimum of fatigue: a most important factor in an aircraft liable to pull up to 9 g in an air-to-air combat. All flying controls are electrically operated through a 'fly-by-wire' system that replaces the old-fashioned mechanical linkages, enabling the aircraft to respond faster and more accurately to pilot commands, whilst also simplifying maintenance. A head-up display, side-stick controller and zero-zero ejection seat are also included in the cockpit.

Specification

Type: single-seat tactical fighter (F-16A) and two-seat combat trainer (F-16B)
Powerplant: one 23,810-lb (10800-kg) Pratt & Whitney F100-PW-100(3) afterburning turbofan
Performance: maximum speed 914 mph (1455 km/h) or Mach 1.2 at sea level, and 1,320+ mph (2124+ km/h) or Mach 2 at altitude; initial climb rate 60,000+ ft/min (18288+ m/min); service ceiling about 60,000 ft (18288 m); combat radius 575 miles (925 km); ferry range with drop tanks 2,303 miles (3705 km)
Weights: (F-16A) operational empty 14,567 lb (6607 kg); internal fuel 6,972 lb (3162 kg); maximum external load 15,200 lb (6894 kg); design take-off gross, clean 22,500 lb (10205 kg); maximum take-off without external tanks 22,785 lb (10335 kg), with external load 33,000 lb (14968 kg)
Dimensions: span (over missiles) 32 ft 10 in (10.01 m); length 47 ft 7¾ in (14.52 m); height 16 ft 5¼ in (5.01 m); wing area 300 sq ft (27.87 m²)
Armament: one 20-mm General Electric M61A-1 multi-barrel cannon in left wing/body fairing, with 500 rounds; one AIM-9J/L Sidewinder infra-red homing missile at each wingtip (radar-homing Sparrow or AMRAAM later) for air-to-air interception; six underwing hardpoints and one under fuselage for up to 15,200 lb (6894 kg) of attack weapons or drop-tanks (10,500 lb/4763 kg if full internal fuel is carried). Stores under wings/fuselage can include four more Sidewinders or Sparrows, Pave Penny laser tracking pod, single or cluster bombs, flare pods, air-to-surface missiles, laser-guided and electro-optical weapons
Operators: Belgium, Denmark, Israel, the Netherlands, Norway, USAF

General Dynamics F-16 Fighting Falcon

The weapons illustrated comprise triplets of free-fall bombs (typically Mk 82) and four Sidewinders (AIM-9J depicted but operational standard will be the 9L).

General Dynamics (Convair) F-106 Delta Dart

General Dynamics (Convair) F-106A Delta Dart of the 159th Fighter Interceptor Squadron, Florida National Air Guard.

History and notes

In the early 1950s it became clear that the 'Ultimate Interceptor' being developed by Convair would not be operational by its 1954 deadline. Faced with this problem, the US Air Force decided to procure from Convair a less sophisticated, interim interceptor. This became designated the F-102A Delta Dagger: the original MX-1554 Ultimate Interceptor was then designated the F-102B, and it is this aircraft which became eventually the F-106 Delta Dart.

It was fortunate that the USAF adopted such a policy, for the F-102A ran into serious development problems, and it was not until April 1956 that the first production examples of this 'interim' aircraft entered service. In the same period the F-102B was virtually at a standstill, starved of funds and still awaiting its Wright J67 powerplant, though the Hughes MX-1179 electronic control system (ECS) was ready before the airframe. When the F-102A tests were seen to be successful the US Air Force contracted for 749 examples; at the same time, November 1955, an order was placed for 17 F-102Bs.

On 17 June 1956 the F-102B was redesignated officially as the F-106, reflecting the fact that the original requirement had now changed considerably.

Two YF-106A prototypes made their first flights on 26 December 1956 and 26 February 1957, but flight tests were disappointing, and it was painfully obvious that there were still many shortcomings. Maximum speed was some 15% below the required figure, but causing greater concern was the slow rate of acceleration, and neither of these factors were helped by delays in the Pratt & Whitney J75-P-9 turbojet which had been substituted for the Wright J67 chosen originally.

To salvage something from this difficult situation, the USAF decided to reduce its planned procurement of 1,000 F-106s by some 65%. So much had already been spent on the programme that it seemed sensible to continue development so that the US Air Force would acquire eventually a smaller but high quality force of interceptors. Engine intake modifications, and eradication of some of the bugs from engine and avionics, made it possible for the first deliveries of aircraft with an initial operational capability to be made to the 498th Fighter Interceptor Squadron at Geiger AFB, Washington, in October 1959. Production of 277 F-106As and 63 F-106B two-seat combat trainers (which retained full combat capability), ended in December 1960.

Late production F-106As differed in equipment from those which entered service in 1959, which meant that modification programmes to bring all aircraft to a common standard were running concurrently with the production of new aircraft. This was but the tip of the iceberg, for the need to retain the F-106s in front-line service with Aerospace Defense Command (ADC) has meant the updating programmes have been almost continuous since that time. These have included the installation of ejection seats operable in supersonic flight, the provision of flight refuelling capability and of drop tanks suitable for supersonic operations; improved radar, automatic flight control and DC power system under the MEISR (Minimum Essential Improvement in System Reliability) programme; introduction of an M-61 20-mm multi-barrel gun, lead-computing gunsight, clear cockpit canopy, and radar homing and warning (RHAW) system under ADC's Sixshooter programme; and the installation of a Hughes solid-state digital computer.

In early 1979, ADC still retained six squadrons of F-106 aircraft to defend the United States from conventional attack, these being supported by five F-106, three F-101 and two F-4 squadrons flown by the Air National Guard. During 1978, one of the ANG's F-106 squadrons was replaced by the second F-4 squadron.

Current events show that the USAF did well to persevere in its efforts to get the F-106 into service in 1959, believing in its capability sufficiently to accept and make the best possible use of some 35% of the number planned originally. It is now twenty years since that decision, and the F-106s are still in the front-line of the nation's defence: they are likely to remain there until the early 1980s when sufficient advanced fighter/interceptors will become available to take over this role.

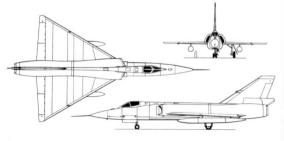

Convair F-106A Delta Dart

General Dynamics (Convair) F-106 Delta Dart

The General Dynamics F-106A Delta Dart is another willing old bird soldiering on through lack of a replacement, this one is operating from the Air Defense Weapons Center at Tyndall AFB.

Specification

Type: supersonic all-weather interceptor
Powerplant: one 24,500-lb (11113-kg) reheat Pratt & Whitney J75-P-17 turbojet
Performance: maximum speed Mach 2.3 or 1,519 mph (2445 km/h) at 36,000 ft (10970 m); combat radius with external fuel tanks 729 miles (1173 km)
Weights: empty 23,646 lb (10726 kg); maximum take-off (F-106A, area interceptor mission) 38,700 lb (17554 kg)
Dimensions: span 38 ft 3½ in (11.67 m); length 70 ft 8¾ in (21.56 m); height 20 ft 3¼ in (6.18 m); wing area 631.3 sq ft 58.65 m²)
Armament: one Douglas AIR-2A Genie or AIR-2B Super Genie rocket, and four Hughes AIM-4F or AIM-4G Super Falcon air-to-air missiles carried in internal weapons bay; many aircraft have also one 20-mm gun
Operator: US Air Force

General Dynamics F-111/FB-111

History and notes

It needs no more than a glance at the current inventory of the Soviet air force to see how one country, at least, has moved heavily in favour of variable-geometry or 'swing-wing' aircraft in the past 10 to 15 years. For the nation that first put this principle into practice in a production aircraft, however, the progress from prototype to successful service warplane made a far from happy story. The major advantages offered by a variable-geometry aircraft are a high supersonic performance with the wings swept back; economical subsonic cruising speed with them fully spread; a long operational or ferry range; and relatively short take-off and landing runs at very high weights. So, when the US Air Force's Tactical Air Command was seeking a strike aircraft to replace the Republic F-105 Thunderchief, as outlined in its SOR (Specific Operational Requirement) 183 of 14 June 1960, it was very interested in the results of experiments with variable-geometry wing configurations that had recently been conducted by NASA's Langley Research Center at Hampton, Virginia. The US Navy, at the same time, was looking for a new fleet air defence fighter to succeed the

McDonnell Douglas F-4 Phantom, and eventually the Department of Defense decreed that the two requirements should be combined in a single programme known as TFX, or Tactical Fighter, Experimental.

The Defense Secretary, Robert McNamara, stuck to this decision despite strong objections from both services, and his department rejected all six designs originally submitted in late 1961. However, a design from Boeing, and a joint offering by General Dynamics and Grumman, were considered worthy of study contracts. At three subsequent 'paper' evaluation conferences, after successive refinements of the two designs, the Boeing contender appeared to be a clear favourite and was almost universally recommended for adoption. To McNamara, however, it was technologically too advanced and lacked the commonality between the air force and navy versions that he believed was essential. He therefore overruled his advisers, and on 24 November 1962 a development contract for 23 aircraft was awarded to General Dynamics. Of these, 18 were to be basic tactical F-111As for the USAF and five were F-111Bs, developed primarily by Grumman for the US Navy.

The F-111B began to run into trouble almost immediately; despite a long and intensive flight development programme the type was eventually cancelled in July 1968. The aircraft had consistently proved overweight, quite unable to meet the performance required of it, and only seven examples were completed: the five development machines, plus two of the 231 production F-111Bs which the US Navy had planned to order.

The F-111A, on which all subsequent models were based, had an almost equally unhappy early history after its first flight on 21 December 1964, but eventually it was cleared for service and deliveries of 141 production examples began in October 1967, to the 474th Tactical Fighter Wing at Nellis AFB, Nevada. In spring 1968 the 428th Tactical Fighter Squadron took six F-111As to Thailand for operational trials over Vietnam — and lost three of them in four weeks. Groundings and modifications followed, and when 48 more F-111As were sent to Vietnam in 1972-73, they flew over 4,000 combat sorties in seven months for the loss of only six aircraft. One of the modifications was to the engine air inlet geometry; the next 94 aircraft were built with an enlarged inlet (to suit more powerful engines which were not fitted) and designated F-111E.

Meanwhile, the designation F-111C had been applied to 24 aircraft ordered by the Royal Australian Air Force in 1963, but as a result of extensive modifications and escalating costs the delivery of these did not begin until 1973. They have the increased-span wings of the FB-111A and a strengthened landing gear. Another export order was placed in 1966 when the Royal Air Force ordered 50 F-111Ks, but these were cancelled two years later and the two that were almost complete became YF-111As for the USAF, the rest becoming FB-111As.

The third production tactical version for the USAF (96 were built) was the F-111D, which combined a slightly more powerful engine with the modified inlets of the E model. It also introduced 'Mk II' avionics, which included an AN/APQ-30 attack radar, a digital (instead of analogue) computer, AN/APN-189 Doppler navigation equipment, and head-up displays for both crew members; several other installations were improved versions of the 'Mk I' systems in the F-111A and E.

The fourth and last tactical production version, the F-111F, has been described as 'the aircraft that the F-111 should have been from the beginning'. It has a much more powerful TF30 engine, with which it first flew in May 1973, and 'Mk IIB' avionics which, while more advanced than those in the A and E, are less complex than those in the F-111D. In this form the F-111 finally emerged as the superb combat aeroplane that it was planned to be, with excellent range, efficiency and reliability in the worst possible weather.

The other major basic version, serving with the Strategic Air Command, is the FB-111A. This has, in effect, the F-111D fuselage and intakes, the larger wings of the F-111B/C, strengthened landing gear, and yet another variant of the TF30 engine. For the strategic role, the avionics are related to the Mk IIB fit.

Specification

Type: two-seat all-weather attack aircraft (F-111), electronic warfare aircraft (EF-111) and strategic bomber (FB-111)

Powerplant: two Pratt & Whitney TF30 afterburning turbofans: TF30-P-3s of 18,500-lb (8390-kg) static thrust in A and C; TF30-P-9s of 19,600-lb (8890-kg) static thrust in D and E; TF30-P-100s of 25,100-lb (11385-kg) static thrust in F; TF30-P-7s of 20,350-lb (9230-kg) static thrust in FB-111

Performance: maximum speed (clean) at 35,000 ft (10670 m) and above, Mach 2.2 (1,450 mph/2335 km/h); maximum speed (clean) at low level Mach 1.2 (800 mph/1287 km/h); range with internal and external fuel (A and C) 3,165 miles (5093 km); (F) more than 2,925 miles (4707 km), (EF) 2,416 miles (3889 km); service ceiling (clean) (A) 51,000 ft (15550 m), (F) 60,000 ft (18300 m), (EF) 50,000 ft (15250 m)

Weights: empty (A) 46,172 lb (20943 kg), (C) 47,300 lb (21455 kg), (D and E) about 49,000 lb (22226 kg), (F) 47,175 lb (21398 kg), (FB) about 50,000 lb (22680 kg), (EF) 53,600 lb (24313 kg); maximum take-off (A) 91,500 lb (41504 kg), (C) 114,300 lb (51846 kg), (D and E) 99,000 lb (44906 kg), (F) 100,000 lb (45359 kg), (FB) 119,000 lb (53977 kg), (EF) 87,800 lb (39825 kg)

Dimensions: span fully spread (A, D, E and F) 63 ft 0 in (19.20 m), (C and FB) 70 ft 0 in (21.34 m); span fully swept (A, D, E and F) 31 ft 11½ in (9.74 m), (C and FB) 33 ft 11 in (10.34 m); length 73 ft 6 in (22.40 m), (EF) 77 ft 0 in (23.47 m); height 17 ft 1½ in (5.22 m), (EF) 20 ft 0 in (6.10 m); wing area fully spread (A, D, E and F) 525 sq ft (48.77 m²), (C and FB) 550 sq ft (51.10 m²); wing area fully swept (A, D, E and F) 657.3 sq ft (61.07 m²)

Armament: (F) two 750-lb (341-kg) B-43 bombs, or one 20-mm M61 multi-barrel cannon and one B-43 bomb, in internal weapons bay; three underwing hardpoints on each outer wing panel, the inner four pivoting to keep stores aligned as wings sweep, the outer two non-pivoting and jettisonable. All six wing points 'wet', for carriage of drop-tanks instead of weapons; maximum ordnance load (E) 29,000 lb (13154 kg), (FB) 37,500 lb (17010 kg) as fifty 750-lb (341-kg) bombs, two in internal bay and 48 on wing pylons

Operators: Australia, USAF

This drawing shows an aircraft from the final production block of F-111As, the original model with low-thrust engines and small-area inlets. It is shown with weapon-bay doors open, though the bay usually carries items other than weapons and in a few aircraft houses the M61 gun. Countermeasure pods, such as the ALQ-119, are carried immediately to the rear of the main gears on ventral pylons which are unavailable for other loads.

Grumman A-6 Intruder

History and notes

During the Korean War the US services flew more attack missions than any other type, in the case of the US Navy and US Marine Corps mostly with elderly piston-engined. aircraft. What they learned during this conflict convinced them of the need for a specially-designed jet attack aircraft that could operate effectively in the worst weather. In 1957 eight companies submitted 11 designs in a US Navy competition for a new long-range, low-level tactical strike aircraft. Grumman's G-128, selected on the last day of the year, was to fulfil that requirement admirably, becoming a major combat type in the later war in South-East Asia, and leading to a family of later versions.

Eight development A-6As (originally designated A2F-1) were ordered in March 1959, a full-scale mockup was completed and accepted some six months later, and the first flight was made on 19 April 1960. The jet-pipes of its two 8,500-lb (3856-kg) static thrust Pratt & Whitney J52-P-6 engines were designed to swivel downwards, to provide an additional component of lift during take-off, but this feature was omitted from production aircraft, which instead have jet-pipes with a permanent slight downward deflection. The first production A-6As were delivered to US Navy Attack Squadron VA-42 in February 1963, and by the end of the following year deliveries had reached 83, to VA-65, VA-75 and VA-85 of the US Navy and VMA(AW)-242 of the US Marine Corps. First unit to fly on combat duties in Vietnam was VA-75, whose A-6As began operating from the USS *Independence* in March 1965, and from then onwards Intruders of various models became heavily involved in the fighting in South-East Asia. Their DIANE (Digital Integrated Attack Navigation Equipment) gave them a first-class operating ability and efficiency in the worst of the humid, stormy weather offered by the local climate, and with a maximum ordnance load of more than 17,000 lb (7711 kg) they were a potent addition to the US arsenal in South-East Asia.

Production of the basic A-6A ran until December 1969 and totalled 482 aircraft, plus another 21 built as EA-6As, retaining a partial strike capability but developed primarily to provide ECM (electronic countermeasures) support for the A-6As in Vietnam and to act as Elint (electronic intelligence) gatherers. The first EA-6A was flown in 1963, and six A-6As were also converted to EA-6A configuration. A more sophisticated electronic warfare version, the EA-6B, is described separately.

The next three variants of the Intruder were also produced by the conversion of existing A-6As. First of these (19 converted) was the A-6B, issued to one USN squadron and differing from the initial model primarily in its ability to carry the US Navy's AGM-78 Standard ARM (anti-radiation missile) instead of the AGM-12B Bullpup. For identifying and

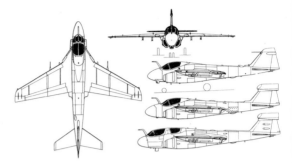

Grumman A-6E Intruder
(side views of A: A-6E; B: EA-6A; C: EA-6B Prowler)

acquiring targets not discernible by the aircraft's standard radar, Grumman then modified 12 other A-6As into A-6Cs, giving them an improved capability for night attack by installing FLIR (forward-looking infra-red) and low light level TV equipment in a turret under the fuselage. A prototype conversion of an A-6A to KA-6D in-flight refuelling tanker was flown on 23 May 1966, and production contracts for the tanker version were placed. These were subsequently cancelled, but 62 A-6As were instead converted to KA-6D configuration, equipped with Tacan (tactical air navigation) instrumentation and mounting a hose-reel unit in the rear fuselage to refuel other A-6s under the 'buddy' system. The KA-6D is also able to operate as a day bomber, or as an air/sea rescue control aircraft, and since the withdrawal of the EKA-3B from seagoing duty has been the standard carrier-based tanker.

On 27 February 1970, Grumman flew the first example of the A-6E, an advanced, upgraded development of the A-6A, which the A-6E succeeded in production. Procurement of nearly 350 of this version is planned for USN and USMC squadrons, of which some 120 are newly-built and about 230 are converted from A-6As. The basis of the A-6E, which retains upgraded forms of the airframe and powerplant of the earlier models, is a new avionics fit, founded on the addition of a Norden AN/APQ-148 multi-mode navigation/attack radar, an IBM/Fairchild AN/ASQ-133 computerized navigation/attack system, Conrac armament control unit, and an RCA video-tape recorder for assessing the damage caused during a strike mission. The Norden radar provides ground mapping, terrain avoidance/clearance, and target identification/tracking/rangefinding modes, with cockpit displays for both the pilot and navigator/bombardier, who sit side by side in the well-forward cockpit. It replaces the two older radars of the A-6A.

Following the first flight of a test aircraft on 22 March 1974, all US Navy and US Marine Corps Intruders are to be progressively updated still further under a programme known as TRAM (Target Recognition Attack Multisensor). To the A-6E-standard Intruder, this adds a Hughes turreted

This Grumman A-6A is assigned to attack squadron VA-35 "The Panthers" aboard CVA-65 *Enterprise*. Its outboard wing and centreline pylons are fitted with multiple ejector racks for tandem triplets of 500 lb bombs (Mk 82).

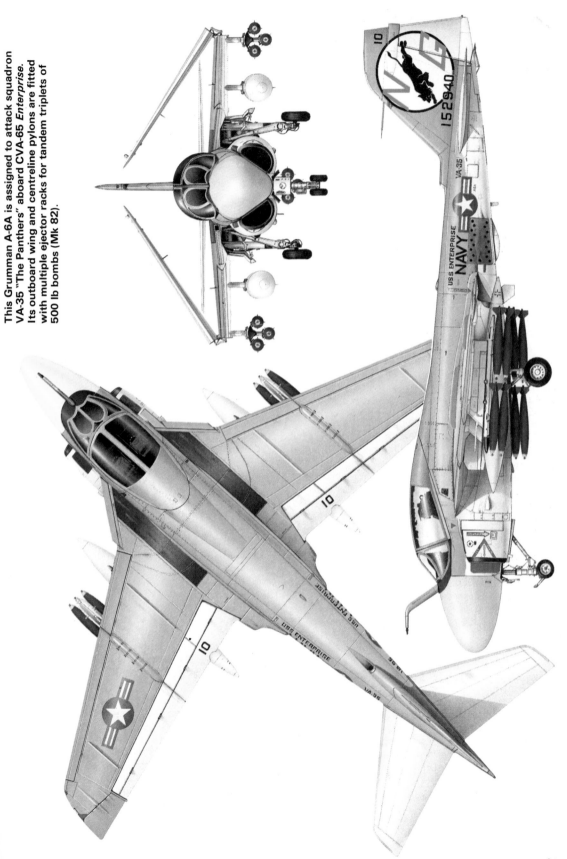

Grumman A-6 Intruder

Grumman's KA-6D Intruder is the standard seagoing tanker of the 13 US Navy Carrier Air Wings. Distinguished chiefly by its hose-reel fuselage, it can transfer over 21,000 lb (9526 kg) of fuel; alternatively it can fly day attack or control missions.

electro-optical package of FLIR and laser detection equipment, integrated with the Norden radar; adds CAINS (Carrier Airborne Inertial Navigation System) to the existing navigation equipment; provides the capability for automatic landings on carrier decks; and incorporates provisions for the carriage and delivery of automatic-homing and laser-guided air-to-surface weapons. The first US Navy squadron to be equipped with the A-6E/TRAM version was VA-165, which was deployed aboard the USS *Constellation* in 1977.

Including training squadrons, the Intruder equipped some 20 US Navy and US Marine Corps squadrons in the late 1970s, and it is expected that eventually all aircraft will be brought up to the A-6E standard. The title of 'miniature B-52' (bestowed by the North Vietnamese and Viet Cong) is well earned, for the Intruder's maximum weapon load, all carried externally, represents about 30 per cent of its maximum land take-off weight, and can be made up of a greater variety of weapons, nuclear or conventional, than any previous US naval attack aircraft. With its truly all-weather operating ability, plus a highly sophisticated set of avionics for navigation and pinpoint precision bombing by day or night, it is certain to maintain a highly important contribution to US naval air power on land or at sea for many years to come.

Specification

Type: two-seat carrier or shore-based attack aircraft

Powerplant: two 9,300-lb (4218-kg) static thrust Pratt & Whitney J52-P-8A or -8B turbojets
Performance: maximum speed at sea level (A-6A, clean) 685 mph (1102 km/h), (A-6E, clean) 648 mph (1043 km/h); maximum speed at high altitude (A-6A, clean) 625 mph (1006 km/h); range with full weapon load (A-6E) 1,924 miles (3096 km); ferry range with maximum internal and external fuel (A-6E) 2,723 miles (4382 km); maximum rate of climb at sea level (A-6E, clean) 9,200 ft (2804 m) per minute; service ceiling (A-6A) 41,660 ft (12700 m), (A-6E, clean) 47,500 ft (14480 m)
Weights: empty (A-6A) 25,684 lb (11650 kg), (EA-6A) 27,769 lb (12596 kg), (A-6E) 25,740 lb (11675 kg); maximum take-off (A-6E, catapult) 58,600 lb (26580 kg), (A-6E, field) 60,400 lb (27397 kg)
Dimensions: span 53 ft 0 in (16.15 m); span folded 25 ft 4 in (7.72 m); length 54 ft 9 in (16.69 m); height 16 ft 2 in (4.93 m); wing area 528.9 sq ft (49.1 m²)
Armament: one underfuselage and four underwing attachments for maximum external load of 15,000 lb (6804 kg) in A-6A, or 18,000 lb (8165 kg) in A-6E; wide variety of nuclear or conventional weapons, typical loads ranging from thirty 500-lb (227-kg) bombs, in clusters of six, to three 2,000-lb (907-kg) bombs plus two 250-gallon (1135-litre) drop-tanks; air-launched missiles can include Bullpup (A-6A), Standard ARM (A-6B) or Harpoon (A-6E)
Operators: US Marine Corps, US Navy

Grumman EA-6B Prowler

Electronic warfare is the role of the Grumman EA-6B Prowler. This example is from VAQ-134, US Navy, operating from the USS Enterprise.

Grumman EA-6B Prowler

History and notes

A US Navy requirement for a carrier-based strike aircraft resulted, in 1956, in a number of submissions to satisfy the specification. The submissions were no easy task to finalise, for whilst the US Navy was seeking a subsonic aircraft with long range and/or endurance, it was not really the aeroplane but what it contained that mattered. Experience gained in Korea had shown that the real need was for a strike aircraft that could fly at tree-top height to slip beneath the curtain of enemy radar, and then have the capability to find and attack any target by day or night in all weather conditions.

Grumman's G-128 submission was chosen for development from 11 proposals, and this materialised as the A-6A, which first flew in prototype form on 19 April 1960. When it entered service on 1 February 1963, it was the world's first all-weather day/night attack aircraft with the capability of detecting and identifying tactical and strategic targets under zero-visibility conditions, and against which it could launch conventional or nuclear weapons.

This very advanced aircraft did not come cheaply, for the ability to get to a target in any weather is not provided by the airframe, but rather by the very sophisticated electronics which it carries, and the avionics to make such performance possible can cost perhaps two or three times as much as the aircraft. Neither is it an ultimate weapon, for from the moment that an aircraft like this is deployed, the enemy is working to overcome the temporary operational lead the new system provides.

To offset such defence, there has been extensive development of electronic countermeasures (ECM) aircraft able to mislead or suppress enemy radars, and as an interim ECM escort aircraft for A-6 Intruders a special EA-6A version was developed and first flown as a prototype in 1963. Retaining some strike capability, this is primarily equipped for the ECM role, with more than 30 different aerials to detect, locate, classify and jam the radiations from enemy radar systems. A total of 27 EA-6As were procured for the US Marine Corps pending development of an even more specialized variant for this role.

Thus, Grumman's EA-6B Prowler has been evolved to satisfy this requirement, an advanced version of the EA-6A which has been completely redesigned to carry the extra avionics necessary for it to fulfil this demanding role. Externally it looks little different from the basic A-6A, but it has a nose section which has been extended by 4 ft 6 in (1.37 m), and a distinctive fin pod housing highly sensitive surveillance receivers. The major changes are internal and these include accommodation for two additional crew members, reinforced wings and strengthened landing gear to match higher gross weight and extended fatigue life, reinforced underfuselage structure, greater fuel capacity, and more powerful J52-P-408 engines.

It is expected that a total of 90 of the aircraft will be acquired to equip at least 12 squadrons. The first production aircraft was delivered in January 1971, and production was continuing in 1979.

Specification

Type: four-seat carrier or land-based advanced ECM aircraft

Powerplant: two 11,200-lb (5080-kg) Pratt & Whitney J52-P-408 turbojets

Performance: (no external jammers) maximum speed at sea level 651 mph (1048 km), cruising speed at optimum altitude 481 mph (774 km/h), combat range with maximum external fuel 2,399 miles (3861 km), range (with maximum payload, 5% reserves plus 20 minutes at sea level) 1,099 miles (1769 km); (with five tactical jamming pods) maximum speed 623 mph (1003 km/h), cruising speed at optimum altitude 481 mph (774 km/h), ferry range 2,022 miles (3254 km)

Weights: empty 32,162 lb (14588 kg); stand-off jamming configuration take-off 54,461 lb (24703 kg); ferry range configuration take-off 60,610 lb (27492 kg); maximum take-off 65,000 lb (29484 kg)

Dimensions: span 53 ft 0 in (16.15 m); span (wings folded) 25 ft 4 in (7.72 m); length 59 ft 5 in (18.11 m); height 16 ft 2 in (4.93 m); wing area 528.9 sq ft (49.13 m²)

Armament: none

Operators: US Marine Corps

Grumman E-2 Hawkeye

History and notes

The original concept of AEW (airborne early warning) was developed during World War II, when it was realised that an airborne surveillance radar could overcome the range limitations imposed by the curvature of the Earth on such detectors on land or on board ship. Early attempts to provide such an 'eye in the sky' were not particularly successful, but over the next three decades both the equipment and the AEW concept have developed to a considerable extent.

One company associated with AEW since its earliest days is Grumman, which claims with some justification that its E-2 Hawkeye was the first, as well as remaining the only, aircraft in service today that was designed from the outset as an AEW/tactical airborne command and control aircraft. Following a lineage that began with the TBF-3W Avenger, and continued with the AF-2W Guardian and the E-1B Tracer, the Hawkeye was the winner of a US Navy competition for a radar-carrying aircraft that would form part of an overall Naval Tactical Data System, the requirement for which was issued in 1956. The radar operator in the TBF-3W was quickly overwhelmed by the number of targets which he had to track on the face of the radar scope with a waxed pencil; the AF-2W and E-1B added video relays, so that the radar picture was on several scopes at a ground site or on board a parent aircraft carrier, but a high density of targets could still overshadow any number of assigned manual operators. In any case, manual operation restricted the number of tracks and interceptions the operators could handle.

What was needed was an aircraft of sufficient size to carry not only the radar but also digital computers which could detect targets automatically, select the best available means of interception, and generally keep a task force commander fully informed at all times of the disposition of friendly or hostile ships and aircraft in his area. Automation was the key: the operators had to be free of all routine activities in order to give their full attention to the tactical situation.

Grumman won the competition on 5 March 1957 with a design for a twin-turboprop aircraft carrying a crew of five (two pilots, radar operator, air control officer and combat information centre officer) and mounting a General Electric AN/APS-96 surveillance radar in a 24-ft (7.32 m) discus-shaped revolving radome on a pylon above the fuselage. To even out the airflow disturbed by this enormous excrescence, a wide-span dihedral tailplane was fitted, bearing four fins and twin rudders. Known originally as the W2F-1, the first prototype made its initial flight on 21 October 1960, powered by two Allison T56-A-8 turboprops. This was an aerodynamic prototype only: the full electronics systems were installed in the second Hawkeye, which made its maiden flight on 19 April 1961. In 1962 the designation was changed to E-2A, and the first of 62 examples of this version (including prototypes) was delivered to Squadron VAW-11 on 19 January 1964.

Beginning in 1969 (a prototype conversion was flown on 20 February), all operational E-2As were modified to E-2B standard, differing mainly in having an improved computer, the microelectric Litton L-304, and provision for flight-refuelling. Over the next five years these were re-delivered to equip Squadrons VAW-113, -116, -125 and -126. They normally operate in teams of two or more aircraft, flying at altitudes of 30,000 ft (9150 m) to provide long-range early warning of potential threats from hostile surface vessels and fast-flying aircraft. The dorsal radome rotates once every 10 seconds while the Hawkeye is in flight; to facilitate stowage when on board its parent carrier, the telescopic pylon can be lowered 2 ft (0.61 m).

In the summer of 1971, following the first flight of a prototype on 20 January, Grumman began production of a new Hawkeye model, the E-2C. This heralded a significant improvement in operational capability, with a major upgrading of the principal avionics, and entered service in November 1973 with VAW-123. The initial order by the US Navy was for 11 E-2Cs, since increased to 47, including some TE-2C trainers. The E-2C has also been ordered by Israel (four) and Japan; the US Navy plans to acquire a further 36 by the end of 1984.

Major ingredients of the E-2C are the APS-125 radar, APA-171 radar and IFF (identification, friend or foe) antennae in the dorsal radome; an air-data computer in addition to the L-304; plus a carrier aircraft inertial navigation system (CAINS). The APS-125, developed jointly by General Electric and Grumman, is capable of detecting airborne targets in a 'land clutter' environment, at ranges up to 230 miles (370 km). It provides automatic detection and tracking over land or water, with simultaneous surveillance (though displayed separately if required) of air as well as surface traffic. The on-board data processing gear can track, automatically and simultaneously, more than 250 targets; it can also control over 30 airborne interceptions. As an addition to its radar system, the E-2C carries a passive detection system (PDS) which automatically detects the presence, direction and identity of any traffic in a 'high signal density' environment. The PDS can alert its operators to the presence of electronic emitters at distances up to almost 500 miles (805 km), establish the location of the emission, and identify the threat. At the same time, the E-2C's own radar system incorporates ECCM (electronic counter-countermeasures) to help ensure its own continued effectiveness in the face of hostile jamming. Despite the additional avionics, the E-2C still carries only a five-man crew.

The C-2 Greyhound is a transport derivative of the E-2.

Grumman E-2 Hawkeye

Specification

Type: airborne early-warning and control aircraft

Powerplant: two 4,910-shp (3661-kW) Allison T56-A-425 turboprops

Performance: maximum speed 374 mph (602 km/h); cruising speed for maximum range 310 mph (499 km/h); patrol endurance 6 hours; maximum ferry range 1,605 miles (2583 km); service ceiling 30,800 ft (9390 m)

Weights: empty 37,678 lb (17090 kg); internal fuel load 12,400 lb (5624 kg); maximum take-off 51,569 lb (23391 kg)

Dimensions: span 80 ft 7 in (24.56 m); length 57 ft 7 in (17.55 m); height 18 ft 4 in (5.59 m); wing area 700.0 sq ft (65.03 m²)

Armament: none

Operators: Israel, Japan, US Navy

The use of substantial numbers of Hawkeye aircraft allows the US Navy to deploy major naval task forces well outside the range of land-based long-range radar systems, providing the fleet defence fighter force with adequate warning of impending attacks at all possible altitudes. The Hawkeye illustrated is an aircraft of AEW squadron 114.

nman F-14A Tomcat

ıestionably one of the finest warplanes in the world today, the Grumman F-14 Tomcat is fulfilling the role that, in the mid-1960s, it was hoped would be undertaken by the naval version of the General Dynamics F-111 variable-geometry strike aircraft. By the time that the F-111B programme was eventually cancelled in the summer of 1968, Grumman (also responsible for developing the F-111B version) had already reached an advanced stage in designing a new swing-wing carrier fighter, following a US Navy competition in which four other designs were in contention. From these, the US Navy selected Grumman's G-303 proposal in January 1969 to fill this major gap in its front-line inventory. In the following May a detailed mock-up was completed for US Navy evaluation, and in the same year an initial contract was placed for six development aircraft (later increased to 12). The first of these made its maiden flight on 21 December 1970, but nine days later, on only its second flight, this prototype was coming in to land when the complete hydraulic system failed, resulting in the loss of the aircraft, although both crew members were able to eject to safety. Despite this setback, however, the development programme proceeded without further serious mishap, the second aircraft making its first flight on 24 May 1971.

Designed to later technology than the pioneering F-111, the F-14A was designed from the outset for operation from USN fleet carriers, and is unique among variable-geometry aircraft so far designed in having, in addition to variable-sweep outer wings, a smaller moveable foreplane (Grumman calls it a glove vane) inside the leading-edge root of the fixed inboard portion of each wing (the glove box). The outer wings pivot to give a leading-edge sweep of 68° when in the fully-aft position, reducing to 20° when the wings are in the fully-forward position. As the main wings pivot backwards, the glove vanes can be extended forward into the airstream to regulate any alterations in the centre of pressure and prevent the aircraft from pitching. By deploying its variable-sweep wings to the best advantage, the Tomcat is thus able to vary its flying configuration to the different aerodynamic and performance requirements needed when taking off from, or landing on, a carrier, taking part in an air-to-air dogfight, or carrying out a low-level attack mission against a surface target. In air-to-air fighting, the variation of wing sweep can be undertaken by the in-built automatic flight control system, relieving the pilot of this task and enabling him to concentrate on out-manoeuvring and shooting down his opponent. With additional control surfaces which include full-span trailing-edge flaps, spoilers, leading-edge slats and all-moving horizontal tail surfaces, the Tomcat is a superbly manoeuvrable warplane; longitudinal stability is assured by the use of twin outward-canted fins and rudders. It is also very strong structurally, many of the airframe components being manufactured of boron-epoxy or other composites, or titanium.

The primary role of the Tomcat is to provide long-range air defence of the US fleet, and the two-man crew (pilot and naval flight officer) are seated in tandem on zero-zero ejection seats under a single long, upward-opening canopy, which affords a fine all-round view. An excellent weapons platform, the Tomcat's armament for the air defence role includes air-to-air missiles such as the medium-range AIM-7 Sparrow and close-range AIM-9 Sidewinder (the latter being mounted on launchers attached beneath the glove box on each side), and for unexpected dogfights a Gatling-type multi-barrel cannon. Primary interception armament, however, consists of six Hughes Phoenix air-to-air missiles, four of which are mounted on pallets which fit into the semi-recessed Sparrow positions under the aircraft's belly, with an additional Phoenix underneath each wing glove box alongside the underwing Sidewinders. The Phoenix is currently the longest-range air-to-air missile in use anywhere in the world (more than 124 miles/200 km), and the Tomcat is the only combat aircraft equipped to carry it. In conjunction with the extremely powerful Hughes AWG-9 radar mounted in the nose, it provides the Tomcat with the unique ability to detect and attack an airborne target while it is still 100 miles (160 km) away. The F-14A also has a secondary capability in the low-level attack role, in which event the air-to-air missiles can be replaced by up to 14,500 lb (6577 kg) of externally-mounted bombs or other weapons.

The initial F-14A model of the Tomcat has been in service with the US Navy since October 1972, when the first deliveries were made to squadrons VF-1 and VF-2. It was an aircraft of the latter unit which, in March 1974, flew the first operational Tomcat sortie from the carrier USS *Enterprise*. Subsequent acceptance of the fighter into regular USN service was both enthusiastic and without major incident until 1975, when a series of powerplant, structural and systems problems were encountered. However, these have been largely resolved, one resultant modification being an increase in available thrust with the afterburners on. (Shortage of power and other propulsion problems have threatened replacement with different engines, however.) The US Navy plans to acquire some 570 Tomcats, about 55 per cent of which had been delivered by the beginning of 1979 to equip more than a dozen US Navy and US Marine Corps squadrons. At that time the Naval Air Training Center at Patuxent River, Maryland, was developing a tactical air reconnaissance pod system (TARPS) to extend further the versatility of the F-14A, seen as the interim replacement for the Rockwell RA-5C Vigilante.

Eighty F-14As were exported to the Imperial Iranian Air Force in the mid-1970s, but cost escalation

Grumman F-14A Tomcat

mainstay of the US Navy's fleet defence thanks to its combination of an advanced airframe and engines with the powerful weapon system formed by the AIM-54 missile and AWG-9 radar. The aircraft illustrated is from Navy Fighter Squadron 1, based on the USS *Enterprise*.

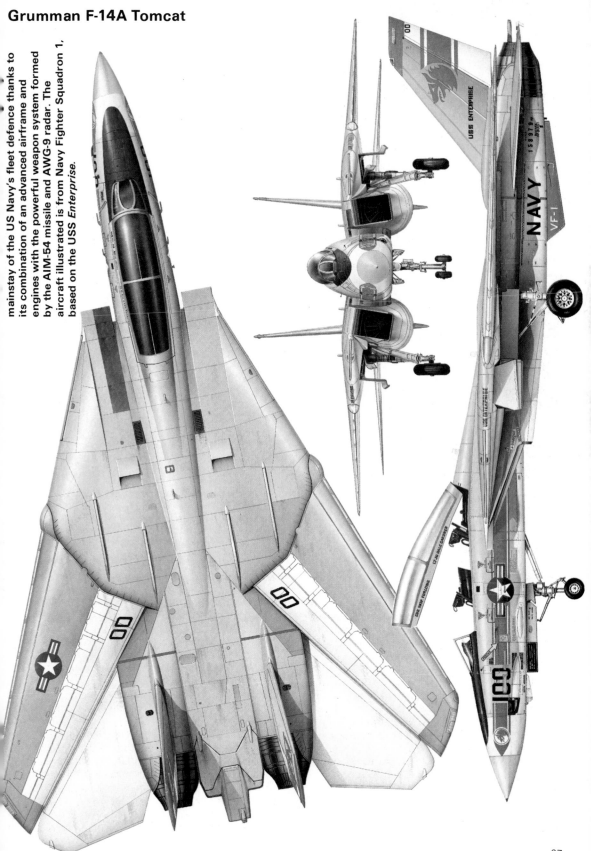

Grumman F-14A Tomcat

curtailed the development of the proposed F-14B and F-14C models for the US Navy. Two prototypes of the former were produced by refitting F-14As with 28,090-lb (12741-kg) static thrust Pratt & Whitney F401-P-400 turbofans, the first of these making its initial flight on 12 September 1973. Development of the F-14C, with the same engines plus new avionics and weapons, was also halted.

Current US Navy fears about the reliability and power of the TF30 are reflected in the fact that in 1981 it is planned to fly an evaluation programme with an F-14A re-engined with the General Electric F101 Derivative Fighter Engine.

Specification

Type: tandem two-seat carrier-borne multi-role fighter

Powerplant: two 20,900-lb (9480-kg) static thrust Pratt & Whitney TF30-P-412A afterburning turbofans

Performance: maximum speed at altitude Mach 2.34 or 1,564 mph (2517 km/h); maximum speed at sea level Mach 1.2 or 910 mph (1470 km/h); range (interceptor, with external fuel) about 2,000 miles (3200 km); service ceiling over 56,000 ft (17070 m); maximum rate of climb at sea level (normal gross

This Grumman F-14A Tomcat, probably recovering aboard the first nuclear carrier, CVA-65 *Enterprise*, is painted in an unusual scheme which embraces the radome, which most units do not paint. The ship's fore/aft axis is shown by the direction of the wake.

weight) over 30,000 ft (9145 m) per minute

Weights: empty 39,310 lb (17830 kg); normal take-off 58,539 lb (26553 kg); take-off with four Sparrows 58,904 lb (26718 kg); take-off with six Phoenix 69,790 lb (31656 kg); maximum take-off 74,348 lb (33724 kg)

Dimensions: span unswept 64 ft 1½ in (19.45 m); span swept 38 ft 2½ in (11.65 m); length 61 ft 2 in (18.89 m); height 16 ft 0 in (4.88 m); wing area 565.0 sq ft (52.49 m^2)

Armament: one General Electric M61A-1 20-mm multi-barrel Vulcan cannon in forward fuselage with 675 rounds; four AIM-7 Sparrow or AIM-54 Phoenix air-to-air missiles under fuselage; two AIM-9 Sidewinder air-to-air missiles, or one Sidewinder plus one Phoenix or Sparrow, under each wing glove box; tactical reconnaissance pod containing cameras and electro-optical sensors; or up to 14,500 lb (6577 kg) of Mk 82/83/84 bombs or other weapons

Operators: Iran, US Marine Corps, US Navy

Grumman OV-1 Mohawk

US Army Grumman OV-1B Mohawk of the 23rd Special Warfare Aviation Detachment.

History and notes

In the mid-1950s, both the US Army and US Marine Corps drew up specifications for a battlefield surveillance aircraft. Their requirements were generally similar: to carry a variety of reconnaissance equipment, to have rough-field capability, and be able to operate on a STOL basis. It proved possible for both services to agree on a common design. Thus, in 1957 the US Navy, acting as programme manager for both the US Army and the US Marine Corps, ordered nine examples of Grumman's G-134 design for test and evaluation. These were designated initially YAO-1A, subsequently YOV-1A, and the first of these aircraft made its maiden flight on 14 April 1959.

Early evaluation left little doubt of the excellence of the design, but even before the prototype had made its first flight the US Marine Corps had withdrawn from the initial contract, and no examples of that service's OF-1s were built. Instead, the flight-test programme was speeded up, and before the end of 1959 the US Army had placed production contracts for OV-1A and OV-1B aircraft, the basic OV-1 acquiring the name Mohawk.

First turboprop-powered aircraft to enter service with the US Army, the OV-1 is comparatively slow but highly manoeuvrable, and to help offset its vulnerability as a result of its speed and role, has a well-armoured cockpit with a 0.25-in (0.64-cm) thick aluminium-alloy floor, flak curtains on both fore and aft bulkheads, and bullet-resistant windscreens. Although conventional in its basic configuration, detail design has produced an easily identified and unusual-looking aircraft. The mid-set monoplane wing is quite normal, but the two turboprop engines mounted high on each wing have their centrelines canted outward and upward. The tail unit, with three sets of fins and rudders, has considerable dihedral so that, while the centre fin is vertical, the endplate fins are canted in. Moreover, because it is desirable to provide the two-man crew with the best possible downward view, the sides of the cockpit are deeply bulged.

The basic version is the OV-1A, equipped for day and night visual or photo reconnaissance, and provided with dual controls. The OV-1B which followed has increased wing span, SLAR and an internal camera with in-flight processor; the dual controls have been deleted. Next production version was the OV-1C, similar to late production version OV-1As but with the AN/AAS-24 infra-red (IR) surveillance system. Final version was the OV-1D with side

Grumman OV-1B Mohawk (with SLAR)

loading doors to accept a pallet with SLAR, IR, or other sensors; in addition to production aircraft, more than 80 OV-1B/-1Cs were converted to OV-1D standard. The designations RV-1C and RV-1D apply respectively to OV-1C and OV-1D aircraft modified permanently for electronic-reconnaissance missions.

Specification

Type: two-seat multi-sensor observation aircraft
Powerplant: (OV-1D) two 1,400-shp (1044-kW) Lycoming T53-L-701 turboprops
Performance: (OV-1D) maximum speed at maximum rated power (SLAR mission) 289 mph (465 km/h) at 10,000 ft (3050 m), (IR mission) 305 mph (491 km/h); maximum range with auxiliary fuel (SLAR mission) 944 miles (1519 km), (IR mission) 1,011 miles (1627 km); maximum endurance at 161 mph (259 km/h) at 15,000 ft (4570 m) on a SLAR mission 4 hours 20 minutes, on an IR mission 4 hours 32 minutes
Weights: (OV-1D) empty equipped 12,054 lb (5468 kg); normal take-off (SLAR mission) 15,741 lb (7140 kg), (IR mission) 15,544 lb (7051 kg); maximum take-off (SLAR mission) 18,109 lb (8214 kg), (IR mission) 17,912 lb (8125 kg)
Dimensions: span (OV-1A/-1C) 42 ft 0 in (12.80 m), (OV-1B/-1D) 48 ft 0 in (14.63 m); length 41 ft 0 in (12.50 m); height 12 ft 8 in (3.86 m); wing area (OV-1A/-1C) 330 sq ft (30.66 m²), (OV-1B/-1D) 360 sq ft (33.44 m²)
Armament: normally none, but bombs, rockets and Minigun pods have been carried on underwing pylons
Operators: Israel and US Army

Grumman S-2 Tracker/E-1 Tracer/C-1 Trader

History and notes

In the years immediately after World War II, the US Navy's carrier-based ASW effort was based upon the use of twin-aircraft hunter/killer teams. Typical was the twinning of the Grumman Avenger, with TBM-3W or TBM-3W-2 radar-equipped search aircraft locating enemy submarines for the TBM-3S or TMB-3S-2 aircraft which made the attack with suitable anti-submarine weapons. There were clearly some snags to such a twin-aircraft attack: for example, malfunction of one meant that the second was virtually useless. Furthermore, the location problem was aggravated by the introduction into service of deeper-diving nuclear-powered submarines. A larger amount of more sophisticated avionics was needed for their detection, as well as for the launch and guidance of air-to-underwater weapons.

In the late 1940s the US Navy finalised its ideas on the kind of single hunter/killer aircraft which it needed to fulfil this role, and Grumman designed a fairly large twin-engine high-wing monoplane, designated G-89, to meet this requirement. The high-wing configuration maximized the cabin space to provide room for on-board equipment, and additional stowage space for expendable sonobuoys was provided in the rear of the engine nacelles. Other features included a large weapons bay, retractable search radar in the rear fuselage, MAD boom in a retractable fairing, searchlight beneath the starboard wing, plus folding wings and arrester hook for carrier operations.

On 30 June 1950 Grumman was awarded a contract to build for evaluation a single prototype of the G-89, the US Navy designation for this aircraft being XS2F-1, and this aircraft flew for the first time on 4 December 1952. S2F Tracker, WF Tracer and TF Trader versions were to appear in due course, and under the 1962 tri-service rationalisation of designations these became respectively S-2, E-1, and C-1 series aircraft. The S-2A, the first production version of the Tracker, began to enter service with the US Navy's Anti-Submarine Squadron VS-26 in February 1954. In addition to the 500-plus examples built for the US Navy, more than 100 S-2As were exported to friendly nations. A number of these aircraft were used in a training role under the designation TS-2A.

The designation S-2B applied to S-2A aircraft which had been modified to carry AQA-3 Jezebel passive long-range acoustic search equipment, working in conjunction with Julie active acoustic echo-ranging by explosive charge. S-2C was the designation of the next production version, which had an enlarged weapons bay with an offset extension on the left side, and these also had a larger tail to compensate for a higher gross weight.

The second major production version was the S-2D, of which the initial example flew for the first time on 21 May 1959. This had a wing of increased span, still larger tail surfaces, plus greater fuel

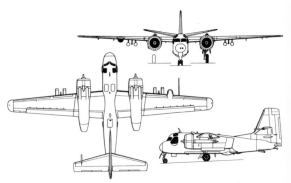

Grumman S-2 Tracker

capacity and stowage for double the number of sonobuoys in each engine nacelle, for a combined total of 32. In addition, the forward fuselage was lengthened and widened to improve accommodation for the four-man crew. S-2Ds began to enter service in May 1961, and eventually equipped at least 15 US Navy squadrons. Those modified later to carry more advanced search equipment had the designation S-2E, and production of these ended in 1968 with a batch of 14 for the Royal Australian Navy. S-2F was the designation of S-2Bs retrofitted with the same advanced search equipment as that installed in the S-2Es. The de Havilland Aircraft of Canada company built 100 Trackers for the Royal Canadian Navy, the first 43 as CS2F-1s and the remainder with improved equipment as CS2F-2s.

The final version of the Tracker was designated S-2G, and is similar to the S-2E, but with advanced equipment which enabled the type to serve on US Navy's CVS-class aircraft-carriers until the Lockheed S-3A Viking entered service.

Specification

Type: naval anti-submarine aircraft
Powerplant: two 1,525-hp (1137-kW) Wright R-1820-82WA Cyclone radial piston engines
Performance: (S-2E) maximum speed at sea level 265 mph (426 km/h); patrol speed 150 mph (241 km/h) at 1,500 ft (455 m); ferry range 1,300 miles (2092 km); endurance with maximum fuel (10% reserves) 9 hours.
Weights: (S-2E) empty 18,750 lb (8505 kg); maximum take-off 29,150 lb (13222 kg)
Dimensions: (S-2E) span 72 ft 7 in (22.12 m); length 43 ft 6 in (13.26 m); height 16 ft 7 in (5.05 m); wing area 496 sq ft (46.08 m^2)
Armament: one Mk 47 or Mk 101 nuclear depth bomb or similar store in weapons bay, 60 echo-sounding depth charges in fuselage, 32 sonobuoys in engine nacelles, plus a variety of bombs, rockets or torpedoes on six underwing hardpoints
Operators: Argentina, Australia, Brazil, Canada, Italy, Japan, Netherlands, Taiwan, Thailand US Navy, Uruguay

Grumman S-2 Tracker/E-1 Tracer/C-1 Trader

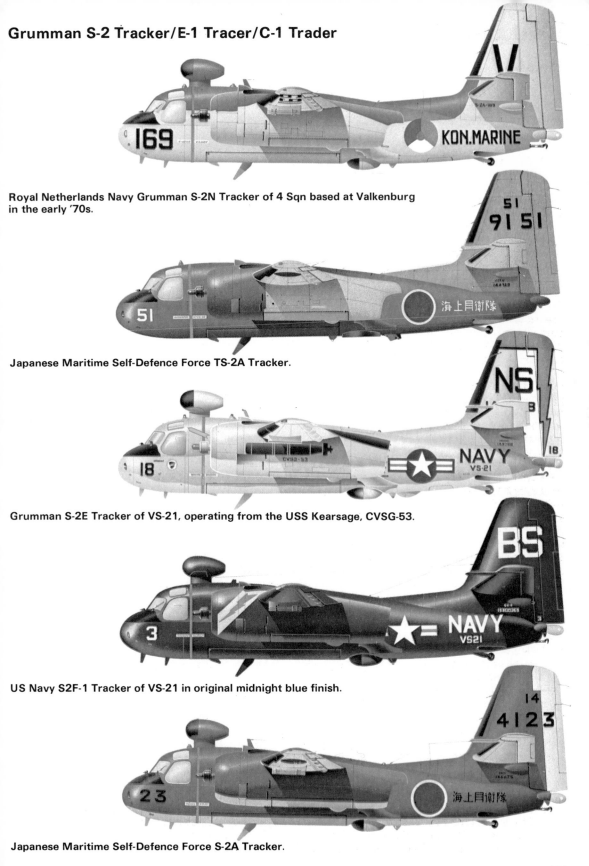

Royal Netherlands Navy Grumman S-2N Tracker of 4 Sqn based at Valkenburg in the early '70s.

Japanese Maritime Self-Defence Force TS-2A Tracker.

Grumman S-2E Tracker of VS-21, operating from the USS Kearsage, CVSG-53.

US Navy S2F-1 Tracker of VS-21 in original midnight blue finish.

Japanese Maritime Self-Defence Force S-2A Tracker.

Hindustan Aeronautics HF-24 Marut

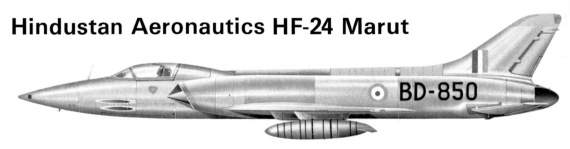

Hindustan Aeronautics HF-24 Marut Mk 1 figher of the Indian Air Force; three squadrons operate the type in the IAF.

History and notes

India's first, and so far only, indigenous jet fighter, the HAL HF-24 Marut (wind spirit) has not been an unqualified success. Development was protracted, performance disappointing, and the search for an engine capable of carrying it to its intended Mach 2 maximum speed unfruitful.

The lack of home-produced experience in designing jet aircraft was offset by acquiring the services of a team of German engineers, headed by Dipl-Ing Kurt Tank, the brilliant wartime technical director of Focke-Wulf. This team began work on the HF-24 in June 1956 and stayed until 1967, after which development was continued by an all-Indian team. After preliminary trials with a full-size two-seat glider built to the same basic configuration, two prototype HF-24s were built, making their initial flights on 17 June 1961 and 4 October 1962 respectively.

The two prototypes were followed in 1963-64 by 18 pre-production aircraft, before series manufacture began of the Marut Mk I as a ground-attack fighter. A token delivery of two of these aircraft was made to the Indian air force on 10 May 1964; 12 others were delivered later, the remaining four being retained for various test purposes. Of all-metal low-wing configuration, the Marut has 45° swept wings, twin Orpheus 703 non-afterburning turbojets side by side in the fuselage, and a Martin-Baker Mk 84C zero-height ejection seat for the pilot. The first production Mk I was flown on 15 November 1967, and by the time of the December 1971 war with Pakistan Maruts equipped three IAF squadrons (Nos 10, 31 and 220), acquitting themselves well in operations, without loss. Mk I production, including development aircraft, totalled 129, but no additional squadrons were equipped with the type.

In addition to the single-seater, HAL also developed a two-seat combat proficiency trainer version of the Marut, known as the Mk IT. The first of two Mk IT prototypes was flown on 30 April 1970, and 18 were eventually built, with the two seats in tandem under a long, one-piece canopy, and dual controls for the occupants.

Production of the Marut ended in 1977. Over the years a number of attempts have been made to push the performance up to Mach 2, one of which involved the conversion of a pre-production Marut to Mk IA standard by fitting afterburners to the existing Orpheus 703 engines. Entirely new powerplants

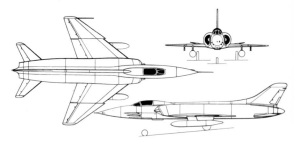

Hindustan Aeronautics HF-24 Marut

studied have varied from the German-designed, Egyptian-built Brandner E300 turbojet in the latter half of the 1960s to the more recent study of the Turbo-Union RB.199 turbofan which powers the Panavia Tornado. None of these has yielded satisfactory results, and the idea of a Mach 2 Marut now seems to have been abandoned.

Specification

Type: single-seat ground-attack fighter (Mk I); two-seat operational trainer (Mk IT)
Powerplant: two 4,850-lb (2200-kg) static thrust HAL-built Rolls-Royce Orpheus 703 turbojets
Performance: maximum speed at 39,375 ft (12000 m) (Mk I) Mach 1.02 or 675 mph (1086 km/h), (Mk IT) Mach 1.00 or 661 mph (1064 km/h); maximum indicated airspeed at sea level (Mk I) 691 mph (1112 km/h); combat radius (Mk IT) at low level 148 miles (238 km), at 39,375 ft (12000 m) 246 miles (396 km); ferry range (Mk IT) at 30,000 ft (9150 m) 898 miles (1445 km); time to 40,000 ft (12200 m), aircraft clean 9 minutes 20 seconds
Weights: empty (Mk I with ventral drop-tank) 13,658 lb (6195 kg), (Mk IT) 13,778 lb (6250 kg); maximum take-off (Mk I) 24,048 lb (10908 kg), (Mk IT) 23,836 lb (10812 kg)
Dimensions: span 29 ft 6¼ in (9.00 m); length 52 ft 0¾ in (15.87 m); height 11 ft 9¾ in (3.60 m); wing area 301.4 sq ft (28.00 m²)
Armament: four 30-mm Aden Mk 2 cannon with 120 rounds per gun, two on each side of forward fuselage; retractable Matra Type 103 pack of fifty 68-mm SNEB air-to-air rockets in belly (not in Mk IT); four underwing points for 1,000-lb (454-kg) bombs, Type 116 SNEB rocket pods, T10 air-to-surface rocket clusters, napalm, or drop-tanks
Operator: India

Hughes Model 500M Defender

History and notes

Hughes announced on 21 April 1965 that it was the company's intention to market a commerical equivalent of the military OH-6A. Three versions were to be available: the basic Model 500, a five-seat executive; the utility Model 500U (later 500C), which would carry seven persons or up to 1,710 lb (776 kg) of freight; and a military Model 500M, basically the same as the US Army's OH-6A, but configured for sale to foreign military customers. These variants differed from the military OH-6A mainly in their powerplant. The Models 500 and 500M retained the same basic Allison T63-A-5A, but in these applications rerated to 278 shp (207 kW) for take-off, and with a maximum continuous rating of 243 shp (181 kW). The 500C has the commercial 400-shp (298-kW) Allison Model 250-C20 turboshaft, derated to the same levels as the T63-A-5A, but giving improved 'hot and high' performance. Deliveries of these helicopter models began in 1968, and the 500M proved an attractive buy for many foreign air forces, including those of Colombia, Denmark, Mexico, the Philippines, and Spain. In addition, licence manufacture of the Model 500 has been undertaken by BredaNardi in Italy, Kawasaki in Japan and RACA in Argentina.

The development of a more advanced version began in 1974, introducing a number of changes to enhance performance. The more powerful Allison 250-C20B was introduced: this develops a maximum of 420 shp (313 kW), but is derated in this application to 375 shp (280 kW) for take-off, and has a maximum continuous rating of 350 shp (261 kW). There are two readily noticeable external changes, the first being the provision of a T-tail, with a small-span horizontal stabilizer, with diminutive end-plate fins, mounted at the tip of the dorsal fin. This replaces the earlier unit which had a similar ventral/dorsal fin arrangement, but had also a fixed stabilizer with considerable dihedral mounted on the starboard side of the fin. The other major external change is the introduction of a five-blade main rotor similar to that installed on the experimental OH-6C. In fact, as early as April 1976 Hughes had been working on a modified OH-6A which was known as 'The Quiet One', and it was for this aircraft that the slower-rotating five-blade main rotor had originally been developed. This latter aircraft also had a four-blade tail rotor, but to avoid excessive weight that of the 500D, as this new helicopter is known, has only two blades of slightly increased diameter, plus a longer and strengthened tail boom.

During 1976 Hughes made extensive studies of armed helicopters, from which the conclusion was reached that the Model 500D could, with minimal modification, be marketed as a low-cost multi-mission combat helicopter. The resulting Model 500M-D Defender created a favourable impression and is currently being manufactured extensively by Hughes and its licensees.

Hughes 500M-D Defender equipped with a TOW missile system.

Hughes Model 500M/Defender

Specification

Type: lightweight commercial/military helicopter
Powerplant: (500M-D) one 420-shp (313-kW) Allison 250-C20B turboshaft, derated to 375 shp (280 kW), and with a maximum continuous rating of 350 shp (261 kW)
Performance: maximum cruising speed at sea level 160 mph (257 km/h); range at sea level (with allowance for 2-minute warm-up, standard fuel and no reserves) 300 miles (483 km)
Weights: empty 1,320 lb (599 kg); maximum take-off 3,000 lb (1361 kg)
Dimensions: main rotor diameter 26 ft 5 in (8.05 m); length (rotors turning) 30 ft 6 in (9.30 m); height 8 ft 3½ in (2.53 m); main rotor disc area 547.81 sq ft (50.89 m²)
Armament: (500M-D) includes 2.75-in (69.9-mm) rockets, 7.62-mm (0.3-in) Minigun, 30-mm Chain Gun; Mk 44 or Mk 46 homing torpedoes; or four TOW air-to-surface missiles
Operators: Argentina, Colombia, Denmark, Italy, Israel, Japan, Mauritania, Mexico, South Korea, Spain

Ilyushin Il-38 May

History and notes

The Soviet Union was a latecomer in the field of specialized maritime reconnaissance and anti-submarine-warfare (ASW) aircraft, as it came late to the manufacture of airborne early warning systems. For this reason it is usually assumed that Soviet systems such as the Ilyushin Il-38 'May' and the Tu-126 'Moss' are not up to the same standards as Western counterparts; but their operational effectiveness depends on hard-to-assess details of their sensors and internal equipment.

The closest Western equivalent of the Il-38 is the Lockheed P-3 Orion. Both were developed from medium-range airliners of about the same vintage, although the Il-18 which forms the basis of the Il-38 is a rather larger aircraft than the Lockheed Electra. However, the histories of the two types are different. The first Orion entered service some 10 years before the Il-38 appeared, and by the time the Soviet aircraft had entered service the P-3's systems had been modernized twice to keep abreast with the growing threat from Russian ballistic-missile-firing submarines (SSBNs). More recently, the P-3C has undergone various Update programmes, acquiring new types of sensor and improved versions of systems already fitted. None of this development effort has been paralleled visibly on the Il-38, no changes in equipment having been observed since the type entered service.

Neither has the Soviet Union the benefit of the West's long experience of ASW, dating back to the Battle of the Atlantic in World War II. The Lockheed Neptune, for example, had no known equivalent in the Soviet Union. Jet aircraft such as the Tu-16 were too inefficient at low speeds and altitudes to be used effectively in the ASW role, which was mainly the province of flying-boats such as the Beriev Be-6 and M-12, with relatively short range.

In the early 1960s, when the United States Navy's force of Polaris-armed SSBNs was being built up, there was no aircraft in the Soviet naval air force (AVMF) which could counter the increasing threat. With the development of the Poseidon missile, the area from which US SSBNs could threaten large sectors of the Soviet Union increased well beyond the area which could be covered, even partially, by Be-6s and M-12s. The need for a specialized ASW aircraft grew with the deployment of the longer-ranged missile to replace the Polaris, and Il-38 development appears to have coincided with the introduction of Poseidon. The aircraft was first observed in 1974, but by that time it appears to have been in service for some years, and so design probably began in about 1965. About 100 Il-38s have been delivered to the AVMF, and some have been supplied to India; it is possible that the latter aircraft have a reduced standard of equipment, like the Lockheed P-3F supplied to Iran.

The airframe of the Il-38 is certainly stronger than that of the Il-18 airliner, in order to withstand the stresses of manoeuvring at low altitude in gusty weather. It is also likely that the ASW aircraft can take off at a higher gross weight than the airliner (the P-3C for instance, is very much heavier than the Electra) and it would be logical to expect the engines to be similar to the uprated AI-20s fitted to the Antonov An-32 STOL freighter.

A highly significant feature of the Il-38 design is the fact that the wing is set much farther forward than on the airliner. This indicates that the forward fuselage contains a concentration of heavy equipment. On either side of the fuselage, ahead of the wing, there is fitted what appears to be an air intake and outlet. One explanation for this feature, and for the short front fuselage, is that a large processor is installed forward, with the main tactical control compartment above the wing and extending towards the rear. The aft fuselage presumably includes sleeping accommodation for relief crews and galley facilities, which account for little weight.

Unlike that of the Orion, the main radar of the Il-38 is mounted under the forward fuselage immediately aft of the nosewheel bay. Radar is a major search aid for an ASW aircraft, but in these days of nuclear-powered submarines it has to be of high performance if it is to be effective.

The weapon bay of the Il-38 is installed well forward; this feature does not in itself account for the forward shift of the wing, as it is shared by the P-3, where the wing is in the same relative position as on the original Electra. The weapon bay houses sonobuoys as well as offensive weapons, whereas the P-3 has separate sonobuoy stowage in the rear fuselage. Underfloor capacity immediately ahead of the wing is probably used for fuel tankage. The Il-38 carries the symbol of the ASW aircraft's trade: a magnetic anomaly detector (MAD) installed in a long tailboom.

Radar, MAD and acoustic sensors appear to be the main sources of raw data for the Il-38, but its effectiveness will also depend on the processing equipment fitted and its ability to select and pass information to the crew. Electronic surveillance measures (ESM) are not conspicuous, although there is a fin-top antenna. Also apparently absent are infra-red and low-light level visual sensors, both standard on the latest Western types. Going purely on external signs, the Il-38 as so far observed appears to be a first-generation type in terms of its operational equipment; however, it can be expected that more effective versions are under development and will appear in AVMF service in due course.

Development of a large, long-range subsonic military aircraft was reported in 1979, with both the strategic missile-launching and ASW roles apparently in mind. However, the new type may be intended more for the high-altitude surveillance role formerly undertaken by the Tu-142 than for ASW of the sort carried out by the Il-38 and its Western equivalents.

Illyushin Il-38 May

Compared with the Il-18 airliner the Il-38 has the wing further forward, balancing heavy equipment loads in the forward fuselage. The main weapon bay is ahead of the wing, where it can extend up to floor level. The ECM/Elint version called 'Coot-A' carries its equipment here.

Specification

Type: maritime reconnaissance and ASW aircraft
Powerplant: four 5,200-shp (3879-kW) Ivchenko AI-20M turboprops
Performance: maximum speed 400 mph (640 km/h); patrol speed 290 mph (460 km/h); endurance 16 hours; range 5,200 miles (8300 km)
Weights: empty 90,000 lb (40000 kg); maximum take-off 150,000 lb (68000 kg)
Dimensions: span 122 ft 9 in (37.4 m); length (including MAD boom) 129 ft 10 in (39.6 m); height 33 ft 4 in (10.3 m); wing area 1,500 sq ft (140 m²)
Armament: internal weapons bay for homing torpedoes, nuclear and conventional depth charges and sonobuoys
Operators: India, USSR

Ilyushin Il-76 Candid

History and notes

Superficially similar to the Lockheed C-141 StarLifter, the Ilyushin Il-76 'Candid' is in fact a heavier and more powerful aircraft, more capable of operations from short, unpaved runways. It is replacing the Antonov An-12 'Cub' as the main tactical transport of the Soviet VTA (air transport force); it is also in service with Aeroflot, and Il-76s of both operators have been used to supply arms to Soviet client states.

The design of the Il-76 started in the late 1960s, to meet a joint civil/military requirement. Aeroflot needed an aircraft smaller and more flexible than the An-22 'Cock', while the VTA could presumably see a requirement for a faster aircraft than the big Antonov turboprop for use in forward areas. The requirement which emerged was for an aircraft which could carry twice the maximum payload of the An-12 over sectors longer than the older aircraft's maximum range. The new transport had to be able to use the same short and semi-prepared strips as the An-12, setting problems in undercarriage and wing design.

There is little room for flexibility in the design of a heavy military freighter. Loading and unloading requires a rear ramp and a floor at truck-bed height, so that a low wing is ruled out; wing wake then makes a low-set tailplane risky, so that aircraft of this type tend to have T-tails. The Ilyushin design bureau, headed from the mid-1960s by General Designer Novozhilov, adopted this generally conventional layout for the Il-76. It was the first Soviet transport to have podded engines, hung on low-drag pylons reminiscent of those of the Douglas DC-8-62. The engines are set well inboard compared with those of Western airliners, and are probably set too low to have any blowing effect on the flaps. The wing is fitted with extensive high-lift devices, including slats, triple-slotted trailing-edge flaps, and spoilers for low-speed roll control.

A unique feature of the Il-76 is its rough-field landing gear, more complex than that of the C-141. The main gear comprises four units, each a single axle with four wheels abreast, while the nose gear also has four wheels abreast. The original Il-76 was designed to have a 'footprint pressure' no higher than that of the An-12.

Internally, the Il-76 is equipped with a cargo roller floor, two 6,500-lb (3000-kg) winches and two roof cranes with a total capacity of 22,000 lb (10000 kg).

In addition to the normal crew of two pilots, a flight engineer and a navigator, there is accommodation for a loadmaster and a radio operator. The navigator occupies a cabin below the flight deck, with a glazed nose. Production Il-76s have two radomes similar to those of late-production An-22s, one housing a weather radar and the other containing mapping equipment. The final member of the crew, on military Il-76s, is the tail gunner: the apparently archaic armament of twin 23-mm cannon

fitted to the An-12 is retained on its jet replacement. Unlike the An-12, however, the jet aircraft carries a tail-warning radar.

The first Il-76 was flown in March 1971, and was demonstrated at the Paris air show two months later. Prototype and early production aircraft were designed closely to the original specification, which demanded 3,100-mile (5000-km) range with 88,000-lb (40000-kg) payload, and had a maximum take-off weight of 346,000 lb (157000 kg). This is believed to have been matched by limited fuel capacity. From 1977 production appears to have concentrated on the Il-76T, with some 20 per cent more fuel. It is likely that more of the Il-76T wing is wet, allowing payload to be traded for extra range.

Take-off and landing runs for the lighter early Il-76 are quoted at 2,800 ft (850 m) for the 1,500 ft (450 m) respectively; these are almost certainly ground rolls, but still suggest that the Il-76 could comfortably use a 5,000 ft (1500 m) strip. This performance is impressive, if not in the class of the US Advanced Medium STOL Transport (AMST) prototypes, and makes the Il-76 a tactical transport to be reckoned with. It has also been used extensively in the airlift role, and air-dropping trials have been carried out.

About 100 Il-76s are now in service; production is continuing at about 30 aircraft/year, and the VTA is probably replacing all its 600 An-12s with the new type. Reports of a tanker version under development may have been premature: the Il-86 wide-body airliner would seem to be a more suitable basis for such a development and would now be available in the same timescale. Deliveries to Aeroflot appeared to be gaining momentum in 1978, suggesting that the VTA was relaxing some of its demands for priority in deliveries.

The Il-76T is probably the definitive version of the type for the time being, in the absence of any more advanced Soviet powerplant.

Specification

Type: strategic or tactical freighter

Powerplant: four 26,500 lb (12000 kg) Soloviev D-30KP turbofans

Performance: maximum speed 530 mph (850 km/h) or Mach 0.8; economical cruising speed 500 mph (800 km/h) or Mach 0.75; range with 77,000-lb (35000-kg) payload 4,000 miles (6500 km); ceiling 42,000 ft (13000 m)

Weights: empty 135,000 lb (62000 kg); maximum payload about 88,000 lb (40000 kg); maximum take-off 375,000 lb (170000 kg)

Dimensions: span 165 ft 8 in (50.5 m); length 152 ft 10½ in (46.59 m); height 48 ft 5 in (14.76 m); wing area 3,230 sq ft (300 m²)

Armament: (when fitted) two 23-mm cannon in radar-directed manned tail turret

Operators: Iraq, USSR

Illyshin Il-76 Candid

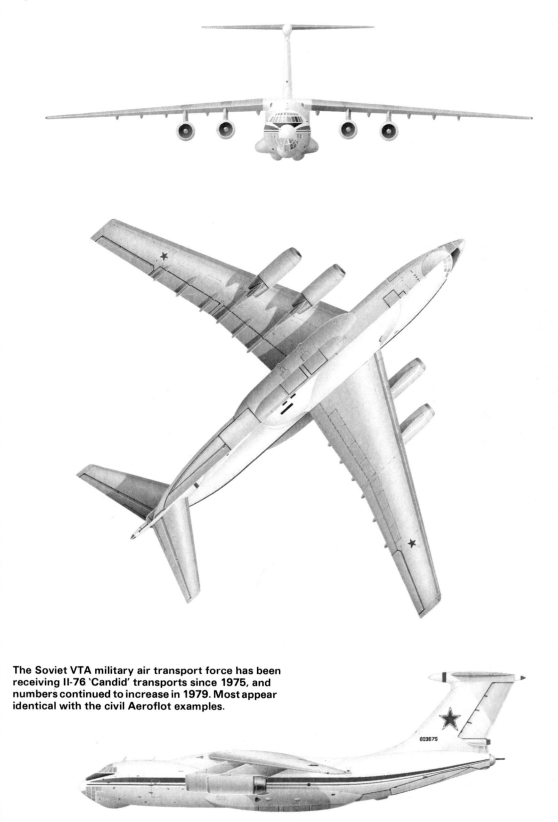

The Soviet VTA military air transport force has been
receiving Il-76 'Candid' transports since 1975, and
numbers continued to increase in 1979. Most appear
identical with the civil Aeroflot examples.

Israel Aircraft Industries Kfir

History and notes

Kfir (Lion Cub) has been developed by IAI to succeed the Dassault Mirage III in the interceptor and ground-attack roles. The Israeli Air Force received 72 single-seat Mirage IIICJs from April 1972, mainly for use as air-superiority fighters and for interception. In late 1966 Israel ordered 50 Mirage 5Js to complement the Mirage IIIs by concentrating on ground-attack, but following the Six-Day War in June 1967 the French government placed an embargo on the delivery of the Mirage 5Js, which were eventually put into service with France's *Armée de l'Air*. The Israeli Air Force therefore had to look elsewhere for equipment and, although the United States began to supply McDonnell Douglas F-4 Phantoms and McDonnell Douglas A-4 Skyhawks, the Israeli authorities decided to set up an indigenous production line to build combat aircraft.

The basic Mirage III/5 airframe was adopted as a starting point, with a General Electric J79 turbojet — the engine used in the Phantom — replacing the SNECMA Atar employed in the Mirage series. Mating the US powerplant with the Dassault-designed airframe proved difficult, however, and IAI produced the Nesher (Eagle) as an interim fighter to fill the gap until the new type was available. The Nesher was a locally built copy of the Mirage III/5, with some modifications but retaining the Atar 9C engine. The prototype Nesher is thought to have made its maiden flight in September 1969 and deliveries of production aircraft, equipped with Israeli avionics, began in 1972. About 40 Neshers are reported to have fought with the Israeli Air Force during the Yom Kippur War in October 1973.

The Kfir was revealed in April 1975, when two examples were put on display. The aircraft closely resembles the Mirage 5 but has a number of differences apart from the use of a US engine and Israeli equipment. The rear fuselage is fatter and shorter than in the French-designed aircraft, with the variable exhaust nozzle protruding from the afterbody. The afterburner is cooled by air drawn from a scoop in the root of the fin. The forward section of Kfir's fuselage is larger than that of the Mirage, and the undersurface is flatter, while the nose itself has been lengthened. The leading edges of the 60° delta wing are also modified, and the strengthened landing gear uses long-stroke oleos.

The adoption of the J79-17 turbojet in place of an Atar has improved specific fuel consumption by about 20 per cent, and the higher mass flow demanded by the US engine has necessitated an increase in intake inlet and duct area. The J79 also runs hotter than the French engine, which was one of the major difficulties encountered as a result of the substitution.

In July 1976 the Israeli Air Force revealed the existence of the Kfir-C2, the major external difference between this model and the original Kfir-C1 being the addition of canard surfaces. The addition of canards, slightly ahead of and above the wing, has a number of effects: it increases the lift available at a given angle of attack, allows the aircraft to operate over a greater range of angles of attack, and reduces stability because the centre of lift and centre of gravity are moved closer together. The canards have been fitted mainly to improve manoeuvrability in combat, but they also allow the aircraft to operate from shorter runways. The Kfir-C2 has saw-teeth in the wing leading edges and small strakes along the nose, both these features complementing the canard surfaces in improving manoeuvrability. The Kfir-C1 and -C2 are otherwise identical, or nearly so, and the original aircraft are being converted to bring them up to the definitive -C2 standard.

The Kfir carries two internally mounted 30-mm DEFA cannon with their muzzles protruding below the engine air intakes, as in the Mirage 5. The front of the barrel is fitted with specially developed gas-deflecting baffles which, according to the Israeli Air Force, allow the guns to be fired over the complete performance envelope without the risk of engine compressor stall. The aircraft can also carry a variety of external stores totalling more than 8,500 lb (3856 kg), including Rafael Shafrir air-to-air missiles, rocket pods, conventional or anti-runway bombs, and guided air-to-surface weapons such as Maverick, Hobos and Shrike.

The Israeli Air Force is expected to receive a total of about 160 Kfirs, and the type is also being offered for export. At least one proposed sale, to Ecuador, has however been embargoed by the United States, which refused to supply engines in support of such a deal. Some of the Israeli Air Force's Kfirs will be two-seat trainers.

Specification

Type: single-seat fighter and ground-attack aircraft

Power Plant: one General Electric J79-GE-17 (modified) turbojet rated at 17,900 lb (8119 kg) thrust with afterburning

Performance: maximum design speed (clean) at least Mach 2.2 or 1,450 mph (2335 km/h) at high altitude; tactical radius (as interceptor with two drop tanks) up to 330 miles (535 km); time to 36,000 ft (11000 m) 1.5 minutes

Weights: maximum combat for ground attack 32,120 lb (14600 kg); typical combat as interceptor with two Shafrir missiles 20,470 lb (9305 kg)

Dimensions: span 27 ft (8.23 m); length 50 ft 4 in (15.34 m); height 17 ft 1 in (5.22 m); wing area 392 sq ft (36.43 m²)

Armament: two 30-mm DEFA cannon and two Shafrir AAMs or air-to-ground weapons including bombs, rockets or missiles (such as Maverick, Hobos and Shrike)

Operator: Israel

Israel Aircraft Industries Kfir

The most prominent external difference between the Kfir-C2 and the original Kfir and Mirage is the fixed canard, a pair of sweptback foreplanes above the engine inlet ducts which greatly improve field length, combat manoeuvrability, control about all axes and landing behaviour.

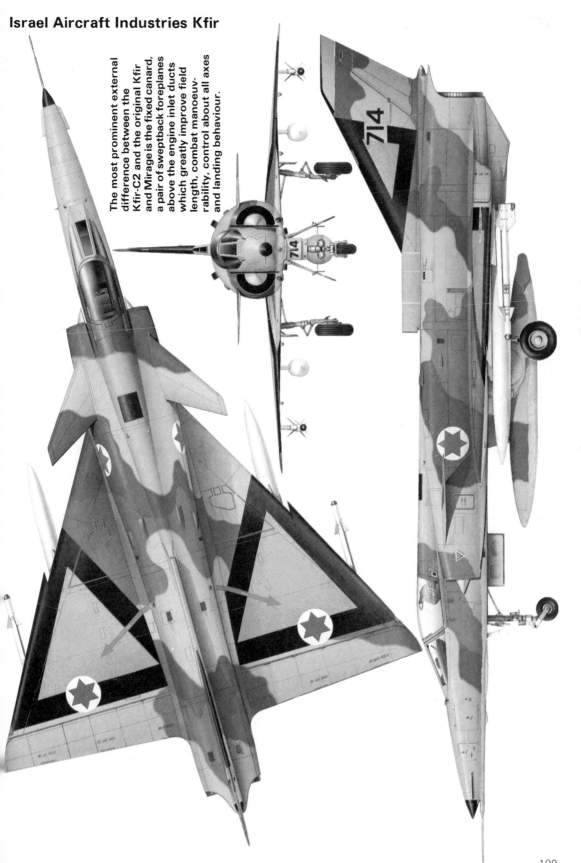

Kamov Ka-25 Hormone

History and notes

The Soviet naval air arm (AVMF) has for many years been a loyal customer of the design bureau named after Nikolai Kamov. Like the similarly named Kaman concern in the United States, the Kamov bureau has been associated with compact helicopters of close-coupled twin-rotor layout, but whereas Kaman developed the Flettner intermeshing rotor concept, the Soviet team chose the co-axial layout, originally applied to the experimental pre-World War II Breguet-Dorand. With no need for a long tail boom to counter torque, the fuselage of the co-axial helicopter can be made small and compact. This renders it particularly suitable for shipboard use, and all the helicopters operated by the AVMF from ships have been Kamov co-axial types.

The Ka-8 and Ka-10 'flying motorcycle' designs of 1945-55 aroused naval interest in the potential of shipboard helicopters for over-the-horizon target spotting; this 'airborne crow's nest' concept had been explored by the German navy in World War II. The Ka-15 cabin helicopter and the improved Ka-18 were ordered for AVMF service, but appear to have been used only on a small scale for experimental shipboard operations.

The Soviet Union's definitive shipboard helicopter, however, made its public debut in 1961, at the Tushino air display. More than four times as heavy as the Ka-15, the new helicopter was powered by twin turbines, six times as powerful as the piston engine of the older type, with scarcely any increase in weight and volume. As with land-based helicopters, the availability of the turboshaft engine vastly increased what could be achieved.

Details of the Ka-25 design probably reflect lessons learned in trials with smaller helicopters. The twin-engine layout presumably confers a degree of security in the event of an engine failure, although the type does not seem over-endowed with power unless the engines can be run at a contingency rating higher than the figure quoted for the Ka-25K civil derivative. Both engines, however, have their own independent fuel supplies, a feature not always found on Soviet land-based helicopters; the type is fitted with autostabilization, powered controls, comprehensive communications and full all-weather navigation equipment. Most Ka-25s are fitted with emergency flotation 'boots' on each of the four landing gear legs, which inflate automatically in the event of a ditching.

The 'missile-armed' prototype seen in 1961 was codenamed 'Harp' by NATO, but for some reason best known to NATO the very similar production version was christened 'Hormone'. The first version of the Ka-25 to see service appears to have been the 'Hormone-B' fitted with a large chin radome broader than that of the 'Harp' prototype. The 'Hormone-B' is deployed on 'Kresta I' class cruisers and 'Kiev' class aircraft-carriers, and appears to be associated with long-range surface-to-surface cruise missiles

such as the SS-N-3 'Shaddock' (on the cruisers) and the SS-N-12 fitted to the 'Kiev' class. (The lead ship of the latter class, *Kiev*, made her maiden voyage in 1976, followed by *Minsk* in 1979.) The 'Hormone-B' seems to be a modern extension of the 'flying crow's nest' principle, using its radar to provide guidance and targeting information for the long-range missiles. The 'Kresta I' class appeared in 1967, marking the first shipboard deployment of the Ka-25. It would be logical for the 'Hormone-B' to lack some of the ASW equipment of the 'Hormone-A', in order to increase its range and ceiling and hence the area over which it can offer missile guidance.

The 'Hormone-A', the basic ASW variant, appeared shortly after the 'Hormone-B' on the helicopter-carriers *Moskva* and *Leningrad*, and on the new 'Kresta II' and 'Kara' cruiser classes. It also equips the 'Kanin' class destroyers. It forms the bulk of the helicopter complement of the 'Kuril' class carriers, which also carry a number of 'Hormone-B' radar pickets.

Little is known about the operational equipment of the 'Hormone-A', and equipment standards appear to vary; some aircraft are fitted with a box-like container on the fuselage side, while others have been seen with nose aerials possibly connected with ESM (electronic surveillance measures). As well as radar, the 'Hormone-A' almost certainly carries dunking sonar equipment in the cabin, and is likely to be fitted with a magnetic anomaly detector (MAD) in a towed 'bird'. The radome is smaller than that of the 'Hormone-B' and the radar is presumably less powerful. There may be an internal weapons bay, but usually the 'Hormone-A' crew would leave the 'kill' to the SS-N-14 ASW missiles of the mother ship.

A new naval helicopter is expected to appear shortly, but there would seem to be no need in the immediate future for a Ka-25 replacement.

Specification

Type: multi-role shipboard helicopter
Powerplant: two 900-shp (671-kW) Glushenkov GTD-3 turboshafts
Performance: maximum speed 135 mph (220 km/h); cruising speed 120 mph (200 km/h); hovering ceiling 2,000 ft (600 m); service ceiling 16,500 ft (5000 m); maximum endurance 4 to 5 hours; range with external fuel 400 miles (650 km)
Weights: empty about 10,500 lb (4750 kg); normal maximum 15,500 lb (7100 kg); overload 16,500 lb (7500 kg)
Dimensions: rotor diameter 51 ft 8 in (15.75 m); fuselage length about 34 ft (10.35 m); height 17 ft 8 in (5.4 m); rotor disc area 4,193 sq ft (389.7 m^2)
Armament: two homing torpedoes or depth charges in internal weapons bay
Operator: India, Jugoslavia, Syria, USSR

Kamov Ka-25 Hormone

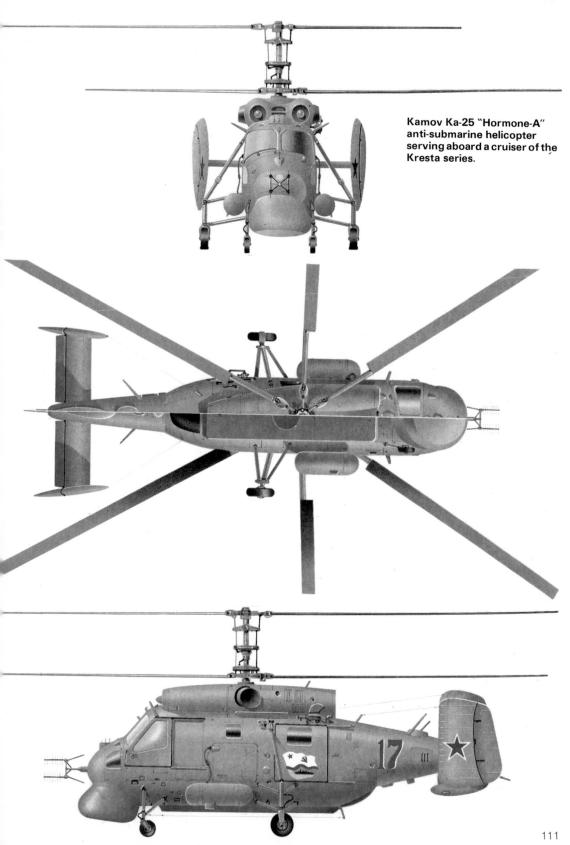

Kamov Ka-25 "Hormone-A"
anti-submarine helicopter
serving aboard a cruiser of the
Kresta series.

Kaman H-2 Seasprite

History and notes

In 1956 the US Navy initiated a design competition to procure a high-speed all-weather utility helicopter. Kaman's design proved sufficiently attractive to be selected as the winner later in 1956, and on 29 November 1957, the company received a contract for four prototypes plus an initial batch of 12 production aircraft. The service designation was HU2K-1 (changed in 1962 to UH-2A) and the name Seasprite. The prototype flew for the first time on 2 July 1959, but it was rather more than three years later that the first UH-2A production aircraft entered service with the US Navy's Helicopter Utility Squadron 2 (HU-2) at Lakehurst NAS, on 18 December 1962.

Initial production version was the UH-2A, powered by a single 1,250-shp (932-kW) General Electric T58-GE-8B turboshaft, and these aircraft first went to sea aboard USS *Independence* on 4 June 1963. They were followed into service by the UH-2B with reduced navigation avionics, and the first detachment of these went to sea with USS *Albany* on 8 August 1963. Service deployment under active conditions highlighted the desirability of providing increased engine power, and in March 1965 Kaman completed the first of two twin-engine conversions for evaluation. These had two T58-GE-8B turboshafts mounted in pods on each side of the rotor pylon, providing improved performance, plus the added reliability of a twin-engine installation. The success of this conversion meant that all surviving UH-2A and UH-2B aircraft were converted from 1967 onwards, and at the same time tail surface areas were increased slightly, and minor modifications made to the rotor pylon and cockpit. The resulting aircraft was designated UH-2C.

Next version to enter service was the HH-2C, an armed and armoured variant of the UH-2C, having a chin-mounted 7.62-mm (0.3-in) Minigun turret, waist-mounted machine-guns, extensive armour, and changes such as uprated transmission and dual wheels on the main landing gear to cater for the higher gross weight. They were followed by HH-2Ds with armament and armour deleted.

Increasing concern with the problem of nuclear submarines caused the US Navy to think hard and long about ways and means of coping with this

Kaman's SH-2F Seasprite is a vastly more capable helicopter than the original single-engined Seasprites, with radar, sonics, MAD bird and torpedoes.

menace, and in 1971 two HH-2Ds were modified to carry an experimental under-nose radar system. Two more were modified subsequently, and the results of their testing were incorporated into the US Navy's important Light Airborne Multi-Purpose System (LAMPS) programme.

While these HH-2Ds were being modified, Kaman was testing two other Seasprites with even more advanced avionics, and deliveries of this SH-2F version began in May 1973, with initial deployment on board USS *Bagley*. SH-2Ds and HH-2Ds have since been uprated to this SH-2F configuration.

Specification

Type: naval ASW, anti-ship missile defence, search and rescue and utility helicopter
Powerplant: (SH-2F) two 1,350-shp (1007-kW) General Electric T58-GE-8F turboshafts
Performance: (SH-2F) maximum speed at sea level 165 mph (266 km/h); cruising speed 150 mph (241 km/h); range with maximum fuel 422 miles (679 km)
Weights: (SH-2F) empty 7,040 lb (3193 kg); take-off 12,800 lb (5806 kg)
Dimensions: (SH-2F) main rotor diameter 44 ft 0 in (13.41 m); tail rotor diameter 8 ft 2 in (2.49 m); length (rotors turning) 52 ft 7 in (16.03 m); height (rotors turning) 15 ft 6 in (4.72 m); main rotor disc area 1,520.5 sq ft (141.25 m²)
Armament: can include air-to-surface missiles, homing torpedoes, guns and rockets
Operators: US Navy

Kaman SH-2F Seasprite

Kiang A-5 Fantan

Kiang 5 tactical strike fighters of the Air Force of the People's Liberation Army serve both in overall natural metal finish.

Changes transforming the MiG-19S into the Kiang 5 tactical strike fighter are the new forward fuselage with sharply pointed conical nose, forward-positioned cockpit and lateral air intakes, internal ordnance bay, taller vertical tail surfaces and paired ventral strakes.

History and notes

Unlicensed Communist Chinese production of the Mikoyan-Gurevich MiG-19 fighter began in 1961 and has continued up into the 1980s, with numerous improvements incorporated to keep the type up to date. Using the same basic design philosophy and technology, the Chinese have also developed an attack derivative, the Kiang A-5. Although the existence of this aircraft type has been known for some time, its proper designation has only recently been revealed: poor intelligence and research had earlier resulted in the inappropriate designation F-9 'Fantan'.

Development of the A-5 began in the 1960s with a requirement for a low-level interdictor based on the F-6. Although the F-6 has twin engines fed from a single intake, the location of the engines well to the rear meant that the central fuselage could be turned into a small but adequate bomb-bay if the nose intake were replaced by a pair of lateral intakes. This resulted in the A-5's main external difference to the F-6. Large-area intakes were decided upon, and the final design adopted (intakes of high aspect ratio leading into long ducts) allowed much of the original fuselage and all of the wing structure to be retained unaltered. To what was basically the fuselage of the MiG-19 was grafted, therefore, a new front section with a conical nose leading into a flattened oval section by the intakes.

A number of other detail improvements have been made (the relocation of the nosewheel gear relative to the cockpit to increase usable fuselage volume, modification of the flaps, revision of the dorsal spine to increase speed, alteration of the cockpit canopy, increase in the height of the vertical tail surfaces, and improvements to the underwing hardpoints). Prototype testing of the A-5 probably began in the early 1970s, and the type is now in regular service with the Chinese air force. A-5s were used opera-

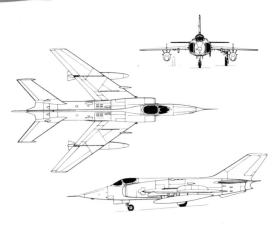

Kiang-5

tionally in the Sino-Vietnamese border conflict of 1979.

Specification

Type: single-seat tactical fighter-bomber/interdiction aircraft

Powerplant: two 7,165-lb (3250-kg) WP-6A afterburning turbojets (improved copies of the Tumansky RD-9B)

Performance: (estimated) maximum speed Mach 1.35 at 32,800 ft (10000 m) and Mach 0.95 at sea level; radius of action (hi-lo-hi) 404 miles (650 km); initial climb rate 20,000 ft (6100 m) per minute

Weights: empty about 13,100 lb (5940 kg); maximum not known

Dimensions: not known

Armament: two 30-mm cannon plus four 551-lb (250-kg) bombs and rocket pods

Operator: China

Lockheed C-5 Galaxy

One of the 76 Lockheed C-5A Galaxy long-range transports in service with Military Airlift Command, USAF.

History and notes

In 1963 the USAF's Military Air Transport Service (MATS), since redesignated Military Airlift Command (MAC), began to investigate the procurement of a very large strategic transport which would not only supplement the Lockheed C-141s in service, but would also have the capability of operating from the same airfields.

Requests for Proposals were issued in May 1964, and Boeing, Douglas and Lockheed were subsequently awarded contracts for development of their designs. At about the same time, General Electric and Pratt & Whitney were given contracts for the design and construction of prototype powerplants suitable for use by this large aircraft, which by then was expected to have a maximum take-off weight of around 700,000 lb (317515 kg). In August 1965, General Electric's GE1/6 turbofan engine prototype was selected for development: in its final form, this engine was designated TF39-GE-1. Two months later, Lockheed was named prime contractor for the airframe, and construction of the prototype began in August 1966, by which time the aircraft had been designated C-5A and named Galaxy. Major structural design, including the wing, was handled by a special company formed by 'brain drain' designers in Britain. This aircraft flew for the first time on 30 June 1968, and it and seven other examples were assigned to a test programme which extended into mid-1971. The ninth aircraft off the line, the first production/operational example, was delivered to MAC on 17 December 1969. Successful testing resulted in contracts for a total of 81 C-5As to equip four squadrons, and the last of these were delivered in May 1973. The original intention had been to acquire 115 of these aircraft to equip six squadrons, but cost escalation resulted in procurement of the reduced number.

Operational deployment of the Galaxy started in 1970, when the first of these aircraft began to supplement the airlift capability then provided by Lockheed C-141A StarLifter transports. It was discovered very quickly that they were a valuable addition to MAC's air fleet, operating reliably on supply missions from the United States to Europe and south-east Asia. In this latter area C-5As made their first deliveries to South Vietnam in August 1971, and in the months which followed, and particularly in the spring of 1972, made a major contribution to MAC's capability in south-east Asia. By comparison with the C-141A StarLifter which was then, and still is, an important component of the strategic airlift

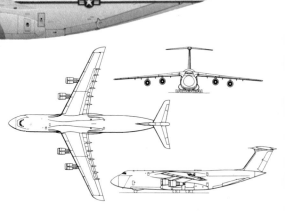

Lockheed C-5A Galaxy

fleet, the Galaxy can lift a payload which is more than twice as heavy. More importantly, its lower deck has an unobstructed length of 121 ft 1 in (36.91 m) and width of 19ft 0 in (5.79 m), which gives this aircraft the ability to carry practically any piece of the US Army's equipment, including self-propelled howitzers, personnel carriers, and tanks, none of which can enter the constricted hold of the C-141. Typical of outsize loads which have been carried over transoceanic ranges are two M48 tanks, with a combined weight of 198,000 lb (89811 kg), and three Boeing Vertol CH-47 Chinook transport helicopters.

Despite the fact that, at the time of their introduction into service, the USAF had to cope with what were dimensionally the largest in-use aircraft in the world, they encountered few problems in handling the C-5A on a worldwide basis. In-flight refuelling capability makes possible their deployment with the heaviest of loads over whatever range is necessary.

Specification

Type: heavy logistics transport aircraft
Powerplant: four 41,000-lb (18597-kg) thrust General Electric TF39-GE-1 turbofans
Performance: maximum speed at 25,000 ft (7620 m) 571 mph (919 km/h); average cruising speed 518 mph (834 km/h); range with design payload 3,749 miles (6033 km); range with 112,600-lb (51075-kg) payload 6,529 miles (10507 km)
Weights: basic operating 337,937 lb (153286 kg); design payload 220,967 lb (100229 kg); maximum take-off 769,000 lb (348813 kg)
Dimensions: span 222 ft 8½ in (67.88 m); length 247 ft 10 in (75.54 m); height 65 ft 1½ in (19.85 m); wing area 6,200 sq ft (576.00 m²)
Armament: none
Operator: US Air Force

Lockheed C-130 Hercules

Lockheed C-130B Hercules of 28 Sqn, South African Air Force, based at Waterkloof.

One of two Lockheed C-130B Hercules delivered to 3 Sqn, Royal Jordanian Air Force, from USAF stocks. They are based at King Abdullah Air Base, Amman.

History and notes

Surely one of the most ubiquitous of all post-World War II aircraft, Lockheed's Model 382 was certainly well named, for it has proved itself able to perform far more and diverse labours than the 12 attributed to the Greek hero Heracles, known to the Romans as Hercules. Furthermore, it is another of the small number of types which, in 1980, will have been in production for one-third of the entire period of powered flight.

Its origin came in 1951 when the USAF made the decision to acquire a fleet of turboprop transports for use by the Military Air Transport Service (MATS), later the Military Aircraft Command (MAC), and by Tactical Air Command (TAC). This policy set in motion the design of three aircraft, designated C-130, C-132 and C-133. The second was a heavy logistic transport to be built by Douglas, but this was cancelled. This company did, however, build the C-133 Cargomaster, a heavy strategic freighter which served with MATS/MAC.

The tactical transport was originally known to USAF planners as the Logistic Carrier Supporting System SS-400L. The initial contract for two prototypes, placed on 11 July 1951, used the designation YC-130. Just over three years later, on 23 August 1954, the first of these made its first flight, and these two aircraft, like early series C-130As, were powered by four 3,750-shp (2796-kW) Allison T56-A-1A turboprop engines. The C-130, popularly called the 'Herky-Bird', was designed by Lockheed-California, but all production has been handled by Lockheed-Georgia. The first production contract was awarded in September 1952, and the first production C-130A flew for the first time at Marietta, Georgia, on 7 April 1955. Initial production

deliveries went to TAC units in December 1956, these including the 463rd Troop Carrier Wing, and the 322nd Division USAFE.

The Hercules, as it became named, set a wholly new standard in tactical airlift. New features were pressurization, very good flight performance, and a full-section rear ramp-door. A high setting of the monoplane wing ensured that the cabin had minimal loss of capacity from the wing carry-through structure, and for the same reason, the main landing gear when retracted was enclosed in fairings built onto each side of the fuselage. Provision of weather radar altered the nose profile after only a few production aircraft had been constructed, and two other early modifications were carried out to increase fuel capacity and strengthen the floor and fuselage to cater for heavier loads. Access to the main cargo hold, 41 ft 5 in (12.62 m) in length, and with a maximum width of 10 ft 3 in (3.12 m), is via a hydraulically-operated loading ramp which, when closed, forms the undersurface of the rear fuselage. This represents the basic configuration of the C-130A, and a listing of the wide range of variants will trace the usage and purpose of a transport aircraft of which more than 1,600 examples have been built, and which was still in production in 1980.

Variants of the C-130A have included a single AC-130A gunship which was tested in Vietnam: armament included four 20-mm guns and four 7.62-mm (0.3-in) Miniguns. Two GC-130A (later DC-130A) aircraft were converted to carry up to four RPVs, and provided with electronics equipment to launch, control and monitor their flight. Eleven JC-130As were converted for the tracking of missiles and spacecraft, and additional fuel and oil capacity con-

Lockheed HC-130H Hercules air search, rescue and recovery aircraft; seven examples are in service with the US Coast Guard. These have a nose-mounted recovery system able to pick up from the ground persons, or objects weighing up to 500 lb (277 kg).

ferred an endurance of 12 to 13 hours; seven of these were reconverted as AC-130A gunships and deployed operationally in Vietnam in 1968–69. Seventeen RC-130As were equipped with TV viewfinder, cameras, mapping equipment, galley and five additional crew positions and delivered by the end of 1959 to MAC's 1,370th Photo Mapping Wing.

Next major version was the C-130B, the first of which entered service with the TAC on 12 June 1959. These had extra fuel capacity, strengthened landing gear, and 4,050-shp (3020-kW) Allison T56-A-7 turboprops driving four-blade propellers (standard on later versions). A total of 230 were built and, as well as being delivered to the USAF, were supplied also to the Indonesian, Pakistani, Canadian and South African air forces. Variants of the C-130B have included 12 HC-130B search and rescue aircraft for the US Coast Guard, these having extra accommodation for a radio operator, two search observers and 22–44 passengers. Six C-130Bs were equipped with air-snatch satellite recovery equipment for use in connection with the Discoverer programme, and supplied to the USAF's 6,593rd Test Squadron based at Hickam AFB, Hawaii, in mid-1961. NC-130B was the designation applied to a single aircraft converted for STOL research, this having two turbojet engines pod-mounted beneath the outer wing to provide large volumes of bleed air for BLC blowing. RC-130B was the designation for survey and reconnaissance versions, similar to the earlier RC-130A. Under the

designation WC-130B, 17 aircraft were converted for weather reconnaissance and research, and were distributed between the USAF's 53rd Squadron in Puerto Rico, the 54th Squadron on Guam, and the 55th Squadron in California. The designation C-130D applied to 12 wheel/ski-equipped version of the C-130A for operation in the Antarctic, or other ice/snowbound areas.

The C-130E was another major version, with increased fuel tankage to increase range, of which 503 examples were built. Derivatives included eight AC-130Es, an improved close-support gunship with extensive weapons and night sensors for service in Vietnam; DC-130E RPV launch and control aircraft, converted by Lockheed Aircraft Service Company (LASC); one special duty EC-130E for the US Coast Guard; three HC-130E SAR aircraft for the USAF. Two 'oddities', so far as alphabetical designation is concerned, are the C-130F, similar to the KC-130F assault transport with flight refuelling equipment to serve as a tanker, but without the refuelling equipment and underwing pylons: both versions were re-engined subsequently with 4,508-shp (3362-kW) Allison T56-A-15 turboprops.

Current production version is the C-130H, powered by T56-A-15 turboprops, of which well over 500 had been ordered and a lesser quantity delivered by early 1979. Variants include HC-130H long-range SAR aircraft with pick-up gear to lift persons or objects from the ground; JC-130H, four modified from HC-130H, for retrieval of space capsules on re-entry; DC-130H, one modified by LASC for RPV

All AC-130 "Herky gunships" were rebuilt from (mostly C-130E) transports. Camouflage was similar to that of the B-52D/F bombers, with sides green/brown or, as here, black. Although it had a relatively brief combat life the Lockheed AC-130 was probably the most effective truck killer of the entire war in SE Asia. This example served with a group of interdiction units in 1969-73.

Lockheed C-130 Hercules

Libyan Arab Republic Air Force Lockheed C-130H Hercules, one of eight received before a US arms embargo was enforced on the country.

USAF HC-130P Hercules operated by the Aerospace Rescue and Recovery Service for specialised SAR duties and capable of refuelling helicopters in flight.

One of three C-130H Hercules of 721 Sqn, Royal Danish Air Force, based at Vaerlose.

launch and recovery; KC-130H flight refuelling tankers; C-130K, designation of 66 aircraft for service with the RAF; HC-130N SAR aircraft for retrieval of space capsules; HC-130P helicopter refuelling tankers; EC-130Q command communication aircraft for the US Navy; KC-130R tankers for the US Marine Corps; and LC-130R wheel/ski landing gear transport for service with the US Navy in the Antarctic. Japan has ordered the PC-130H maritime patrol variant, while an Indonesian order is for the C-130H(S) with a fuselage stretch of 15 ft (4.57 m). Britain has 66 C-130 tactical transports, 30 of which are to be modified to Hercules C.3 standard by the insertion of two fuselage plugs to increase length by 15 ft (4.57 m).

In addition to the military versions of the Hercules, lengthened-fuselage but otherwise generally similar civil transports are manufactured under the designation L 100 series.

Specification

Type: military/civil medium/long-range transport
Powerplant: (C-130H) four 4,508-shp (3362-kW) Allison T56-A-15 turboprops

Performance: (C-130H) maximum cruising speed 386 mph (621 km/h); range with maximum payload, 5% reserve and allowances for 30 minutes at sea level 2,487 miles (4002 km); range with maximum fuel, reserve and allowances as above 5,135 miles (8264 km)
Weights: (C-130H) operating (empty) 75,331 lb (34170 kg); maximum normal take-off 155,000 lb (70307 kg); maximum overload take-off 175,000 lb (79379 kg)
Dimensions: span 132 ft 7 in (40.41 m); length (except HC-130H) 97 ft 9 in (29.79 m); height 38 ft 3 in (11.66 m); wing area 1,745 sq ft (162.11 m²)
Armament: (gunship versions) has included 20-mm and 40-mm guns, a 105-mm howitzer, and 7.62-mm (0.3-in) Miniguns
Operators: Argentina, Australia, Belgium, Bolivia, Brazil, Cameroon, Canada, Chile, Colombia, Denmark, Ecuador, Egypt, Gabon, Greece, Indonesia, Iran, Israel, Italy, Japan, Jordan, Libya, Malaysia, Morocco, New Zealand, Nigeria, Norway, Pakistan, Philippines, Portugal, Saudi Arabia, Singapore, South Africa, Spain, Sudan, Sweden, Turkey, UK, USA, Venezuela, Zaïre (C-130 models only)

Lockheed C-141 StarLifter

Lockheed C-141B StarLifter, prototype long-fuselage conversion of the standard C-141A, of Military Airlift Command, USAF.

History and notes

Victory in battle often goes to the contestant who gets there 'firstest with the mostest', and the Lockheed C-141 StarLifter transport was developed to enable the United States to deploy large quantities of troops and heavy equipment very quickly indeed.

The aircraft was designed to specification SOR-182 (Specific Operational Requirement 182) issued for a turbofan-powered freighter and troop carrier for operation by the US Military Airlift Command, and was selected in a competition in which Boeing, Douglas and General Dynamics were contenders. The transport is the flying element of the US Logistics Support System 476L, the purpose of which is to provide global-range airlift for the MAC, and strategic deployment capabilities at jet speeds for the US Strike Command, which includes the Strategic Army Corps and the Composite Air Strike Forces of Tactical Air Command.

Of conventional construction, the StarLifter is of swept-wing configuration, the wing being mounted high on top of the fuselage to minimise cabin obstruction. The four engines are mounted on pylons carrying them well below and forward of the wing leading edge. A distinctive feature is the tall T-tail.

The 70 ft 0 in (21.34 m) long cabin has a maximum width of 10 ft 3 in (3.12 m) and a maximum height of 9 ft 1 in (2.77 m), and can accommodate 154 troops or 123 fully-equipped paratroops, or 80 stretchers with seats for up to 16 walking wounded or attendants.

The StarLifter demonstrated its load-carrying potential when it established a world record for heavy cargo drops by delivering 70,195 lb (31840 kg). Several aircraft were modified to carry the Minuteman ICBM in its special transport container, a total weight of 86,207 lb (39103 kg).

The StarLifter began squadron operations with MAC in April 1965 and soon demonstrated its usefulness in war when it was used extensively to carry troops and supplies across the Pacific to Vietnam and carry wounded back to the USA. This and other operational experience indicated the need to provide the StarLifter with a flight-refuelling capability. It was frequently found, moreover, that when loaded with a bulky rather than weighty load, the aircraft had not reached its maximum weight; that is to say, it could have carried still more. Though nothing could be done to enlarge the cross-section of the StarLifter's fuselage, the latter could

Lockheed C-141B StarLifter

be lengthened.

Accordingly, in mid-1976 Lockheed was awarded a contract to develop an extended C-141 with in-flight refuelling equipment. Designated YC-141B, a converted aircraft first flew on 24 March 1977. The fuselage extension consists of a 13 ft 4 in (4.06 m) plug inserted in front of the wing and a similar 10 ft 0 in (3.05 m) plug immediately aft of the wing. At the same time refined wing-root fairings were fitted. These not only reduce drag, thus permitting high speed and reducing fuel consumption, but also change the lift distribution, permitting the carriage of increased loads without affecting the fatigue life of the wing.

The enlarged cabin can accommodate 13 standard pallets, instead of the previous 10. The US Air Force plans to convert all of its 271 operational StarLifters (out of 284 built) to the new configuration by 1982, in effect adding the equivalent of an extra 90 aircraft.

Specification

Type: (C-141B) long-range logistics jet transport
Powerplant: four 21,000-lb (9525-kg) Pratt & Whitney TF33-P-7 turbofans
Performance: maximum level speed at 25,000 ft (7620 m) over 570 mph (920 km/h); maximum cruising speed over 560 mph (900 km/h); range with maximum fuel about 5,000 miles (8500 km); range with maximum payload about 4,000 miles (6450 km)
Weights: operating weight 149,848 lb (67970 kg); maximum payload (2.25 g) 89,152 lb (40439 kg); or (2.5 g) 68,877 lb (31242 kg); maximum ramp weight 344,900 lb (156444 kg)
Dimensions: span 159 ft 11 in (48.74 m); length 168 ft 4 in (51.3 m); height 39 ft 3½ in (11.98 m); wing area 3,228 sq ft (299.9 m²)
Operator: USAF

Lockheed F-104 Starfighter

History and notes

Although by the early 1950s, just over a decade after the first jet aircraft had flown, NACA (the National Advisory Committee for Aeronautics, now known as NASA) had flown a series of experimental Mach1+ aeroplanes to push back the speed and altitude frontiers, the fastest US service fighter was the Mach 0.8 North American F-86 Sabre, and the first true transonic fighter, the North American F-100 Super Sabre, had not yet flown.

This was the situation facing C.L. 'Kelly' Johnson, chief engineer of Lockheed, when in 1952 he set out to produce a fighter superior to anything being flown by the Communists over Korea. It was to be as small as possible, reversing the trend towards ever heavier aircraft exemplified by the Republic XF-91, McDonnell XF-88 Voodoo, and Lockheed's own XF-90. Small size, he reasoned, would permit a maximum speed about twice the speed of sound and great manoeuvrability on the power of only one engine, so cutting down on size, cost and complexity.

At that time designers were limited by the relatively low power available from the early jet engines. The best at the time was the Wright J65, a licence-built version of Britain's Armstrong Siddeley Sapphire. But General Electric was just about to launch the J79, the engine that was to become one of the most widely used of all Western turbine powerplants.

With the promise of this engine to come, Johnson went ahead with his design. He chose Mach 2.2 as the flat-out level speed, and investigated some 300 different shapes to find one that would provide the best compromise between speed, range, manoeuvrability, and landing and take-off performance. Throughout 1953, as the bitter air war finally ended in the Korean skies, Johnson continued to interview pilots just back from combat, to find out what they wanted; meanwhile model after model went through the Lockheed wind tunnels.

Since the discovery in Germany that swept wings produced less drag than straight ones at speeds around Mach 1, virtually all designers had gone over to them. But later work by NACA showed that swept wings were actually 'draggier' at speeds around Mach 2, and so Johnson chose a tiny straight wing only 4 inches (10.16m) thick at the deepest part, and with so sharp a leading edge that it had to be covered with a protective sheet on the ground to prevent injury. The wing was heavily anhedralled to overcome the 'aileron' effect of the large rudder. To increase the lift producd by the tiny wing, high-pressure air from the engine was blown over the flaps when they were depressed for landing. The tailplane was set high on the fin in an effort to avoid pitchup, a serious aerodynamic characteristic that was known to affect jet fighters when pulling very tight turns. There was very little room for equipment, and no attempt was made to incorporate AI (Airborne Interception) radar. Most controversially,

Lockheed F-104S Starfighter

the pilot was given a downward-firing ejector seat on the grounds that a conventional upward-firing one might hit the tailplane.

On 4 March 1954 the XF-104 prototype made its first flight with simple inlets feeding a J65 engine. There were many problems to overcome, and some 50 production F104As with advanced inlets feeding a J79 engine were assigned to the test programme in addition to the prototypes and pre-production aeroplanes. Development in fact took four years to accomplish, twice the anticipated duration, and far longer than any other US fighter up to that time. Clearance for use by the squadrons was granted in January 1958, but accidents and continued difficulties were so prolific that the F-104A was grounded three months later. In July 1958 the type was again cleared to fly.

During 1958 F-104As of the USAF Air Defense Command (responsible for the defence of the continental United States) set up international speed and altitude records. But the US Air Force was losing interest in the lightweight fighter formula, despite the efforts of Lockheed to turn the F-104 into a workable combat aircraft, and in 1959 they were transferred to the Air National Guard, the part-time reserve organisation.

The F-104 progamme by now had assumed considerable momentum, however, and the USAF was obliged to accept the next model, the greatly improved F-104C (the F-104B had been a two-seat version of the F-104A). This time, however, they went to the Tactical Air Command, where they stayed till 1965.

The F-104 story might have ended there had it not been for the decision of a group of NATO countries led by West Germany to build under licence a totally redesigned version. While the European aircraft industry was slowly regaining strength, there was certainly not enough experience to build a fighter guaranteed to match anything the Russians could put up. In the largest international programme up to then Germany, Italy, Holland, Denmark, Norway, Canada and Japan investigated a dozen or so air-

Lockheed F-104 Starfighter

Spain's Ejercito del Aire operated 21 Lockheed F-104G Starfighters in the '60s, based at Torrejon.

Luftwaffe F-104G of Jagdgeschwader 71 "Richthofen".

Royal Canadian Air Force Canadair-built F-104G Starfighter of 441 Sqn, No 1 Fighter Wing based at Marville, France, 1965. The aircraft has a Vicom camera pod.

craft, and in February 1959 chose what had already become the most controversial of them, the F-104, for its new multimission attack fighter, to replace a variety of earlier types such as Gloster Meteors, Lockheed Shooting Stars, North American Sabres, and Republic Thunderstreaks. Lockheed's sales tactics in the matter were to be widely criticised over the next 20 years.

So the F-104G (G for Germany, with more than 700 aircraft) was launched, to keep production lines in many countries busy for the next seven years. The Super Starfighter was the most advanced fighter anywhere at the time of its introduction; apart from being the first Mach 2+ fighter outside the USA, Britain, Soviet Union and Sweden, it had a proper fire-control radar and the world's first miniature, high-accuracy inertial navigation system for squadron service.

But in the hands of its chief customer the F-104G was destined to become as controversial as the F-104A before it. The number of accidents, which might have been expected to decrease with increasing familiarity, began to rise alarmingly, to the extent that in 1965 one Super Starfighter was being lost every 10 days. Eventually, however, the Luftwaffe pilots grew in experience and the ground crews learned how to maintain its aircraft more efficiently, and loss rates have been reduced.

The most recent version of the F-104 family is the F-104S, an advanced interceptor for the Italian and Turkish air forces. This is basically the same as the -G model, but incorporates refinements developed over years of experience with the earlier models. But the main change was the substitution of a weapon system for air fighting rather than for ground attack. The main external differences were the addition of two wingtip-mounted Sparrow missiles (hence the 'S' in the designation), and appearance of a pair of additional strakes under the rear fuselage. It first flew in 1968, and the 245 aeroplanes built in Italy were the last Starfighters to be built.

Lockheed's last big effort to sell the F-104 took place in 1970, when it proposed a version for the IFA (International Fighter Aircraft) competition, subsequently won by Northrop with its F-5E, and again a few years later in the LWF (Light-Weight Fighter) programme. The latter produced the General Dynamics F-16, which is to become the F-104's successor.

Specification

Type: single-seat multimission fighter
Powerplant: one General Electric J79-GE-11A of 10,000-lb (4536-kg) thrust, increasing to 15,800 lb (7167 kg) with afterburning
Performance: maximum speed 1,300 mph (2092 km/h) at 40,000 ft (12192 m); radius of action 690 miles (1110 km); service ceiling 55,000 ft (16764 m)
Weights: empty 14,0821-lb (6388 kg); maximum 28,779 lb (13054 kg)
Dimensions: span 21 ft 11 in (6.68 m); length 54 ft 9 in (16.69 m) height 13 ft 6 in (4.15 m); wing area 196.1 sq ft (18.22 m²)
Armament: one 20-mm General Electric M61 six-barrel cannon, wingtip-mounted Sidewinder air-to-air missiles; various external stores to total weight of 4,000 lb (1814 kg)
Operators: (all F-104 versions) Belgium, Canada, Denmark, Greece, Italy, Japan, the Netherlands, Norway, Taiwan, Turkey, West Germany

Lockheed P-2 Neptune

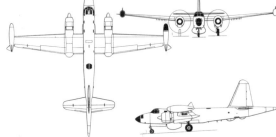

Kawasaki P-2J version of the Lockheed Neptune fitted with advanced ASW systems and powered by T64 turboprops.

History and notes

Originating from design studies made in the early years of World War II, Lockheed's land-based Neptune patrol aircraft was destined, from 1947 to 1962, to represent the foundation of the US Navy's land-based patrol squadrons. Strangely enough, the original design studies were made at a time when the US Navy had not envisaged that a land-based patrol aircraft would be included in its inventory of operational types.

The initial studies were made by Lockheed's Vega subsidiary in 1941, but at that time the impact of America's involvement in World War II concentrated most activities of the nation's aviation industry into the production of aircraft essential for the prosecution of the war in the Pacific, and support of the Allies in Europe and the Middle East. By 1944, however, there was an increasingly important requirement for a new land-based patrol bomber, and Lockheed dusted the cobwebs off its earlier designs and took a new look at the US Navy's requirement.

These, in fact, were basically similar to Lockheed's Model 26 design which had been formulated in 1941, and with but comparatively slight changes two prototypes and 15 production aircraft were ordered by the US Navy on 4 April 1944 under the designation P2V, the PV family having been the Ventura and Harpoon. The letter 'V' suffix denoted the Vega origin, despite the fact that Vega had lost its identity when absorbed into the Lockheed parent company in 1943. The first prototype XP2V-1 flew for the first time on 17 May 1945. It was seen to be fairly large aircraft, able to accommodate a crew of seven, and possessing a weapons bay which could carry two torpedoes or 12 depth charges, and armed with three pairs of 0.5-in (12.7-mm) machine-guns in nose, dorsal and tail positions. The powerplant comprised two 2,300-hp (1715-kW) Wright R-3350-8 Duplex Cyclone radial piston engines. The initial 15 production aircraft ordered were designated P2V-1, and though almost identical to the prototypes, had underwing mountings for up to 16 rockets. In September 1946 one of these aircraft, stripped of all unessential equipment and provided with tankage for 50,400 lb (22861 kg) of fuel, set a world distance record. this was the *Truculent Turtle*, which between 29 September and 1 October 1946 completed a non-stop flight of 11,235 miles (18081 km) from Perth, Western Australia, to Columbus, Ohio.

Lockheed P-2E Neptune

Second production version was the P2V-2 with more powerful R-3350-24W engines, six nose-mounted 20-mm cannon and, in later examples, 20-mm guns in dorsal and tail positions. The following P2V-3, which had only the dorsal and tail guns plus advanced ASW avionics, proliferated into the P2V-3C for carrier-launched nuclear-weapon delivery, P2V-3Z armoured transports, and P2V-3Ws with APS-20 search radar. The P-2D (formerly P2V-4) had improved electronics and APS-20 search radar. Extensively built as a result of war in Korea was the P-2E (formerly P2V-5) with many changes. The powerplant comprised two 3,250-hp (2424-kW) Wright R-3350-30W Turbo-Compound engines, and variants included: the P2V-5F with two 3,400-lb (1542-kg) thrust Westinghouse J34-WE-34 turbojets mounted beneath the wing to improve performance for take-off and maximum speed; the P2V-5FE with advanced avionics; the P2V-5FS with Jezebel passive underwater detection equipment; the P2V-5FD for drone (RPV) control; and the AP-2E for tactical land reconnaissance over Vietnam. The type was supplied also to the RAAF and RAF, and of those supplied to the latter most were transferred subsequently to Argentina (6), Brazil (14), and Portugal (12). P-2F (formerly P2V-6) designated a version of the P-2E with advanced avionics and minelaying capability, and when equipped with J34-WE-36 auxiliary turbojets this became the P-2G. MP-2Fs carried mines or Petrel AUM-N-2 air-to-surface missiles, and TP-2Fs were utilised in a training role. Final Lockheed production version was the P-2H (formerly P2V-7), first flown on 26 April 1954, of which many remain in service. This was the only Neptune to have underwing auxiliary turbojets as standard on all production aircraft, plus many of the

Lockheed P-2 Neptune

refinements introduced on P-2E and P-2F aircraft. SP-2H aircraft had Julie explosive echo-sounding and Jezebel acoustic search equipment, and LP-2Js were equipped for Arctic photo-reconnaissance. The USAF operated seven P2V-7Us in Vietnam as RB-69A ECM test and training aircraft, on loan from the US Navy, and also acquired a small number of AP-2H aircraft for special duties. Kawasaki in Japan built 48 P-2H ASW aircraft under licence, and has since developed a new ASW aircraft for the JMSDF under the designation P-2J, plus one UP-2J for target towing.

Specification

Type: naval patrol bomber and ASW aircraft
Powerplant: (P-2H) two 3,500-hp (2610-kW)
Wright R-3350-32W radial piston engines, plus two 3,400-lb (1542-kg) Westinghouse J34-WE-34 turbojets
Performance: (P-2H) maximum speed 403 mph (649 km/h) at 10,000 ft (3050 m); cruising speed 207 mph (333 km/h) at 8,500 ft (2950 m); ferry range 3,685 miles (5930 km)
Weights: (P-2H) empty 49,935 lb (22650 kg); maximum take-off 79,895 lb (36240 kg)
Dimensions: (P-2H) span 103 ft 10 in (31.65 m); length 91 ft 4 in (27.84 m); height 29 ft 4 in (8.94 m); wing area 1,000 sq ft (92.90 m²)
Armament: variations of 20-mm cannon, 0.5-in (12.7-mm) machine-guns, mines, torpedoes, depth charges, and air-to-surface missiles
Operators: Argentina, France, Japan, the Netherlands

Lockheed P-3 Orion

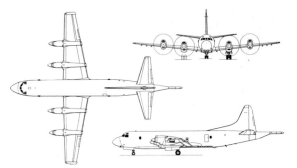

Iranian Air Force Lockheed P-3F Orion, one of six based at Bandar Abbas for maritime reconnaissance.

History and notes

In early December 1957 the prototype of a new four-turboprop civil transport was flown by Lockheed. This had the company designation L.188, and the first deliveries of L.188A production aircraft to US airlines began in the autumn of 1958. Named Electra, about 170 were built in L.188A and L.188C versions, and these were supplied mainly to US and South American airlines.

In August 1957 the US Navy called for design proposals to meet Type Specification 146. This concerned the supply of a new advanced aircraft for maritime patrol and ASW (Anti-Submarine Warfare), and in order to save cost and, more importantly, to permit service introduction as quickly as possible, the US Navy suggested that a variant of an aircraft that was already in production would receive favourable consideration if generally suitable. Thus, Lockheed proposed a developed version of the civil Electra as its submission for the USN competition, and in April 1958 the US Navy announced that this had been selected. The initial research and development contract was awarded on 8 May 1958, and Lockheed proceeded immediately to modify the third civil Electra airframe as an aerodynamic prototype for US Navy evaluation of flight characteristics. This had a mock-up of the MAD (Magnetic Anomaly Detection) boom as an extension of the rear fuselage and a simulated weapons-bay,

Lockheed P-3C Orion

and made its first flight on 19 August 1958. An operational prototype with full avionics flew for the first time on 25 November 1959, this having the designation YP3V-1, and the name of Orion was adopted for these aircraft in late 1960. The first production P3V-1 made its initial flight on 15 April 1961, and six aircraft were involved in flight testing, operational evaluation and acceptance trials before the first deliveries of production aircraft to USN Patrol Squadrons VP-8 and VP-44 began on 13 August 1962. By that time the P3V-1 had been redesignated as the P-3 Orion.

During more than 17 years of service there has been very considerable revision of the avionics

Lockheed P-3 Orion

US Navy Lockheed RP-3D version of the Orion employed for Project Magnet, the investigation of the Earth's magnetic field.

Royal Norwegian Air Force P-3B Orion, named "Fridtjof Nansen", operated by 333 Sqn at Andoya; five are in service.

equipment, as a result of changing threats and the inevitable progressive evolution of ASW equipment over this period. In other respects there have been few changes, except that the original 4,500-hp (3356 kW) Allison T56-A-10W turboprop was replaced by a more powerful version.

Orions are operated normally by a crew of 10, five of these being regarded as tactical specialists who work in a compartment within the main cabin which contains electronic, magnetic and sonic detection equipment. And because these aircraft have a patrol endurance of up to 10 hours, a large crew rest area with galley is provided in the main cabin.

The initial P-3A production aircraft are being replaced in USN squadron service progressively by new production P-3Cs. It is planned that P-3A/B aircraft released from active service will, as they become available, be used to modernise the US Navy's reserve forces, gradually replacing the Lockheed P-2 Neptunes which at present are used by the reserve.

For an aircraft which has given good service over a period of more than 17 years, it is inevitable that a number of versions and variants have evolved. The major production versions are the P-3A, -3B and -3C.

Current production version is the P-3C. This has the same power plant as the -3B, but has an advanced system of sensors and control equipment identified as A-NEW. Heart of the system is a digital computer which processes all ASW information, and this then becomes available for retrieval or display at any time. Under the Update and Update II programmes, P-3Cs have been given even more advanced systems. Update III was under development in 1978 and 1979 to provide new ASW avionics for installation in the early 1980s and service entry in 1984. Variants include two RP-3A special project reconnaissance aircraft, four WP-3As for weather reconnaissance, EP-3Bs for electronic reconnaissance, one RP-3D for a worldwide magnetic survey, two WP-3Ds to serve as airborne research

centres, 10 EP-3E electronic reconnaissance aircraft for service with VQ-1 and VQ-2 squadrons, and six P-3Fs as long-range surveillance aircraft for the Royal Iranian Air Force. During the period 1979-90, Japan is to assemble four and build under licence 41 P-3Cs for the Japanese Maritime Self-Defence Force. The Canadian Armed Forces' CP-140 Aurora, of which 18 have been ordered (the first flying in 1979), combines the airframe of the P-3C and an avionics fit derived from that of the Lockheed S-3A Viking. Provision for the Harpoon anti-ship missile is being made on all Update II Orions of the US Navy.

Specification

Type: ASW patrol/attack aircraft
Power Plant: (P-3B/C) four 4,910-ehp (3661-kW) Allison T56-A-14 turboprop engines
Performance: (P-3B/C) maximum speed at 15,000 ft (4750 m) at AUW of 105,000 lb (47627 kg) 473 mph (761 km/h); patrol speed at 1,500 ft (457 m) at above AUW 237 mph (381 km/h); mission radius 3 hr on station at 1,500 ft (457 m) at 1,550 miles (2494 km); maximum mission radius, no time on station, at maximum normal take-off weight, 2,384 miles (3836 km)
Weights: (P-3B/C) empty 61,491 lb (27892 kg); maximum normal take-off 135,000 lb (61235 kg); maximum permissible weight 142,000 lb (64410 kg)
Dimensions: span 99 ft 8 in (30.38 m); length 116 ft 10 in (35.61 m); height 33 ft 8½ in (10.27 m); wing area 1,300 sq ft (120.77 m²)
Armament: (weapons bay) one Mk-25/39/ 55/56 mine, or three Mk-36/52 mines, or three Mk-57 depth-bombs, or eight Mk-54 depth-bombs, or eight Mk-43/44/46 torpedoes; (underwing pylons) mines and rockets, torpedoes for ferrying, and a searchlight under the starboard wing. Maximum weapons load (P-3C) is 20,000 lb (9070 kg)
Operators: Australia, Canada, Iran, Japan, the Netherlands, New Zealand, Norway, Spain, and the US Navy

Lockheed SR-71

History and notes

Perhaps the most enigmatic aircraft in service, the delta-winged Lockheed SR-71 'Blackbirds' go about their clandestine business of keeping watch on the world's more serious trouble spots for the US Department of Defense and Central Intelligence Agency. Flying at altitudes of more than 80,000 ft (24384 m) they remain out of sight throughout their missions, showing up only as fast-moving traces on the radar screens of countries below, and perhaps occasionally revealing their presence as a sonic bang.

It is a reflection on their phenomenal performance that the many and continuing optical and electronic intelligence and surveillance tasks across the globe can be accomplished with so few aircraft flying so infrequently. The final and largest members of the 'Blackbird' family, so named for their midnight-blue thermally emissive finish, the SR-71As were built for the United States Air Force Strategic Air Command and are incorporated as a single squadron into the 9th Strategic Reconnaissance Wing based at Beale Air Force Base in California. The total number of aircraft has never been publicly disclosed, but is certainly more than 30 and has been augmented at lease once.

Two Pratt & Whitney J58 continuous bleed turbojet engines are at the heart of the highly complex propulsion system. It is rightly so-called; at low speed the efflux from the engines provides the force that drives the Blackbird through the sky, but as the speed increases the situation changes and at Mach 3 the engine produces only 18% of the thrust, the rest being generated at suction in the intakes (54%) and from the special ejector nozzles at the rear of the multiple-flow nacelles, (28%). The J58 burns special JP-7 fuel, supplied in flight by the purpose-equipped Boeing KC-135Q tankers at Beale.

The SR-71 went into service in 1966. Two other

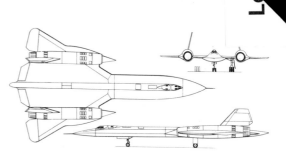

Lockheed SR-71A

versions, the SR-71B and SR-71C, are dual-control trainers with reduced performance because of the extra drag produced by the projecting second cockpit. While SR-71s have made headlines with their record-breaking performances, their professional careers have always been shrouded in secrecy. It is likely that they observed the Arab/Israeli wars of 1967 and 1973, the Greek/Turkish flare-up, various parts of the war in Vietnam, deliveries of arms to Cuba, and many other crisis spots. Their information is supplemented by data from reconnaissance satellites because even the SR-71A is vulnerable to the most recent missiles.

Specification

Type: two-seat reconnaissance aircraft
Powerplant: two 32,500-lb (14700-kg) Pratt & Whitney J58 afterburning bleed turbojets
Performance: maximum speed Mach 3 to 3.5 at 80,000 ft (24384 m); maximum sustained cruising speed Mach 3; range 2,590 miles (4168 km)
Weight: (estimated) maximum operational 140,000 – 170,000 lb (64000 – 77000 kg)
Dimensions: span 55 ft 7 in (16.94 m); length 107 ft 5 in (32.74 m); height 18 ft 6 in (5.64 m)
Armament: none
Operator: US Air Force

Fastest aircraft in the world (now the X-15s are grounded), the Lockheed SR-71 equips the 9th Strategic Reconnaissance Wing at Beale AFB, California. The wing has nominal strength of nine, but several times that number have been built, in several versions.

ockheed S-3 Viking

History and notes

The evolution of nuclear-powered submarines, able to remain submerged for long periods and to range across the world's oceans, posed an entirely new threat to defence planners of all nations. When it became possible to launch ballistic missiles, with nuclear warheads, from a submerged submarine, it seemed that the ultimate weapon had been created. Clearly, the submarine had become a major weapon, and the US Navy considered it essential that no effort should be spared to develop a new generation of carrier-based hunter-killer aircraft to replace their Grumman S-2 Trackers which were no longer able to detect the more sophisticated, quieter and deeper-diving submarines being put into service by the Soviet Union.

Consequently, in 1967 the US Navy initiated a design competition to which submissions were received in April 1968 from Convair, Grumman, McDonnell Douglas, North American Rockwell, and Lockheed-California collaborating with LTV Aerospace. Following evaluation by Naval Air Systems Command, General Dynamics and Lockheed were requested in August 1968 to provide further contract definition and to make additional refinement. When these final proposals were evaluated in early 1969, Naval Air Systems Command selected that submitted by Lockheed.

When the initial $461 million contract was awarded by the US Navy in August 1969, Lockheed announced that the new anti-submarine aircraft, already designated S-3A, would be developed in partnership with Vought Aeronautics Division of LTV Aerospace and Univac Federal Systems Division of Sperry Rand. Vought was to design and build the wings, tail unit, landing gear and engine pods; Univac was responsible for an advanced digital computer to provide the high-speed data processing which would be the key to the effectiveness of this new aircraft; and Lockheed was to build the fuselage, integrate the avionics system, and carry out final assembly and system integration.

The first prototype made its initial flight on 21 January 1972, and because of the urgency to put these aircraft into service additional funding was added to the initial contract to provide for eight research and development aircraft. Within little more than a year all eight were involved in the development programme, working to such effect that initial deliveries to the US Navy were made on 20 February 1974, the first aircraft going to Squadron VS-41. By that time the S-3A had acquired the name Viking, and when the US Navy ordered 13 production aircraft, on 4 May 1972, it had already been planned to equip 13 squadrons, each with 10 aircraft. Additional contracts placed since that date have covered the production of 187 aircraft in total, comprising the original eight R & D S-3As, plus 179 production aircraft, of which the last were delivered during 1978.

To carry out its ASW role, the Viking has a comprehensive range of the most advanced sonobuoys, and a MAD boom extendable from the rear fuselage. Non-acoustic sensors include the outstanding Texas Instruments APS-116 high-resolution radar, a forward-looking infra-red scanner in a retractable turret, and passive ECM in wingtip pods. Accurate navigation is ensured by an advanced inertial navigation system, augmented by doppler, Tacan and UHF/DF. HF and UHF communication systems are provided, and an ACLS (Automatic Carrier Landing System) is installed to facilitate all-weather operations. Heart of the ASW data processing is the Univac 1832A digital computer which receives inputs from all sensors, stores information for instant recall, and carries out weapon-trajectory calculations based on information from the sensors. It can also provide pre-flight navigation details.

In July 1975 Squadron VS-21, on board the USS *John F. Kennedy*, made the first operational deployment of the S-3A, and since that time all planned squadrons have been equipped with these aircraft.

S-3A squadrons are deployed on carriers of the US Navy Atlantic and Pacific fleets, with each deployment lasting approximately six months. In the event of a major conflict it is envisaged that each carrier directly engaged would be provided with two squadrons of Vikings (20 aircraft), the additional squadrons coming from carriers undergoing overhaul, or withdrawn from those unlikely to operate in areas of severe submarine threat.

Specification

Type: carrier-based ASW patrol/attack aircraft
Power Plant: two 9,275-lb (4207-kg) thrust General Electric TF34-GE-2 high by-pass ratio turbofan engines
Performance: maximum speed 518 mph (834 km/h); maximum cruising speed 426 mph (686 km/h); loiter speed 184 mph (296 km/h); combat range more than 2,300 miles (3700 km)
Weights: empty 26,650 lb (12088 kg); maximum design gross 52,539 lb (23831 kg); normal ASW mission take-off 42,500 lb (19278 kg)
Dimensions: span 68 ft 8 in (20.93 m); span (folded) 29 ft 6 in (8.99 m); length 53 ft 4 in (16.26 m); length (tail folded) 49 ft 5 in (15.06 m); height 22 ft 9 in (6.93 m); height (tail folded) 15 ft 3 in (4.65 m); wing area 598 sq ft (55.55 m^2)
Armament: (weapons bay) four Mk-36 destructors, or four Mk-46 torpedoes, or four Mk-82 bombs, or two Mk-57 or four Mk-54 depth-bombs, or four Mk-53 mines; (underwing pylons) SUU-44/A flare launchers, Mk-52, -55 or -56 mines, Mk-20-2 cluster bombs, LAU-68/A, -61/A, -69/A or -10A/A rocket pods, Mk-20 cluster bombs, Mk-76-5 or -106-4 practice bombs, or Aero 1D auxiliary fuel tanks
Operator: US Navy

Lockheed S-3 Viking

This Lockheed S-3A Viking is assigned to fixed-wing ASW squadron VS-21 (it is almost certainly the commander's aircraft), embarked aboard "JFK". It is carrying two 300-US gal external fuel tanks.

Lockheed U-2

History and notes

When it became vital for the West to know the extent of military developments in the Soviet Union, and the deployment of that country's armed forces, the USA initiated a major programme of aerial reconnaissance. Initially, specially adapted versions of aircraft such as the Convair B-36 and Boeing B-47 bombers were used. In time, however, the Mikoyan-Gurevich MiG-15 began to intercept these aircraft, and in December 1954 the US decided to produce a specialized reconnaissance aircraft.

The result was the Lockheed U-2, built virtually by hand in the Lockheed company's secret 'Skunk Works' in Burbank.

The U-2 had a remarkable high-flying and long-range performance as a result of powerplant and configuration. The former was a Pratt & Whitney engine with wide-chord compressor blades for flight at high altitudes, and specially adapted to run on low-volatility fuel. The configuration, employing a high aspect ratio, glider-like wing, enabled the range to be extended by shutting down the engine to flight-idle and gliding.

Despite payload restrictions, the aircraft bristled with data-gathering devices, including a long-focus camera, which scanned through seven apertures and could record on 4000 pairs of photographs an area some 125 miles (200 km) wide by 2,200 miles (3540 km) long, and an Elint receiver which monitored radio and radar transmissions from the ground.

In April 1960 a set of U-2 prints taken over the Soviet Union revealed what appeared to be the first Russian ICBM installation. Plans were made for another mission to be made and accordingly a U-2 was ferried to a base in Pakistan, ready for a long over-land flight of 2,900 miles (4700 km) over the Soviet Union, which was to have ended in Norway. During the flight, however, the U-2, piloted by Gary Powers, was knocked into a spin by the explosion of a ground-to-air missile and crashed.

Some U-2s have been used for high-altitude weather reconnaissance and research. Designated

Lockheed U-2D

U-2D and having two seats, these are instrumented with equipment supplied by NASA and the Wright Air Development Center.

In the 1960s one of 19 new versions was the U-2CT dual conversion with a separate cockpit for the instructor. Another new version was designated U-2R. This had a lengthened fuselage and redesigned wing of increased span, able to hold more fuel. From the U-2R has been developed the TR-1. This is being produced openly as a high-altitude tactical surveillance and reconnaissance aircraft for the USAF Tactical Air Command, with funds allocated for the production of an initial batch of 25 aircraft.

Specification

Type: (TR-1) high-altitude reconnaissance aircraft
Powerplant: one 17,000-lb (7711-kg) Pratt & Whitney J75-P-13 turbojet
Performance: maximum speed at 40,000 ft (12200 m) 430 mph (692 km/h); cruising speed 460 mph (740 km/h); service ceiling over 70,000 ft (21335 m); range 3,000 miles (4830 km)
Weights: unknown
Dimensions: span 103 ft 0 in (31.39 m); length 63 ft 0 in (19.20 m)
Operators: NASA, US Air Force

This dark stranger is a Lockheed U-2R, much larger than other versions of the clandestine U-2 mystery ship and in this case operating in black out of Davis-Monthan AFB with no marking save tail-number 10333 in red.

Martin B-57 Night Intruder

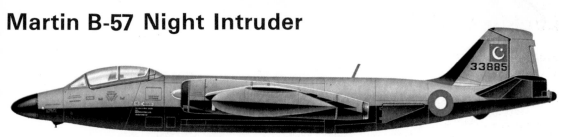

Pakistan Air Force Martin B-57B of 7 Sqn, based at Masroor and camouflaged for the night attack role.

History and notes

On 21 February, 1951, the third production English Electric Canberra B.2 flew to Baltimore, setting a transatlantic record and also becoming the first jet aircraft to complete an unrefuelled Atlantic crossing. The flight was historic in another way because The Martin Company was to undertake licence-production of the type for the USAF — the first foreign design built for US combat deployment since the end of World War I.

As the Martin Model 272, the initial US-built aircraft comprised a pre-production batch of eight to establish the line. They incorporated numerous engineering changes. The designation B-57A was given to this batch, fitted with Wright J65-W-1 (licence-built Armstrong Siddeley Sapphire) engines, and the first flew on 20 July 1953. These were followed by 67 externally similar RB-57As with

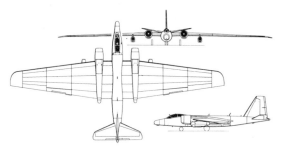

Martin RB-57F Night Intruder

cameras behind the bomb bay; the first of these went to Shaw AFB in early 1954. For the next three years the RB-57A served with the 363rd Tactical Reconnaissance Wing.

This grotesque WB-57F was developed from the British Canberra by Martin and General Dynamics for extreme-altitude reconnaissance.

The Martin B-57 in SE Asia did a tremendous job, often in close partnership with such diverse platforms as the O-2 slow-FAC Cessna and AC-130K night gunship. This example is being readied for a mission at Da Nang AB in May 1966. Attrition was low.

The first major change came with the next model, the B-57B night intruder, of which 202 were built — half of Martin's total of 403. The cockpit was changed to a tandem configuration. A rotary bomb bay was fitted (see specification) and the first B-57B flew on 28 June, 1954.

A transition trainer version, the B-57C, served alongside the B-57B in TAC service, and 38 were built following the first flight on 30 December, 1954.

One other variant with a similar airframe was the B-57E, flown in April 1956. This was a multi-role version, capable of use as a bomber, reconnaissance aircraft, trainer or target tug, for which purpose a detachable container was carried beneath the fuselage; 68 were produced, the last being completed in 1959.

The two final versions were so far removed from the original Canberra design that the ancestry was almost unrecognisable. First was the RB-57D, of which 20 were built for high-altitude work, six as two-seat reconnaissance aircraft (RB-57D2) and the remainder as single seaters, of which several were used for electronic reconnaissance missions under the designation RB-57D(C), having enlarged bulbous nose and tail radomes increasing the length by 2 ft 4 in (71.12 cm) and wingtip fairings which, together with a completely new wing, raised the span to 107 ft 6 in (32.76 m). The RB-57Ds served for several years with the TAC. Pacific Air Forces, MATS (MAC) for air sampling, and the Aerospace Defense Command calibrating the NORAD radar network.

If the long-span RB-57D looked odd, the RB-57F was grotesque. General Dynamics was given a USAF contract to convert 12 B-57Bs into reconnaissance platforms capable of operating at up to 100,000 ft (30480 m). A completely new wing of 122 ft 5 in (37.32 m) span and 2,000 sq ft (185.8 m²) was designed. A new vertical tail increased the height to 19 ft (5.79 m), and length became 69 ft (21.03 m). The RB-57F had two 18,000-lb (8165-kg) Pratt & Whitney TF33-P-11 turbofans supplemented by two underwing 3,300-lb (1500-kg) Pratt & Whitney J60-P-9 turbojets. The first RB-57F was delivered on 18 June 1964.

The war in South-East Asia gradually brought the B-57 out of retirement and into the forefront of the battle as a FAC, ground attack, night reconnaissance, multi-sensor reconnaissance and early warning platform. Unfortunately, the multi-sensor B-57G never got into production (as conversions), but surviving B-57Bs were rebuilt as EB-57s of three subtypes used chiefly by the Aerospace Defense Command as standard EW platforms for tasks such as threat-evaluation and simulation, fighter affiliation, and jamming tests on NORAD.

Specification

Type: originally reconnaissance bomber
Powerplant: (B-57B) two 7,200-lb (3265-kg) Wright J65-W-5 turbojets
Performance: (B-57B) maximum speed at 40,000 ft (12192 m) 582 mph (937 km/h); maximum speed at sea level 520 mph (837 km/h); rate of climb at sea level 3,500 ft (1066 m) per second; service ceiling 48,000 ft (14630 m); range 2,300 miles (3700 km) (RB-57D) maximum speed at 40,000 ft (12192 m) 632 mph (1017 km/h); service ceiling 60,000 ft (18288 m)
Weights: (B-57B) empty 26,000 lb (11793 kg); maximum loaded 55,000 lb (24948 kg)
Dimensions: (B-57B) span 64 ft (19.5 m); length 65 ft 6 in (19.9 m); height 15 ft 7 in (4.75 m); wing area 960 sq ft (89.18 m²) (RB-57D) span 106 ft (32.30 m); length 65 ft 6 in (19.9 m); height 14 ft 10 in (4.51 m)
Armament: (B-57B) eight 0.50-in (12.7-mm) Colt-Browning machine-guns or four 20-mm cannon in wings; underwing racks can accommodate mixed loads such as two 500-lb (227-kg) bombs and eight 5-in (12.7-cm) rockets, or napalm tanks; A rotary weapons bay in the fuselage has a capacity of up to 5,000 lb (2268 kg) of bombs or rockets, and these can be mounted on the bomb bay door as an internal load and rotated to provide an external load when approaching a target
Operators: Pakistan, US Air Force

Messerschmitt-Bölkow-Blohm BO105

The Netherlands Army Light Aircraft Group (Gp LV) operates a total of 30 MBB BO 105C light observation helicopters in 300 Sqn.

History and notes

Rigid non-articulated rotor, two engines, compact size — all these combine to make the Messerschmitt-Bölkow-Blohm BO105 a particularly impressive helicopter. It is fully aerobatic and highly manoeuvrable, but also comparatively expensive. Its safety and versatility have made the BO105 a successful civil helicopter, and a few military forces find the type equally suitable. It is assigned multiple roles and can operate in all weathers. Nap-of-the-earth flying is a speciality to which the BO105 is well suited, the rigid rotor allowing it to hug contours like a leech. A conventional helicopter can tolerate no negative-g, restricted as it is by a much more mobile rotor assembly, but the BO105 can be pushed down the other side of such obstacles as trees, having been pulled up over them conventionally. Armed with up to six HOT or TOW missiles, the BO105 is a formidable opponent to any tank. West Germany's army air corps, the *Heeresflieger*, is receiving 212 BO105Ps each armed with six HOT anti-tank missiles, and a further 227 BO105Ms have been procured to replace Aérospatiale Alouette IIs in the liaison and communications role.

The BO105 started life in 1962, the radical rotor system having been tested earlier on a ground rig. Government contracts covered this initial testing and also the construction of prototypes in 1964. Dipl Ing E. Weiland conceived the rotor, which in its developed, production form uses rigid, glass-fibre, folding blades. Sud Aviation (now part of Aérospatiale) was involved, and it was one of this company's helicopters, a Turboméca Astazou-powered Alouette II, which was used as a test bed for the initial trials. The first prototype BO105 was fitted with a conventional rotor assembly (from the Westland Scout) and a pair of Allison 250-C18 turboshafts but was destroyed following resonance during ground trials; the second aircraft, similarly powered, pioneered the rigid rotor on the BO105. MTU-München Turbo 6022 engines were tried on the third development aircraft, but production machines are now all powered by the Allison turboshaft. Customers previously had the option of two versions of this engine: the 317-shp (236-kW) C18, now out of production, or the 400-shp (298-kW) C20, now standard. The *Heeresflieger's* PAH-1s are powered by a pair of 405-shp (302-kW) T63-A-720 turboshafts. German land forces will have had some

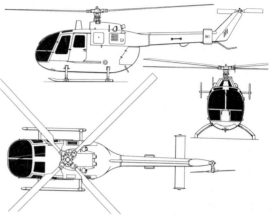

Messerschmitt—Bölkow—Blohm BO.105C

two years experience with the Euromissile (Aérospatiale/MBB) HOT when the PAH-1s enter service, as the German army's RJpz-2 tank destroyers have been converted to carry the new missile in place of Aérospatiale SS.11s.

Specification

Type: twin-engined, multi-role, all weather helicopter
Powerplant: two 400-shp (298-kW) Allison 250-C20 turboshafts; (PAH-1) two 405-shp (302-kW) Allison T63-A-720 turboshafts
Performance: maximum speed at sea level 167 mph (270 km/h); maximum cruising speed at sea level 144 mph (232 km/h); range with standard fuel and no reserves 363 miles (585 km) at sea level, 388 miles (625 km) at 5,000 ft (1525 m); maximum range with auxiliary tanks at sea level 621 miles (1000 km), at 5,000 ft (1525 m) 658 miles (1060 km); maximum rate of climb at sea level 1,870 ft (570 m) per minute; maximum rate of climb at sea level, on one engine 197 ft (60 m) per minute
Weights: empty equipped 2,645 lb (1200 kg); maximum take-off 5,070 lb (2300 kg)
Dimensions: rotor diameter 32 ft 2¾ in (9.82 m); length (rotors turning) 38 ft 10¾ in (11.84 m); height 9 ft 9½ in (2.98 m); main rotor disc area 811.2 sq ft (75.4 m²)
Armament: up to six Euromissile HOT or Hughes TOW anti-tank missiles with stabilized sight, plus various other options
Operators: Netherlands, Nigeria, Philippines, Sudan, West Germany

Donnell Douglas A-4 Skyhawk

History and notes

In 1950 the US Navy was busy preparing its specification for an advanced attack aircraft. Early experience in the Korean War, which started in mid-1950, had shown that such an aircraft was needed for deployment from aircraft-carriers, the mobile airfield/maintenance base that service planners then considered vital for global policing. The US Navy decided it needed a turboprop-powered aircraft, with a maximum weight of 30,000 lb (13607 kg), and capable of carrying a 2,000 lb (907 kg) bomb load.

When the Douglas Aircraft Company at El Segundo received a request for proposals the divisions's chief engineer, Ed Heinemann, had for some time been investigating the possibility of producing an advanced aeroplane which would be far less complex and much lighter in weight than the attack/fighter aircraft then in service. The US Navy's requirement provided a first opportunity to put these ideas into practice and it is unlikely that, in even his wildest dreams, he could have imagined in 1951 that his brain child would still be in production 28 years later.

In its original form the Skyhawk was a small single-seat aircraft of delta-wing configuration, although a number of two-seat variants have been produced subsequently. Like many classic designs it happened to be right first time, and the XA4D-1 prototype which first flew on 22 June 1954 is superficially almost identical to single-seat production aircraft which are still in service.

The engine selected to power the prototype was a 7,200 lb (3266 kg) thrust Wright J65-W-2 (a licence-built Armstrong Siddeley Sapphire), but the first production A4D-1s, subsequently A-4As, of which deliveries to Navy Squadron VA-62 began on 26 October 1956, were powered by the 7,700 lb (3493 kg) thrust Wright J65-W-4 or -4B.

Not surprisingly, for an aircraft with such a long production history, there have been many versions and variants. A brief mention of each of these will show the steady development of the type from the first production series to the A4-M/N Skyhawk IIs being built up to early 1979.

The A-4A was followed by the A-4B (A4D-2) which had an engine of the same power, a Wright J65-W-16A or -20. Major changes included provision for carrying Bullpup missiles; introduction of a navigation computer, flight refuelling capability, and dual hydraulic system. Examples of this version used for training purposes, in the absence of a special-purpose trainer, were given the designation TA-4B.

The A-4C (A4D-2N) had the fuselage nose extended to accommodate new equipment necessary to improve all-weather capability, including an advanced autopilot, terrain clearance radar, and a low-altitude bombing system. Deliveries of 638 aircraft for USN and USMC began in December 1959.

The next production version was the A-4E (A4D-5) with an 8,500 lb (3855 kg) thrust Pratt & Whitney J52-P-6A turbojet, and this engine was fitted retrospectively to A-4A, -4B and -4C aircraft in operational service. The A-4E introduced a zero-height/90 knot (104 mph/167 km/h) ejection seat, and new underfuselage/underwing pylons enabling this version to carry 8,200 lb (3719 kg) of weapons.

The A-4F attack bomber with the 9,300 lb (4218 kg) thrust Pratt & Whitney J52-P-8A turbojet, introduced lift spoilers to reduce landing run, nosewheel steering, a zero-zero ejection seat, improved protection against ground fire, and new avionics installed in a 'hump' fairing aft of the cockpit. Because of the hump, this and other recent versions are called 'Camels'; in S.E. Asia the A-4 served widely with the USN, USMC and USAF, and was popularly called the 'Scooter'.

It was followed by a TA-4F two-seat trainer (all two-seaters have one large canopy except for the TA-4S), TA-4J two-seat trainer, and the A-4M Skyhawk II in production in 1979. This latter version has a braking parachute as standard, and a number of detail improvements. Also in production is the A-4N, similar to the -4M, which is being built for Israel. A-4Gs and TA-4Gs for the Royal Australian Navy, and A-4Ks and TA-4Ks for the RNZAF, are both similar to the A-4F and TA-4F respectively. The A-4H and TA-4H have been supplied to Israel, A-4KU and TA-4KU to Kuwait, A-4P and A-4Q to the Argentine Air Force & Navy respectively. A-4S and TA-4S (two separate canopies) are designations for updated A-4Bs for the Singapore Air Defence Command, modified by Lockheed Aircraft Service Company. Remaining versions are the A-4L, a modified A-4C with uprated engine for the US Navy Reserve, and A-4Y, an updated A-4M, to which specification all -4Ms are to be modified. This has a new Head Up Display, redesigned landing gear, and Hughes Angle Rate Bombing system.

Specification

Type: single-seat attack bomber
Power Plant: (A-4M) one 11,200-lb (5080-kg) Pratt

McDonnell Douglas A-4 Skyhawk

A McDonnell Douglas A-4F Skyhawk of Navy attack squadron VA-212, formerly embarked aboard CVA-19 *Hancock*. This model introduced the dorsal "camel" hump for additional avionics.

McDonnell Douglas A-4 Skyhawk

& Whitney J52-P-408 turbojet
Performance: (A-4M) maximum speed with
4,000-lb (1814-kg) bombload, 646 mph (1040 km/h);
maximum ferry range 2,000 miles (3219 km)
Weights: (A-4M) empty 10,800 lb (4899 kg), take
off 24,500 lb (11113 kg)
Dimensions: (A-4M) span 27 ft 6 in (8.38 m);
length 40 ft 4 in (12.29 m); height 15 ft 0 in
(4.57 m); wing area 260 sq ft (24.15 m²)
Armament: (A-4M) underfuselage hardpoint with a
capacity of 3,500 lb (1588 kg); two inboard

underwing hardpoints each with a capacity of
2,250 lb (1021 kg); two outboard underwing
hardpoints each with a capacity of 1,000 lb
(454 kg) Extensive range of weapons can be
carried, including conventional or nuclear bombs,
air-to-air and air-to-ground rockets, missiles and
gunpods. Two 20-mm guns in wing roots are
standard (Israeli have 30-mm)
Operators: Argentina, Australia, Indonesia, Israel,
Kuwait, Malaysia, New Zealand, Singapore, US
Marine Corps and US Navy

McDonnell Douglas AV-8B Advanced Harrier

History and notes
Strong interest in the British Aerospace Harrier by
the US Marine Corps resulted in an initial order for
12 examples in 1969, under the designation AV-8A,
and these were equipped to carry AIM-9 Sidewinder
missiles. Subsequent orders brought the total for
USMC use to 102, of which eight were two-seat
trainers designated TAV-8A, and all had been
delivered by 1977. They were used to equip three
USMC squadrons (VMA 231, VMA 513 and VMA
542) at Cherry Point, North Carolina.

Deployment by the US Marine Corps of the AV-8A
Harrier jet V/STOL concept was operationally attractive. They needed, however, an aircraft with this
capability that had virtually double the weapons
payload/combat radius of the AV-8A, and the Corps
was encouraged in this belief by McDonnell Douglas,
the type's US foster-parent. In late 1973 the British
and US governments started to consider joint
development of an AV-16A 'Advanced Harrier', but
by early 1975 the British government had decided
that there was 'not enough common ground' to take
part in a joint programme. Instead, the USMC and
McDonnell Douglas initiated a programme to convert two AV-8As as prototype YAV-8Bs, AV-8B
being the designation allocated to the new US
development.

These prototypes differ from the British-built AV-
8A by the introduction of a supercritical wing of
graphite/epoxy construction, a lift-improvement
device to contain the engine exhaust air as it re-
bounds from the ground, increased-area trailing-
edge flaps, drooped ailerons, redesigned engine air
intakes, strengthened landing gear, and completely
different subsystems and equipment. The first of
these prototypes made its first flight at the McDonnell plant at St Louis, Missouri on 9 November 1978,
and the second first flew in early 1979.

At that time it was anticipated that, subject to
satisfactory flight testing, the USMC would initiate
production of the first batch of a stated requirement
for 350 aircraft, and a similar quantity was a possible requirement of the US Navy. Despite the operational need, the AV-8B has been politically handicap-

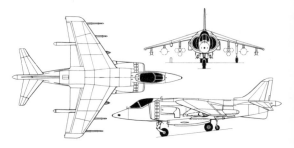

McDonnell Douglas AV-8B Advanced Harrier

ped by being 'foreign' and the Carter administration
hoped to terminate the programme by eliminating it
from the FY80 Defense Budget. The US Marines
hoped in early 1980 to get this decision reversed.

Specification
Type: V/STOL strike aircraft
Powerplant: one 21,500-lb (9752-kg) thrust Rolls-
Royce Pegasus Mk 803 (F402-RR-402) vectored-
thrust turbofan
Performance: (estimated) operational radius (VTO)
with 3,000-lb (1361-kg) external load 57 miles (92
km); operational radius (STO) with same external
load 414 miles (666 km); ferry range over 2,000
miles (3220 km)
Weights: basic operating empty 12,470 lb (5656
kg); maximum take-off (VTO) 18,850 lb (8550 kg);
maximum take-off (STO) 29,750 lb (13495 kg)
Dimensions: span 30 ft 4 in (9.25 m); length 46 ft
4 in (14.12 m); height 11 ft 7¾ in (3.55 m); wing
area 230 sq ft (21.37 m²)
Armament: twin underfuselage gun/ammunition
packs each mounting a US 20-mm cannon or
30-mm Aden gun; three underfuselage and six
underwing hardpoints with combined capacity of
9,200 lb (4173 kg): weapons carried can include
MK-82 Snakeye bombs and laser or electro-optical
guided weapons, and AIM-9L Sidewinders for air-
to-air use
Operator: (1979) US Marine Corps prototypes only

McDonnell Douglas F-4 Phantom II/RF-4

F-4E at the time of the Israeli Holy Day war in 1973 when the type undertook
long-range strike missions as well as air superiority tasks.

McDonnell Douglas RF-4B Phantom of the US Marine Corps
Reconnaissance Squadron VMCJ-2.

Luftwaffe RF-4E (97448) of Aufklarungsgeschwader 51 "Immelmann"
at Bremgarten.

History and notes

Even before the 5,000th McDonnell Douglas F-4
Phantom II was delivered in mid-1978, the aircraft
had a production history which far outstripped that
of any other recent combat jet aircraft in the
Western world. Only the Mikoyan-Gurevich MiG-21
can challenge its astonishingly large production
total. The Phantom's success, originally attributable
to its excellent fighter and strike aircraft qualities,
was boosted by the demand for the type during the
Vietnam war. During 1967 the production rate at
McDonnell Douglas's St Louis factory peaked at 72
aircraft per month. The Phantom has been used as a
front-line aircraft by 12 nations — and remains in
service with 11 countries.

In 1953 McDonnell failed to win the contract for
the first US Navy supersonic shipborne fighter. A
new design was started in-house in the same year,
tailored to a specification which the company
evolved from its contacts with leading naval personnel. After seeing a mock-up the US Bureau of
Aeronautics (BuAer) ordered McDonnell to build
two prototype F3H-Gs. After four months' work, in
April 1954, the design was drastically revised to provide more internal fuel capacity, a two-seat cockpit
and more comprehensive fire-control equipment.
The strike/fighter which emerged from this revision
was called the F-4 Phantom II (the Roman numeral
initially distinguishing it from McDonnell's first jet
fighter with the same name). The first flight took
place on 27 May 1958 and the F-4 soon proved that it
could live up to its claims. It could operate over a
290-mile (467-km) radius of action, loiter for up to

two hours, and was the first aircraft which could
detect, intercept and destroy any target which came
within radar range.

The US Navy ordered only 375 aircraft initially,
but it was evident from its earliest days that the
Phantom was a good basic airframe for a wide variety of roles. The first 24 production aircraft eventually entered service as F-4A Phantoms, and were
followed into US Navy and Marine Corps service by
the F-4B. This version had raised cockpits, higher-
thrust J79 engines, a larger radar and several structural modifications. F-4B production eventually
totalled 649 aircraft, plus 46 RF-4B reconnaissance
versions for the US Marine Corps.

The US Air Force, which traditionally did not
order US Navy aircraft, ordered the first of 583
minimum-change F-4Cs in July 1963, and later added 505 examples of the RF-4C tactical reconnaissance version. With a more powerful radar the
aircraft became the F-4D, and no fewer than 825 examples of this type were built. Most of these were
delivered to the US Air Force between 1965 – 68,
although 32 examples went to Iran and 36 to Korea.
Of the original F-4Cs, 36 were later sold to Spain.

Even more were to come. It was the F-4E Phantom which eventually became the most numerous
version. This has more powerful engines, extra rear-
fuselage fuel, APQ-120 solid-state radar and, in all
but the first production blocks, a 20-mm M61 cannon
under the nose. The first F-4E flew on 7 August
1965 and production deliveries began in 1967. About
1,477 examples were built, 949 for the US Air Force,

McDonnell Douglas F-4 Phantom II/RF-4

RAF Phantom FGR.2 (XT901) in the markings of 17 Sqn before it converted to Jaguars.

F-4D Phantom of the 306th Fighter Squadron, Imperial Iranian Air Force.

and the rest for export. A large leading-edge slat on all late-model F-4Es improves manoeuvrability, and safety in ground-attack missions, and has been retrofitted to many of the earlier F-4Es. Australia operated 24 F-4Es while waiting delivery of its General Dynamics F-111s, and is the only former Phantom operator. Export orders for the F-4E, with the approximate order sizes, came from: West Germany (10), Greece (56), Iran (177), Israel (86), Japan (154), South Korea (19) and Turkey (40). The Japanese order includes 138 F-4EJs which are being licence-built by Mitsubishi. Other versions of this Phantom variant include the RF-4E (130 built for export) and F-4F (175 for West Germany), the latter being a simplified F-4E.

Some 116 US Air Force F-4Es are being converted to F-4G Wild Weasel aircraft, packed with electronic countermeasure (ECM) equipment to locate and either disrupt or attack enemy electronic stations. The first aircraft flew in 1975, and conversions will continue until 1981.

The F-4J is a further version for the US Navy and Marine Corps. Although similar to the F-4B it has improved AWG-10 radar and fire-control electronics, more powerful engines, and more internal fuel, and was the first version to have a leading-edge slot on the tailplane. Deliveries of 522 aircraft were spread over 1966 – 72. The type is being improved in service, stronger wing-root components and leading-edge wing slats being added to 302 aircraft, which are redesignated F-4S. A similar improvement programme for the F-4B did not incorporate the wing slats, but has brought 228 of the original aircraft up to F-4N standard.

Britain took delivery of 52 F-4K and 118 F-4M Phantoms to equip Fleet Air Arm and Royal Air Force squadrons. Both types have Rolls-Royce Spey 202/203 turbofan engines and several equipment modifications.

Total Phantom production, to early 1979, was 5,177 aircraft, comprising 1,264 for the original

customer (US Navy and Marine Corps), 2,650 for the US Air Force, 1,135 for export and 138 built under licence in Japan. The type is still in production in Japan, where the last delivery should be made in 1981. During 1980 Egypt received the last of its 35 ex-USAF F-4E Phantoms.

Specification

Type: (F-4E) two-seat shipboard/land-based multi-role fighter/strike aircraft
Powerplant: two 17,900-lb (8127-kg) General Electric J79-GE-17 afterburning turbojets
Performance: maximum design speed (clean) Mach 2.17 or 1,430 mph (2304 km/h) at 36,000 ft (10973 m); cruising speed with full internal fuel, four AIM-7E missiles and two 308-gallon (1400-litre) drop tanks 572 mph (924 km/h) at 33,000 ft (10050 m); typical combat radius on hi-lo-hi mission with two 308-gallon (1400-litre) drop tanks and four AIM-7E missiles 520 miles (840 km); ferry range 1,610 miles (2593 km); service ceiling (clean) 58,750 ft (17907 m); maximum rate of climb (clean) 49,800 ft (15179 m) per minute
Weights: empty equipped 31,853 lb (14461 kg); normal take-off (internal fuel, four AIM-7E missiles and two 308-gallon/1400-litre drop tanks) 53,814 lb (24430 kg); maximum take-off 61,795 lb (28055 kg)
Dimensions: span 38 ft 4 in (11.68 m); length 63 ft 0 in (19.20 m); height 16 ft 5 in (5.00 m); wing area 530 sq ft (49.24 m^2)
Armament: one 20-mm M61A1 rotary cannon with 640 rounds, four AIM-7E Sparrow missiles semi-recessed under fuselage, or up to 3,020 lb (1371 kg) on centreline pylon, plus various combinations of missiles and stores on four wing pylons up to a weight of 12,980 lb (5888 kg)
Operators: Egypt, Greece, Iran, Israel, Japan, South Korea, Spain, Turkey, UK, US Air Force, US Marine Corps, US Navy, West Germany

McDonnell Douglas F-4 Phantom II/RF-4

The McDonnell Douglas F-4E was a dramatically improved land-based variant of the justly celebrated Phantom II fighter: it introduced a slatted wing, inbuilt M61 20mm cannon, uprated powerplant and many avionics improvements.

Donnell Douglas F-15 Eagle

ry and notes

Now spearheading the defence of the Western world, and likely to stay there well into the next century, the McDonnell Douglas F-15 Eagle has a flight performance unsurpassed by any other fighter. It is probably the only US fighter capable of catching the Soviet Union's very fast and high-flying Mikoyan-Gurevich MiG-25, and indeed very early in its career was being openly talked about as the 'Foxbat killer'. Israel and Iran are two countries that have raged impotently as this formidable Soviet spy-plane and long-range interceptor has streaked high along their borders (and even over their territory), photographing military installations. With typical early-warning times quite long, as they have been in the mid-1970s, it has been immune from the efforts of the McDonnell Douglas F-4 Phantoms to bring them down. In at least one case Sparrow missiles from Israeli F-4s launched against 'Foxbats' operating from Libya have fallen impotently into the sea.

But all this has now changed. F-15s are now operational in Europe, Israel, Japan and Saudi Arabia, and the Mach 3/80,000-ft (24385-m) cruise performance of the MiG-25 will no longer be adequate to protect it over these areas. Although armed with the same Sparrow and Sidewinder combat missiles as its predecessor, the Phantom, the F-15 behaves as a much more powerful 'first stage', giving the missiles considerably greater speed and height at launch.

In the early 1960s, while the fabulous F-4 was still fresh to the US Navy (its sponsor and first customer), American defence experts were beginning to plan a fighter to follow it. Both the US Navy and US Air Force wanted an air-superiority aircraft, and many people saw the possibility of a common design. But as time went by the two services evolved substantially different requirements and with the example of the disastrous General Dynamics F-111A/F-111B fresh in their minds the planners let the two services have their own ways.

For several years the USAF and the companies studied a number of projects without any conviction that any of them were worth pursuing. The trouble was that not enough was known about the new generation of combat aircraft known to be under development in the Soviet Union. Then, in July 1967, the Soviet air force unveiled at Domodedovo airport near Moscow a whole fleet of new military aircraft. Two of them, the MiG-23 variable-geometry fighter, soon to be code-named 'Flogger, and the clearly for-

Trio of Eagles over the Arctic demonstrate that US airpower has not yet entirely vanished. These three F-15As of the 36th TFW, based at Bitburg in West Germany, were photographed on detachment to Bodo Air Station, Norway, for 'Arctic Express 78'.

McDonnell Douglas
F-15 Eagle

The wing commander's aircraft of the 49th TAC Fighter Wing at Holloman AFB, Albuquerque, New Mexico is painted in low-visibility grey (one of at least five colour schemes experimented with on Tactical Air Command Eagles). In 1979 it appeared likely that, while the RAF may switch to grey for interceptors, the F-15s are more likely to end up with two-tone blue. The objective is low visibility "eyeball" combat.

McDonnell Douglas F-15 Eagle

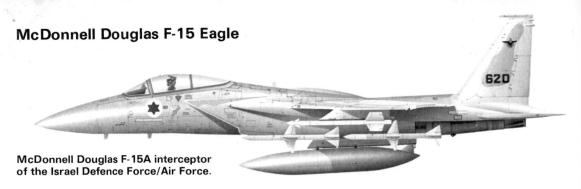

McDonnell Douglas F-15A interceptor of the Israel Defence Force/Air Force.

midable MiG-25 'Foxbat', crystallised the suspicions long held by US defence experts.

In September 1968, after running its rule over the new Soviet designs, the USAF commissioned three companies to produce another set of competitive designs. They were McDonnell Douglas, Fairchild and North American, and in December 1968 the first-named was declared the winner. Undoubtedly its F-4 background helped, but all three companies put up extraordinarily detailed schemes. The winner, for example, had conducted no fewer than 13,000 hours of wind-tunnel testing, compared with 900 hours on which the F-4 had been chosen, and had submitted 37,500 pages of technical, industrial, commercial and administrative documentation. The new fighter was designated the F-15 Eagle, and the first of 20 test aeroplanes made its initial flight in July 1972. The type entered service in November 1974 and the first squadron was declared operational in January 1976.

A thrust/weight ratio far greater than used in any previous fighter was specified. This was necessary for two reasons: to permit a rate of climb sufficient to catch any intruding MiG-25 with its Sparrow and Sidewinder anti-aircraft missiles, and to out-turn any likely foe in combat in order to bring its gun to bear.

To exploit fully the new fighter designs being studied by the US Air Force and US Navy, the Defense Department decided the time was right for new propulsion systems, and accordingly a third competition was held, between Pratt & Whitney and General Electric, the two top US engine companies. The former's F100 engine, after some initial problems, is shaping up to be a worthy successor to the General Electric J79, probably the most widely used military powerplant in the western world. As with most combat aircraft designed since the late 1960s, twin engines rather than one were chosen for better chances of survival.

The decision to carry only one crew member (its naval contemporary, the F-14, has a crew of two) meant that the F-15 had to be easy to fly and automated as far as possible. In particular it meant that the Hughes APG-63 pulsed-Doppler radar had to be easy to operate and read; pilots in combat or scanning the skies cannot afford to be looking down into the cockpit all the time.

In a word, the F-15 is designed for 'seat-pants' operation: the pilot flies the machine instinctively,

his eyes constantly scanning the sky and seeing only one instrument, the head-up display. This instrument is a cathode-ray tube fed with information from the radar, showing the actual position of the target in the sky, its range, closing speed, missile safe firing distance and all the other information the pilot needs to attack the target.

The F-15B is the two-seat trainer version of the F-15A single-seat fighter. The current Eagle models are the F-15C and F-15D single- and two-seater. These both carry an additional 2,000 lb (907 kg) of internal fuel, increasing combat radius by up to 115 miles (185 km). Both models also feature provision for a programmable signal processor for the APG-63, greatly enhancing the radar's air-to-air and air-to-ground capabilities.

Such is the importance of the F-15 in Europe that less than two years later three squadrons had been deployed to Germany to face the growing fleet of Soviet and eastern bloc warplanes ranged along the East German border. Export F-15s are now also finding their way to Israel, Saudi Arabia and Japan. So potent was the Eagle considered that the decision to permit export to Israel was long held up because of political implications in the Arab world.

Specification

Type: single-seat air-superiority fighter
Powerplant: two Pratt & Whitney F100-PW-100 turbofan engines, each of 23,800-lb (10976-kg) thrust with afterburning **Performance:** maximum speed 921 mph (1482 km/h) at low altitude, Mach 2.5 at altitude; maximum radius of action, 2,878 miles (4631 km) with three 600 US gallon tanks; maximum rate of climb 40,000 ft/min (12192 m/min); service ceiling 63,000 ft (19203 m)
Weights: empty 28,000 lb (12700 kg); maximum take-off 56,000 lb (25401 kg)
Dimensions: span 42 ft 10 in (13.05 m); length 63 ft 9 in (19.43 m); height 18 ft 8 in (5.63 m); wing area 608 sq ft (56.5 m²)
Armament: one 20-mm M61A1 rotating-barrel gun and up to eight air-air missiles (normally four AIM-7F Sparrow III and four AIM-9L Sidewinder) under guidance of APG-63 pulsed-Doppler radar with search range of 150 miles (241 km)
Operators: United States, Israel, Saudi Arabia, Japan

(the specification applies to the F-15A)

McDonnell Douglas F-18 Hornet

Artist's impression of what the F-18A Hornet will look like in operational markings, here VF-114 US Navy.

History and notes

In the years between World Wars I and II the US Army Air Corps usually contracted for the manufacture of competitive prototypes of designs which were considered to be the most suitable submissions to meet a specific requirement. There were many advantages from such a policy, especially when manufacturers were seeking anxiously for military contracts, not the least of which was the fact that the prototypes could be test flown and evaluated, and even flown competitively, one against the other. World War II brought an end to this procedure, and many years were to elapse before this competitive prototype procurement method was reinstated.

One requirement for which this policy was used arose in the early 1970s, when the USAF was seeking what it chose to identify as a Lightweight Fighter (LWF). Early excursions into the design and development of supersonic combat aircraft had resulted in hardware which was big, heavy, complex and costly. The USAF's LWF project sought to investigate whether it was possible to evolve a lightweight, low-cost, high-performance air-superiority fighter. Competitive prototypes were considered essential to assist in evaluating the operational potential of such an aircraft, as well as making it possible to establish the role which an LWF would best be able to satisfy. Thus, Requests For Proposals were sent out in 1971, and by 28 February 1972 submissions had been received from five companies. From these, General Dynamics and Northrop were awarded contracts on 13 April 1972 to build two prototypes each, under the respective designations YF-16 and YF-17. First to fly, on 2 February 1974, was the General Dynamics YF-16, Northrop's first YF-17 flying on 9 June 1974. During the evaluation which followed, terminating at the end of December 1974, the YF-16s had flown in excess of 400 hours, the YF-17s more than 200. In September 1974 the USAF announced that the winner of the competition would be declared in January 1975, and at that time identified the aircraft as the Air Combat Fighter (ACF). On 13 January 1975 it was duly announced that the YF-16 had been selected for production by General Dynamics.

Northrop's YF-17 prototype was a markedly different aeroplane from the single-engine YF-16, being identified by its combination of a mid-wing monoplane configuration, outward-canted twin vertical tails, and with underwing air intakes for its two

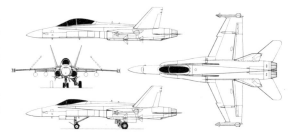

McDonnell Douglas F-18A Hornet

14,000-lb (6350-kg) thrust General Electric YJ101-GE-100 afterburning by-pass turbojet engines. The rejection of this prototype was a disappointment to Northrop, for the company had devoted considerable time and funding since 1963 in the evaluation of an advanced tactical fighter derived from their P-530 Cobra project. There was, however, a silver lining to this particular cloud.

In early 1974 the US Navy initiated the study of a low-cost lightweight multi-mission fighter, then identified as VFAX, but in August 1974 the VFAX concept was terminated by the US Congress, which directed instead that the US Navy should investigate the YF-16/17 prototypes which had been built for the USAF. McDonnell Douglas had taken a close look at both of the competing prototypes, coming to the conclusion that Northrop's design most nearly met the US Navy's original requirement, and teamed up with Northrop to arrive at a new aircraft derived from the YF-17, with much greater fuel capacity and gross weight, which could be submitted to the US Navy for consideration.

This proposal, for what was identified initially as the Navy Air Combat Fighter (NACF), was received enthusiastically by the US Navy, and on 2 May 1975 it was announced that McDonnell Douglas (as prime contractor), Northrop and General Electric had all been awarded short-term contracts to refine their proposals. Less than 12 months later, on 22 January 1976, the US Navy announced that full-scale development was being initiated of this new naval combat/strike fighter, under the designation F-18 Hornet, and that 11 aircraft were to be produced initially for the flight test programme.

McDonnell Douglas and Northrop have planned carefully their joint participation, and in respect of the F-18 Northrop will develop and build the centre and aft fuselage, this representing about 40% of the total task. McDonnell Douglas will develop and build the remainder, and be responsible for final assembly and marketing of these naval aircraft. An international land-based version designated F-18L, with reduced fuel capacity and weight, is also planned, and Northrop will be responsible for sales and 60% of the construction of these aircraft.

This advanced naval aircraft is not only capable of high performance, but has avionics and equipment to enhance its combat/strike capabilities. It has part-graphite structure and fly-by-wire control system. Without moving his hands from the throttle or control stick the pilot has within the compass of his fingers every switch necessary to engage in air-to-air combat or ground-attack. The array of instruments once commonplace in high-performance aircraft is replaced by cathode-ray tube displays, and all vital information is available on the head-up display (HUD) which enables the pilot to be aware of the state of his aircraft without taking his eyes from the target. The Hughes AN/APG-65 tracking radar is able to track accurately multiple targets, so that the Hornet will be able to 'sting' to great effect.

The first F-18 was rolled out on 13 September 1978 and made its first flight on 18 November 1978. The US Navy plans to acquire at least 1,366 of these aircraft, the first becoming operational in 1982. It is planned also to develop an attack version, still designated F-18, chiefly for the US Marine Corps, with sensors and instruments configured for surface attack, as well as the dual-control TF-18 trainer with reduced internal fuel. These are all included in the 1,366 total, increased from the original 800 to cover the USMC's non-receipt of the AV-8B V/STOL aircraft, as well as to cater for attrition and to replace the F-14A TARPS reconnaissance models of the Grumman Tomcat. The F-18A has also been short-listed by several ·countries seeking a new strike fighter, and was chosen by Canada in early 1980.

Specification
Type: single-seat carrier-based combat/strike aircraft
Powerplant: two 16,000-lb (7257-kg) General Electric F404-GE-400 afterburning turbofans
Performance: (estimated) maximum speed (clean) Mach 1.8; maximum speed at intermediate power Mach 1.0; ferry range (unrefuelled) more than 2,300 miles (3700 km)
Weights: take-off (fighter) 33,585 lb (15234 kg); take-off (fighter escort) 35,000 lb (15875 kg); maximum take-off more than 44,000 lb (19958 kg)
Dimensions: span 37 ft 6 in (11.43 m); length 56 ft 0 in (17.07 m); height 15 ft 3½ in (4.66 m); wing area 400 sq ft (37.16 m²)
Armament: carried on nine external weapon stations, with a maximum capacity of 13,700 lb (6214 kg) for high-g missions: weapons can include AIM-9 Sidewinder air-to-air missiles, AIM-7 Sparrow air-to-air missiles (F-18 only), bombs and rockets; sensor pods and fuel tanks can also be carried on these weapons stations; M61 20-mm six-barrel gun mounted in nose
Users: (from 1982) US Marine Corps, US Navy

McDonnell Douglas F-101 Voodoo

History and notes
Detail design of a new penetration fighter to escort bombers of the USAF's newly formed Strategic Air Command was entrusted to the McDonnell Aircraft Company in 1946. Two prototypes were ordered under the designations XF-88 and XF-88A, both swept-wing aircraft with two turbojet engines, but the latter was to have afterburners to boost the thrust of its Westinghouse J34-WE-22 engines. Both prototypes flew, but the XF-88 contract was cancelled in 1948. Primary reasons for this was a shortage of funds, for with US defence plans which hinged on greater use of the nuclear deterrent, all available funding had to be concentrated on the continued procurement of the Convair B-36 pending the availability of a new generation of strategic bombers.

Nevertheless, the requirement for a long-range fighter to escort the B-36 was equally vital, and on 6 February 1951 the USAF issued a general operational requirement for such an aircraft. From the ensuing submissions McDonnell's was chosen as most

McDonnell Douglas F-101B Voodoo

suitable. The submission was for an improved version of the XF-88. However, no decision for production was made, and it was not until the shortcomings of in-service fighters as escorts for Boeing B-29 bombers involved in the Korean War became painfully clear that the USAF decided that it wanted

McDonnell Douglas F-101 Voodoo

F-101B Voodoo

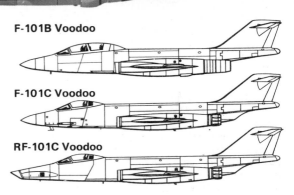

F-101C Voodoo

RF-101C Voodoo

McDonnell's new fighter urgently.

Consequently, the McDonnell aircraft was ordered in 1951 to provide Strategic Air Command (SAC) with the long-range fighter escort which it required for its B-36s, except that, as it could fly only one-fifth as far as the B-36, it was seen then as an interim interceptor which by some strange metamorphosis would develop at some stage into the anticipated long-range escort. On 30 November 1951 the aircraft was designated F-101 and christened Voodoo. But even before the first F-101 flew, on 29 September 1954, SAC had cancelled its requirement for this aircraft. It was decided, however, that subject to satisfactory evaluation, production of the Voodoo would continue for the Tactical Air Command.

Thus, on 2 May 1957, the first production F-101As were delivered to the SAC's 27th Fighter-Bomber Wing at Bergstrom AFB, Texas. Both the unit and its aircraft were due for transfer to Tactical Air Command (TAC) on 1 July 1957, and ultimately all the operational F-101As produced went to form the equipment of three squadrons of the TAC's 81st Tactical Fighter Wing. Of the total of 77 F-101As built, 27 were allocated for experimental and test purposes.

The operational F-101As were about twice as powerful as other current fighters, being powered by two 14,880-lb (6749-kg) thrust Pratt & Whitney J57-P-13 afterburning turbojets, and its large internal fuel capacity could be supplemented by three external tanks to provide a range in excess of 1,500 miles (2414 km). Its standard armament of four M-39 20-mm revolver cannon could be supplemented by three Falcon air-to-air missiles in the internal weapon bay. So far as speed was concerned, the F-101A could attain Mach 1.5 or 1,002 mph (1613 km/h) at 35,000 ft (10670 m). It gained the world absolute speed record of 1,208 mph (1944 km/h).

The F-101A was succeeded by the F-101C (only 47 built) which had structural strengthening for low-altitude operation and was provided with flight-refuelling capability. Most of the foregoing versions were modified subsequently for use by the US Air National Guard as the RF-101G and RF-101H respectively, equipped with nose-mounted cameras. Special-purpose reconnaissance versions were also built; RF-101As with six cameras in place of armament, and an improved RF-101C, combined production of these models totalling 200 aircraft.

For use by the Air Defense Command (ADC) a two-seat long-range interceptor was developed under the designation F-101B. The first of 480 entered service with the 60th Fighter Interceptor Squadron at Otis AFB, Massachussetts, on 5 February 1959, and some of these were equipped with dual controls as TF-101Bs. Following service with ADC (later ADCOM) 66 of these aircraft were transferred to the Royal Canadian Air Force, which shares with ADC defence responsibility within the NORAD command. When modified for Canadian use they were designated F-101F and TF-101F respectively, but were redesignated in RCAF service as CF-101B and CF-101F. They were exchanged subsequently for 66 similar aircraft with more advanced electronics.

Specification

Type: long-range all-weather interceptor
Powerplant: (F-101B) two 14,880-lb (6749-kg) afterburning Pratt & Whitney J57-P-55 turbojets
Performance: (F-101B) maximum speed Mach 1.85 or 1,221 mph (1965 km/h) at 40,000 ft (12190 m); range 1,550 miles (2494 km)
Weight: (F-101B) maximum take-off 46,500 lb (21092 kg)
Dimensions: span 39 ft 8 in (12.09 m); length 67 ft 4¾ in (20.54 m); height 18 ft 0 in (5.49 m); wing area 368 sq ft (34.19 m²)
Armament: (F-101B) three AIM-4D Falcon air-to-air missiles in internal weapon bay, plus two AIR-2A Genie air-to-air missiles under fuselage
Operators: Canada, US Air National Guard

Mikoyan-Gurevich MiG-15 Fagot/ 15UTI Midget

MiG-15 of the Air Force of the People's Liberation Army (China).

History and notes

Although obsolete in its basic fighter version, the Mikoyan-Gurevich MiG-15 'Fagot' survives in considerable numbers in its two-seat trainer version and will remain in use, in some countries, until it is replaced by the Aero L-39 Albatros.

German and Russian research gave rise to the design of the MiG-15 in 1945-46, and the first prototype was not unlike the Focke-Wulf Ta 183 study of the late war years. Early difficulties occasioned by the lack of a suitable powerplant for the proposed fighter were solved when the British government decided to supply the Soviet Union with a batch of Rolls-Royce Nene turbojets. A copy was produced by the Klimov bureau under the designation RD-45; later uprated versions were designated in the VK-1 series.

The first prototype was lost soon after its first flight in July 1947, but a second and extensively revised prototype flew towards the end of the same year, and the aircraft was ordered into production in March 1948. Deliveries started in 1949, by which time the improved MiG-15SD, better known as the MiG-15bis, was flying in prototype form. The MiG-15UTI conversion trainer flew shortly afterwards.

The combat debut of the MiG-15 in Korea in November 1950 proved an unpleasant shock to the West. There was only one Allied fighter in the same class, the North American F-86 Sabre. Its better equipment, and the better training of the US pilots, allowed the US Air Force to achieve superiority over the MiG-15, but the Soviet fighter had a better climb rate, ceiling and acceleration even than this outstanding US type.

China, Poland and Czechoslovakia built MiG-15s, (the first-named under the designation F-2) and the latter two countries converted many single-seaters into two-seaters after the MiG-15 was phased out of first line service. In the absence of any production trainer version of the MiG-17 or MiG-19, the MiG-15UTI moved out of its original role as conversion trainer and became the Eastern bloc's standard advanced trainer. Even today it is found in service all over the world.

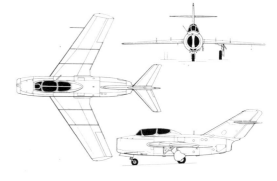

Mikoyan-Gurevich MiG-15UTI Midget

Specification

Type: single-seat fighter and (MiG-15UTI) two-seat advanced trainer

Powerplant: one 5,950-lb (2700-kg) Klimov VK-1 centrifugal-flow turbojet

Performance: maximum speed 668 mph (1076 km/h) at 39,500 ft (12000 m); ferry range 1,250 miles (2000 m); initial climb rate 9,050 ft (2760 m) per minute; ceiling 51,000 ft (15500 m)

Weights: empty 7,500 lb (3400 kg); normal loaded 11,000 lb (4960 kg); maximum take-off 12,750 lb (5786 kg)

Dimensions: span 33 ft 1 in (10.08 m); length 35 ft 7½ in (10.86 m); height 11 ft 1¾ in (3.4 m); wing area 221.7 sq ft (20.6 ²)

Armament: one 37-mm N-37 and two 23-mm NS-23 cannon (later aircraft had the NS-23s replaced by NR-23 revolver cannon); underwing hardpoints for slipper tanks or up to 1,100 lb (500 kg) of stores

Operators: Albania, Algeria, Angola, Bulgaria, China, Cuba, Czechoslovakia, East Germany, Egypt, Finland, Guinea, Hungary, Iraq, Mali, Mongolia, Nigeria, North Korea, Poland, Romania, Somalia, South Yemen, Sri Lanka, Syria, Tanzania, Uganda, USSR, Vietnam

Mikoyan-Gurevich MiG-17 Fresco

MiG-17F of the Syrian Arab Air Force. This jet has all but been replaced in service with more modern aircraft.

History and notes

The Mikoyan-Gurevich MiG-17 'Fresco' was a completely redesigned development of the MiG-15, intended to remove the maximum speed restriction of Mach 0.92 which affected the earlier type. During flight trials the MiG-17 is claimed to have exceeded Mach 1 in level flight, but this performance was not attained in service.

Early production MiG-17s were fitted with the same VK-1 engine as the MiG-15, but the main production model, the MiG-17F, introduced the VK-1F with a simple afterburner. The wing of the MiG-17 was thinner and more sharply swept than that of its forebear, and the rear fuselage was slightly extended to reduce drag. First seen in 1955 was the MiG-17PF, a limited all-weather interceptor with radar in a central inlet bullet and the inlet lip. A further development was the MiG-17PFU, armed with four AA-1 'Alkali' guided air-to-air missiles, the Soviet Union's first missile-armed interceptor.

Although the MiG-17 was in theory obsolete by the mid-1960s, the type gave a good account of itself over Vietnam, being flown by most of the leading North Vietnamese pilots. Its US adversaries were hampered by rules under which they had to close to within visual range before firing, and unlike the MiG-17 they were not designed for close-range dogfighting.

The MiG-17 has been built in Poland (as the LIM-5 and -5P), Czechoslovakia (as the S-104) and China (as the Shenyang F-4 and all-weather F-5). China has also developed a two-seat trainer version of the aircraft. A special close-support version was developed in Poland as the LIM-6, with a deeper, longer-chord inner wing section, and dual mainwheels, rocket-assisted take-off gear and a braking parachute for operation from unprepared fields.

Specification

Type: single-seat fighter
Powerplant: one 7,500-lb (3400-kg) Klimov VK-1 afterburning turbojet
Performance: maximum speed 710 mph (1145 km/h) at 10,000 ft (3000 m); range 1,400 miles

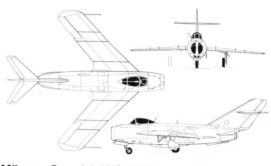

Mikoyan-Gurevich MiG-17F Fresco

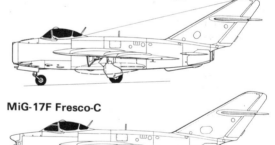

MiG-17F Fresco-C

MiG-17PF Fresco-D

(2250 m); rate of climb 12,795 (3900 m) per minute; ceiling 54,500 ft (16600 m)
Weights: empty 9,000 lb (4100 kg); maximum take-off 14,750 lb (6700 kg)
Dimensions: span 31 ft 7 in (9.63 m); length 36 ft 4½ in (11.09 m); height 11 ft (3.35 m) wing area 243.3 sq ft (22.6 m²)
Armament: (MiG-17P, PF) three 23-mm NR-23 cannon and/or four AA-1 'Alkali' AAMs; two underwing hardpoints for drop tanks or stores up to 1,100 lb (500 kg)
Operators: Afghanistan, Albania, Algeria, Angola, Bulgaria, China, Cuba, Czechoslovakia, East Germany, Egypt, Guinea, Hungary, Iraq, Mali, Nigeria, North Korea, Poland, Romania, Somalia, South Yemen, Sri Lanka, Sudan, Syria, Tanzania, Uganda, USSR, Vietnam, Yemen

Mikoyan-Gurevich MiG-19 Farmer

MiG-19PM limited all-weather interceptor of the Polish Air Force.

History and notes

The Mikoyan-Gurevich MiG-19 'Farmer', the world's first production supersonic fighter, remained in production in 1980, and currently forms the backbone of the Chinese tactical air force in its Shenyang F-6 version. In the hands of Pakistan air force pilots it has proved its worth against considerably more modern and more costly opponents, with agility in combat which would do credit to a contemporary air-superiority fighter.

Development of the MiG-19 started in the late 1940s, with a requirement for a new fighter designed around the newly developed Lyulka AL-5, the Soviet Union's first large axial-flow jet engine. Disappointing progress with this powerplant, however, led to the decision to redesign the Mikoyan prototype around two small-diameter Mikulin AM-5s. The first aircraft, the I-360, was distinguished by a T-tail, but was destroyed in flight-testing as a result of tailplane flutter. The I-350(M) was completed with a low-set tailplane, and was flown in late 1952. It was soon followed by the production MiG-19F with afterburning AM-5Fs, the first version to go supersonic in level flight in early 1953.

The initial MiG-19F and limited-all-weather MiG-19PF were less than successful, and were eventually withdrawn from service as a result of high accident rates. They were replaced by the MiG-19S, with an all-moving tailplane, refinements to flying controls and systems, and RD-9 engines. The latter was a largely redesigned development of the AM-5 produced by the Tumansky bureau, and was the first of many Tumansky engines believed to power all MiG fighters up to the MiG-27 'Flogger-D'. Deliveries of the definitive MiG-19S started in mid-1955 and the basic airframe thereafter continued almost completely unchanged to the end of the type's Russian production life.

The MiG-19S was rapidly followed by the MiG-19P, with Izumrud radar in an intake bullet fairing and the inlet lip, and from this version was developed the Soviet Union's first missile-armed fighter.

Production of the MiG-19 was transferred from the Soviet Union to Czechoslovakia in 1958, the Aero works producing some 850 aircraft between 1958 and 1961. In that year, the Chinese Shenyang works produced the first examples of an unlicensed copy of the MiG-19S, designated F-6. By the mid-1970s at least 1,800 F-6s had been built in

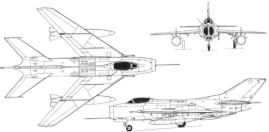

Mikoyan-Gurevich MiG-19 Farmer

China. A substantial number of F-6s was supplied to Pakistan in 1965-66 and 1972; Vietnam, Albania and Tanzania have also taken delivery of similar aircraft. The MiG-19 has also formed the basis for the Chinese F-6bis or A-5 strike fighter, an enlarged Mig-19 with side air intakes.

The Pakistani aircraft have been modified with launch pylons for AIM-9 Sidewinder missiles, and Chinese aircraft probably carry a version of the equivalent K-13 'Atoll'.

Specification

Type: single-seat fighter and limited all-weather interceptor

Powerplant: two 7,165-lb (3250-kg) after-burning Tumansky RD-9B turbojets

Performance: maximum speed (clean) 900 mph (1450 km/h) at 33,000 ft (10000 m) or Mach 1.4; maximum speed with external fuel tanks 715 mph (1150 km/h) at 33,000 ft (10000 m); initial climb rate 22,640 ft (6900 m) per minute; ceiling 57,400 ft (17500 m); ferry range with external fuel 1,350 miles (2200 km)

Weights: empty 11,400 lb (5172 kg); loaded (clean) 16,300 lb (7400 kg); maximum take-off 19,600 lb (8900 kg)

Dimensions: span 29 ft 6½ in (9.0 m); length (excluding pitot tube) 41 ft 4 in (12.6 m); height 12 ft 9½ in (3.9 m); wing area 269 sq ft (25 m^2)

Armament: three 30-mm NR-30 cannon plus rocket pods on underwing pylons; Pakistani aircraft have AIM-9 Sidewinders; MiG-19PM has no cannon but four K-5M 'Alkali' AAMs

Operators: Afghanistan, Albania, Bangladesh, Bulgaria, China, Cuba, Iraq, North Korea, Pakistan, Somalia, Sudan, Tanzania, Uganda, USSR, Vietnam, Zambia

Mikoyan-Gurevich MiG-21 Fishbed/ MiG-21U Mongol

One of the few MiG-21Rs in the Czech Air Force carrying unit insignia.

MiG-21PFMA serves in five regiments of the Egyptian Air Force.

History and notes

The Mikoyan-Gurevich MiG-21 'Fishbed', still in pro- duction and apparently under development more than 25 years after it first flew, must be judged a classic combat aircraft. Although its combat record has been mixed, it has had a profound influence on Western fighter design. At the time of writing, it re- mains the principal low-level tactical air defence fighter of the Eastern bloc, working in conjunction with MiG-23s, and is unlikely to be fully replaced before the second half of the 1980s, even in Soviet service.

The origins of the MiG-21 lie in Korean War ex- perience as do those of the Lockheed F-104. Both types stemmed from demands from pilots for an 'air- superiority' fighter from which all unneccessary equipment would be eliminated, and in which all aspects of the design would be subordinated to com- bat performance. Armament would be the minimum needed to knock down an enemy fighter.

The Mikoyan design bureau went even further in the direction of miniaturization than Lockheed, pro- ducing in 1955 the first of a series of prototypes designed around an engine not much larger than the Tumansky RD-9; two of the latter powered the MiG-19, itself not a large aircraft. The new engine, also of Tumansky design, was not available by 1955, so the swept-wing E-50 of that year was powered by an uprated RD-9E and a booster rocket.

In the following year the design bureau flew the swept-wing E-2A and the tailed-delta E-5, both powered by the newly developed RD-11 and armed with three 30-mm cannon. The tailed-delta layout of the E-5 resembled that of the Douglas Skyhawk in plan view, but featured a mid-set wing in line with the tailplane. The advantages of the layout included low drag and, as it turned out, excellent handling; on

the debit side, its low-speed performance was not good and it was structurally complicated. However, the E-5 offered generally better performance than the E-2, and the tailed-delta was selected for produc- tion.

The first series aircraft were developed from the E-6 production prototype and were themselves designated E-66 by the Mikoyan bureau. They car- ried a simple radar-ranging sight and two K-13 'Atoll' air-to-air missiles in addition to two 30-mm cannon, but with only 11,250-lb (5100-kg) maximum thrust they were underpowered. A few aircraft of the type entered service with a trials unit in late 1957, with the designation MiG-21. The first large- scale production variant was the MiG-21F, powered by an uprated Tumansky R-11F-300 of 12,600-lb (5750-kg) thrust, which entered service in late 1959. Most of these had the left gun removed to save weight, and had a fin of longer chord than that of the early MiG-21.

After the appearance of the MiG-21F, the process of improving the MiG-21 began in earnest. The early MiG-21 was a clear-weather interceptor with little payload, range and armament. However, there were strict limits to what could be done to rectify the situation, because any extra equipment could have disastrous effects on the perfomance of what was basically a small aircraft.

The MiG-21F was delivered to India and Finland as well as to Warsaw Pact states, and was put into production in China (as the F-7) and Czechoslovakia. By the time it was established in service, develop- ment of a limited-all-weather version was under way, an aero-dynamic prototype being demonstrated at Tushino in 1961. This was the MiG- 21PF, with an R1L radar in the centrebody of a

Mikoyan-Gurevich MiG-21 Fishbed/MiG-21U Mongol

Indian Air Force Hindustan-built MiG-21PFM hastily camouflaged for service in the 1971 India-Pakistan war.

redesigned inlet. Guns were removed, and the cockpit was faired into the fuselage, sacrificing rear vision for low drag.

Between 1964 and 1970 the MiG-21PF formed the basis for numerous modified subvariants. In the course of production, a new brake-chute installation was added at the base of the fin. On the MiG-21SPS, plain flaps blown by engine-bleed air replaced the chord-extending Fowler flaps. Later the fin was again extended forwards, and some aircraft had provision for a GP-9 gun-pack containing the newly developed GSh-23 cannon. Also covered by the MiG-21PF designation was the introduction of the 13,700-lb (6200-kg) R-11F2S-300 engine and improved R2L radar.

The next recognisable modification produced the MiG-21PFM, with a conventional sideways-hinged canopy and separate windscreen replacing the forward-hinged one-piece hood of the MiG-21F. It was followed by the MiG-21PFMA, with a deeper dorsal spine and four wing pylons, which formed the basis for the MiG-21R reconnaissance version with optical and electronic sensors in ventral and wing-tip pods. The next major modification came in 1970, with the service introduction of the MiG-21MF. This has an internal GSh-23 and the new Tumansky R-13 rated at 14,500 lb (6600 kg). The equivalent reconnaissance version is designated MiG-21RF. Egypt and India have both fitted MiG-21s with British avionics, and Egyptian MiG-21s may be modified to carry Sidewinder missiles.

In 1973 there appeared the first examples of a new MiG-21 development, the MiG-21SMT, with internal fuel and avionic equipment in a bulged dorsal spine. It has been followed by the structurally redesigned and simplified MiG-21bis, with the Tumansky R-25 and further improved avionics including a new gunsight; the new type may also carry the AA-8 Aphid missile. Despite the development of the MiG-21 in the direction of multi-role capability, it is now mainly used for air defence of tactical air bases.

However, the MiG-21 is limited in range and payload by comparison with the MiG-27, while its dogfighting performance is not in the class of the latest Western fighters. The MiG-21bis may be an interim development, pending production of a new aircraft to fill the air-to-air slot in the Soviet air arm. Meanwhile, the MiG-21bis has become the standard

export version. Another MiG-21 development is reported to be the Chinese fighter designated F-8.

Other versions of the MiG-21 have included the MiG-21M, generally similar to the MiG-21MF but powered by the older R-11, which was built under licence in India and has been superseded on the Indian production lines by the MiG-21bis. All trainer versions of the MiG-21 have similar forward fuselages and lack search radar: the MiG-21U is basically equivalent to an early MiG-21PF, the MiG-21US is equivalent to the MiG-21PFS and the MiG-21UM is derived from the MiG-21MF. It is likely that a MiG-21bis-derived trainer will emerge in due course.

Specification

Type: fighter/light strike and (MiG-21M variants) conversion trainer
Powerplant: (MiG-21bis, to which subsequent details refer) one 16,500 lb (7500 kg) Tumansky R-25 afterburning turbojet
Performance: maximum speed clean 1,320 mph (2125 km/h) or Mach 2 at 36,000 ft (11000 m); maximum speed with external stores at medium altitude 1,000 mph (1600 km/h) or Mach 1.5; maximum speed at sea level just over Mach 1; service ceiling about 50,000 ft (15000 m); hi-lo-hi combat radius about 300 miles (500 km)
Weights: empty 13,500 lb (6200 kg); maximum loaded 22,000 lb (10000 kg)
Dimensions: span 23 ft 6 in (7.16 m); length 51 ft 9 in (15.75 m); height 14 ft 9 in (4.49 m); wing area 247 sq ft (22.9 m²)
Armament: one twin-barrel 23-mm GSh-23 cannon, plus four wing hardpoints for 3,300 lb (1500 kg) of ordnance, including up to four K-13 (AA-2 'Atoll') or AA-8 'Aphid' air-to-air missiles, AS-7 'Kerry' air-to-surface missiles or unguided rockets; outer wing pylons or centreline pylon can be used for drop tanks
Operators: Afghanistan, Albania, Algeria, Angola, Bangladesh, Bulgaria, China, Cuba, Czechoslovakia, East Germany, Ethiopia, Egypt, Finland, Hungary, India, Iraq, Laos, Malagasy, Mozambique, Nigeria, North Korea, Poland, Romania, Somalia, Sudan, Syria, Tanzania, Uganda, USSR, Vietnam, Yemen, Yugoslavia, Zambia

Mikoyan-Gurevich MiG-21 Fishbed/MiG-21U Mongol

This MiG-21 bis shows the three-colour camouflage apparently coming into increasing use among Warsaw Pact air forces for tactical use.

Mikoyan-Gurevich MiG-23 Flogger-A, B, C, E, G

History and notes

The Mikoyan-Gurevich MiG-23 'Flogger' is almost certainly the most important of Soviet tactical warplanes, and production of this aircraft and of its derivative the MiG-27 was reported to have attained a rate of 300 aircraft a year by 1976-77. The type has replaced many MiG-21s and Sukhoi Su-7s, and in 1978 was first deployed by the PVO air defence force. It has no direct Western equivalent, the near-contemporary Dassault-Breguet Mirage G being almost identical in concept but never put into production. The most closely comparable type in service is perhaps the Saab 37 Viggen, but the MiG-23 can probably best be likened to a 'miniaturised Phantom', later in timescale and more advanced, but intended for the same spectrum of roles. Modification fairly late in its development produced a type with better air-superiority characteristics than at first intended, but the MiG-23 cannot be compared in this respect with later specialized Western fighters. Its most significant feature, however, is that the same basic airframe serves as a dedicated air-to-ground aircraft ('Flogger D' and 'Flogger F') as well as an interceptor/air superiority fighter.

Develoment of the MiG-23 was almost certainly initiated in 1963-64, before the Vietnam war and most Middle East experience of air combat. The aim was to produce for Frontal Aviation (FA) a tactical fighter which could match the payload/range of types such as the Lockheed F-104G, Republic F-105 and McDonnell Douglas F-4 Phantom without demanding massive runways. The last concern was also a feature of Western thinking at the time, leading to development of the Viggen and a short-lived NATO enthusiasm for V/STOL strike aircraft.

The Mikoyan evaluated at least two approaches to the FA requirements: the swing-wing MiG-23 and a tailed-delta type with a battery of Kolesov lift jets amidships (the latter codenamed 'Faithless' by NATO). It is also possible that a canard type was test-flown. The swing-wing prototype was the first such aircraft to fly in the Soviet Union, as distinct from the mid-span pivot principle used on the Su-17 and Tupolev Tu-26. Both the aircraft evaluated were designed to accept the Tumansky R-27, the first Soviet afterburning turbofan for military use.

The Mikoyan prototypes were evaluated in 1966-67, and the decision to go ahead with the swing-wing type was probably taken in 1968. By that time, however, the importance of the air combat regime was being recognised; the MiG-23 may also have demonstrated generally unacceptable handling characteristics, as well as needing improvement in the air-to-air regime. In any event, although a few aircraft basically similar to the prototype (designated 'Flogger-A' by NATO) were put into service with trials units, several years elapsed before the highly modified MiG-23S 'Flogger-B' was introduced.

Compared with the prototype, the MiG-23S

Mikoyan-Gurevich MiG-23S (Flogger-B)

features an extremely large saw-toothed leading-edge extension which increases wing area and taper, reducing the shift of aerodynamic centre with wing sweep. The planform was also altered, the tail surfaces being moved aft. Together, most of the modifications would tend to make the aircraft more stable, while the additional wing area might restore some of the manoeuvrability thus sacrificed.

The notched wing planform distinguishes the MiG-23 series from other variable-sweep aircraft. Other unusual features include a folding ventral fin and a complex but space-saving main landing gear. Movable surfaces include simple leading-edge droops on the outer sections of the moving wing panels, plain trailing-edge flaps and spoilers. The outermost of the three flap sections operate in conjunction with the four-section spoiler/dumpers and tailerons for roll control. Western testing shows strongly that variable-geometry wings should be matched with sophisticated high-lift systems.

Whereas design of the MiG-23 was biased towards the strike role, development was aimed at improving handling and manoeuvrability in the air-combat regime. No effort was made, however, to improve visibility, beyond the installation of rear-view mirrors.

Development of the MiG-23S equipment and armament went hand in hand with airframe and power-plant work. The aircraft is fitted with a radar (codenamed High Lark) considerably larger and more powerful than that fitted to the MiG-21, and is armed with specially developed medium-range and dogfighting missiles. All examples in FA service also carry a laser (or possibly infra-red) sighting or ranging aid beneath the nose.

The MiG-23S entered service in 1971-72. Early aircraft were powered by the 23,150-lb (10500-kg) Tumansky R-27, but by the time the aircraft was established in service work was under way on the more powerful R-29 engine: this was probably another example of development aimed at improving air-to-air combat capability. The R-27 is, however, still used in the MiG-23U 'Flogger-C' conversion trainer and the export 'Flogger-E'; the latter has a much-reduced standard of equipment, including

Mikoyan-Gurevich MiG-23 Flogger-A, B, C, E, G

Libyan Air Force MiG-23U Flogger-C

Flogger-B (MiG-23MF) of the Air Force of the DDR with rocket pods on outboard fuselage pylons and AAM launching shoes on glove pylons.

Flogger-F (MiG-23BM) of the Czechoslovak Air Force of a unit based at Pardubice, some 60 miles (100 km) east of Prague. The two-tone upper surface camouflage scheme with pale blue undersurfaces has been standardised by most non-Soviet WarPac air forces.

AA-2-2 'Advanced Atoll' missiles and like the trainer, a radar apparently derived from the R2L of the MiG-21. The AA-2 'Atoll' formed the interim armament of the MiG-23S until the newly developed AA-7 and AA-8 entered service in the mid-1970s.

The current standard air defence version of the MiG-23 is identified by Nato as 'Flogger G'. Companies with examples of the 'Flogger B' type observed in 1973-74, the 'Flogger G' is distinguished externally by a smaller dorsal fin extension and the fact that the nose radome is very slightly drooped. This is in addition to a number of features which may have been phased in during the course of production rather than being specific to the 'Flogger G':
*Installation of the more powerful R-29B engine, improving acceleration, sustained turning ability and field performance
*Development of a pulse-Doppler attack radar capable of directing missiles against targets flying lower than the launching aircraft. The represents a considerable advance over the original High Lark radar, which was described by US sources as being comparable to that of the late1960s F-4J Phantom
*Provision for jettisonable overload fuel tanks on non-swivelling wing pylons

The 'Flogger G' is in production for the FA and PVO but has not been exported. Compared with aircraft now being delivered to the Western air forces, it is not a "visual-range" fighter so much as an intercepter designed to fire at radar range, closing for cannon and short-range-missile engagement only as a second resort. It is assumed that Soviet superiority in numbers in the central region of Europe is so great that the air force is prepared to accept losses due to misidentification.

Specification

Type: air combat fighter and interceptor with secondary strike role or (MiG-23U) conversion trainer
Powerplant: (current production) one 25,350-lb (11500-kg) Tumansky R-29B afterburning turbofan
Performance: maximum speed 1,450 mph (2350 km/h) or Mach 2.2 at 36,000 ft (11000 m); maximum speed at sea level 840 mph (1350 km/h) or Mach 1.1; service ceiling 55,000 ft (17000 m); ferry range 1,750 miles (2800 km); combat radius 575 miles (930 km)
Weights: empty 25,000 lb (11300 kg); internal fuel 10,140 lb (4600 kg); normal take-off 38,000 lb (17250 kg); maximum 41,000 lb (18500 kg)
Dimensions: span (unswept) 46 ft 9 in (14.25 m); span (swept) 27 ft 2 in (8.3 m); length 59 ft 10 in (18.25 m); height 14 ft 4 in (4.35 m); wing area 400 sq ft (37.2 m^2)
Armament: one internal 23-mm GSh-23 twin-barrel cannon, two glove hardpoints for AA-7 'Apex' medium-range air-to-air missiles, or air-to-surface weapons, two belly hardpoints for AA-8 'Aphid' dogfight air-to-air missiles. The export 'Flogger-E' carries four AA-2-2 'Advanced Atoll' air-to-air missiles
Operators: Algeria, Bulgaria, Czechoslovakia, Egypt, Ethiopia, Iraq, Libya, USSR

Mikoyan-Gurevich MiG-25 Foxbat

History and notes

Unquestionably the most impressive military aircraft to appear from the Soviet Union, the MiG-25 is unique in combining spectacular speed and climb performance with simplicity and ruggedness. Only built in limited numbers, it is near to replacement in the Soviet Union but is becoming a Third World status-symbol.

In early 1979 the US Department of Defense commented that the MiG-25 'Foxbat' was being produced 'mainly for export'. At that time the only known foreign recipients were Libya and Algeria. Their MiG-25s give these nations the ability to defy all but the most sophisticated defence systems by virtue of sheer height and speed of penetration. Long ago the appearance of MiG-25s stimulated purchases of advanced weapon systems by the United States, Israel and the former Iranian regime, making the 'Foxbat' the best sales aid for McDonnell Douglas and Grumman yet devised. The type is also reported to form the basis of the Soviet Union's new air-defence system for the 1980s, but it is likely that the airframe is so highly modified for this role that a new designation will be applied.

The basic design goes back to 1957-59, when it seemed possible that the US Air Force would introduce a Mach 3, 70,000-ft (21350-m) bomber (the North American B-70) by 1964.

The design of the E-266, as the Mikoyan bureau designated the new type, was influenced by that of the North American A-5 Vigilante. The two types both have large, thin-section shoulder wings of moderate sweep, vertical ramp inlets and identical fuselage and propulsion layouts.

However, the Mach 3 requirement demanded a unique approach to structure and propulsion. The E-266 is constructed largely of fabricated steel sections, and the fuel tanks are of continuously welded steel sheet so that they can expand and contract with temperature without leaking. (Fuel-tank sealing proved to be a major problem with Mach 3 aircraft.) Power is provided by two extremely simple turbojets optimized for high-Mach performance; static pressure ratio is low, but at high speeds is multiplied by compression in the inlet ducts. The powerplant thus has some of the characteristics of a turbo-ramjet. At low speeds its efficiency is extremely poor, a factor exacerbated by the fact that only at high speeds is a substantial part of the lift generated by the intakes.

The propulsion system, possibly including an early version of the electronic inlet control system, was tested on a modified Mikoyan-Gurevich I-75 interceptor, designated E-166, which is claimed to have exceeded Mach 2.8 on a 1,665 mph (2681 km/hr) official record run in 1965. However, it was not until 1967 that similar record speeds were set by E-266 development aircraft. By that time the airframe and engine appeared to be fully developed, with methanol-water injection for high-speed flight.

However, it was another three years before production MiG-25s appeared in service, indicating protracted development of the offensive systems. The type received the NATO name 'Foxbat'.

There are two main versions, both deployed around 1970. The PVO air defence force operates the interceptor, possibly designated MiG-25P and known to NATO as 'Foxbat-A'. The radar and missile system is designed mainly for interceptions controlled from the ground or the Tupolev Tu-126 'Moss' AWACS aircraft. Although the 'Fox Fire' radar appears to be based on the 'Big Nose' radar of the two-seat Tu-28P, which operates with greater autonomy, the MiG-25 relies to a great extent on communication links and ground-guided trajectories rather than inertial or Doppler radar systems.

By the time the interceptor entered service, however, the MiG-25 had found a new role as a reconnaissance aircraft, using electronic and optical sensors. Although the range and sensor capacity of the MiG-25R are markedly inferior to those of the Lockheed SR-71, the aircraft can penetrate many defence systems in safety provided that there is a safe base close at hand. MiG-25Rs have been based in Egypt for uninterceptable overflights of Israel, and have flown from Poland in missions along the East German border for Elint probing of NATO defences. Two versions of the MiG-25R appear to exist: one, designated 'Foxbat-B' by NATO, has cameras as well as Elint dielectric panels, while the 'Foxbat-D' has more extensive Elint equipment but no cameras.

The third confirmed variant is the MiG-25U 'Foxbat-C' conversion trainer, with a separate second cockpit in an extended nose. It has no operational systems.

Specification

Type: interceptor and reconnaissance aircraft
Powerplant: two 27,000-lb (12250-kg) Tumansky R-31 afterburning turbojets
Performance: maximum speed (clean) Mach 3.0, equivalent to just under 2,000 mph (3200 km/h) at medium and high altitudes; maximum speed with external stores Mach 2.8; maximum sustained altitude 75,000 ft (23000 m); typical intercept radius 460 miles (740 km); range at Mach 3 900 miles (1500 km); initial climb rate 30,000 ft (9000 m) per minute
Weights: empty 44,000 lb (20000 kg); maximum take-off 82,500 lb (37500 kg)
Dimensions: (interceptor) span 46 ft (14 m); length 73 ft 2 in (22.3 m); height 18 ft 6 in (5.64 m); wing area 605 sq ft (56.2 m^2)
Armament: up to four AA-6 'Acrid' air-to-air missiles (two radar and two infra-red) plus optional ventral gunpack probably containing GSh-23 cannon
Operators: Algeria, Libya, Syria, USSR

Mikoyan-Gurevich MiG-25 Foxbat

A MiG-25 "Foxbat-A" in the usual unpainted livery of IA-PVO interceptors. Dielectric areas (aerials) are grey (in some "Foxbats" the main "Fox Fire" radome has a dark green colour).

Mikoyan-Gurevich MiG-27 Flogger-D, F

History and notes

With the increasing optimization of the Mikoyan-Gurevich MiG-23 for the air-to-air role, it became increasingly attractive to develop a specialized version of the type for strike duties rather than employing the type as a multi-role aircraft as had been intended. This was the rationale behind the MiG-27, known to NATO as the 'Flogger-D', which presumably flew in 1972-73 (development having been initiated once the MiG-23 was reasonably well settled in service) and entered service with the Soviet Union's 16th Air Army in East Germany in 1975.

The main difference between the MiG-23 and the MiG-27 lies in the forward fuselage. The MiG-27 dispenses with the nose radar and has a slimmer nose giving a much better downward view. The nose cap houses a simple ranging radar; aft of this is a small window for a laser ranger, a radome which may cover a terrain-avoidance radar, and a Doppler aerial. Several other aerials appear on the leading edge of the wing gloves and on either side of the forward fuselage.

In order to save weight the variable inlets of the MiG-23 are dropped in favour of simple fixed structures; the medium-altitude high-speed performance thus sacrificed is not needed by the MiG-27 in any case. The secondary power nozzle of the engine is also simplified, probably to balance the weight saved in the forward fuselage. Weapon pylons are installed beneath the inlet ducts, rather than on the fuselage underside as on the MiG-23. The quoted weapon load is small by comparison with smaller Western aircraft, but represents an operating standard rather than the all-out "Christmas-tree" figure used in Western brochures. The twin-barrel GSh-23 gives way to a much harder-hitting six-barrel weapon, probably of 23-mm calibre although some reports claim that it is a 30-mm gun. The mainwheel tyres are fatter, to cope with greater weights, and the type can be fitted with auxiliary RATO (rocket-assisted take-off) units on rear-fuselage racks.

Interestingly, it is the specialised ground-attack version of the MiG-23 that has been chosen for export to the Soviet Union's satellites in Eastern Europe. This export model, the 'Flogger F', has the F-4-style ramp inlets and variable nozzle of the air-defence 'Floggers', which presumably endow it with a considerably higher top speed than the FA's 'Flogger D'; however, this performance is academic because it can only be used for air-to-air combat, for which purpose the export aircraft is quite useless due to its lack of air-intercept (AI) radar. The nose is similar to that of the FA strike aircraft, but the export types lack some of the 'domestic' model's antannae and dielectrics. The cannon of the export model is the fighter's twin-barrel GSh-23, while the underfuselage pylons are located under the belly (as on the fighter) rather than under the inlet ducts, probably precluding ASM armament. The export aircraft have RATO attachments. All in all, the 'Flogger F' seems to be less well optimised for the strike role than the 'Flogger D' and although it has been seen in service with Soviet units it is basically a downgraded version. It is probably powered by the R-27.

There is no direct trainer equivalent to the MiG-27, conversion being carried out on MiG-23Us despite the different propulsion systems. Some MiG-23Us have similar aerials to those of the MiG-27, suggesting that they are used for MiG-27 weapons training.

The closest Western equivalent to the MiG-27 is the smaller Jaguar, and like the Western aircraft it is probably intended for the medium-depth strike role rather than close-support duties or interdiction. However, with the aid of jetisonable drop tanks and rocket-assisted take-off, the MiG-27 can threaten a considerable area of Europe from dispersed forward bases in East Germany, being vastly more effective in payload range terms than its predecessors.

Weapons developed for the MiG-27 include cluster and fuel-air munitions as well as laser-guided and electro-optical 'smart' glide bombs. It is the first Soviet type to be seen with multiple stores racks: tandem racks can be fitted to both centreline and wing stations. The number of aerials on the airframe bear witness to an extensive internal ECM suite, augmented by external pods.

Specification

Type: tactical attack fighter
Powerplant: one 25,350-lb (11500-kg) Tumansky R-29B afterburning turbofan
Performance: maximum speed 1,050 mph (1700 km/h) or Mach 1.6 at 36,090 ft (11000 m); maximum speed (clean) at sea level 840 mph (1350 km/h) or Mach 1.1; service ceiling 55,775 ft (17000 m); ferrry range 1,750 miles (2800 km); combat radius 575 miles (930 km)
Weights: empty 24,250 lb (11000 kg); internal fuel 10,140 lb (4600 kg); normal take-off 39,685 lb (18000 kg); overload take-off 44,310 lb (20100 kg)
Dimensions: span (spread) 46 ft 9 in (14.25 m); span (swept) 27 ft 2 in (8.3 m); length 58 ft (17.7 m); height 14 ft 4 in (4.35 m); wing area 400 sq ft (37.2 m²)
Armament: one six-barrel rotary cannon, two multiple weapon points under each inlet duct and two multiple racks under gloves for maximum external weapon load estimated at the very low value of 6,614 lb (3000 kg), including ASMs
Operators: Cuba, Egypt, Iraq, Syria, USSR

Mikoyan-Gurevich MiG-27 Flogger-D, F

MiG-27 Flogger-D of the V-VS Frontovaya Aviatsiya based in the DDR (Group of Soviet Forces in Germany). This displays the standard three-colour upper surface camouflage scheme employed by FA tactical fighters, but the exact pattern varies marginally from aircraft to aircraft.

Mil Mi-6 Hook/Mi-10 Harke

History and notes

When the first of five prototypes of the Mil Mi-6 'Hook' was flown in September 1957, it was by far the largest helicopter in the world; what is more surprising is that with one exception (the same design bureau's abortive Mi-12) it has retained that distinction up to the appearance of its 1980s descendant, the Mil 'Halo' (see introduction).

The Mi-6 was the result of a joint military and civil requirement for a massive helicopter that would not only bring a new dimension to mobile warfare, with the ability to transport light armoured vehicles, but would also help in the exploitation of previously uncharted areas of the Soviet Union. Thus the requirement was not only demanding in terms of payload, calling for a disposable load half as great again as the fully loaded weight of the Mi-4, but also in terms of range.

The requirement was met by the first use of turbine power in a Soviet helicopter, and also by the provision of variable-incidence wings, first fitted in 1960 to the 30 pre-series aircraft, which carry 20% of the weight of the aircraft in cruising flight. Unusually the Mi-6 can make a rolling take-off at a weight greater than that at which it can take-off vertically. The engineering problems were formidable — the R-7 gearbox and rotor head alone weigh 7,055 lb (3200 kg), more than both the engines.

Like the Mi-4, the Mi-6 has clamshell doors at the rear of the cabin and can accommodate small armoured vehicles. Even larger loads can be lifted by the specialized flying-crane derivative of the Mi-6, the Mi-10 'Harke'; this features a much shallower fuselage than the Mi-6, and in its initial version is fitted with a vast quadricycle landing gear which allows it to straddle and lift loads as large as a motor-coach or a prefabricated building. The later Mi-10K has a shorter, lighter landing gear and rear-facing gondola beneath the nose for a crewman to direct lifting operations.

The Mi-6 and Mi-10 are not as widely used as the Mi-8 by the Soviet armed forces, possibly because such large helicopters are vulnerable in combat. However, they were used to carry heavy weapons in support of Soviet-backed forces in Africa in 1978.

Specification

Type: heavy transport helicopter and (Mi-10) crane helicopter (specification Mi-6)
Powerplant: two 5,500-shp (4103-kW) Soloviev D-25V turboshafts
Performance: maximum speed 186 mph (300 km/h); crusing speed 155 mph (250 km/h); range with 26,500-lb (12000-kg) payload 125 miles (200 km); range with 8,800-lb (4000-kg) payload 620 miles (1000 km); service ceiling at maximum gross weight 14,500 ft (4400 m); hovering ceiling 8,200 ft (2500 m)
Weights: empty 60,050 lb (27240 kg); maximum internal payload 26,500 lb (12000 kg); normal take-

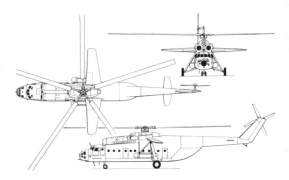

Mil Mi-6 Hook

Mil Mi-10 Harke

off 89,300 lb (40500 kg); maximum vertical take-off 93,700 lb (42500 kg)
Dimensions: main rotor diameter 114 ft 10 in (350 m); fuselage length 108 ft 10¼ in (33.18 m); wing span 50 ft 2½ in (15.3 m) height on ground 30 ft 1 in (9.16 m); main rotor disc area 10,356.8 sq ft (962 m²)
Armament: in tactical role, one machine-gun in nose compartment
Operators: Algeria, Bulgaria, Egypt, Ethiopia, Iraq, Libya, Peru, Syria, USSR, Vietnam

Mil Mi-6 supplied by the Soviet Union in 1978 to the Fuerza Aerea del Peru.

Mil Mi-8 Hip

The Mil Mi-8 Hip remains the most numerous of helicopters in the Egyptian inventory with nearly 70 currently on strength.

History and notes

The Mil Mi-8 'Hip' relates to the earlier, piston-engined Mi-4 'Hound' as the Mi-2 'Hoplite' relates to the Mi-1 'Hare'. As in the case of the smaller helicopter, development started as a turbine-powered adaptation of the original design and proceeded to a point where there was little if any commonality between the new helicopter and its predecessor.

The first prototype of the Mi-8 was flown in 1961, with the four-blade rotor of the Mi-4 and a single Soloviev turboshaft of 2,700-shp (2014-kW). In 1962, however, the second prototype flew with the production standard twin-engine installation, and in 1964 a five-blade rotor was added. It was this version which went into production as the standard Warsaw Pact medium transport helicopter in about 1967.

The Mi-8 is widely used by the Soviet air force and other Warsaw Pact forces, apparently by the tactical units rather than by the VTA military transport force. It is broadly comparable with the land-based transport versions of the Sikorsky S-61 family, although there is so far no evidence that the type is used in the long-range rescue role as are the US Air Force's HH-3s. Its usefulness in military service is increased by its rear-loading doors, which allow the full width of the cabin to be used for bulky or awkward loads. The Mi-8 can, for instance, accommodate small military vehicles or infantry weapons such as anti-tank guns. Another standard feature is a four-axis (roll, pitch, yaw and altitude) autopilot.

Most military Mi-8s in Warsaw Pact service are armed, usually carying two weapon pylons on outriggers on each side of the fuselage. These are generally used for carrying rocket pods. Machine-guns do not seem to be permanently installed on the Mi-8, but it is reported that Soviet airborne troops are trained to fire their own small-arms from pivoted mountings in the windows. The current standard version is Hip E, with attachments for up to six rocket pods, surmounted by four launchers for AT-2 Swatter anti-tank guided weapons. The export Hip F carries six AT-3 Sagger ATGWs.

The Mi-8's armament is presumably intended for self-defence in the form of fire suppression during landings in hostile territory. The type is too large for aggressive use in combat, its size and conventional rotor system making it less manoeuvrable than a

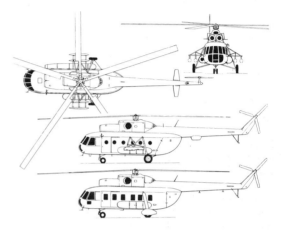

Mil Mi-8 Hip

specialized attack helicopter.

A specialized role in which the Mi-8 has been seen is minesweeping, a number of aircraft of this type having been ferried to Egypt in 1974 to assist in the clearing of the Suez Canal.

Specification

Type: twin-engined medium transport helicopter
Powerplant: two 1,500-shp (1119-kW) Isotov TV-2-1117A turboshafts
Performance: maximum speed 145 mph (230 km/h); cruising speed 125 mph (200 km/h); range with 6,500-lb (3000-kg) payload 265 mph (425 km); hovering ceiling 14,765 ft (4500 m)
Weights: empty 15,780 lb (7420 kg); maximum payload 8,800 lb (4000 kg); maximum take-off (VTO) 26,500 lb (12000 kg)
Dimensions: main rotor diameter 69 ft 10¼ in (21.29 m); fuselage length 60 ft 1 in (18.31 m); height 18 ft 4½ in (5.6 m); main rotor disc area 3,828 sq ft (355 m²)
Armament: normally, up to four 16×57-mm rocket pods on fuselage pylons
Operators: Afghanistan, Bangladesh, Czechoslovakia, East Germany, Egypt, Ethiopia, Finland, Hungary, Iraq, North Korea, Libya, Pakistan, Peru, Poland, Romania, Somalia, South Yemen, Syria, USSR, Vietnam, Yugoslavia

Mil Mi-14 Haze

Becoming the standard shore-based Soviet Naval Aviation ASW helicopter, the Mil Mi-14 "Haze-A" has been developed from the Mi-8 "Hip".

History and notes

It is not surprising that the Soviet Navy's land-based anti-submarine warfare (ASW) helicopter, the Mil Mi-14 'Haze' should be derived from the Mi-8 'Hip'; what is surprising, however, is that its development should have taken so long to come about. Once the requirement was formulated, the evolution of the type was fairly rapid; the prototype, designated V-14, was reported to be flying in 1973, and the operational version was seen in service in 1977. It is steadily replacing such aircraft as the ASW version of the Mi-4 'Hound' (possibly designated Mi-4MA), while the Kamov Ka-25 'Hormone' will probably continue to be the Soviet navy's standard shipboard helicopter.

The powerplant, rotor system and much of the air-frame of the Mi-14 appear closely similar to those of the Mi-8, the structural difference between the two types being confined mainly being found in the lower part of the fuselage. The Mi-14 has a flying-boat-type bow, a watertight hull, and rear-set sponsons carrying stabilising floats. Unlike that of its land-based progenitor, the undercarriage of the Mi-14 is retractable. The Mi-14 is clearly capable of water landings, although like the closely comparable Sikorsky SH-3 series it may be designed for water landings only in an emergency. This is also suggested by the location of the search radar under the nose; repeated immersion in salt water in hardly calculated to extend the life of electronic equipment, while the radome would not improve stability on the water. The tail bumper of the Mi-8 is retained, and carries a small pontoon to prevent the tail rotor from striking the water. The sponsons presumably contain fuel, supplanting the side-mounted tanks of the land-based aircraft.

Externally visible operational equipment includes the search radar beneath the nose and a magnetic anomaly detector "bird" carried on the rear of the pod. The "bird" is towed on a long cable when in use, well away from the magnetic disturbances produced by the airframe of the helicopter. It is likely

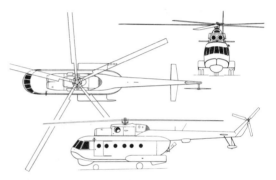

Mil Mi-14 Haze

that, like the SH-3, the Mi-14 carries a "dunking sonar" in the fuselage, and that the helicopter can lower this into the water while hovering. Weapons can presumably be carried on the lower fuselage sides forward of the sponsons, close to the centre of gravity.

The effectiveness of the Mi-14 is difficult to assess, depending as it does on the quality of its sensors and the data-processing equipment installed. It is likely that the systems are similar to those of the Ka-25, with the addition of extra processes, displays and crew positions, and that both aircraft will be steadily updated and improved in service. The main advantage of the larger helicopter over the Ka-25 is its greater range, and its ability to strike targets without the assistance of a surface vessel.

Specification

Type: Amphibious (?) anti-submarine warfare (ASW) helicopter. Powerplant, weights, performance and dimensions not known, but generally assumed to be similar to Mi-8
Armament: Offensive stores almost certainly include mines, depth charges and homing torpedoes
Operator: Soviet Navy

Mil Mi-24 Hind

The Mil Mi-24 "Hind-D" is a formidable battlefield helicopter now in widespread production for Soviet and allied air forces: the stub wings can carry four AT-6 "Spiral" anti-tank missiles and four pods each with thirty-two 57mm rocket projectiles, a four-barrel cannon is installed under the nose, and the capacious fuselage can accommodate a complete infantry squad.

History and notes

One of the most significant developments in the Soviet Union's tactical air power recently has been the development of a powerful force of heavily armed helicopters. The Mil Mi-24 'Hind' is a large and intimidating armed helicopter, and has been a cause for controversy and a source of puzzlement in the West since it was first observed in 1973. At first it was thought to be a straightforward armed version of the Mi-8, but it soon became clear that the new helicopter was rather smaller than its predecessor, although apparently using the same engines. The early 'Hind-A' appeared to be a conventional squad-carrying helicopter, with the addition of rocket pods and missile rails. This sort of combination had been experimentally used by the US Army in Vietnam, but had led to the development of specialized armed helicopters with automatic turreted armament and small silhouette, designed to escort the troop carriers, while other helicopters armed with guided weapons took on the enemy armour. The 'Hind-A', however, appeared to combine all three elements into one unwieldy package: a troop carrier with guns for self-defence, but equipped with rockets for defence suppression and anti-tank missiles for attacking enemy armour.

The conundrum of how the Mi-24 was to be used became even more perplexing with the arrival in 1975 of the 'Hind-D', adding to the earlier versions' armament a highly complex nose gun installation. The 'Hind-D' and the similar 'Hind E' and 'Hind F, also feature a more heavily protected cockpit, considerably less spacious than that of its predecessor. One fear was that the gun armament is intended for use against NATO's own anti-tank helicopters in Western Europe. By early 1980 it had been estimated that more than 1,000 'Hinds' were in service, both 'Hind-A and -C' and later variants being in volume production at a total rate of 30 units a month. The 'Hind-C' lacks provision for anti-tank guided weapons, while the 'Hind-B' was an early variant which does not appear to have entered service.

The Mi-24 seems to combine the powerplant and transmission of the Mi-8 with a smaller rotor and airframe, retaining the fan-cooled transmission characteristic of large Mil turbine helicopters. The cabin is considerably smaller than that of the 28-seater Mi-8, but should be able to accommodate a 12-man infantry section without difficulty, off-loading them via a large side door forward of the anhedralled stub wings.

The forward fuselage of the 'Hind-A' comprises a spacious 'greenhouse' canopy for the crew of three. Access to the flight-deck is via two large sliding windows, which can be opened in flight and may be used for defensive machine-guns. Visible avionic equipment includes a small blister under the forward fuselage (probably a missile sight) and an electro-optical head on the left inner pylon.

The 'Hind-D' forward fuselage features two tandem blown canopies on separate cockpits, reducing the chance of both crewmen being disabled with one hit. The windscreens are made of flat armour glass. In the extreme nose is a turret mounting a four-barrel gun; early models carried a 12.7-mm weapon, but a 23-mm cannon is fitted to current aircraft. Aft of the turret are two installations: a blister very similar to that under the nose of the 'Hind-A' and a larger installation which appears to contain a sensor slaved in elevation to the gun. This may be an assisted gunsight (either infra-red or TV). A large low-airspeed probe juts from the forward (gunner's) windscreen.

Now entering service on a version of the helicopter identified as 'Hind-E' is a new heavy anti-tank missile designated AT-6 'Spiral' by NATO, possibly weighing as much as 200 lb (90 kg) per round and with a 6-mile (10-km) range. It is likely to be laser-guided, with semi-active seeking, rather than wire/infra red guided like the AT-2 'Swatter' previously carried by 'Hind-D'. It is also believed to be tube-launched, and it is possible that more than four could be carried on one helicopter. Export

customers get a downgraded gunship known as 'Hind-E', armed with wire-guided AT-3 Sagger missiles.

Performance figures for the Mi-24 are difficult to assess, but records established by Soviet women pilots in a helicopter known as the 'A-10' may give a clue. Given that the Mi-24 has as much power as the larger Mi-8, the performance of the 'A-10' — including top speed of 228.9 mph (368.4 km/h) — is roughly what might be expected. However, its power/weight ratio is considerably less than that of the latest US armed helicopters, and with its relatively old-technology rotor system (similar to that of the Mi-8) the Mi-24 is not likely to be agile. Its large size compared with the Western ideal of a combat helicopter will also make it vulnerable to hostile fire. A surprising feature of the design, which will adversely affect its survivability, is its complete lack of infra-red signature suppression; the exhausts are open from all aspects. Counter-attack rather than stealth seem to be the keys to survivability.

The Mi-24 has been described as a 'helicopter battle-cruiser' and this may not be too bad a summing-up of what the machine does. Its main advantage is its ability to fight in several different ways: by dropping an anti-tank platoon, complete with missiles, while defending itself against ground fire with the nose gun (or in the case of the 'Hind-A', with side guns); by acting as its own escort on troop-carrying flights; by acting as a tank-killer pure and simple, with a vast capacity for even the heaviest reload rounds; or by carrying a squad of troops armed with man-portable surface-to-air missiles. An inevitable corollary of this 'combination of all arms' in a single aircraft, however, is that the vehicle's size and weight rule out evasive flying, and render it difficult to escape alert and well-equipped defences.

Specification

Type: ('Hind-A to-C') assault helicopter and ('Hind-D to F') gunship

Powerplant: (early versions) two 1,500-shp (1119-kW) Isotov TV-2 turboshafts, later aircraft two 2,200-shp (1640 kW) TV-3 turboshafts

Performance: maximum speed 200 mph (320 km/h); cruising speed 160 mph (260 km/h); service ceiling 18,000 ft (5500 m)

Weights: empty 14,000 lb (6500 kg); loaded 22,000 lb (10000 kg)

Dimensions: main rotor diameter 56 ft (17 m); length of fuselage 56 ft (17 m); height 14 ft (4.25 m); main rotor area 2,463 sq ft (227 m²)

Armament: ('Hind-D') four-barrel cannon of 14.5-or 20-mm calibre in nose turret; (all versions) up to four pods each containing thirty-two 57-mm rockets, plus up to four anti-tank missiles on stub wings; the 'Hind-A' has nose- and side-mounted guns

Operators: Algeria, Libya, Syria, USSR

Mitsubishi F-1

Mitsubishi F-1 figher of 3 Sqn, 3rd Air Wing, Japanese Air Self-Defence Force,
based at Misawa and formed in March 1978.

History and notes

Mitsubishi's F-1 close-support fighter is an adaptation of the same company's T-2 supersonic trainer
for the Japanese Air Self-Defence Force. Design
work on the fighter, which was originally designated
FS-T2-*Kai*, began in 1972 and the second and third
production T-2 trainers (59-5106 and 59-5107) were
converted to prototype F-1s. The first flight of
59-5107 in modified form was made on 3 June 1975,
with the second machine following it into the air four
days later.

The prototype retained the rear cockpit and
canopy of the T-2, with a fire-control system and test
equipment in place of the instructor. In the summer
of 1975 the fighter prototypes were delivered to the
JASDF Air Proving Wing at Gifu for service
testing, which was satisfactorily concluded in
November 1976.

The first production aircraft (70-8201) made its
maiden flight on 16 June 1977, and was handed over
to the JASDF at Mitsubishi's Komaki factory in
September that year. In early 1979 production
orders for 64 aircraft had been placed, against an
anticipated requirement of 70.

Power is provided by two Iskikawajima-Harima
TF40-IHI-801A turbofans (licence-built Rolls-
Royce/Turboméca Adours). Internal fuel is housed in
seven fuselage tanks with a total capacity of 841 Imperial gallons (3823 litres). In addition, 180-Imperial
gallon (821-litre) auxiliary fuel tanks can be carried
on two underwing pylons, with a third beneath the
fuselage.

The F-1's avionics fit includes dual UHF, IFF/SIF,
head-up display, radio altimeter, attitude and
heading reference system, air-data computer,
Tacan, Ferranti inertial navigation system, and a
radar warning and homing system. Mitsubishi Electric supplies the multi-mode radar and a fire control
system and bombing computer. Built-in armament
comprises a 20-mm JM-61 (General Electric) multi-
barrel cannon, while four underwing hardpoints, fitted with multiple-ejector racks, allow up to twelve
500-lb (227-kg) bombs to be carried. Alternative
loads include rocket pods, drop tanks or two Mitsubishi ASM-1 anti-ship missiles. For self-defence,
the F-1 can carry two or four Sidewinder or Mitsubishi AAM-1 air-to-air missiles on wingtip mountings.

Behind the cockpit is an avionics compartment
(housing a bombing computer) and an inertial
navigation system, and on the fin are radar warning

Mitsubishi F-1

aerials. The fuselage structure is basically that of the
T-2. The wing has leading-edge flaps, the outer
segments of which are extended to create a 'dog
tooth', and single-slotted flaps ahead of which are
slotted spoilers for roll control.

The first JASDF unit to equip with the F-1 was the
3rd *Hiko-tai*, formerly a North American F-86F
unit, which reformed with the Mitsubishi fighter at
Misawa air base in the spring of 1978; the 8th *Hiko-
tai* will follow. The JASDF's original plans called for
three 18-aircraft squadrons, but more recent thinking favours a squadron strength of 25. This means
that current procurement plans will provide aircraft
for only two squadrons.

Specification

Type: ground attack fighter
Powerplant: two 7,070-lb (3206-kg) Ishikawajima-
Harima TF40-IHI-801A afterburning turbofans
Performance: maximum speed at 36,090 ft (11000
m) Mach 1.6; maximum rate of climb at sea level
35,000 ft (10670 m) per minute; service ceiling
50,000 ft (15240 m); combat radius with 4,000-lb
(1814-kg) warload and external tanks 218 miles
(351 km)
Weights: empty equipped 14,017 lb 66358 kg);
maximum take-off 30,146 lb (13674 kg)
Dimensions: span 25 ft 10¼ in (7.88 m); length 56
ft 9½ in (17.31 m); height 14 ft 4¼ in (4.38 m);
wing area 228 sq ft (21.18 m²)
Armament: one 20-mm JM-61 cannon and 6,000 lb
(2720 kg) of external stores, including bombs,
rockets, drop tanks or Mitsubishi ASM-1 air-to-
surface missiles; wingtip attachments for up to
four Sidewinder or Mitsubishi AAM-1 air-to-air
missiles
Operator: Japan

Myasishchev M-4/201 Bison

Myasishchev M-4 strategic bomber, code-named "Bison-C", operated by the Aviatsiya Del'nevo Deistviya (Long Range Aviation) of the Soviet Air Force.

History and notes

One of the Soviet Union's most underestimated aircraft, the Myasishchev bomber usually known as the M-4 'Bison' has probably been at least as important to the development of Long-Range Aviation (DA) and the AVMF (Soviet Naval Aviation) as the better known Tupolev Tu-95 'Bear'. The type is often dismissed as a near-failure, partly because it was not appreciated for many years that what had been identified as a special record-breaking version was in fact the difinitive production model of the aircraft.

The availability of the massive Mikulin AM-3 turbojet made it a logical step to incorporate four of these engines in a heavy bomber, as well as using them in the twin-engined Tu-16 'Badger'. The Myasishchev bureau was formed in 1951 to build such an aircraft, and the first prototype flew in early 1953, shortly after its US contemporary, the Boeing B-52 Stratofortress. However, by that time it was clear that the original version would have inadequate range, and it appears that only a few of the AM-3-powered aircraft (designated 'Bison-A' by NATO) went into service. The heavier and considerably more powerful Myasishchev 201M 'Bison-B' flew in early 1955. Among other changes, two of the five gun turrets fitted to the original aircraft were removed to save weight.

The 'Bison-B' was one of the first Soviet types to carry a flight-probe, and many of the old 'Bison-As' were converted to tankers with a hose-reel in the bomb bay. With the rise of the Soviet navy, many of the 'Bison-Bs' were transferred to the AVMF as long-range reconnaissance aircraft, and a later development, the 'Bison-C', carried a large search radar in an extended nose. All 'Bisons' have ventral radar installations and observation blisters, and some appear to be equipped for electronic intelligence (Elint) operations. AVMF aircraft have now been retired, but the M-4 remains in service as a bomber and tanker with the SA.

The 201M established a series of impressive world records in 1959, although at that time the designation was thought to apply to the M-52 supersonic bomber; only in 1967 was it realised that the 201M was a 'Bison' variant. One aircraft attained 638 mph (1028 km/h) on a 1000-km (621-mile) closed circuit with a 59,525-lb (27000-kg) payload, simultaneously setting a record for zero payload over the same course. The 201M lifted a 121,275-lb (55000-kg) payload to 43,036 ft (13121 m), a record unmatched by any aircraft until the appearance of the Lockheed C-5A.

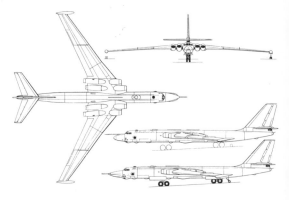

Myasischev M-4 Bison C

The 201M has not been seen with air-to-surface missiles, possibly because its twin-bogie undercarriage design results in a lower ground clearance than that of the Tu-95. As a free-fall bomber, it was probably obsolete almost as soon as it entered service, the increasing performance of interceptors and missile systems rendering it a relatively easy target. As far as is known, the 'Bison' has never been converted for low-level attack as have the B-52 and BAe Vulcan. It is most unlikely that any of the 201Ms are still equipped as bombers, serving instead as tankers and reconnaissance aircraft. The old AM-3-powered 'Bison-As' have probably all been retired.

Specification

Type: strategic bomber, tanker and maritime reconnaissance aircraft (specification for Myasishchev 201 'Bison-C')
Powerplant: four 28,500 lb (13000 kg) Soloviev D-15 (almost certainly bypass) turbojets
Performance: maximum speed 680 mph (1100 km/h) or Mach 0.95 at 10,000 ft (3000 m); cruising speed 560 mph (900 km/h); service ceiling 56,000 ft (17000 m); range with 11,000-lb (5000-kg) weapon load 11,200 miles (18000 km)
Weights: empty 198,500 lb (90000 kg); normal take-off 365,000 lb (165000 kg); overload take-off 463,000 lb (210000 kg)
Dimensions: span 172 ft 2 in (52.5 m); length 175 ft 2 in (53.4 m); wing area 3,440 sq ft (320 m²)
Armament: Six 23-mm NR-23 cannon in dorsal, ventral and tail barbettes, and up to 33,000 lb (15000 kg) of internal stores
Operators: USSR

North American F-100 Super Sabre

F-100C-5-NA (54-1798) Super Sabre of 111th Sqn, Turk Hava Kuvvetleri, 1st Jet Air Base, Eskisehir, 1973.

History and notes

The first of the USAF's so-called 'Century-series' fighters, because their designations were 100 or over, the North American F-100 is also regarded as being the world's first operational fighter capable of sustaining a speed in excess of Mach 1 in level flight. Its design originated as a private venture by North American Aviation for an improved successor to the North American F-86 Sabre, and was identified originally by the company as the Sabre 45 because of the aircraft's 45° of wing sweepback.

In October 1951 the USAF requested North American to proceed with development of the Sabre 45 design, resulting in a rapidly produced mockup which, when inspected in November, brought a demand for more than 100 detail changes. The company's involvement in accelerated production of the F-86 for deployment in Korea meant that reduced priority was given to the Sabre 45 project, and it was not until 21 March 1952 that inspection of the revised mockup could take place. This was then designated F-100A, as the result of an order for two YF-100A prototypes placed by letter contract on 3 January 1952, followed by an order for 23 production F-100As in 11 February 1952.

The initial flight of the first prototype was made on 25 May 1953, and in a subsequent flight this aircraft demonstrated a speed of Mach 1.05 although powered by a derated prototype engine. The second prototype flew on 14 October 1953, and the first production F-100A on 29 October 1953: all three aircraft confirmed shortcomings in respect of flight control, stability, and pilot visibility.

Interim modifications were made to correct these deficiencies and on 27 September 1954 F-100As entered operational service with the Tactical Air Command's 479th Fighter Day Wing at George AFB, California. By early November all F-100s were grounded following serious accidents. The major problem was that at high speed and under high-g the aircraft had a tendency to yaw: if this instability was not recognised immediately and corrected the result was loss of control and break-up. Electronic and aerodynamic 'fixes' including extended wings and a taller vertical tail, were a temporary paliative; but it was not until introduction of a hydraulically-actuated electrically-controlled yaw damper on the subsequent F-100C, plus a pitch damper, that the problem was regarded as solved.

By the time that production ended in 1959, the USAF had accepted 2,249 Super Sabres for its own

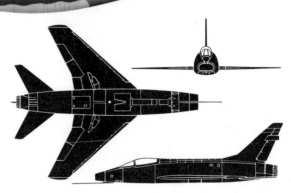

North American F-100D Super Sabre

use, fewer than had been expected. The F-100A had been followed by the F-100C fighter-bomber with a strengthened wing for external loads, the F-100D fighter-bomber with an autopilot and other improved equipment and detail changes, and the longer-fuselage two-seat F-100F combat trainer with full operational capability. F-100s saw extensive service in Vietnam, and seven F-100Fs were equipped with anti-SAM (surface-to-air missile) avionics, under the designation Wild Weasel I, to counter North Vietnamese weapons, and in April 1966 were deployed to attack 'Fan-Song' fire-control radar systems.

Specification

Type: supersonic tactical fighter/fighter-bomber/combat trainer

Powerplant: (F-100D) one 17,000-lb (7711-kg) afterburning thrust Pratt & Whitney J57-P-21A turbojet

Performance: (F-100D): maximum speed Mach 1.3 or 864 mph (1390 km/h) at 36,000 ft (10970 m); cruising speed 565 mph (909 km/h) at 25,000 ft (7620 m); combat radius 530 miles (853 km)

Weights: (F-100D) empty 21,000 lb (9525 kg); maximum take-off 34,832 lb (15800 kg)

Dimensions: span 38 ft 9 in (11.81 m); length (F-100D) 47 ft 0 in (14.33 m); span (F-100F) 52 ft 6 in (16.00 m); wing area 385 sq ft (35.77 m²)

Armament: (F-100D) four M39 20-mm cannon, with six underwing hardpoints for rockets, bombs, air-to-air and air-to-surface missiles, or drop tanks

Operators: Denmark, France, Taiwan, Turkey, US Air National Guard (1980 Denmark, Taiwan and Turkey only)

North American Rockwell OV-10 Bronco

The US Marine Corps uses the Rockwell OV-10A Bronco for observation missions. This example has a low infra-red paint scheme.

History and notes

In 1956 Grumman designed a battlefield surveillance aircraft to satisfy a joint US Army and Marine Corps requirement, and in the following year the US Navy, acting as joint programme manager, ordered nine of these aircraft for test and evaluation. The Marine Corps had allocated the designation OF-1 to its version of what became the Grumman G-134 Mohawk, but withdrew from the project before the first prototype was completed.

Experience of limited-warfare engagements, following cancellation of the OF-1, convinced US Marine planners that they had an urgent need for a light multi-purpose aircraft which could, if and when required, be operated in a counter-insurgency (COIN) role. Accordingly, a specification was drawn up for a light armed reconnaissance aircraft (LARA) and Requests For Proposals were issued by the US Navy. Submissions were received from nine US manufacturers, and in August 1964 North America's NAH300 design was announced as the winner.

Following the selection of North American's design, seven YOV-10A prototypes were ordered for test and evaluation, and the first of these made its maiden flight on 16 July 1965. Features included two crew in tandem with near-perfect view, STOL wing and rough-field landing gear, armament on sponsons on the nacelle-type fuselage, and a rear door for casualties or cargo.

Production aircraft began to enter service in 1967 and the USAF's OV-10As, of which 157 were acquired, were used operationally in Vietnam at the beginning of 1968. The US Marine Corps received 114 OV-10As, with deliveries to VMA-5 beginning on 23 February 1968. To enhance their capabilities for operations in Vietnam, 15 of the USAF's OV-10As were equipped with special equipment under the Pave Nail programme. This provided a stabilized night periscope, a laser range-finder/target illuminator, a Loran receiver and co-ordinate converter. Such aircraft proved valuable for locating targets at night, which could then be illuminated for attack by laser-seeking missiles.

Other versions of the OV-10 Bronco include six OV-10Bs, similar to the OV-10A, supplied to the German forces for target towing, plus 18 OV-10B(Z) aircraft supplied in 1970 for improved performance in the same mission, these having a 2,950-lb (1338-kg) General Electric J85-GE-4 turbojet pylon-mounted above the wing.

Two OV-10As were modified under a 1970 US

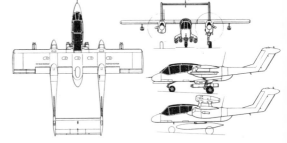

Rockwell OV-10 Bronco

Navy contract to YOV-10D NOGS (Night Observation/Gunship System) aircraft to provide the Marine Corps with a new night operational capability. Special equipment included a 20-mm gun turret beneath the aft fuselage, and a forward-looking infra-red (FLIR) sensor and laser target illuminator in a turret beneath an extended nose. Under-wing pylons carry a wide range of stores. Following extensive tests, 17 USMC OV-10As were delivered to Rockwell's Columbus Division in early 1978 for conversion to OV-10D NOS (night observation surveillance) aircraft with developed equipment and avionics as installed in the YOV-10D NOGS prototypes, plus the provision of 1,040-hp (776-kW) T76 engines. Initial deliveries began in early 1979.

Specification

Type: multi-purpose counter-insurgency aircraft
Powerplant: (OV-10A) maximum speed at sea level without weapons 281 mph (452 km/h); combat radius with maximum weapons 228 miles (367 km); ferry range with maximum auxiliary fuel 1,382 miles (2224 km)
Weights: (OV-10A) empty 6,893 lb (3127 kg); normal take-off 9,908 lb (4494 kg); overload take-off 14,444 lb (6552 kg)
Dimensions: span 40 ft 0 in (12.19 m); length 41 ft 7 in (12.67 m); height 15 ft 2 in (4.62 m); wing area 291 sq ft (27.03 m)
Armament: four weapons attachment points beneath the sponsons and one beneath centre fuselage with combined capacity of 3,600 lb (1633 kg); two 7.62-mm (0.3-in) M60C machine-guns in each sponson; USMC aircraft can carry one AIM-9D Sidewinder beneath each wing
Operators: Germany, Indonesia, Thailand, US Air Force, US Marine Corps, Venezuela

Northrop F-5A/F-5B Freedom Fighter

F-5A-40 of the 341st Squadron 111th Wing, Hellenic Air Force, Achialos.

History and notes

In 1954 the US government initiated a study to determine Asian and European requirements for a lightweight and comparatively inexpensive high-performance fighter, to be supplied to friendly nations via the Military Assistance Programme. As a result of this interest, Northrop began investigation of the requirement, identifying their initial work as the N-156 concept. Two years of private development followed before the USAF and Navy showed interest in a supersonic trainer derived from this work and this, designated T-38, was developed in parallel with the private venture N-156C. First flight of the prototype N-156C was made on 30 July 1959, and during which a speed in excess of Mach 1 was attained.

However, it was not until 23 April 1962 that the US Secretary of Defense approved USAF selection of the N-156C, this being designated subsequently F-5, the first single-seat F-5A prototype flying initially in May 1963. A two-seat version for fighter/trainer duties was developed and built simultaneously under the designation F-5B, and this entered operational service four months before the F-5A, with the 4441st Combat Crew Training Squadron at Williams AFB, Chandler, Arizona, on 30 April 1964.

To evaluate the combat potential of the F-5A, a 12-aircraft unit of the Tactical Air Command's 4503rd Tactical Fighter Wing was deployed to South-East Asia in October 1965, under the codename Project Skoshi Tiger. It was from this project that the F-5 acquired the nickname 'Tiger'. The aircraft deployed to Da Nang were diverted from the Military Assistance Programme, and provided with in-flight refuelling capability, armour protection, jettisonable pylons, additional avionics, and finished in camouflage paint. In a period of four months these aircraft flew more than 2,500 hours, in roles which included close support, interdiction and reconnaissance. In early 1966 the unit was moved to Bien Hoa AB, from where interdiction, armed reconnaissance and combat air patrols against enemy MiG fighters were flown over North Vietnam.

Versions of the F-5 include the basic F-5A, the two-seat F-5B and the reconnaissance version RF-5A, which carries four KS-92A cameras mounted in the fuselage nose. The Royal Norwegian Airforce flies modified F-5As under the designation F-5G and reconnaissance versions under the designation RF-5G. Versions of the F5A/B built jointly by Canada

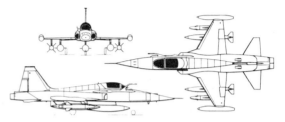

Northrop F-5A Freedom Fighter

and The Netherlands for their armed forces, are known as CF5A/D and NF-5AB respectively. Spanish versions of the F5 built under licence by AISA (CASA) are known as the C-9 and the CE-9.

Specification

Type: tactical fighter, fighter/trainer, and reconnaissance aircraft

Powerplant: two 4,080 lb (1850 kg) afterburning General Electric J85-GE-13 turbojets

Performance: maximum speed (F-5A) Mach 1.4 or 924 mph (1488 km/h) at 36,000 ft (10970 m); (F-5B) Mach 1.35 or 891 mph (1435 km/h) at 36,000 ft (10970 m); maximum cruising speed without afterburning (both versions) Mach 0.97 or 640 mph (1031 km/h) at 36,000 ft (10970 m); combat radius with maximum payload, plus allowances for 5 minutes combat at S/L (F-5A) 195 miles (314 km), (F-5B) 201 miles (323 km); combat radius with maximum fuel, plus allowances for 5 minutes combat at S/L (F-5A) 558 miles (898 km),(F-5B) 570 miles (917 km)

Weights: empty equipped (F-5A) 8,085 lb (3667 kg), (F-5B) 8,361 lb (3792 kg); maximum military load 6,200 lb (2812 kg); maximum take-off (F-5A) 20,677 lb (9379 kg), (F-5B) 20,500 lb (9298 kg)

Dimensions: span 25 ft 3 in (7.70 m); length (F-5A) 47 ft 2 in (14.38 m), (F-5B) 46 ft 4 in (14.12 m); height (F-5A) 13 ft 2 in (4.01 m), (F-5B) 13 ft 1 in (3.99 m); wing area 170 sq ft (15.79 m²)

Armament: two 20-mm M-29 guns (F-5A/B), two M-39 guns (RF-5A), two AIM-9B Sidewinders; plus AGM-12B Bullpup ASMs; LAU-3/A and LAU-10/A rocket pods; Mk-81, Mk-82, Mk-83, Mk-84, M-117 and BLU-1/B bombs

Operators: Brazil, Canada, Ethiopia, Greece, Jordan, Morocco, the Netherlands, North Yemen, Norway, Philippines, South Korea, Spain, Taiwan, Thailand, Turkey, Venezuela, Vietnam

Northrop F-5E/F Tiger II

History and notes

While production of the Northrop F-5A/B was in progress, the company developed as a private venture an improved version of the F-5, using as a prototype an F-5A airframe. First flown in March 1969, it was powered by two 5,000-lb (2267-kg) afterburning General Electric J85-GE-21 turbojets, providing almost 23% more power than the engines of the F-5. This higher-performance aircraft was offered to the USAF who were acting as the US government's instrument in the IFA competition for foreign customers as a follow-on to the F-5, but this force was unprepared to accept this as a replacement for the satisfactory and effective F-5 without extended flight testing to establish whether the new engines offered any really significant advantages. There were other factors which at that time caused some concern to the Secretary of Defense and the USAF. If Northrop's new fighter introduced new engines and some degree of advanced ideas, would it retain the proven capability of the F-5A/B to be operated and maintained successfully by nations which did not aspire to the technological experience of the USAF? Conversely, the USAF wanted a fighter with expanded performance, for the primary requirement was for a fighter able to fly air superiority missions against aircraft such as the Soviet-built MiG-21. The tentative name of Advanced International Fighter was attached to the new design but, effective or not, the USAF could not expect to receive funding for its development and production without the normal Congressional procedure of selecting a contractor. Thus, requests for proposals were sent to eight US manufacturers on 26 February 1970, and in the following month four companies replied, each offering a version of a fighter aircraft already in production. Ling-Temco-Vought proposed a variant of the F-8 Crusader, Lockheed of the F-104 Starfighter, McDonnell Douglas of the F-4 Phantom II and, of course, Northrop the advanced F-5. It was the last which was chosen for production to meet the requirements for what had by then become known as the International Fighter Aircraft (IFA), and on 20 November 1970 the USAF announced selection of Northrop as the prime contractor for this programme.

The effectiveness of the F-5E in service use can perhaps be judged best by the fact that the top air combat training schools in the US, the Navy's Fighter Weapon School and the Air Force's Aggressor Squadron, both use F-5Es as 'enemy' aircraft in combat training against US squadrons of first-line operational tactical fighters.

By early 1978 orders for the F-5E/F totalled just over 1,000, in ratio of approximately 9:1, of which about 75% had then been delivered. An RF-5E reconnaissance version was approved for development on 31 March 1978, the prototype making its first flight on 29 January 1979. This has a longer nose, the usable volume of 23 cu ft (0.65m³) allowing

Northrop F-5E Tiger II

the carriage of palletized reconnaissance equipment such as cameras and infra-red sensors. It is intended that during the flight test programme of the RF-5E both day and night photo-reconnaissance missions will be flown.

Northrop is currently developing from the F-5E an F-X (intermediate export) fighter. With the designation F-5G this is to be powered by a single General Electric F404 turbofan, increasing available power by some 60% and so enhancing the type's air combat capabilities.

Specification

Type: tactical fighter, fighter/trainer, and reconnaissance aircraft

Powerplant: two 5,000-lb (2267-kg) afterburning General Electric J85-GE-21 turbojets

Performance: maximum speed (F-5E) Mach 1.64 or 1,083 mph (1743 km/h) at 36,000 ft (10970 m); (F-5F) Mach 1.56, or 1,030 mph (1657 km/h) at 36,090 ft (11000 m); maximum cruising speed (F-5E) Mach 0.98 or 647 mph (1040 km/h) at 36,000 ft (10970 m); combat radius with maximum fuel, two AIM-9E Sidewinders, plus allowances for 5 minutes combat with maximum afterburning power at 15,000 ft (4570 m) 656 miles (1056 km); combat radius with 5,200-lb (2358-kg) weapons load, two AIM-9E Sidewinders, maximum fuel, plus allowances for 5 minutes combat at military power at S/L 138 miles (222 km)

Weights: empty (F-5E) 9,683 lb (4392 kg), (F-5F) 10,567 lb (4793 kg); maximum take-off (F-5E) 24,664 lb (11187 kg), (F-5F) 25,147 lb (11406 kg)

Dimensions: span 26 ft 8 in (8.13 m); span over missiles 27 ft 11¾ in (8.53 m); length (F-5E) 48 ft 2 in (14.68 m), (F-5F) 51 ft 7 in (15.72 m); height (F-5E) 13 ft 4 in (4.06 m), (F-5F) 13 ft 1¾ in (4.01 m); wing area 186 sq ft (17.3 m²)

Armament: two Colt-Browning M-39 20-mm guns (F-5E), one M-39 (F-5F); two AIM-9E Sidewinders; LAU-3/A and LAU-59/A rockets; Mk-82, Mk-84, Mk-117A1, BLU-27/B, BLU-32/B, and CBU-24/49 bombs

Operators: Brazil, Chile, Egypt, Ethiopia, Indonesia, Iran, Jordan, Kenya, Malaysia, North Yemen, Saudi Arabia, Singapore, South Korea, Sudan, Switzerland, Taiwan, Thailand, and the USAF and USN (as trainers)

Northrop F-5E/F Tiger II

"Lizard" camouflage applied to an F-5E (01528) of the 64th FITS, 57th FWW at Nellis AFB.

Fuerza Aerea de Chile F-5E of Grupo 7 at Antofagasta AFB. Delivered in 1976, the 15 F-5Es in Chilean service have a dorsal fin extension housing the ADF antenna.

Chinese Nationalist Air Force F-5E (74-00959) "Chung Cheng" of 2nd Fighter Wing, Taiwan. Example illustrated is one of initial batch supplied direct from Northrop.

The Royal Saudi Air Force operated 70 Northrop F-5E Tiger IIs in four squadrons based at Taif and Khamis Mushayt.

Forca Aerea Brasileira F-5E (4820) of the 1° Escuadrao, 1° Grupo de Aviacao de Caca, at Santa Cruz AFB, Rio de Janeiro.

Northrop F-5E (159881) of the US Naval Fighter Weapons "Top Gun" School at Miramar NAS, Calif. Soviet style numbers adorn the nose and the school emblem is on the fin.

Northrop T-38A Talon

T-38A of the 64th Fighter Weapons School USAF.

History and notes

As mentioned briefly in the description of the Northrop F-5A/B, the evolution of that tactical fighter had begun with Northrop's N-156 concept which, after two years of development as a private venture, had resulted in a supersonic trainer which in 1956 was identified as the N-156T and submitted as a proposal to the USAF. Three prototypes were ordered in December 1956 for development as a two-seat supersonic basic trainer (the first and, except for the Mitsubishi T1B, only such aircraft in the world). The first of these made its initial flight on 10 April 1959 at Edwards AFB, California. By that time there had been a contract revision, concluded in June 1958, for the supply of six aircraft under the designation YT-38, plus one airframe for static testing.

Powerplant of the first two prototypes comprised two 2,100-lb (953-kg) thrust non-afterburning General Electric YJ85-GE-1 turbojets, but the remainder of the YT-38 trials aircraft had 3,600-lb (1633-kg) afterburning thrust YJ85-GE-5 engines. Whilst testing of the first two prototypes was satisfactory, early evaluation of the YT-38s with the more powerful engines left little doubt that the US Air Force was about to acquire an exceptional trainer, and the first contract was for 13 T-38As, which were given the name Talon. The first was delivered for service with the USAF's 3510th Flying Training Wing, at Randolph AFB, on 17 March 1961.

When it entered service, no aircraft could have looked less like a trainer than the Talon. Its slender area-ruled fuselage, narrow-span sharp-edged wings, and tailplane with anhedral, identified it at a glance as an advanced combat aircraft: many pupils wondered just what they were taking on. But despite its high-performance capability, with a Mach 1.3 speed at altitude, its stalling speed was as low as 146 mph (235 km/h) and very considerable design effort had been directed to make it an aeroplane which would not be too demanding on the pupil in the front seat. Both pupil and instructor are accommodated on rocket-powered ejection seats, the latter raised 10 in (0.25 m) higher than the pupil to improve the instructor's forward view. All flying controls are hydraulically powered by a duplicated system; directional and longitudinal stability augmenters are installed in series with the control system; and aileron design and area are such that the Talon can be flown and landed safely with one aileron inoperative.

Northrop T-38 Talon

The cumulative effect of such attention to the safety aspect, plus the inherent reliability of the entire aircraft and its systems, enabled the US Air Force to report in 1972 that the T-38 had maintained consistently the highest safety record of any supersonic aircraft in USAF service. During 1971 the T-38A accident rate was 1.2 per 100,000 flying hours, which was below half the average for the Air Force.

When production ended in early 1972, a total of 1,187 T-38s had been delivered to the USAF. Other users included the US Navy, which acquired five from the US Air Force, and NASA, which obtained a total of 24 from Northrop to serve as flight-readiness trainers for astronauts. In addition, 46 were supplied through the USAF for use by the German *Luftwaffe* in the training of German student pilots in the United States: these aircraft retain USAF military insignia.

Specification

Type: two-seat supersonic basic trainer
Powerplant: two 3,850-lb (1746-kg) afterburning thrust General Electric J85-GE-5A turbojets
Performance: maximum speed Mach 1.3 or 858 mph (1381 km/h) at 36,000 ft (10970 m); maximum cruising speed 627 mph (1009 km/h) at 36,000 ft (10970 m); range with maximum fuel, with 20 minutes reserve at 10,000 ft (3050 m) 1,140 miles (1835 km)
Weights: empty 7,164 lb (3250 kg); maximum take-off and landing 11,820 lb (5361 kg)
Dimensions: span 25 ft 3 in (7.70 m); length 46 ft 4½ in (14.14 m); height 12 ft 10½ in (3.92 m); wing area 170 sq ft (15.79 m²)
Armament: none
Operators: NASA, US Air Force, US Navy, Turkey, West Germany

Panavia Tornado

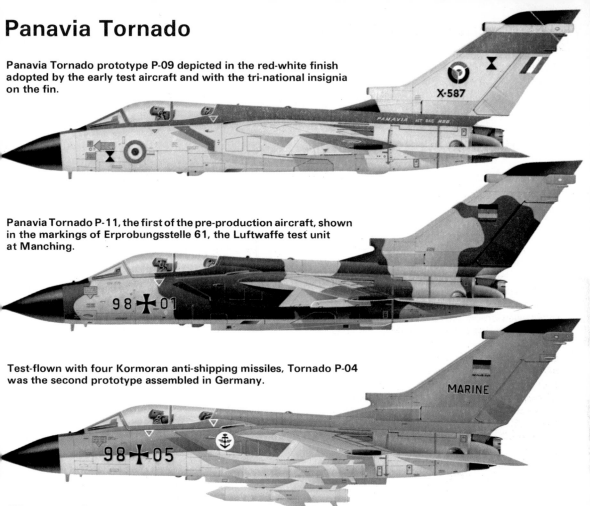

Panavia Tornado prototype P-09 depicted in the red-white finish
adopted by the early test aircraft and with the tri-national insignia
on the fin.

Panavia Tornado P-11, the first of the pre-production aircraft, shown
in the markings of Erprobungsstelle 61, the Luftwaffe test unit
at Manching.

Test-flown with four Kormoran anti-shipping missiles, Tornado P-04
was the second prototype assembled in Germany.

History and notes

The tri-national Panavia Tornado fighter-bomber,
previously known as the MRCA (Multi-Role Combat
Aircraft), has been developed to equip the air forces
of Britain, Germany and Italy, together with the
German navy. The manufacuturer, Panavia, was
formed in March 1969 and comprises a consortium
of British Aerospace, Messerschmitt-Bölkow-Blohm
(MBB) and Aeritalia. The complementary engine
organisation, Turbo-Union, was set up in September
1969 and consists of Rolls-Royce, Motoren- und
Turbinen-Union (MTU) and Fiat.

The Tornado has resulted from the need to replace
a wide variety of earlier types used for several roles.
These include German and Italian Lockheed F-104G
Starfighters, together with the Royal Air Force's
HS Vulcans, BAC Canberras and HS Buccaneers.
These are all due to be superseded by the Tornado
IDS (interdictor/strike) version, called Tornado
FG.1 by the RAF. In addition, the Tornado F.2 or
ADV (Air-Defence Variant) is being developed to
succeed the RAF's BAC Lightning and McDonnell
Douglas Phantom interceptors.

The abandonment of earlier studies, such as the
AFVG (Anglo-French Variable-Geometry) and joint
US-German projects, led to the adoption of Tornado

as a tri-national programme in an effort to increase
the production run and thus reduce unit costs.
Canada, Belgium and the Netherlands also took part
in the early studies but subsequently withdrew, leaving the present three sponsoring countries. Development began in mid-1970, following the completion of
the feasibility and project-definition phases.

The Tornado is a twin-engined, two-seat aircraft
which is intended to perform six major roles covering the requirements of the four initial operating
services. These are close air support and battlefield
interdiction, interdiction/counter-air operations, air
superiority, interception, naval attack and reconnaissance. A dual-control trainer version with secondary combat responsibilities is also in production.

A variable-geometry (swing-wing) layout was
adopted to give the Tornado the maximum operating
flexibility. This includes the ability to use dispersed
semi-prepared airfields, loiter for long periods with
the wings swept forwards, cruise for long distances
at high and medium altitudes, and fly at high speed
just above the ground or sea with its wings swept
back for the best gust-response characteristics and a
smooth ride. An extremely sophisticated navigation-
attack system is installed, but a two-man crew was

Panavia Tornado

nevertheless selected to maximize the aircraft's efficiency. The Tornado will perform its attack role at least as well as the much larger General Dynamics F-111 and provide an effective all-weather counter to the build-up of Warsaw Pact forces.

The first of nine prototypes made its maiden flight in August 1974, this series being followed by six pre-production Tornadoes. Four of these are to be refurbished to operational standard and will enter service alongside 805 new production aircraft: 324 for the *Luftwaffe* and German navy, 385 for the RAF (of which 165 will be ADVs) and 100 for the Italian air force. Delays have resulted in the service-entry timetable being put back, but delivery for service test began in February 1977, and the Tri-National Training Establishment at RAF Cottesmore began work in 1980, the first production Tornado having been delivered in the middle of the year.

The shoulder-mounted wings are swept by 25° when fully forward and 66° when swung completely aft; the angle is controlled manually by the pilot, although a semi-automatic arrangement is likely to be adopted (certainly for the F.2) to relieve the crew's workload in air combat. The navigation-attack system includes a Texas Instruments multi-mode radar for terrain following, ground mapping, air-to-air acquisition and lock-on, navigation fixes and air-to-ground target ranging. The Ferranti inertial navigator and Decca doppler radar feed navigation information to the main computer, a Litef Spirit 3. Data are communicated to the navigator on his combined radar/projected-map and television displays, and to the pilot on a projected-map repeater. Flight-director and weapon-aiming symbology is presented to the pilot on his head-up display, and any other information required by the navigator can be extracted from the central computer using television tabular displays.

This avionic equipment, including a retractable derivative of the Ferranti LRMTS (Laser Ranger and Marked-Target Seeker) also used in the SEPECAT Jaguar and BAe (HS) Harrier, allows the Tornado to carry out single-pass attacks at high speed and deliver its weapons extremely accurately. During low-level trials the aircraft has demonstrated a sustained indicated airspread of 920 mph (1472 km/h), which is well above the limit of almost all other types at present in existence.

The demanding specification laid down for the Tornado called for an advanced new engine, the RB.199-34R. This three-spool turbofan, two of which are installed, is designed for an economic fuel consumption at maximum dry thrust and a high maximum afterburning thrust. This combination of attributes is necessary if the aircraft is to be able to take off from a short run, have a top speed of more than Mach 2 and good combat manoeuvrability, yet also have a worthwhile range during low-level interdiction missions at transonic speeds with heavy weapon loads. Thrust reversers and anti-skid brakes provide a short-landing capability.

The F.2 Air-Defence Variant, an interceptor designed specifically for the RAF, incorporates a number of modifications for its role of patrolling the East German border and defending the large sea areas around Britain. Marconi Avionics and Ferranti are collaborating on development of a new air-interception radar, known unofficially as Foxhunter, which will be able to detect intruders at distances of more than 115 miles (185 km). The Tornado F.2 will also be fitted with a Marconi Avionics long-range visual identification system to sort out targets from friendly aircraft, and it will carry British Aerospace Sky Flash air-to-air missiles which, operating in conjunction with the radar, can seek out and destroy intruders at ranges of 25 miles (40 km) or more regardless of their height. In addition to the four Sky Flash missiles mounted in semi-recessed belly positions, the Tornado F.2 will be armed with two or four AIM-9L Super Sidewinder air-to-air missiles and will carry a single built-in 27-mm Mauser cannon of the same type as is installed in the IDS aircraft, which are fitted with two guns.

Despite these changes, the ADV is 80% common with the IDS. The major obvious difference is a 4 ft (1.2 m) extension to the forward fuselage to accommodate the new radar (with a pointed radome), different avionics and extra fuel. Three ADV prototypes are being built, and the first flew on 27 October 1979. The aircraft is due to enter service with the RAF in about 1982.

Specification

Type: multi-role combat aircraft
Powerplant: two 15,000-lb (6805-kg) Turbo-Union RB.199-34R afterburning turbofans
Performance: maximum level speed at altitude over Mach 2.2 or 1,450 mph (2335 km/h); level speed (clean) at low altitude about Mach 1.2 or 810 mph (1305 km/h); tactical radius at least 870 miles (1390 km) with heavy weapon load; ceiling 50,000 ft (1520 m)
Weights: empty about 25,000 lb (11350 kg); maximum take-off about 60,000 lb (27200 kg)
Dimensons: span (wings swept) 28 ft 2 in (8.60 m); span (wings forward) 45 ft 7 in (13.90 m); length 54 ft 9½ in (16.70 m); height 18 ft 8½ in (5.70 m)
Armament: (IDS) two 27-mm Mauser cannon and up to more than 18,000 lb (8180 kg) of stores, including bombs, Martel air-to-surface missiles Kormoran and P3T anti-ship missiles, Sparrow, Aspide, Sky Flash and Sidewinder air-to-air missiles, MW-1 submunition dispensers, BL755 and other cluster bombs, JP233 anti-runway bombs, etc; (ADV) one 27-mm Mauser cannon and four Sky Flash air-to-air missiles, plus up to four AIM-9L Super Sidewinder air-to-air missiles
Operators: on order for Italy, UK, West Germany

Panavia Tornado

This example is one of the original nine flight prototypes, P.06 (XX948), assembled at Warton by BAe and used for various stores-separation and gun-firing trials. In addition to the eight 1,000 lb bombs it is shown with two 1500-litre (396 US gal) drop tanks and ECM jammer pods. Defensive electronics are said to include the EL-73 radar warning system, Ajax pods, ALQ-101(V) pods, ARI.18228 fin aerials and various dispensers.

Rockwell T-2 Buckeye

History and notes

In 1956 the US Navy required a jet training aircraft which, once a student had completed his *ab initio* period on a less potent and less costly to operate machine, would be suitable for continuous instruction in stages up to advanced training, fighter tactics, and carrier operation. The winner of the competition was North American Aviation (now North American Aircraft Group of Rockwell International). North American was then producing the T-28 Trojan for both the US Navy and US Air Force, and the fact that the new design included a control system similar to that used in the T-28, plus the utilization of many proven components, may have influenced the US Navy's decision.

In late 1956 North American received a contract for 26 production aircraft under the designation T2J-1, later changed to T-2A, and it was decided to dispense with construction of a prototype. The first T-2A Buckeye flew on 31 January 1958, and initial deliveries went to NAS Pensacola, Florida. Production totalled 217, used mainly by VT-7 and VT-9 at NAS Meridian, Missouri, whose students had already completed 35 hours on the T-34.

The T-2A has a wing in the mid-position, with pupil and instructor in tandem on rocket-powered zero-altitude ejection seats. The single 3,400-lb (1542-kg) Westinghouse J34-WE-36 turbojet is mounted in the belly, and fed by twin intakes.

Under a US Navy contract two T-2As were rebuilt

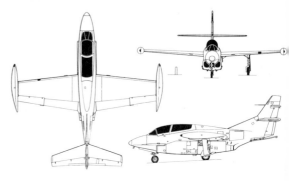

Rockwell T-2C Buckeye

in 1960 with two 3,000-lb (1361-kg) Pratt & Whitney J60-P-6 turbojets. The first of these YT-2Bs flew on 30 August 1962; the first of 10 T-2Bs flew on 21 May 1965, entering service at Meridian in May 1966. A total of 97 T-2Bs were built, the 34th and subsequent aircraft having additional fuel capacity.

Most extensively built was the T-2C, with two 2,950-lb (1338-kg) General Electric J85-GE-4 engines. The first flew on 10 December 1968, and all of 231 had been delivered by 1976. The T-2D has been supplied to the Venezuelan air force; this variant differs in its avionics and in the deletion of the carrier equipment. T-2Es for the Greek air force have six wing stations with a combined capacity of 3,500 lb (1588 kg) of ordnance, plus protection for the fuel tanks from small-arms fire. The standard T-2C has one store station beneath each wing, with a combined capacity of 640 lb (290 kg).

Specification

Type: general-purpose jet trainer
Powerplant: (T-2C) two 2,950-lb (1338-kg) General Electric J85-GE-4 turbojets
Performance: (T-2C) maximum level speed 530 mph (853 km/h) at 25,000 ft (7620 m); maximum range 1,070 miles (1722 km)
Weights: (T-2C) empty 8,115 lb (3681 kg); maximum take-off 13,191 lb (5983 kg)
Dimensions: span (over wingtip tanks) 38 ft 1½ in (11.62 m); length 38 ft 3½ in (11.67 m); height 14 ft 9½ in (4.51 m); wing area 255 sq ft (23.69 m²)
Armament: (T-2C) can include gun packs, target-towing gear, practice bombs and rockets
Operators: Greece, US Navy, Venezuela

A Rockwell T-2A of the US Navy.

Rockwell (North American) T-39 Sabreliner

Rockwell T-39 Sabreliner operated by Strategic Air Command, USAF, on VIP and communications duties.

24497

U.S.AIR FORCE

History and notes

In August 1956 the USAF specified a requirement for a general utility/trainer aircraft, then identified as UTX, signifying utility/trainer experimental, and in sending out its requests for proposals stipulated that interested manufacturers would be required to design, build and fly a prototype as a private venture. At that time North American Aviation had more or less completed the design study of a small pressurized jet transport aircraft, and was thus in a position to offer this design to the US Air Force with but few changes to make it capable of meeting their specification.

The original design had placed the engines in the wing roots, but as detail design proceeded during early 1957 the configuration was changed to a rear-engine layout, with two turbojet engines attached to the sides of the rear fuselage. Construction was virtually complete in May 1958, but the first flight was delayed until four months later, as the result of the non-availability of suitable engines. It was with two 2,500-lb (1134-kg) General Electric J85 turbojet engines that the prototype flew on 16 September 1958, and the type completed its USAF flight test evaluation at Edwards AFB, California in December. Early in 1959 North American received an initial production order for seven aircraft.

The first of these, which by then had the USAF designation T-39A, made its initial flight on 30 June 1960. This had two Pratt & Whitney J60-P-3 turbojets of increased power, and some internal changes, and initial deliveries for the Air Training Command, on 4 June 1961, went to Randolph AFB. Subsequent contracts brought total orders for the T-39A to 143, and these were delivered for service with the Air Training Command, Strategic Air Command, Systems Command, and to the Headquarters of the USAF for command duties. From June 1967 the USAF also took delivery of a number of T-39As, which had been modified with strengthened landing gear and provided with seven, instead of four, passenger seats.

In the period February – June 1961, six aircraft designated T-39B were delivered to the Tactical Air Command for training duties at Nellis AFB, Nevada. These were equipped with a doppler navigation system and the NASARR all-weather search and range radar which was installed in the Republic F-105, and were used to train crews who were to fly the Thunderchief.

The designation T3J-1, subsequently T-39D, was

Rockwell T-39 Sabreliner

allocated to 42 Sabreliners ordered from North American in 1962 by the US Navy. Required for the training of maritime radar operators, these had Magnavox radar systems installed, and delivery to the Naval Air Training Command HQ, at NAS Pensacola, Florida, began in August 1963. The US Navy acquired also seven Series 40 commercial Sabreliners, under the designation CT-39E, for high-priority transport of passengers, ferry pilots and cargo, and since 1973 has procured 12 of the longer-fuselage Sabreliner 60s under the designation CT-39G. These are used by both the US Marine Corps and US Navy for fleet tactical support duties. Under the designation T-39F, a number of USAF T-39As were modified to make them suitable for the training of Wild Weasel ECM operators for service with the USAF's F-105Gs and McDonnell Douglas F-4Gs.

Specification

Type: twin-engine utility transport/trainer
Powerplant: (T-39A) two 3,000-lb (1361-kg) thrust Pratt & Whitney J60-P-3 turbojets
Performance: (T-39A) maximum speed 595 mph (958 km/h) at 36,000 ft (10970 m); cruising speed 452 mph (727 km/h) at 40,000 ft (12190 m); design range 1,725 miles (2776 km)
Weights: (T-39A) empty 9,300 lb (4218 kg); maximum take-off 17,760 lb (8056 kg)
Dimensions: span 44 ft 5¼ in (13.54 m); length (T-39A/B/D) 43 ft 9 in (13.34 m); length (CT-39E/G) 46 ft 11 in (14.30 m); height 16 ft 0 in (4.88 m); wing area 342.05 sq ft (31.78 m²)
Armament: none
Operators: US Air Force, US Marine Corps, US Navy

Saab 35 Draken

Saab S 35XD Draken of ESK 729 of the Danish
Flyvevaben based at Karup.

History and notes

Although designed as a bomber interceptor, the
Draken (dragon) has been developed for a wide
variety of roles including ground attack and reconnaissance. The radical double-delta wing, designed
in the late 1940s for lightness and strength so that
supersonic speed could be achieved, was tested on
the Saab 210 research aircraft in 1952 and the layout
proved practicable. The Draken was designed
around this arrangement, with fuel and equipment
distributed along the fuselage and long wing-root to
compensate for the small volume available within
the wing, and the first prototype made its maiden
flight in October 1955. The three prototypes,
powered by Rolls-Royce Avon 200 turbojets, were
followed by the first production aircraft in February
1958. Initial production J35As were powered by
RM6Bs — Avons built under licence by Svenska
Flygmotor (now Volvo Flygmotor).

The J35A entered service with the Swedish air
force in March 1960 and was armed with up to four
Sidewinder air-to-air missiles, designated Rb24 in
Sweden, together with an Aden 30-mm cannon in
each wing.

The second version was the J35B, which incorporated Saab's S7 fire-control radar; some were
built as J35Bs from scratch, and others were converted from J35As. The J35D, similar to the B
model but powered by an RM6C (Avon 300) producing 12,790 lb (5800 kg) of dry thrust and 17,650 lb
(8000 kg) with afterburner compared with the
15,190 lb (6890 kg) achieved by the RM6B, first flew
in 1960. The variant built in the largest numbers was
the J35F. The first, a converted J35D, took to the air
in 1965 and the type will remain in service until the
late 1980s. The J35F is fitted with a Hughes weapon
system, comprising a pulse-Doppler radar,
automatic fire-control system and Falcon air-to-air
missiles, built under licence in Sweden by LM
Ericsson and other companies.

A large number of the original J35As were converted into SK35C two-seat trainers, and the S35E
reconnaissance version was developed for overland
operations; it has since been replaced by the Saab
SF37 Viggen. Nearly 550 Drakens have seen service
with the Swedish air force, and the production run
was extended by export orders received just as the
line was about to be closed. Denmark ordered
fighter-bomber, trainer and reconnaissance versions
of the Saab 35X export model and designated them

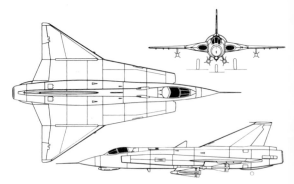

Saab J35F Draken

F-35, TF-35 and RF-35 respectively. The 35X is
similar to the J35F but has a larger internal fuel
capacity and can carry up to 9,920 lb (4500 kg) of external armament. The RF-35s are fitted with the
FFV Red Baron night reconnaissance pod.

Specification

Type: (35X) single-seat fighter-bomber
Powerplant: one 17,650-lb (8000-kg) Volvo
Flygmotor RM6C (licence-built Rolls-Royce Avon
300) afterburning turbojet
Performance: maximum level speed at 40,000 ft
(12190 m) 1,320 mph (2112 km/h) or Mach 2;
maximum rate of climb 34,450 ft (10500 m) per
minute; time to 49,200 ft (15000 m) 5 minutes;
radius of action (hi-lo-hi) with two 1,000-lb (454-kg)
bombs and two drop tanks 623 miles (1000 km);
ferry range with external fuel 2,020 miles (3250
km)
Weights: take-off (clean) 25,130 lb (11400 kg);
maximum take-off 33,070 lb (15000 kg); overload
35,275 lb (16000 kg); normal landing 19,360 lb
(8800 kg)
Dimensions: span 30 ft 10 in (9.40 m); length 50 ft
4 in (15.35 m); height 12 ft 9 in (3.89 m); wing area
538 sq ft (50.0 m²)
Armament: two 30-mm Aden cannon and up to
9,920 lb (4500 kg) of external stores including
Rb24 Sidewinder air-to-air missiles, pods
containing nineteen 75-mm air-to-air rockets each,
twelve 135-mm Bofors air-to-ground rockets, nine
1,000-lb (454-kg) or 14 500-lb (227-kg) bombs, and
other weapons
Operators: Denmark, Finland, Sweden

SAAB-91 Safir

A Saab-91 Safir of the Osterreichische Luftstreitkrafte (Austrian air force).

History and notes

Mass production for six of the world's air forces, within a decade or so after a global war in which Sweden had maintained a strict neutrality, was probably not the thought uppermost in the minds of Saab's designers when this attractive little primary trainer first took shape on the drawing board. World War II was then gradually progressing towards its close, and had been over in Europe for less than six months when the Saab-91 Safir (sapphire) prototype made its initial flight on 20 November 1945, a notable feature of the new design being the extremely short retractable tricycle landing gear. Four basic production models appeared subsequently, the first of these being the three-seat Saab-91A, powered by a 145-hp (108-kW) de Havilland Gipsy Major 10 engine. Initial customer for this version was the Royal Swedish Air Force, which ordered 10 for liaison and communications duties under the designation Tp 91. A further 16 were built for the Ethiopian imperial air force, but were later replaced by a similar quantity of the more powerful Saab-91B. Sweden also ordered 75 of this model for training duties, as the Sk 50B, and 25 were purchased by the Royal Norwegian air force. The Saab-91C was similar, except that it was a four-seater, and was ordered by Ethiopia (14) and Sweden (14, designated Sk 50C). The final model was the Saab-91D, also a four-seater but with a lower-powered and more modern engine; this was ordered by the air forces of Austria (24), Finland (35) and Tunisia (15), to bring military production of the Safir, excluding prototypes, to 244. Several major airlines also bought Safirs for pilot training, and overall production exceeded 300. Some B, C and D models remain in service with the air forces of Austria, Ethiopia and Sweden, and can be adapted for light attack duties with two 7.9-mm (0.31-in) machine-guns and eight rockets or small bombs under the wings. A few Safirs were used to flight-test various components for the Saab-29 Tunnan and Saab-32 Lansen combat aircraft, one having swept wings.

Specification

Type: two/four-seat basic trainer and communications aircraft
Powerplant: (91B and C) one 190-hp (142-kW) Lycoming O-435-A flat-six piston engine; (91D) one

Saab-91 Safir

180-hp (134-kW) Lycoming O-360-A1A flat-four piston engine
Performance: (91B) maximum speed 171 mph (275 km/h); maximum cruising speed 152 mph (244 mph); maximum range 670 miles (1078 km); maximum rate of climb at sea level 1,142 ft (348 m) per minute; service ceiling 20,500 ft (6250 m)
Weights: (91B) empty equipped 1,587 lb (720 kg); maximum take-off 2,685 lb (1218 kg)
Dimensions: (91B) span 34 ft 9¼ in (10.60 m); length 25 ft 11¾ in (7.92 m); height 7 ft 2½ in (2.20 m); wing area 146.39 sq ft (13.60 m²)
Armament: normally none (but see text)
Operators: Austria, Ethiopia, Sweden

The Austrian air force currently has 19 Safirs, 18 of them for training and one for liaison purposes.

Saab 37 Viggen

History and notes

Despite her small population and long-standing policy of neutrality, Sweden has maintained a formidable arms industry and the capability of developing combat aircraft. The Saab 37 Viggen (thunderbolt) is the most potent example of this capability, and because of the high cost of developing new advanced weapon systems, may well be the last Swedish-designed type of this complexity. The Viggen forms part of the Swedish air force's System 37: this is a complete weapon system, including support facilities, which is integrated into the STRIL 60 air-defence network. The Viggen is a true multi-role combat aircraft, having been developed to succeed a variety of earlier types used for attack, interception, reconnaissance and training missions. Other parts of System 37 include the aircraft's engine, avionic equipment, armament, ammunition and reconnaissance sensors, together with supporting items for servicing, maintenance, testing and training.

The first of seven Saab 37 prototypes took to the air in February 1967 and the initial production version, the AJ37, began to replace the Saab A32A Lansen (lance) in mid-1971. The AJ37 is a single-seat attack variant which can carry out interceptor and fighter roles as secondary responsibilities. The combination of a large delta wing and foreplanes fitted with flaps allows the Viggen to operate from short runways and lengths of roadway, thus greatly increasing the flexibility of dispersed operations possible in wartime. This ability is enhanced by the use of a powerful engine: the RM8A, a development of the Pratt & Whitney JT8D-22 turbofan built under licence by Volvo Flygmotor, produces 26,015 lb (11800 kg) of thrust with a Swedish afterburner; the engine is also provided with a Swedish thrust-reverser, which cuts in automatically as the Viggen's nosewheel strikes the ground. The use of automatic speed-control equipment and an advanced head-up display coupled with the Viggen's other STOL features, allows the aircraft to land on strips only 1,640 ft (500 m) long.

The AJ37's sophisticated navigation and fire-control system is based on a Saab CK-37 miniaturized digital computer, which relieves the pilot of much of the workload and allows this single-seat type to carry out an attack as effectively as more normal two-crew aircraft. The CK-37 takes its inputs from an LM Ericsson search and attack radar, together with the air-data computer, Doppler radar, radio altimeter and other sensors, the resulting information being shown on a Marconi Avionics head-up display. The AJ37 carries no built-in armament but can be equipped with a variety of air-to-surface and air-to-air weapons.

Two specialized reconnaissance versions are the SF37 and SH37. The first to enter service was the SH37, in mid-1975. This is a sea-surveillance platform which has replaced the S32C Lansen, using a nose-mounted surveillance radar similar to that in the AJ37 and a pod-mounted forward-looking long-range radar as its main sensors. Other equipment can include the FFV Red Baron infra-red reconnaissance pod or others containing active or passive ECM (electronic countermeasures) equipment. An auxiliary fuel tank may be mounted beneath the fuselage, and lightweight air-to-air missiles such as the AIM-9 Sidewinder can be carried for self defence.

The SF37, which followed the SH37 into service during the first half of 1977, is replacing the Saab S35E Draken (dragon) for overland reconnaissance; each reconnaissance squadron operates aircraft of both types. The SF37's nose section and two pods contain a total of nine cameras looking forwards, vertically downwards and sideways, together with an infra-red camera in the nose and illumination equipment for operations at night. All cameras are controlled by the aircraft's central digital computer, and the amount of information which can be recorded is prodigious. When all cameras are working simultaneously they produce 75 photographs per second, which contain as much data as about 50 black-and-white television cameras operating at the same time. The SF37 is operated in conjunction with a System 37 intelligence platoon, which includes a mobile evaluation centre with briefing, processing, evaluation and interpretation facilities.

The SH37 and SF37, like the SK37 two-seat trainer, are similar to the basic AJ37. The latest version to be developed, the JA37 interceptor, has substantial differences, however. The Volvo Flygmotor RM8B turbofan has a different fan, compressor and afterburner, giving improved climb rates and manoeuvrability, especially at high altitude. An extremely accurate inertial navigator, the Singer Kearfott KT-70L, is one of several new sensors which feeds the same company's central digital computer, built under licence by Saab as Computer 107. Another innovation is the LM Ericsson PS-46 pulse-Doppler radar, which allows two JA37s on fighter patrol along the coast to survey as much airspace as required a whole squadron of earlier aircraft. The new cockpit presentation layout, developed by Saab in collaboration with Svenska Radio, is based on three electronic displays. These can show electronic maps giving the location of air bases and anti-aircraft batteries, together with a tactical plot either received by radio-link from the ground or derived directly from the AJ37's radar. A Smiths Industries head-up display is installed, allowing the pilot to operate his radar and weapon systems while continuing to look outside the aircraft. The HUD also makes for easier transition from fighter to attack missions.

The JA37, unlike earlier versions, carries it own built-in armament. This comprises an underbelly pack containing a 30-mm Oerlikon KCA cannon of enormous power. The gun fires 0.79 lb (0.36 kg) pro-

This AJ37 is assigned to F7 wing at Satenäs, the first unit to equip with the Viggen in 1971. The tail number is that of the individual aircraft. The Flygvapen does not at present use sprayed-on winter camouflage but has conducted extensive research on low-visibility colour schemes. The JA37 fighter will have a different blue/grey scheme.

Saab 37 Viggen

First user of the AJ37A attack Viggen was F7 wing at Satenas whose three squadrons were all fully equipped with the extremely effective new aircraft by the end of 1975. This example is seen carrying four pods of Bofors spin-stabilized rockets (each housing six 135mm projectiles).

jectiles at a rate of 1,350 rounds per minute and a velocity of 3,450 ft (1050 m) per second. These shells have as much penetrating power after 4,920 ft (1500 m) of flight as a conventional 30-mm round has as it leaves the muzzle of an Aden or DEFA weapon, and the small drop due to gravity (because the muzzle velocity is so high) eases problems of sighting in tight manoeuvres.

Deliveries of JA37s to the Swedish air force began in late 1980, and the type will eventually replace all J35F Draken interceptors. There is also the possibility of a new attack version, known as the A20, being developed from the JA37 to replace the AJ37 in due course.

Specification

Type: (AJ37) single-seat attack aircraft with secondary fighter role (also reconnaissance and two-seat trainer versions); (JA37) single-seat interceptor

Powerplant: (AJ37) one 26,015-lb (11800-kg) Volvo Flygmotor RM8A afterburning turbofan; (JA37) one 28,150-lb (12770-kg) Volvo Flygmotor RM8B afterburning turbofan

Performance: maximum level speed Mach 2.0 or 1,320 mph (2112 km/h) at 39,990 ft (12190 m); maximum level speed at low level at least Mach 1.1 or 835 mph (1335 km/h); tactical radius with external armament (AJ37), hi-lo-hi at least 620 miles (1000 km), lo-lo-lo at least 310 miles (500 km); time to 32,810 ft (10000 m) (AJ37) less than 1 minute 40 seconds; ceiling (AJ37) estimated at 49,870 ft (15200 m)

Weights: empty (AJ37) more than 26,015 lb (11800 kg); maximum take-off (AJ37) more than 45,085 lb (20450 kg); normal operating (JA37) 37,480 lb (17000 kg)

Dimensions: span 34 ft 9 in (10.60 m); length (AJ37 excluding probe) 50 ft 8 in (15.45 m); length (JA37 excluding probe) 51 ft 1½ in (15.58 m); height (AJ37) 19 ft (5.80 m); height (JA37) 19 ft 4 in (5.90 m); wing area 495 sq ft (46 m²)

Armament: (AJ37) up to 13,230 lb (6000 kg), including Saab Rb04E or Rb05A or Rb75 Maverick ASMs, Bofors pod-mounted 135-mm rockets, bombs or Aden 30-mm gun pods; (fighter mission) Rb24 Sidewinder or Rb28 Falcon air-to-air missiles; (JA37) one 30-mm Oerlikon KCA (304K) cannon and Rb71 Sky Flash and/or Rb24 Sidewinder air-to-air missiles

Operator: Sweden

Saab 105

Saab-105 (designated Sk60 in service) of the Flygvapen (Swedish Air Force), operated by F5 Training School at Ljungbyhed.

History and notes

The twin-jet Saab 105 was developed as a private venture, primarily as a trainer and light ground-attack aircraft, but with a number of other roles available. These secondary duties include liaison and executive transport (for which the side-by-side ejection seats of the trainer can be removed and four fixed seats substituted), reconnaissance, air survey and air ambulance. The first of two prototypes flew on 29 June 1963, and the following year the Saab 105 was ordered into production for the Royal Swedish Air Force. The initial order was for 130, the first of which flew on 27 August 1965, and a follow-up order for a further 20 was placed in 1964.

In Swedish service the Saab 105 is designated Sk 60, the basic training and liaison version being the Sk 60A. This variant entered service in spring 1966 with F5, the Flying Training School at Ljungbyhed. After delivery most of these aircraft were modified by the addition of armament hardpoints, gunsights and associated equipment, giving them a secondary light ground-attack capability. The Sk 60B has ground-attack as its primary role, and the Sk 60C is equipped for photographic reconnaissance, having a Fairchild KB-18 camera in the nose, while retaining ground-attack capability.

Some 75 Sk 60As serve in the training role with F5, pupils progressing from the Sk 61 Bulldog and flying some 160 hours on the jet before qualifying. In an emergency, these trainers would comprise the equipment of five light ground-attack squadrons. A squadron of F21 based at Lulea within the Arctic Circle, Sweden's most northerly airbase, operates a mixture of Sk 60B attack and Sk 60C reconnaissance aircraft. F20, the Air Force College at Uppsala, also operates these variants, and second-line users include a staff liaison flight (who operate the four-seat version) and F13M who undertake target-tug and weapon-testing duties.

A development of the Sk 60B powered by J85 turbojets, the Saab 105XT first flew on 29 April 1967. Fuel capacity was increased to 451 Imperial gallons (2050 litres) to compensate for the higher fuel consumption, two 110-Imperial gallon (500-litre) underwing drop tanks being available. In addition to enhanced performance from the new powerplant, the Saab 105XT has improved avionics, and a strengthened wing enables the underwing load to be increased to 4,410 lb (2000 kg). In addition to training, reconnaissance and ground-attack duties, this

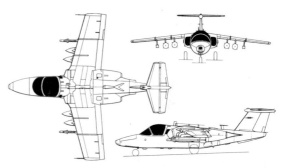

Saab-105G

version can perform the interception and target-towing roles. Infra-red guided missiles such as Sidewinder are carried for day interceptor duties. Forty aircraft, designated Saab 105O were built for the Austrian air force. The Saab 105G is a further refinement of the basic design, with greater improvements in avionics and warload.

Specification
Type: trainer and light attack aircraft
Powerplant: (Sk 60 series) two 1,640-lb (743-kg) Turboméca Aubisque turbofans; (Saab 105O and Saab 105G) two 2,850-lb (1293-kg) General Electric J85-GE-17B turbojets
Performance: maximum speed at sea level 447 mph (720 km/h) for Sk 60, 603 mph (970 km/h) for Saab 105O; maximum permissible diving speed Mach 0.86; climb to 29,525 ft (9000 m) 15 minutes for Sk 60; climb to 32,810 ft (10000 m) 4 minutes 30 seconds for Saab 105O; service ceiling 39,400 ft (12000 m) for Sk 60, 42,650 ft (13000 m) for Saab 105G; range at 29,525 ft (9000 m) 1,106 miles (1780 km) for Sk 60; range at 42,980 ft (13100 m) 1,491 miles (2400 km) for Saab 105O
Weights: empty 5,534 lb (2510 kg) for Sk 60, 5,662 lb (2550 kg) for Saab 105O; maximum take-off 9,920 lb (4500 kg) for Sk 60, 14,330 lb (6500 kg) for Saab 105O
Dimensions: span 31 ft 2 in (9.5 m); length 34 ft 5 in (10.5 m); height 8 ft 10 in (2.7 m); wing area 175 sq ft (16.3 m^2)
Armament: provision for up to 1,543 lb (700 kg) of underwing stores (Sk 60); up to 4,410 lb (2000 kg) of underwing stores (Saab 105O)
Operators: Austria, Sweden

SEPECAT Jaguar

One of the ten single-seat SEPECAT Jaguar international S(O) Mk Is operated by 8 Sqn, Sultan of Oman's Air Force.

History and notes

Developed jointly by BAC in Britain and Breguet in France, the SEPECAT Jaguar was originally intended as a light tactical attack and training machine with supersonic performance. Development resulted in a machine so capable that it seemed pointless to use it only as a trainer, and the tandem dual-control versions are fully combat-ready (though not fitted with the full spectrum of avionics and weapons as the single-seater). The extremely neat afterburning turbofan engine was developed by Turboméca and Rolls-Royce, two being installed in a manner reminiscent of the McDonnell Douglas FH4 Phantom's arrangement.

The engines occupy titanium bays in the lower part of the rear fuselage, with the nozzles just ahead of the tail section. The air ducts have plain fixed inlets of square section on each side behind the cockpit and pass inwards and downwards under the one-piece wing. Fuel is housed in four fuselage tanks and the integral tank formed by the fixed portion of wing on each side of the centreline.

A common requirement for the Jaguar was drafted by the British (RAF) and French (*Armée de l'Air*) in 1965, calling for single-seat attack and dual-control trainer versions to enter service with the *Armée de l'Air* in 1972 and RAF in 1973; a single-seat naval model was also specified for the French *Aéronavale* for use from the two French aircraft-carriers. The first prototype flew on 8 September 1968, and all other variants were developed within the allotted time and budget. Unfortunately the *Aéronavale* abandoned the naval Jaguar M after the prototype had completed its development in favour of an all-French aircraft of substantially lower performance and capability delivered five years later. The other four initial versions all entered service on schedule.

The first to fly and enter service was the Jaguar E (*Ecole* or school) trainer which entered the inventory of the *Centre d'Expériences Aériennes Militaires* at Mont de Marsan in May 1972. This has pupil and instructor seated on old Martin-Baker Mk 4 seats which cannot be used safely at speeds below 104 mph (167 km/h). In most other respects, including armament, it is identical to the next version to enter service, the Jaguar A. The Jaguar A (*Appui* or attack) model is the *Armée de l'Air* single-seat version, with a Mk 9 zero/zero seat, pointed nose without sensors, and a simple nav/attack system based on a Doppler radar navigation system and twin-gyro platform.

Britain's Jaguars are more sophisticated, and have inertial nav/attack systems, HUD (head-up display), projected map display, radar height, laser ranger (in a 'chisel' nose) and more comprehensive ECM including the ARI.18223 radar warning receiver installation near the top of the fin. Called Jaguar S by SEPECAT, the consortium formed by BAC and Breguet and today a joint venture of British Aerospace and Dassault-Breguet, this version is designated Jaguar GR.1 by the RAF and 165 were delivered by 1978.

For export various options have been added, to produce the Jaguar International, these additions including more powerful engines, overwing pylons for Magic, AIM-9L or other dogfight missiles, Agave nose radar with Ferranti 105S laser in a small fairing below the nose, low-light TV and new weapon options including Harpoon and Kormoran for use against ships. One Jaguar was rebuilt by BAe with the Dowty quadruplex fly-by-wire flight control system in 1978. The first two export sales were for aircraft of fairly standard type, though with uprated engines. The third, a very large contract with India involving about £1,200 million and more than 200 aircraft, will take advantage of most of the new options. About 60 Jaguars are to be supplied from the joint production by BAe and Dassault-Breguet, assembly and finally complete licence-manufacture later taking place in India.

Specification

Type: single-seat attack aircraft and two-seat trainer

Powerplant: two Rolls-Royce/Turboméca Adour afterburning turbofans each rated at (Mk 102) 7,305 lb (3314 kg) or (Mk 104) 8,600 lb (3900 kg)

Performance: maximum speed at altitude (clean) 990 mph (1593 km/h) or Mach 1.5; maximum speed at sea level 840 mph (1350 km/h) or Mach 1.1; take-off run with typical tactical load 1,900 ft (580 m); typical attack radius with weapons and no external fuel 507 miles (815 km); ferry range 2,614 miles (4210 km) climb 2 mins 30 secs to 30,000 ft (9144 m); service ceiling 45,000 ft (13716 m)

Weights: empty (A) 15,432 lb (7000 kg); maximum loaded 34,000 lb (15500 kg)

Dimensions: span 28 ft 6 in (8.69 m); length (A,S) 55 ft 2½ in (16.83 m); length (B,E) 57 ft 6¼ in (17.53 m); height 16 ft 0½ in (4.89 m); wing area 258.33 sq ft (24.0 m²)

Armament: see text

Operators: Ecuador, France, India, Oman, UK

This is a SEPECAT Jaguar GR.1 of RAF No 20 Sqn (former Harrier unit) at Brüggen. It is shown fitted with Matra Magic AAMs for trials; AIM-9L Sidewinder may become standard.

Short Skyvan 3M

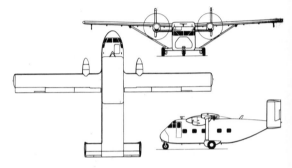

Short Skyvan 3M, one of 15 in transport use with 2 and 5 Sqn, Sultan of Oman's Air Force.

History and notes

The Short Skyvan, a small but capable airlifter, started life with piston engines (two 390-hp/291-kW Continental GTSIO-520s) and first flew on 17 January 1963. These powerplants were subsequently replaced by 520-shp (388-kW) Turboméca Astazou turboprops, and this re-engined version flew for the first time on 2 October 1963. Designated Srs 1 and 1A, these versions were superseded by the Astazou XII-powered Srs 2, of which 16 production aircraft were built. Current Skyvans, Srs 3, are powered by the Garrett AiResearch TPE331 turboprop. The first Srs 3 flew on 15 December 1967, and more than 60 have since been sold to civil operators. Early in 1970 Shorts flew the first military version, the 3M. With a basic layout lending itself to military operation, the Skyvan is used for dropping supplies, evacuating casualties, paratrooping and troop transport, carrying vehicles or ordnance, and assault landings. It is capable of very short take-off and landing (780 ft/238 m and 695 ft/212 m respectively), even under hot and high conditions, and despite its 'workhorse' shape the Skyvan cruises at a useful speed. A large rear-door loading ramp allows carriage of outsize cargo such as light vehicles, and it can be opened in flight for the dropping of supplies up to 4 ft 6 in (1.37 m) in height. Excluding the flight deck, 780 cu ft (22.09 m^3) of cabin volume is available on 120 sq ft (11.15 m^2) of floor area, entered through the rear door which measures 6 ft 6 in (1.98 m) high by 6 ft 5 in (1.96 m) wide. Usable cabin length is 18 ft 7 in (5.67 m). The 3M can accommodate up to 22 fully equipped troops, or 16 paratroops plus dispatcher, or 12 stretcher cases and two attendants, or normally up to 5,200 lb (2358 kg) of freight. Equipment peculiar to the 3M includes a blister window on the port side for the dispatcher and rollers on the floor for facilitating loading and positioning of heavy cargo. The tail is also fitted with a guard rail to prevent fouling of the control surfaces by static lines during dropping. Parachuting fittings include anchor cables for static lines, inward-facing seats with safety nets and a signal light. Many Skyvan 3Ms have nose radar.

Oman is the largest user of the military Skyvan, the Sultan's Air Force operating 16. They fly with No 2 Sqn based at Seeb, and are part of a largely

Short Skyvan 3M

British-made inventory. The Ghana air force flies six 3Ms. Based at Takoradi, they are used for tactical support, communications, coastal patrol and casualty-evacuation duties. No 121 Sqn of the Singapore air force uses six Skyvans for search-and-rescue, and anti-smuggling duties around the island. They are also used for light transport and supply work.

Specification

Type: light STOL utility transport
Powerplant: two 715-shp (533-kW) Garrett AiResearch TPE331-201 turboprops
Performance: maximum design speed 250 mph (402 km/h); maximum cruising speed at 10,000 ft (3050 m) 203 mph (327 km/h); range with 5,000-lb (2268-kg) payload 240 miles (386 km); range at long-range cruising speed 670 miles (1075 km); rate of climb at sea level 1,530 ft (466 m) per minute
Weights: empty equipped 7,400 lb (3356 kg); take-off (normal) 13,700 lb (6214 kg); take-off (maximum) 14,500 lb (6577 kg)
Dimensions: span 64 ft 11 in (19.79 m); length 41 ft 4 in (12.6 m); height 15 ft 1 in (4.6 m); wing area 373 sq ft (34.65 m^2)
Armament: none
Operators: Argentina, Austria, Botswana, Ecuador, Ghana, Indonesia, Lesotho, Malawi, Mauritania, Mexico, Nepal, Oman, Singapore, South Yemen, Thailand

SIAI-Marchetti SF.260

SIAI-Marchetti SF.260WT trainer/counter-insurgency aircraft, one of 12 in service with the Tunisian Republican Air Force.

History and notes

Designed by Stelio Frati as a fast, compact and flamboyant private aircraft, the SIAI-Marchetti SF.260 has found favour with a large number of armed forces. The prototype flew on 15 July 1964 and was known as the F.250. It was built by Aviamilano and was powered by a 250-hp (186.5-kW) Lycoming O-540 six-cylinder piston engine. When SIAI-Marchetti took over the project the aircraft was renamed SF.260 and a 260-hp (192.4-kW) Lycoming O-540 installed. To all intents and purposes merely a three-seater, the SF.260 offers an unusually high level of versatility for its size. It is used for such diverse roles as training, light attack, aerobatic tuition, forward air control, fishery protection, search and rescue, liaison and maritime patrol. SIAI-Marchetti is now directing virtually all its production capacity at military orders, although a civil version is still marketed (at $150,000 basic, the price is a deterrent to most civilians).

There are three military variants. The M, a three-seat trainer developed from the civil A, first flew on 10 October 1970 and pioneered a number of important structural modifications which were subsequently adopted for all versions. Among the changes were stronger wings, which on earlier models had relied on external stiffening. Some 150 Ms have been sold to date. May 1972 saw the first flight of the SF.260W Warrior. Equipped with underwing pylons, this is a light strike platform and has become popular with air forces which cannot afford to risk expensive metal on minor skirmishes. The list of mission profiles is almost limitless for this variant, varying from long-duration sorties close to base (5 hours or so at about 50-mile/80-km range) to 5 minutes over a target 350 miles (565 km) away. A recent innovation is the SF.260SW Sea Warrior maritime-patrol variant, which has enlarged tip-tanks housing (left) lightweight Bendix radar and (right) photo-reconnaissance equipment in addition to fuel.

Specification

Type: three-seat light attack, trainer and maritime reconnaissance aircraft

Powerplant: one 260-hp (192-kW) Avco Lycoming O-540-E4A5 flat-six piston engine

Performance: maximum level speed at sea level (M) 211 mph (340 km/h), (W) 196 mph (315 km/h), (SW) 189 mph (304 km/h); maximum level speed 75% power at 5,000 ft (1524 m) (M) 200 mph (322 km/h), (W) 178 mph (287 km/h), (SW) 171 mph

SIAI-Marchetti SF.260

(275 km/h); radius of action (W) single-crew armed patrol mission at 2,564 lb (1163 kg) 6 hours 25 minutes, with 5 hours 35 minutes over target, 57 miles (92 km); (W) ferry 1,066 miles (1716 km); (SW) 5 hours 17 minutes for two-crew surveillance mission, with 3 hours 40 minutes on station at 120 mph (194 km/h) plus reserves 115 miles (185 km); maximum rate of climb at sea level (M) 1,558 ft (475 m) per minute, (W) 1,099 ft (335 m) per minute, (SW) 885 ft (270 m) per minute

Weights: empty equipped (M) 1,761 lb (799 kg), (W) 1,794 lb (814 kg), (SW) 1,889 lb (857 kg); maximum take-off (M) 2,645 lb (1200 kg), (W, SW) 2,866 lb (1300 kg)

Dimensions: span over tips (M, W) 27 ft 4¾ in (8.35 m), (SW) 28 ft 6½ in (8.7 m); length 23 ft 3½ in (7.1 m); height 7 ft 11 in (2.41 m); wing area 108.7 sq ft (10.10 m²)

Armament: (W) two or four underwing hardpoints with maximum total capacity of 661 lb (300 kg); typical ordnance includes (alternatives) one or two SIAI gun pods each with one 500-round 7.62-mm FN machine-gun; two Simpres AL-8-70 launchers each with eight 2.75-in FFAR rockets; two Matra F2 launchers each with six 68-mm SNEB 253 rockets; two Samp EU 32 275.5-lb (125-kg) general-purpose bombs or EU 13 264-lb (120-kg) fragmentation bombs; two Alkan 500B cartridge throwers for Lacroix 74-mm explosive cartridges, F 725 flares or F 130 smoke cartridges; one Alkan 500B cartridge thrower and one photo-reconnaissance pod with two 70-mm automatic cameras; or two 18.25-gallon (83-litre) auxiliary fuel tanks

Operators: Belgium, Burma, Dubai, Ireland, Italy, Libya, Morocco, Philippines, Singapore, Thailand, Tunisia, Zaire, Zambia

The RAF's Westland Whirlwind HAR Mk 10s performed important rescue duties around Britain's coast until replaced by Sea Kings.

History and notes

Continuing the development of rotary-wing aircraft from the R-4 (the first production helicopter to serve with the US armed forces) via the improved R-5, during 1948 the Sikorsky company evolved the design of a large and more useful helicopter. Details of this design were submitted to the USAF, resulting in a contract for five YH-19 prototypes for evaluation, the first making its maiden flight at Bridgeport, Connecticut, on 10 November 1949.

The basic similarity of the S-55 and the S-51 (R-5, later H-5) was easily seen, but the new design included an unusual powerplant installation, with the engine mounted obliquely in the fuselage nose, a long straight drive-shaft between the pilots connecting the engine and main rotor gearbox, which was immediately beneath the rotor hub. To permit easy examination and maintenance of the engine, it was enclosed by large clamshell doors which allowed good all-round access.

Extensively built for a helicopter of its era, with more than a 1,000 examples being supplied to the US armed services alone, these included the original H-19A for the USAF with 600-hp (447-kW) Pratt & Whitney R-1340-57 engine, similar H-19C Chickasaws for the US Army, and HO4S-1s for the US Navy. With a 700-hp (522-kW) Wright R-1300-3 and increased rotor diameter, the USAF, US Army, US Navy, and US Coast Guard received H-19B, H-19D Chickasaws, HO4S-3s, and HO4S-3Gs respectively. HRS-1s/-2s and -3s, generally similar to the HO4S series, were supplied to the US Marine Corps. H-19B/C/Ds became redesignated UH-19B/C/D respectively in 1962, the US Marines' HRS-3 became CH-19E, and Navy HO4S-3 and Coast Guard HO4S-3G became UH-19F and HH-19G respectively. A few operators have had their machines converted to turbine power with TPE331 or PT6T engines.

In addition to production by Sikorsky for the US armed forces, S-55s were built under licence by SNCASE in France, Misubishi in Japan, and by Westland Helicopters in Great Britain. This last company built a number of variants with US engines but also developed the design and installed the British-built Alvis Leonides Major 14-cylinder engine. Westland-built S-55s had the name Whirlwind and in addition to being supplied to the British armed forces, were exported to France and Yugoslavia, as described separately.

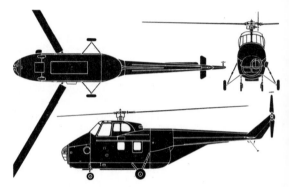

Westland Whirlwind HAR.10

Specification

Type: utility helicopter

Powerplant: (H-19B) one 700-hp (522-kW) Wright R-1300-3 radial piston engine

Performance: (H-19B) maximum speed at sea level 112 mph (180 km/h); cruising speed 91 mph (146 km/h); range 360 miles (579 km)

Weights: (H-19B) empty 5,250 lb (2381 kg); maximum take-off 7,900 lb (3583 kg)

Dimensions: main rotor diameter (H-19A) 49 ft 0 in (14.94 m), (H-19B) 53 ft 0 in (16.15 m); tail rotor diameter 8 ft 8 in (2.64 m); length of fuselage 42 ft 3 in (12.88 m); height 13 ft 4 in (4.06 m); main rotor disc area (H-19A) 1,886 sq ft (175.21 m²), (H-19B) 2,206 sq ft (204.94 m²)

Armament: none, but machine-guns and rockets in Korea, Indo-China, Algeria and elsewhere

Operators: have included Chile, France, Japan, Malaya, UK (Navy), US Air Force, US Army, US Coast Guard, US Marine Corps, US Navy

Sikorsky S-58/H-34 Choctaw/Seabat/Seahorse/ Westland Wessex

Westland Wessex HC Mk 2 XR527 of 28 Sqn, RAF, formerly based at Kai Tak, Hong Kong, but recently moved to Sek Kong.

History and notes

Originating from a US Navy requirement of 1951 for an anti-submarine helicopter, Sikorsky built the prototype S-58, and this has proved to be the most extensively built of all Sikorsky helicopters. The prototype flew on 8 March 1954. The origins of the requirement lay in the US Navy's discovery that the S-55 (in service as the HO4S/HRS) had only limited payload and range too limited for anti-submarine missions.

But the S-55 had proved an efficient design, so the S-58 was basically a larger version with an engine of almost three times the power. Landing gear is of the fixed tailwheel type, instead of a quadricycle unit, and there is accommodation for a pilot and co-pilot above the main cabin, which can accommodate up to 18 passengers, or an equivalent weight in equipment or cargo. The main and tail rotors each have four all-metal blades, and it is claimed that the transmission system has 25% fewer components than those of earlier designs. The US Navy had sufficient confidence in this design to order the production HSS-1 before the prototype had flown. After flight trials had begun, orders began to flow in also from the US Army and US Marine Corps.

The first production SH-34G Seabat (formerly HSS-1) for the US Navy flew on 20 September 1954, entering service with HS-3 in August 1955. The US Navy realised that despite a payload increase of some 70%, it was still not possible for these helicopters to operate singly, and decided to 'pair' them into hunter/killer units.

The SH-34J Seabat was suitable for day or night operation with Sikorsky autostabilization. US Army versions included the CH-34A Choctaw transport, followed by the CH-34C with autostabilization. First version for the US Marine Corps was the UH-34D Seahorse, followed by the UH-34E equipped with pontoons for emergency amphibious operations. Six examples for the US Coast Guard had the designation HH-34F.

Sikorsky built many S-58s for other nations under the Military Assistance Program, as well as for

Sikorsky S-58

direct sale. In addition, Sud-Aviation in France mass-produced S-58s for the French army and navy, plus five for Belgium. Westland Helicopters in Britain built a turbine-powered development as the Wessex.

Specification

Type: general-purpose helicopter

Powerplant: one 1,525-hp (1137-kW) Wright R-1820-84 Cyclone radial air-cooled piston engine

Performance: (CH-34A): maximum level speed 122 mph (196 km/h) at sea level; maximum cruising speed 97 mph (156 km/h); range (with maximum fuel, 10% reserves) 247 miles (398 km)

Weights: empty equipped (CH-34A) 7,750 lb (3515 kg), (UH-34D) 7,900 lb (3583 kg), (SH-34J) 8,275 lb (3753 kg); maximum normal take-off 13,000 lb (5897 kg); maximum permissable 14,000 lb (6350 kg)

Dimensions: main-rotor diameter 56 ft 0 in (17.07 m); tail-rotor diameter 9 ft 6 in (2.90 m); length (rotors turning) 56 ft 8¼ in (17.28 m); height 15 ft 11 in (4.85 m); main-rotor disc area 2,460 sq ft (228.53 m²)

Armament: (SH-34G/J) homing torpedoes carried externally in ASW 'killer' role

Operators: Argentina, Belgium, Brazil, Canada, France, Germany, Italy, Japan, Netherlands, Thailand, US Air Force, US Coast Guard, US Marine Corps, US Navy

Sikorsky S-61A/B/SH-3 Sea King/H-3/Agusta SH-3

Sikorsky S-61A Nuri, Sikorsky-built aircraft of which 38 had been supplied to
Malaysia by late 1979 for multiple military and civil duties.

History and notes

US Navy operation of fixed-wing aircraft in the
ASW hunter/killer role showed that such missions
could be carried out more effectively by single aircraft which combined both roles. As the combination
of hunter/killer capabilities into one vehicle was just
as desirable for a helicopter, at the end of 1957 the
US Navy contracted with Sikorsky for such a
machine.

For the 'hunter' part of its mission the HSS-2 was
equipped with Bendix dipping sonar, the autopilot
holding the required constant altitude, controlled by
Doppler radar and a radar altimeter. All-weather
autostabilization was fitted. For the 'killer' part of
its mission, the HSS-2 could carry up to 840 lb (381
kg) of weapons, including homing torpedoes.

Seven YHSS-2 test aircraft were contracted on 23
September 1957, the first flying on 11 March 1959.
In September 1961 the first deliveries were made to
VHS-3 at Norfolk, Virginia, and VHS-10 at Ream
Field, San Diego. Early examples were powered by
two 1,250-shp (932-kW) General Electric T58-GE-8B
turboshafts, soon replaced by the T58-GE-10 with increased fuel capacity. In 1962 these versions were
redesignated SH-3A and -3D Sea King respectively.

The S-61 has had a long life in many variants.
These include nine RH-3A minesweepers, able to
deploy and recover a variety of MCM (mine
countermeasures)· equipment to deal with the
various types of mines. The HH-3A has Minigun turrets, armour protection, extra fuel capacity, and a
high-speed rescue hoist to provide the US Navy with
an armed search and rescue helicopter (12 were converted by the US Navy at Quonset Point). The Canadian Armed Forces operate the CH-124; four were
delivered by Sikorsky, and 37 assembled in Canada
from 1963. Ten VH-3As of the Executive Flight
Detachment in Washington, providing VIP
transport for the US President and senior ex-
ecutives, were replaced by 11 VH-3Ds. Under the
designation SH-3G, 105 SH-3As were converted as
simple utility helicopters, followed by the multi-
purpose SH-3H with new ASW equipment, advanced radar and magnetic anomaly detection

Sikorsky SH-3 Sea King

(MAD) gear.

SH-3As and S-61As are built under licence by Mitsubishi in Japan for the JMSDF, and SH-3Ds built
under licence by Agusta in Italy have been supplied
to the Italian air force and navy, and to the Iranian
air force. SH-3Ds have been manufactured by Sikorsky for the Brazilian and Spanish navies.
Developments of the S-61 are built by Westland
Helicopters in Britain as the Sea King and
Commando (q.v.)

Specification

Type: amphibious all-weather ASW or general
purpose/transport helicopter
Powerplant: (SH-3D): two 1,400-shp (1044-kW)
General Electric T58-GE-10 turboshafts
Performance: (SH-3D) maximum speed 166 mph
(267 km/h); range (with maximum fuel, 10%
reserves) 625 miles (1006 km)
Weights: (SH-3D) empty 11,865 lb (5382 kg);
maximum take-off 18,626 lb (8449 kg)
Dimensions: main rotor diameter 62 ft 0 in (18.90
m); tail rotor diameter 10 ft 7 in (3.23 m); length
(rotors turning) 72 ft 8 in (22.15 m); height 16 ft
10 in (5.13 m); main rotor disc area 3,019 sq ft
(280.47 m²)
Armament: (SH-3D) provision to carry up to 840
lb (381 kg) of weapons
Operators: Argentina, Brazil, Canada, Denmark,
Iran, Italy, Japan, Malaysia, Spain, US Air Force,
US Marine Corps, US Navy

Sikorsky S-61R/CH-3/HH-3 Jolly Green Giant/ Pelican

A Sikorsky HH-3, of the nosewheel/rear-door S-61R species of the USAF Aerospace Rescue & Recovery Service, retrieves a BQM-34C Firebee II supersonic RPV target during the November 1976 William Tell annual Fighter Weapons meet at Tyndall AFB.

History and notes

The undoubted success of the Sikorsky S-61B in US Navy service provided an indication to the USAF as to which company it should approach when a long-range transport helicopter was required in the early 1960s. In fact, the US Air Force had gained a good insight into the potential of this helicopter when, in April 1962, it had borrowed three HSS-2s fom the US Navy in order to carry supplies to radar units based at 'Texas Towers' in the Atlantic: the USAF found them so useful that it borrowed three more. By that time the US Navy's S-61s had become SH-3As, and those in US Air Force use became designated CH-3B.

In November 1962 the decision was made to acquire similar aircraft for use by the USAF, but a number of design changes were requested to make these more suitable for the transport role, which was the US Air Force's specific requirement. Major change was to the rear fuselage, with the provision of a hydraulically-operated rear loading door/ramp at the rear of the cabin, this making possible the straight-in loading of wheeled vehicles without the need for any other support equipment. Landing gear configuration was changed from that of the S-61B, to more conventional tricycle type, with twin wheels on each unit; a pneumatic 'blow-down' system ensured safe extension of the landing gear in the event of hydraulic failure. Though the planing boat hull

Sikorsky S-61R

was not required, the fuselage was made watertight, with sponsons to house the rear wheels. To ensure that, so far as possible, these aircraft would be able to operate quite independently of ground facilities, pressurized rotor blades simplify inspection, both main and tail rotor hubs are self-lubricating, a gas-turbine auxiliary power unit can supply essential electric and hydraulic power, and equipment is carried to make possible the exchange of all major components without recourse to local facilities, even in the most remote areas. New equipment includes a 2,000-lb (907-kg) capacity winch for internal cargo handling, and considerable care was taken to ensure that the landing gear and rear fuselage modifications did not affect the amphibious capability.

Sikorsky's first S-61R flew initially on 17 June 1963, and just over six months later, on 30 December, the first operational CH-3C was delivered to Tyndall AFB, Florida. A total of 41 were built for the USAF, the powerplant comprising two 1,300-shp (969-kW) General Electric T58-GE-1 turboshaft engines, with standard accommodation for a crew of two and 25 fully equipped troops, or 15 stretchers, or up to 5,000 lb (2268 kg) of cargo.

The CH-3E was introduced in 1966, and differed by having uprated T58-GE-5 engines. A total of 42 were built, and all CH-3Cs were converted later to this standard. An important third variant, which entered service with the USAF's Aerospace Rescue and Recovery Service, has the designation HH-3E, and are equipped to fulfil their role in a combat zone. Their additional equipment includes armour, rescue hoist, a retractable flight-refuelling probe, self-sealing fuel tanks, and defensive armament. Some 50 of these were provided for service in south-east Asia by conversion of CH-3Es. In service these aircraft were known as Jolly Green Giants, and were used mainly to rescue pilots who had been forced down in hostile territory. They were used extensively in North Vietnam, making deep penetrations of enemy airspace, and carrying out successful rescue missions despite heavy gunfire being directed at them.

In 1968 the US Coast Guard received the first 40 HH-3Fs, generally similar to the HH-3E except for deletion of armament, armour and self-sealing tanks. These aircraft, which have the name Pelican, have advanced avionics to facilitate their use in the search and rescue role.

Specification
Type: amphibious transport helicopter
Powerplant: (CH-3E) two 1,500-shp (1119-kW) General Electric T58-GE-5 turboshafts
Performance: (CH-3E) maximum speed 162 mph (261 km/h); range with maximum fuel and 10% reserves 465 miles (748 km)
Weights: (CH-3E) empty 13,255 lb (6012 kg); normal take-off 21,247 lb (9637 kg); maximum take-off 22,050 lb (10002 kg)
Dimensions: main rotor diameter 62 ft 0 in (18.90 m); tail rotor diameter 10 ft 4 in (3.15 m); length (rotors turning) 73 ft 0 in (22.25 m); height 18 ft 1 in (5.51 m); main rotor disc area 3,019 sq ft (280.47 m²)
Armament: (HH-3E) two 7.62-mm (0.3-in) Miniguns on each side
Operators: US Air Force, US Coast Guard

Sikorsky S-64 Skycrane/CH-54 Tarhe

History and notes
The requirement for a heavy lift helicopter was growing in the late 1950s, as it became clear that improving technology concerned with the design of rotary-wing dynamic systems, combined with lightweight high-powered turboshaft engines, should make it possible to build aircraft in this category with entirely new standards of performance. It was at about this same time that development of the Boeing Vertol Model 115 (CH-47 Chinook) began, and Sikorsky initiated its own design for a 'flying crane' that was very different in conception.

It consisted of a basic prime mover comprising a long fuselage beam. At the forward end was suspended a cab to accommodate a crew of three, plus jump seats for two loaders/technicians; at the aft end was a tail with the anti-torque rotor on the left. Above the fuselage two turboshaft engines, main and intermediate gear boxes, main rotor and drive shafts were mounted, leaving the undersurface clear. The tricycle landing gear consisted of a nosewheel beneath the cab, and main legs on outriggers to allow the fuselage to straddle a bulky load. A cargo hook could be lowered by the third, aft-facing crew member.

Sikorsky's concept did not rely purely on the use of cargo hoists, it being intended that the S-64A

Sikorsky S-64 Skycrane/CH-54A Tarhe

would straddle interchangeable pods for a variety of purposes. The fundamental idea was linked closely to the road/ship transit of goods in sealed containers: Sikorsky believed that Skycranes might replace ships over short ranges.

The first of three prototypes made its initial flight on 9 May 1962 and was delivered to the US Army at Fort Benning, Georgia, for test and evaluation. The second and third prototypes were delivered to Germany for evaluation, and VFW-Fokker participated in design and development.

The Army's evaluation was sufficiently successful to gain for Sikorsky a contract for six YCH-54A helicopters for further investigation. The company

Sikorsky S-64 Skycrane/CH-54 Tarhe

The Sikorsky CH-54 Tarhe, called the S-64 by the manufacturer, is the only heavy-lift crane helicopter in the West — and used only by the US Army, despite its universal applicability. This is an early CH-54A, with single mainwheels and less-powerful engines.

designed containers for troop transport, field hospital support, anti-submarine warfare, mine-sweeping, and heavy-lift support operations.

Five of the US Army's prototypes were delivered in 1964-5 as production CH-54A Tarhes. The sixth was retained by Sikorsky to assist FAA certification, which was awarded on 30 July 1965.

Evaluation by the US Army involved deployment in Vietnam with the 478th Aviation Company, where Tarhes performed near-miracles in the retrieval of some 380 damaged aircraft, and the transport of such vehicles as bulldozers and roadgraders, and even armoured vehicles weighing up to 20,000 lb (9072 kg). On one occasion a CH-54A lifted a van containing a total of 90 persons, including 87 combat-equipped troops. Approximately 60 CH-54As were built, powered by two 4,500-shp (3356-kW) Pratt & Witney T73-P-1 engines.

An improved CH54-B was ordered in November 1968, the first two being accepted in 1969. Improvements included more powerful engines, up-rated gearbox, structural strengthening, introduction of a high-lift rotor blade, improved flight-control system, and twin wheels added to the main landing gear. In October 1970, such an aircraft lifted a load of 40,780 lb (18497 kg).

Sikorsky built for the US Army a Universal Military Pod, measuring internally 27 ft 5 in × 8 ft 10 in × 6 ft 6 in high (8.36 × 2.69 × 1.98 m), with a maximum weight of 20,000 lb (9072 kg), for the carriage of troops or field conversion as a surgical unit, command post or communications centre.

Specification

Type: heavy-lift flying-crane helicopter
Powerplant: (CH-54B) two 4,800-shp (3579-kW) Pratt & Whitney T73-P-700 turboshafts
Performance: (CH-54A) maximum speed 126 mph (203 km/h) at sea level; maximum cruising speed 105 mph (169 km/h); range with maximum fuel (10% reserves) 230 miles (370 km)
Weights: (CH-54A) empty 19,234 lb (8724 kg); maximum take-off 42,000 lb (19051 kg)
Dimensions: main rotor diameter 72 ft 0 in (21.95 m); tail rotor diameter 16 ft 0 in (4.88 m); length (rotors turning) 88 ft 6 in (26.97 m); height 25 ft 5 in (7.75 m); main rotor disc area 4,070 sq ft (378.10 m²)
Armament: none
Operator: US Army

ıkorsky S-65/H-53 Sea Stallion

History and notes

American interest in heavy-lift helicopters was not confined to the US Army. As early as 1950 a US Marine Corps requirement had first involved Sikorsky in the design and construction of such a helicopter, this having the company designation S-56. With a maximum take-off weight of 31,000 lb (14061 kg), these HR2S-1 helicopters, subsequently designated CH-37C, were easily the largest rotary-wing aircraft in the West when introduced into service in 1956.

In 1960 the US Marine Corps decided that it needed a more advanced assault-transport helicopter, and Sikorsky produced a new design which utilised the dynamic system which had been developed for the S-64A Skycrane (CH-54 Tarhe), as well as many other components. Completely new, of course, was the watertight hull, provided to permit emergency water-landing capability, rather than being intended for amphibious operations. The emphasis was on good load-carrying capabiity, so rear-loading doors were included in the upswept rear fuselage to simplify loading of bulky items, and hydraulically-operated winches were installed at the forward end of the cabin, with a roller-skid track combination in the floor to make it easy for the loading of wheeled vehicles, a 105-mm howitzer and its carriage, or a wide variety of very heavy cargo.

On 27 August 1962 the US Navy announced that it would procure two prototypes and one static-test airframe, and that Sikorsky were required also to construct a mockup of their S-65A design. The first of these prototypes made its maiden flight on 14 October 1964, and following successful evaluation the first production examples, designated CH-53A and named Sea Stallion, were delivered to USMC units in September 1966. By the beginning of 1967 the type was in operational service in Vietnam.

These aircraft were able to operate in all weathers, had an external cargo system which made possible in-flight pickup and release without any assistance from the ground, and had hydraulically-folded main-rotor blades and tail pylon for shipboard stowage. The powerplant consisted normally of two 2,850-shp (2125-kW) General Electric T64-GE-6 turboshaft engines.

In September 1966 the USAF ordered eight of these aircraft for use by the Aerospace Rescue and Recovery Service, to be equipped similarly to the HH-3E. In other respects they were similar to the CH-53A, except for a powerplant comprising two 3,080-shp (2297-kW) T64-GE-3 turboshafts. The first of these HH-53B helicopters flew on 15 March 1967. An improved version for the USAF had the designation HH-53C, this having 3,925-shp (2927-kW) T64-GE-7 engines, provision for auxiliary fuel tanks, a flight-refuelling probe, rescue hoist, and a 20,000-lb (9072-kg) external cargo hook. The first of these entered service with the USAF on 30 August 1968. Eight HH-53s are being modified under the USAF'S Pave Low 3 programme to provide night search and rescue capability. Completion of these is scheduled for 1980.

The final twin-engined version for the US Marine Corps is the CH-53D, an improved CH-53A. The type differs in having more powerful engines, a special internal cargo handling system suitable for one-man operation, and the capacity to carry 55 equipped troops. The first of this version entered service in March 1969, and when the last was delivered, on 31 January 1972, combined production of the CH-53 then totalled 265 examples. All but the first 34 were equipped with special gear for minesweeping operations, but in October 1972 production was initiated of 30 RH-53D special-purpose minesweeping helicopters, designed to operate with all current and foreseeable equipment for the sweeping of accoustic, magnetic and mechanical mines. First delivery of production aircraft, to the US Navy's HM-12 Squadron, was made in September 1973. Powered currently by two T64-GE-413A turboshafts, it is planned to modify these to 4,380-shp (3266-kW) T64-GE-415 standard.

The designation CH-53G applies to 112 aircraft for the German army with 3,925-shp (2927-kW) T64-GE-7 engines. Two were built and delivered by Sikorsky on 31 March 1969. Of the remainder, 20 were assembled by VFW-Fokker in Germany, using American components, and 90 were manufactured by VFW-Fokker with some 50% of the components being of German manufacture.

Two aircraft were supplied by Sikorsky to the Austrian air force for operation as rescue aircraft in the Alpine regions. Delivered in 1970, these have the designation S-65-Oe. The three-engined CH-53E is described separately.

Specification

Type: heavy assault transport helicopter
Powerplant: (CH-53D) two 3,925-shp (2927-kW) General Electric T64-GE-413 turboshafts
Performance: (CH-53D) maximum speed at sea level 196 mph (315 km/h); cruising speed 173 mph (278 km/h); range (with 4,076-lb (1849-kg) fuel, 2 minutes warm-up, cruising speed, 10% reserves) 257 miles (414 km)
Weights: (CH-53D) empty 23,485 lb (10653 kg); mission take-off 36,400 lb (16511 kg); maximum take-off 42,000 lb (19051 kg)
Dimensions: main rotor diameter 72 ft 3 in (22.02 m); tail rotor diameter 16 ft 0 in (4.88 m); length (rotors turning) 88 ft 3 in (26.90 m); height 24 ft 11 in (7.59 m); main rotor disc area 4,070 sq ft (378.10 m²)
Armament: none
Operators: Austria, Germany, Israel, US Air Force, US Marine Corps, US Navy

In flight a truly impressive machine, the USAF's HH-53C rescue and recovery helicopters are fitted with a flight-refuelling probe, provision for drop tanks, a rescue hoist, a hook for underfuselage sling loads, and a large variety of special avionics systems. A few examples are capable of nocturnal missions with the installation of more equipment under the USAF's Pave Low 3 programme.

Sikorsky S-70/UH-60 Black Hawk/SH-60B

Sikorsky UH-60A Black Hawk utility helicopter, destined for large-scale use with the United States Army.

History and notes

At the beginning of the 1970s the US Army began the somewhat protracted process of procuring a new helicopter. Identified as the Utility Tactical Transport Aircraft System (UTTAS), this is primarily a combat assault helicopter. In August 1972 it was announced that the US Army had selected the submissions received from Boeing Vertol and Sikorsky, and both were contracted to build three prototypes and a static test vehicle of their design for competitive evaluation.

Boeing Vertol's design, designated YUH-61A, was for a conventional helicopter with four-blade main and anti-torque rotors, tricycle landing gear, and two 1,500-shp (1119-kW) General Electric T700-GE-700 engines. Features included a hingeless main rotor, modularized design, and built-in access platforms. The first flew on 29 November 1974.

Sikorsky's competing YUH-60A was generally similar and powered by the same engines. The most noticeable external differences were the tailwheel landing gear and canted anti-torque rotor. The first flight was made on 17 October 1974, the second and third protoypes flying in January and February 1975. The fly-off evaluation of the competing prototypes occupied seven months of 1976, and on 23 December of that year Sikorsky's design was selected for production. The US Army regards the UH-60A Black Hawk as its primary assault helicopter for the immediate future, and hopes to procure a total of 1,107 by 1985. Production of the first 15 began in late 1977, and initial deliveries were made during 1978.

The main rotor is of advanced design, with aft-swept tips; the rotor is designed to survive hits from 12.7-mm or 23-mm armour-piercing shells; and the main-rotor hub has elastomeric bearings needing no lubrication. The fuel system is regarded as crashworthy, as is the fuselage which is designed to survive hits from armour-piercing rounds of up to 7.62-mm calibre. Accommodation is provided for a crew of three and 11 troops, the pilot and co-pilot having armoured seats. Eight seats can be replaced by four stretchers or internal cargo. An external hook of 8,000-lb (3629-kg) capacity is provided for the airlift of artillery and supplies.

The US Navy's continuing search for advanced ASW helicopters resulted in competition for the LAMPS (light airborne multi-purpose system) Mk

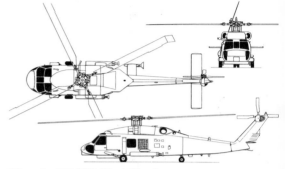

Sikorsky UH-60A Black Hawk

III configuration, in which Boeing Vertol also contended but again lost to a special version of the S-70 designated SH-60B.

The SH-60B has automatic main rotor and tail pylon folding, shorter wheelbase, and naval avionics, including radar, MAD, sonar and ESM. By early 1979 no funding had been allocated for procurement of the SH-60B for the US Navy and, therefore, no estimate can be made for an in-service date.

Specification

Type: (UH-60A) combat assault squad transport; (SH-60B) ship-based multi-purpose helicopter

Powerplant: two 1,543-shp (1151-kW) General Electric T700-GE-700 turboshafts

Performance: (UH-60A) maximum speed 184 mph (296 km/h) at sea level; maximum speed at maximum take-off weight 182 mph (293 km/h); maximum cruising speed 169 mph (272 km/h) at 4,000 ft (1220 m); single-engine speed 149 mph (240 km/h); range at maximum take-off weight with 30-minute reserves 373 miles (600 km)

Weights: (UH-60A) empty 10,900 lb (4944 kg); mission take-off 16,450 lb (7462 kg); maximum take-off 20,250 lb (9185 kg)

Dimensions: main rotor diameter 53 ft 8 in (16.36 m); tail rotor diameter 11 ft 0 in (3.35 m); length (rotors turning) 64 ft 10 in (19.76 m); height 16 ft 10 in (5.13 m); main-rotor disc area 2,261 sq ft (210.05 m^2)

Armament: (UH-60A) provision for one or two 7.62-mm (0.3-in) M 60 machine-guns firing from opened side doors; (SH-60B) two homing torpedoes

Operators: (UH-60A) US Army; (SH-60B) potentially US Navy

SOKO Galeb/Jastreb

Yugoslav Air Force Soko Galeb two-seat trainer of the Flying Training Headquarters at Mostar.

History and notes

SOKO was founded in 1951 and its first indigenous production aircraft was the G2-A Galeb (Seagull), a jet trainer of similar appearance and characteristics to the Italian Aermacchi M.B.326, which pre-dated it by about two years.

Galeb design work began in 1957. The first of two prototypes flew in May 1961 and production began in 1963, initially to meet orders from the Yugoslav air force.

Designed to withstand load factors of + 8 to −4, the Galeb has a fuel system which allows up to 15 seconds inverted flight for aerobatic training. Lightweight HSA (Folland) fully-automatic ejector seats are fitted, and the jettisonable canopy has separate sideways-hingeing sections for the two crew. There is no pressurization, but air-conditioning is available to special order. The jettisonable wing tip tanks each have a capacity of 375 lb (150 kg); for target towing there is a hook beneath the centre fuselage.

The G2-A is the standard version; the Yugoslav air force has about 60, a few of which are believed to be used in the reconnaissance role. The G2-AE export version was flown in late 1974, and production began in 1975 for the Libyan air force, which has received 20. Prior to this, Zambia bought two Galebs and four Jastrebs in 1971, a rather strange purchase since the Zambian air force also bought about 20 of the rival Aermacchi M.B.326.

The J-1 Jastreb (Hawk) is basically a single-seat version with a strengthened airframe and more powerful engine with a built-in starter. The rear canopy is replaced by a metal fairing, and each tip tank houses 485 lb (220 kg) of fuel. The two current production versions are the J-1 attack and RJ-1 tactical reconnaissance models for the Yugoslav air force, which operates about 150 in 12 squadrons, and the equivalent export models, the J-1E and RJ-1E. The former is said to have been ordered, but customers have not been named.

The RJ-1 has a fuselage camera, plus one in the nose of each tip tank.

A Yugoslav air force requirement to provide operational conversion to the Jastreb has been met not by the Galeb but by producing a two-seat trainer version of the Jastreb, the TJ-1. Flying in mid-1974, the variant retains the full operational capability of the ground attack Jastreb and deliveries began in January 1975. At an empty equipped weight of 6,570 lb (2980 kg) the TJ-1 is slightly heavier than its

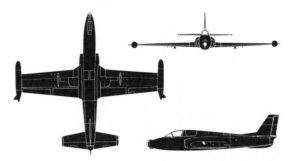

Soko Jastreb

predecessor, and carries only the two tip-tank cameras.

It seems probable that the single- and two-seat versions of the SOKO/CIAR Orao will eventually replace the Galebs and Jastrebs.

Specification

Type: two-seat trainer/single-seat attack aircraft
Powerplant: (Galeb) one 2,500-lb (1134-kg) Rolls-Royce Viper 22-6 turbojet;
Performance: (Galeb) maximum level speed at sea level 470 mph (756 km/h); maximum speed at 20,350 ft (6200 m) 505 mph (812 km/h); cruising speed at 19,680 ft (6000 m) 453 mph (730 km/h); rate of climb at sea level 4,500 ft (1370 m) per minute; service ceiling 39,375 ft (12000 m); take-off run to 50 ft (15 m) 2,100 ft (640 m); landing run from 50 ft (15 m) 2,330 ft (710 m); range at 29,520 ft (9000 m) with full wing tip tanks 770 miles (1240 km).
Weights: (Galeb) empty equipped 5,775 lb (2620 kg); maximum take-off aerobatic trainer 7,438 lb (3374 kg), basic trainer 7,690 lb (3488 kg), navigational trainer 8,439 lb (3828 kg), weapons trainer 8,792 lb (3988 kg), strike version 9,480 lb (4300 kg).
Dimensions: (Galeb) span 34 ft 4 in (10.47 m); span (over tip tanks) 38 ft 1 in (11.62 m); length 33 ft 11 in (10.34 m); height 10 ft 9 in (3.28 m); wing area 209.14 sq ft (19.43 m²).
Armament: (Galeb) two 0.50-in (12.7-mm) machine-guns in nose, underwing pylons for two 220-lb (100-kg) bombs and four 57-mm rockets or two 127-mm rockets or bomb clusters in containers up to 660 lb (300 kg) total.
Operators: Libya, Yugoslavia, Zambia

Sukhoi Su-7 Fitter

Sukhoi Su-7BMK of the Egyptian Air Force. About 100 equip three regiments in ground attack and strike duties.

History and notes

The standard strike fighter of Soviet Air Force Frontal Aviation from the early 1960s to the introduction of the Mikoyan-Gurevich 'Flogger-D' MiG-27 and Sukhoi Su-17 'Fitter-C' and '-D' in the early 1970s, the Sukhoi Su-7 'Fitter-A' has earned a reputation as a reliable and dependable warplane in action in the Middle East and the Indian subcontinent. Its radius of action and warload, however, are not what might be expected of so large an aircraft, and in general it carries fuel or weapons, but not both. The type also relies to a great extent on visual weapon-aiming, which limits its effectiveness.

The Sukhoi and Mikoyan bureaux were each apparently directed by the TsAGI (the Central Hydrodynamic Institute) to develop two alternative fighter designs: one with a wing not dissimilar to that of the MiG-19 'Farmer', then showing great promise, and the other with the newly developed tailed-delta configuration. All four prototype designs shared the mid-wing and circular-section fuselage of earlier Soviet jet fighters, leading to problems for Western intelligence analysts as they tried to determine which of the new types had gone into service.

Both Sukhoi types were ordered in quantity. The Su-7, the swept-wing version, was selected as the strike fighter for Frontal Aviation, and built in large numbers. Points in its favour for this role included reasonable, if not outstanding, field performance; unlike that of the MiG-19, the swept wing of the Su-7 is furnished with area-increasing trailing-edge flaps. Like the definitive MiG-19, the Su-7 has an all-moving tailplane.

Early production Su-7Bs, delivered from 1959, probably had early 20,000-lb (9000-kg) versions of the AL-7. The Su-7BM has the more powerful engine described below, while the later BMK version has low-pressure tyres and twin brake parachutes. Some Su-7BMKs are equipped for take-off rocket boost. Many have been seen operating from rough fields during manoeuvres. Also in service is the Su-7U conversion trainer.

The Su-7BMK is the standard export model, and often mounts two extra pylons aft of the mainwheel wells. Some aircraft of the type have been seen with up to six underwing stations. Egyptian pilots have described their Su-7s as the best aircraft available to

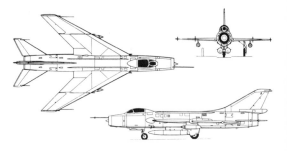

Sukhoi Su-7BM Fitter

them for high-speed combat at low level, where the type is tractable despite the high air loads in such conditions; losses against strong AAA and missile fire in the October 1973 war were remarkably low. The main problems were the lack of efficient navigation and weapon-aiming systems (possibly being rectified by British avionics, though this has yet to be confirmed) and the lack of range and endurance. Just over 1,000 Su-7s were built before production switched to the Su-17 series in 1971-72.

Specification

Type: fighter-bomber
Powerplant: one 15,400-lb (7000-kg) dry or 22,000-lb (10000-kg) afterburning Lyulka AL-7F-1 turbojet
Performance: maximum speed at altitude 1,050 mph (1700 km/h), or Mach 1.6; maximum speed (clean) at sea level Mach 1.1; service ceiling 49,700 ft (15150 m); range with two drop tanks 900 miles (1450 km)
Weights: empty 19,000 lb (8620 kg); maximum loaded 30,000 lb (13600 kg)
Dimensions: length (including probe) 57 ft (17.37 m); span 29 ft 3½ in (8.93 m); height 15 ft 5 in (4.7 m)
Armament: two 30 mm NR-30 cannon in wing roots, plus four wing and two ventral stores pylons, all capable of carrying weapons (rocket pods and bombs form main armament)
Operators: Afghanistan, Algeria, Czechoslovakia, Egypt, Hungary, India, Iraq, North Korea, Poland, Romania, Syria, USSR, Vietnam

Sukhoi Su-9/11 Fishpot

History and notes

Never as widely used or as well known as the contemporary Mikoyan-Gurevich MiG-21 'Fishbed' or Su-7 'Fitter-A', the Sukhoi bureau's delta-wing prototype of 1955-56 nevertheless led to the Su-9 'Fishpot-B' the most numerous supersonic interceptor in the PVO (Air Defence Forces) fleet for many years. The type was supplanted by the Su-15 'Flagon' on the production lines in the late 1960s, but some 600 remain in service.

The Su-9 was designed as an all-weather fighter based on the same tailed-delta configuration as the MiG-21. Entering service in 1958-59, it typified Soviet practice in that it combined a new engine and airframe with an existing weapon, the K-5M 'Alkali' air-to-air missile already in service on the MiG-19P 'Farmer'. The small radar fitted quite simply into the nose of the Su-9, which was closely similar to that of the Su-7. However, the all-weather capability of the Su-9 is fairly limited, as this radar lacks search range. In practice, the type presumably operates in close co-operation with ground control.

The 1961 Tushino air display, however, saw the appearance of a new derivative of the basic type, featuring a longer and less tapered nose. The inlet diameter was considerably larger, and there was a proportionate increase in the size of the centre-body radome to accommodate a new and more powerful radar know to NATO as 'Skip Spin'. The new type replaced the Su-9 on the production lines, and was designated Su-11, with the codename 'Fishpot-C'; it appears to be Sukhoi practice to apply new designations to reflect relatively minor changes, the Su-11 being no more different from its predecessor than contemporary MiG-21 versions differed from the MiG-21F.

Like most Soviet interceptors, the Su-9/11 series has never been exported, even to the Warsaw Pact. The Su-11 is closely comparable to the British Aerospace Lightning, lacking the British fighter's combat performance but possessing radar-guided missiles. It presented a credible defence against the high-flying bomber armed with free-fall weapons,

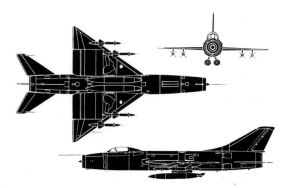

Sukhoi Su-9 "Fishpot" B.

but is increasingly an anachronism in the age of low-level aircraft armed with stand-off weapons, as it lacks the range for long-range patrols. Its importance in combat units, together with that of the Su-9U trainer variant, is likely to decline rapidly in the late 1970s and early 1980s.

Specification

Type: all-weather interceptor
Powerplant: one 22,000-lb (10000-kg) afterburning Lyulka AL-7F turbojet
Performance: maximum (clean) 1,400 mph (2250 km/h), or Mach 2.1; maximum speed with two AAMs and external fuel tanks 1,000 mph (1600 km/h) or Mach 1.5; service ceiling 65,000 ft (20000 m); range about 700 miles (1125 km)
Weights: empty 20,000 lb (9000 kg); maximum loaded 30,000 lb (13500 kg)
Dimensions: span 27 ft 8 in (8.43 m); length (including instrument boom) 60 ft (18.3 m); height 15 ft (4.9 m)
Armament: (Su-9) four K-5M (AA-1 'Alkali') beam-riding air-to-air missiles on wing pylons; (Su-11) two AA-3 'Anab' semi-active AAMs
Operators: USSR

The Sukhoi Su-9/11 series (Su-11 illustrated) is currently available to the number of 600 with the PVO-Strany.

Sukhoi Su-15 Flagon

History and notes

The Sukhoi Su-15 'Flagon' interceptor is a demonstration of the Soviet Union's practice of constantly improving a basic design over a period of many years to produce a highly effective definitive production aircraft. It is now the main interceptor in service with the PVO air-defence force, some 850 being reported to be operational. However, PVO re-equipment needs are now being met partly by the Mikoyan-Gurevich MiG-23S, and with the next generation of interceptor likely to enter service in the early 1980s the importance of the Su-15 could soon decline.

The Mikoyan bureau produced its E-152, which was demonstrated at Tushino is 1961 but not put into service. The Su-15 appears to have evolved rather later, and as flown in 1964-65 appears to have combined the Tumansky R-11 engines, 'Skip Spin' radar and AA-3 'Anab' missiles of the Yakovlev Yak-28P with the delta wing and tail of the Su-9/-11 (almost completely unchanged) and a new fuselage. The two engines were fed by variable-geometry side inlets with auxiliary inlet doors. The Su-15 thus represented a very low-risk development, making use of a large proportion of components from existing aircraft, though it evolved with an uncharacteristically low power-loading and high wing-loading.

A pre-series batch of Su-15s made their appearance at the 1967 Domodedovo air display, but this basic type does not appear to have been built in quantity, probably because it did not represent enough of an advance over the Su-11 to warrant replacement of the single-engined type. Development of the Su-15 was already under way, as indicated by the presence at Domodedovo of an experimental version known to NATO as the 'Flagon-B' (the designation 'Flagon-A' being allotted to the basic aircraft). The 'Flagon-B' was a reduced-take-off-and-landing (RTOL) aircraft similar to the Mikoyan 'Faithless', with three Kolesov lift jets installed in the centre fuselage. The sweep of the outer wing panels was reduced, possibly in order to allow the ailerons to be extended; one of the problems of such RTOL prototypes was the difficulty of control in partially jetborne flight. Although the Soviet Union abandoned research into such aircraft, the wing planform of the 'Flagon-B' foreshadowed the compound sweep of the later Su-15 variants.

The first major production version of the Su-15 is reported to have been the 'Flagon-D', which entered service in the late 1960s or early 1970s. Retaining the radar and missiles of the 'Flagon-A', the 'Flagon-D' probably introduced more powerful engines and compound sweep on the outer wings, separated by a short unswept section from the inner wing. This curious 'soft dog-tooth' is reminiscent of that fitted to the wing of the Ilyushin Il-62 airliner, the only other type to display such a feature. It is likely that the modification to the Su-15 wing is intended to improve low-speed handling and to reduce landing speeds; these were very high on the earlier sub-types, which are considerably heavier than the Su-11 despite having a similar wing area.

The 'Flagon-E', with more powerful R-13 engines, is said to be the most important production version so far. According to the US Department of Defense, it has improved electronics, but these do not appear to have advanced so far as to make the aircraft useful against low-flying targets; this capability was not credited to any PVO aircraft until the introduction of the MiG-23S. Neither are there any firm reports of Su-15s carrying the AA-7 'Apex' missile which arms the MiG-23S, although any new radar fitted to the later 'Flagons' could be the equal of the MiG-23S equipment.

The latest production version of the Su-15 is identified as the 'Flagon-F' by NATO, and is distinguished by a new radome which may be able to accommodate a larger aerial than the unusual conical radome of earlier versions, although it is more likely that the modification has been made for aerodynamic reasons.

Persistent reports that the Su-15 was to be equipped with cannon appear to have been in error. The type seems to be confined to the high-altitude interception role, which it shares with the MiG-25. Like other single-seat Soviet interceptors, it operates under close ground control. There appears, for instance, to be no HUD display, suggesting that the pilot need never see the target except on head-down radar and flight-director displays. In its primary role, the Su-15's attributes include speed and respectable fuel capacity; just how much space there is in the airframe can be judged by the fact that the fuselage of the 'Flagon-B' was little if any wider than standard, despite the battery of lift engines. The engines are tried and proven as is the AAM system.

Specification

Type: interceptor

Powerplant: two 16,000-lb (7500-kg) Tumansky R-13 afterburning turbojets

Performance: maximum speed Mach 2+ at medium altitude, equivalent to 1,320 mph (2120 km/h) at 36,000 ft (11000 m); maximum speed at sea level 680 mph (1100 km/h) or Mach 0.9; service ceiling 55,000 to 60,000 ft (17000 to 18000 m); combat radius 400 miles (650 km)

Weights: empty 27,500 lb (12500 kg); normal loaded 40,000 lb (18000 kg); maximum loaded 45,000 lb (20000 kg)

Dimensions: span 34 ft 6 in (10.5 m); length 70 ft 6 in (21.5 m); height 16 ft 6 in (5 m); wing area 385 sq ft (35.7 m^2)

Armament: two air-to-air missiles, normally AA-3-2 'Advanced Anab'; guns have been reported, but are unconfirmed

Operator: USSR

Sukhoi Su-15 Flagon

This Sukhoi Su-15 "Flagon-F" is unpainted and serving with the air defence IA-PVO. The radar is later than the "Skip Spin" of earler versions, and the large antenna occupies a curved radome of lower drag. Normal armament is two AA-3 "Anab" air-to-air missiles, one IR and the other radar homing. Under the nose are "Odd Rods" IFF and curved ATC/SIF radio antennas; the bulge is caused by the retracted nosewheel.

Sukhoi Su-17/Su-20/Su-22 Fitter-C to -H

History and notes

The Sukhoi Su-17/-20/-22 'Fitter' family of close-support fighters stems from what was apparently a research aircraft, and the three types are the only examples of production variable-sweep aircraft derived from a fixed-geometry design. They reflect the Soviet industry's traditional reluctance to terminate production of an established design, and its talent for filling an operational requirement in a manner which may appear crude but is nonetheless effective. Pending the emergence of a specialized close-support type, the Su-17 and its derivatives continue to fill an important role in the Soviet armoury.

It appears that the development of the Su-17 was a matter of chance. Soviet designers became absorbed in the study of variable sweep in the early 1960s, and discovered the same fundamental problems as had plagued Western designers. Among them was the tendency for the aerodynamic centre to move aft with increasing sweep, causing trim difficulties. The answer, it was discovered, was to set the pivots outboard, but only in the Soviet Union, however, was this trend continued to produce a 'semi-variable-geometry' layout, in which only the outer panels move. This was adopted by the Tupolev bureau for a supersonic bomber in 1965-66, and a Sukhoi Su-7 was apparently modified as a test-bed. This modified aircraft made its public debut at the Domodedovo air display in 1967, and was codenamed 'Fitter-B' by NATO. However, the improvement over the Su-7 was so great that it was decided to place this testbed in production. The first were observed in service in 1970-71.

The basic Su-17 is thought to be powered by the higher-powered AL-21F, while the Su-22 and possibly the Su-20 may have the older AL-7. The Su-17 differs from the Su-7 and the 'Fitter-B' in having a more advanced weapon-aiming system using a complex array of aerodynamic sensors on the nose boom. Control runs are relocated in a dorsal spine, possibly to improve maintainability.

Compared with the Su-7, the Su-17 offers a slight increase in maximum speed in clean condition, but the main advantage comes in weight-lifting and runway capability. The outer wing sections are fitted with slats and trailing-edge flaps, allowing the Su-17 to take off at least 7,500 lb (3500 kg) heavier than the Su-7 from a shorter runway. Two of the pylons, attached to the massive wing fences, are nearly always occupied by large tanks, but even so the Su-17 can still lift more weapons than an Su-7.

The Su-17 is not in the class of the Mikoyan-Gurevich MiG-27, despite its similar thrust, because of its much smaller internal fuel capacity (demanding the carriage of drag-causing external tanks), its less optimized unswept configuration, and its less efficient engine. However, it remains an effective close-support aircraft. At low level with tanks it is probably subsonic, and would use the afterburner only for take-off.

Poland was the first country to take delivery of the Su-20, the initial export model. Some sources suggest that the Su-20 has the AL-7 engine, and it has only two ventral pylons. One possible explanation is that the Poles, lacking MiG-27s, operate their Su-20s as long-range strike aircraft with four tanks, while Russian aircraft are used in the close-support role exclusively, for which wing tanks are adequate.

The second export version is the Su-22, the first Soviet combat aircraft in South America when delivered to Peru in 1977. The Su-22 carries AA-2 'Atoll' missiles, but otherwise is equipped to a very basic standard, lacking radar-warning systems and other items. Peru has had great difficulty in turning the type into an efficient weapon platform.

The Soviet forces, by contrast, are now taking delivery of an even more advanced version, the 'Fitter-D'. First reported in 1977, this appears to have a new weapon-aiming system with an electro-optical device or laser in the centrebody and radar beneath the nose, probably matched with 'smart' weapons similar to those arming the MiG-27. The reporting names 'Fitter G' and 'Fitter H' have also been quoted, implying that at least four more variants (E to H) have deen identified. 'Fitter H' is a reconnaissance aircraft carrying a massive ventral reconnaissance pod. The Su-17 derivatives seem to have proved an unexpected windfall for Soviet close-support units, and a highly successful interim type pending deployment of a specialised close-support fighter such as the RAM-J (see introduction).

Specification

Type: close-support attack

Powerplant: one 24,250-lb (11000-kg) Lyulka AL-21F afterburning turbojet

Performance: maximum speed at 36,000 ft (11000 m) 1,200 mph (1925 km/h) or Mach 1.8: maximum speed at sea level (clean) 830 mph (1340 km/h) or Mach 1.1; maximum speed at sea level with external fuel (almost invariably carried) 650 mph (1050 km/h) or Mach 0.88; service ceiling 55,000 ft (17000 m); ferry range 1,100 miles (1760 km); tactical radius 300 miles (480 km)

Weights: empty 22,000 lb (10000 kg); maximum external load about 7,500 lb (3500 kg); maximum take-off about 37,500 lb (17000 kg)

Dimensions: span (swept) 34 ft 6 in (10.5 m); span (spread) 45 ft (14 m); length (including probe) 58 ft (17.6 m); height 15 ft (4.6 m)

Armament: two wing-root 30-mm NR-30 cannon, plus a total of six (some Su-17s have eight) hardpoints for rockets, air-to-surface missiles or fuel tanks, although 250-Imperial gallon (1130-litre) auxiliary tanks are nearly always carried on outer pylons; some aircraft are fitted to carry AA-2 'Atoll' air-to-air missiles

Operators: Egypt, Peru, Poland, Syria, USSR

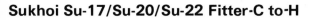

This Sukhoi Su-20 is one of a substantial batch serving with Egypt. Equipment standard is lower than in Soviet Su-17s and engine thrust considerably less. There are also considerable variations in camouflage. The nose carries an instrument air-data boom and, ahead of the blow-in auxilliary inlet doors on the left side, an anti-iced alpha (angle of attack) sensor. The tailcone houses twin brake parachutes. The four drop tanks dominate the head-on appearance, the outers on large fence/pylons aligned with the wing pivots being the largest size used by Soviet tactical aircraft, with finned noses to assist separation.

Sukhoi Su-24 Fencer

History and notes

Backing up the front-line Mikoyan MiG-27s of Frontal Aviation is an increasing force of the heavily-armed, all weather Sukhoi Su-24 strike aircraft. The Nato code-name 'Fencer' applied to these aircraft is something of a misnomer, because the Su-24 (commonly referred to as the Su-19 until the use of the Su-24 designation by the Department of Defense in 1980) has no air-to-air capability to speak of. It is the first Soviet aircraft designed specifically for tactical air-to-ground operations to be put into production since the 1939-45 war, and as such represents an important weapon in the armoury of Frontal Aviation.

Development of the Su-24 presumably got under way shortly after 1965, consequent on the decision to develop Frontal Aviation to the point where it could match and surpass Nato's non-nuclear tactical air capability. It was accepted that operations at night or in adverse weather dictated a two-seater aircraft with avionics systems rather more advanced than those planned for the strike version of the MiG-23, and that this aircraft would have to be generally larger than the single-engined Mikoyan fighter.

The Su-24 made its maiden flight in the early years of the decade and was first observed in 1971-72. Operational units were worked up by mid-1977, and in early 1980 there were eight or nine regiments operational in the Western Soviet Union (equivalent to a total of 280-310 aircraft) and other aircraft of the type were deployed near the Chinese border. Its range, particularly at high altitude, is sufficient for the aircraft to be based in the Western USSR rather than in the more vulnerable (and rather crowded) locations of Eastern Europe. The Su-24 can fly nearly as far in Western Europe on a hi-lo-hi profile from these more secure bases as it could fly lo-lo-lo from Eastern Europe. This explains the fact that the aircraft has not joined the 16th Air Army units in East German; so far the type has been camera-shy, Western Intelligence getting its first clear shots of the aircraft in late 1979.

The development of Fencer was an echo of mid-1950s Soviet design practice in that the wing/tailplane planform was chosen basically similar to that of the MiG-23 'Flogger A'; the modifications applied later to improve the manoeuvrability of the Mikoyan fighter proved unnecessary for the specialised strike bomber, so Fencer lacks the leading-edge extension and claw of the definitive MiG-23/27, and its tailplane tips align with the sweptback wingtips as on the 'Flogger A'.

The Su-24 is about 50 per cent bigger than the MiG-23/27, but has a longer range due to an 80 per cent greater internal fuel capacity. The crew of two are seated side-by-side in what must be a fairly cramped cockpit given the width of the forward fuselage. The nose appears to house radar equipment for terrain-following, and possibly, target tracking and weapon aiming, but the aircraft is not considered to be in the same league for nav/attack capability as the considerably bigger General Dynamics F-111 or the much later Panavia Tornado IDS. Some of the early aircraft may have been fitted with an interim limited all-weather avionics suite similar to that of the MiG-27 'Flogger D'. Internal ECM is probably comprehensive.

Armament of the Su-24 includes a GSh-23 twin-barrel cannon offset to starboard under the fuselage. Other weapons are carried on two swivelling wing pylons, two hardpoints under the wing gloves (which have been seen carrying large external fuel tanks) and three belly pylons. Apart from the range of ordnance carried by the MiG-27, the Su-24 is also expected to carry the longer-range AS-9 anti-radiation missile.

The Su-24 is not regarded as a "deep interdiction" aircraft; in any event, such an aircraft would not fit in with the FA's primary task of contributing directly to the land war. The Su-24 is more accurately classified as an all-weather back-up to the MiG-27, with greater load-carrying capacity but aimed at the same targets: Nato military installations, particularly air bases, in Western Europe. additionally, the Su-24 can strike air bases in Eastern England, but probably not from its normal quarters in the Western USSR. In numbers in service and production rate the type is never likely to match the cheaper and simpler MiG-23/27, but its capability is nevertheless significant to the Frontal Aviation forces.

Specification

Type: two-seat all-weather interdiction/strike aircraft
Powerplant: two unidentified afterburning turbofans, each rating about 19,500 lb (8800 kg) with afterburner
Performance: maximum speed at 36,000 (11000 m) 1,320 mph (2120 km/h) Mach 2; maximum speed at sea level (clean) 900 mph (1450 km/h), Mach 1.2; cruising speed at sea level 600 mph (980 km/h); ferry range 3,750 miles (6000 km); combat radius 700 miles (1100 km) on hi-lo-hi profile
Weights: empty 37,500 lb (17000 kg); maximum normal external load 12,500 lb (5700 kg); normal take-off 65,000 lb (30000 kg); overload take-off 70,000 lb (32000 kg)
Dimensions: span (spread) 56 ft 10 in (17.3 m); (span swept) 32 ft 8 in (10 m); length 72 ft 10 in (22.2 m); height 18 ft (5.5 m); wing area (swept) 485 sq ft (45m²)
Armament: one fixed twin-barrel 23-mm Gsh-23 cannon, up to 12,500 lb (5700 kg) of guided and unguided weapons on two swivelling wing pylons and five other hardpoints under wing gloves and fuselage
Operator: USSR

Sukhoi Su-24 Fencer

The Su-24 is believed to carry the same six-barrel gun as the MiG-27, as well as at least twice the load of external stores on six fixed and two pivoting pylons. The twin engines may have thrust reversers. Head-on, the Su-24 closely resembles a MiG-27, and uses similar aerodynamics, but it is larger and has a wider body, broad cockpit with round-topped canopy and a nose radome. Twin ventral fins slope out. The top and bottom of the right half of the Su-24, emphasize the impressive 16°/72° range of sweep of the swing wings, which are fitted with full-span slats and trailing-edge high-lift flaps.

Transall C.160

History and notes

The Transall (Transporter Allianz or Transport Alliance) group was formed in January 1959 by companies · which now form part of Aérospatiale, Messerschmitt-Bölkow-Blohm and VFW-Fokker, with the aim of producing the C.160 military transport for the French and German air forces. The first prototype made its maiden flight in March 1963, and the initial production aircraft took to the air in April 1967. By the time the production line closed in 1972 the consortium had built 179 examples. The *Luftwaffe* has a large number stored in reserve, but despite this, in October 1977 the programme was relaunched to provide additional aircraft for the French air force and for possible export customers, mainly to maintain employment at Aérospatiale.

The C.160 is a twin-turboprop medium transport which can carry troops, casualties, freight, supplies and vehicles from semi-prepared surfaces. The floor is stressed to take large vehicles and is provided with lashing points of 11,025-lb (5000-kg) and 26,455-lb (12000-kg) capacity. A hydraulically operated rear loading ramp is provided, in addition to a front door on the left side and paratroop doors on each side. A winch and roller conveyor allows loads to be taken aboard, and single loads of up to 17,635 lb (8000 kg) can be dropped from the air.

The new batch of aircraft will incorporate some differences. The loss of French bases in Africa has led to a requirement for additional range, which will

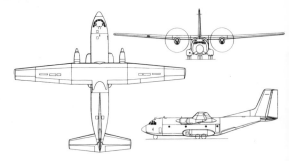

Transall C-160

be met by installing an extra centre-section fuel tank with a capacity of 1,540 gallons (7000 litres) and by fitting a probe so that the aircraft can be refuelled in flight. The new C.160s will additionally have improved avionic equipment, and the left door, which is rarely used, is to be deleted. The French air force is expected to receive 25 new aircraft, and up to 75 may be built in all. First deliveries are likely to take place between 1981 and 1983.

Specification

Type: medium transport aircraft
Powerplant: two 6,100-ehp (4550-kW) Rolls-Royce Tyne 22 turboprops
Performance: maximum level speed at 16,000 ft (4875 m) 368 mph (592 km/h); economical cruising speed at 20,000 ft (6100 m) 282 mph (454 km/h); range with 17,635-lb (8000-kg) payload, 10% reserves and allowances for 30 minutes at 13,125 ft (4000 m) 2,982 miles (4800 km); range as above, but with twice the payload 1,056 miles (1700 km); maximum rate of climb at sea level 1,300 ft (396 m) per minute; service ceiling 25,500 ft (7770 m)
Weights: empty equipped 63,405 lb (28760 kg); maximum take-off 112,435 lb (51000 kg); maximum landing 103,630 lb (47000 kg)
Dimensions: span 131 ft 3 in (40.0 m); length 106 ft 3½ in (32.40 m); height 40 ft 7 in (12.36 m); wing area 1,722 sq ft (160.1 m²)
Payload: up to 35,275 lb (16000 kg), including 93 troops, or 81 paratroops, or 62 stretchers and four attendants
Operators: France, South Africa, Turkey, West Germany

Out of production since 1972, the Transall C.160 has now been brought back into production by France.

Tupolev Tu-16 Badger

One regiment of the Egyptian Air Force still operates the Tu-16 "Badger-G", although serviceability is thought to be low.

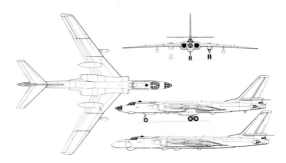

History and notes

The development in the early 1950s of the Mikulin bureau's massive AM-3 turbojet marked the end of the Soviet Union's dependence on Western technology in engines. Rated at 18,000 lb (8200 kg) in its initial version, the AM-3 made possible the design of new bombers with fewer engines than their Western counterparts, being twice as powerful as most contemporary Western engines.

Known as the Tupolev Tu-88 or Samolet N, the prototype of the Tu-16 'Badger' was flown in 1952; it was thus a contemporary of the British V-bombers rather than the American Boeing B-47. Like many Soviet aircraft designs, it was a mixture of the radically new and the conservative in its design philosophy.

The Tu-88 was ordered into production for the DA (Long-Range Aviation) and entered service in 1955. Later versions were equipped with the uprated AM-3M, and most of the type were eventually fitted with flight-refuelling equipment. The system fitted to Tu-16s so far seen is unusual, involving a tip-to-tip connection; other Soviet aircraft have nose probes. Some Tu-16s were completed as specialized tankers with a tip-hose or belly hose-reel.

Soviet production of the Tu-16 probably gave way to the Tu-20 and Tu-22 in the late 1950s, but in 1968 the type was put back into production (as the B-6) in China, as a replacement for the Tu-4. The Tu-16 also formed the basis for the Tu-104, the first Soviet jet airliner.

A new lease of life for the Tu-16 came with the rising power of the Soviet navy in the early 1960s. Tu-16s were steadily transferred from the DA to the AVMF (Soviet Naval Aviation), and became that service's first missile-carriers. The first missile-armed variant, the 'Badger-B', of 1961, carried two turbojet-powered AS-1 'Kennel' missiles under the wings; these aircraft appear to have been converted into 'Badger-Gs' with the more advanced AS-5 'Kelt' missile, and a number of these were delivered to Egypt in the late 1960s and early 1970s. The 'Badger-C' also seen in 1961, carries a single supersonic AS-2 'Kipper' missile, with a large radar installation replacing the glazed nose. A similar radar is featured by the 'Badger-D' maritime reconnaissance aircraft, together with an array of radomes indicating an electronic surveillance capability. The 'Badger-E' and 'Badger-F' are generally supposed to be specialized electronic intelligence (Elint) aircraft, with glazed noses and a plethora of aerials. 'Badger H' is an electronic warfare platform with a specialised role as a chaff

Tupolev Tu-16 "Badger-F".

dispenser; 'Badger J' carries active jamming equipment while 'Badger K' is an Elint platform.

About 400 Tu-16s are still in service with AVMF, including tankers as well as strike aircraft. The reconnaissance and Elint aircraft are likely to be replaced in first-line service by the better-optimized turboprop Ilyushin Il-38 and Il-18 while the missile-armed variants are being replaced by Tu-26s. However, there is life in the 'Badger' yet, as is shown by the re-equipment of some 'Badger-Gs' with a single AS-6 'Kingfish' missile under one wing.

Specification

Type: strategic bomber, missile platform, reconnaissance aircraft, Elint aircraft and flight-refuelling tanker

Powerplant: two 19,200-lb (8700-kg) Mikulin AM-3M turbojets

Performance: maximum speed 620 mph (1000 km/h) or Mach 0.91; cruising speed 530 mph (850 km/h or Mach 0.8; service ceiling 46,000 ft (14000 m); maximum range 4,000 miles (6400 m)

Weights: empty 80,000 lb (36000 kg); maximum take-off 158,500 lb (72000 kg)

Dimensions: span 113 ft 3 in (34.54 m); length 120 ft (36.5 m); height 35 ft 6 in (10.8 m); wing area 1,820 sq ft (170 m²)

Armament: ('Badger-B') two AS-1 'Kennel' ASMs (no longer in service); ('Badger-C') one AS-2 'Kipper'; ('Badger-G') two AS-5 'Kelt'. Bomber versions have provision for 13,000 lb (6000 kg) of internal stores. All versions have seven 23-mm NR-23 cannon: one fixed in forward fuselage, two in tail turret and two each in ventral and dorsal barbettes

Operators: China, Iraq, Indonesia (in storage), Libya, USSR

Tupolev Tu-22 Blinder

History and notes

Often considered a failure, the Tupolev Tu-22 'Blinder' appears in fact to be a workmanlike design, and limited production appears to be a consequence of changing requirements and political factors rather than a technical decision. The figures below reflect the compiler's latest estimates, and in some respects contradict earlier information; the range quoted for the aircraft, for example, has generally been closer to the all-supersonic range capability of the type, rather than reflecting its normal operating profile.

Development of the Tu-22, under the Tupolev bureau designation Tu-105, was initiated in 1955-56. By that time it was clear that the effectiveness of Western air-defence systems was improving rapidly, and that supersonic, missile-armed all-weather interceptors and medium/high-altitude SAMs would be in large-scale service by the end of the decade. The Tu-16, with its modest cruising altitude and defensive gun turrets, was already obsolescent for penetration of hostile territory. The design objectives of the Tu-105 were to produce an aircraft with performance generally comparable with the Tu-16, but with greatly increased penetration altitude and speed.

The Tu-105 was thus designed to incorporate supersonic dash at high altitude without excessively penalizing subsonic efficiency. The engines were mounted high on the rear fuselage in slim cowlings to avoid the weight and drag penalties of long inlet ducts. Sweep was increased relative to that of the Tu-16, but a compound-sweep layout was chosen for minimum subsonic and low speed penalty. The fuselage, wing, landing-gear pods and engine nacelles were positioned and designed in strict accordance with the area rule. The elimination of defensive armament except the tail cannon saved weight and volume and the crew was reduced to three, seated in tandem downward-ejecting seats. For the first time in a Soviet aircraft, bombing/navigation radar displaced the glazed nose.

The source of the engines has long been a mystery, but it appears they are Kolesov VD-7s, similar to the engines fitted to the Myasishchev M-50. The nacelles are fitted with plain inlets; production Tu-22s have narrower inlets than early aircraft, and the lips slide forwards to open an auxiliary annular aperture at low speeds.

The Tu-105 probably flew in 1959, in time for 10 (including one with a missile) to be demonstrated at Tushino in 1961. The type's debut was a complete surprise to Western intelligence, but progress in defence systems had come to the point where a supersonic dash and better cruise altitude were in practice not much of an advantage over the subsonic Tu-16. In addition, the decision to rely solely on missiles for strategic attack had already been taken, leading to the temporary cessation of bomber development, and transfer of many aircraft to the Soviet naval air arm (AVMF).

There was, however, a continuing role for the Tu-22 in the precision strike and missile-carrying role, and about 170 of the type were delivered to Long-Range Aviation (DA) units from about 1964. These were of the variant known to NATO as 'Blinder-B', with a bomb-bay modified to accept the AS-4 'Kitchen' air-to-surface missile, as well as free-fall weapons. The designation 'Blinder-A' was applied to the nine non-missile aircraft seen at Tushino in 1961. The AS-4 is the Soviet equivalent of the defunct British Hawker Siddeley Blue Steel, rocket-powered and with a 200-mile (320-km) range.

The main AVMF variant of the Tu-22 in current service is the maritime-reconnaissance Elint 'Blinder-C'. The 'Blinder-B' and the AS-4 do not appear to be in AVMF service. In the reconnaissance role, the 'Blinder-C' offers payload and flight-refuelled endurance similar to those of the Tu-16, but less space for the crew. Only some 50 are in AVMF service. Both the DA and AVMF operate a few 'Blinder-D' (probably Tu-22U) conversion trainers, with a separate second cockpit above and behind the standard (pupil's) cockpit.

Although the Tu-22 is far from being the failure it has been considered in the West, it has not found an important niche in the Soviet forces. Its main role in the late 1960s and early 1970s was strike in the European region, but its importance in this role has diminished with the introduction of the Sukhoi Su-19 into the FA, and the Tu-26 'Backfire' into the DA and AVMF. The small batches of 'Blinder-Bs' supplied to Libya and Iraq (without AS-4 missiles or nuclear weapons) were probably surplus to DA requirement.

Specification

Type: bomber, reconnaissance and maritime-strike aircraft

Powerplant: probably two 31,000-lb (14000-kg) Kolesov VD-7 afterburning turbojets

Performance: maximum speed at 36,000 ft (11000 m), 1000 mph (1600 km/h) Mach 1.5; cruising speed 36,000 ft (11000 m) 560 mph (900 km/h) or Mach 0.85; service ceiling 60,000 ft (18000 m) with afterburning, 50,000 ft (15000 m) without; maximum range (subsonic) 4,000 miles (6500 km); unrefuelled tactical radius with 250 miles (400 km) supersonic dash 1,750 miles (2800 km)

Weights: empty 90,000 lb (40000 kg); internal fuel 80,000 lb (36000 kg); maximum take-off 190,000 lb (85000 kg)

Dimensions: span 94 ft 6 in (28.8 m); length 136 ft 9 in (41.7 m); height 28 ft 2 in (8.6 m); wing area 1,650 sq ft (155 m^2)

Armament: one 23-mm cannon in radar-directed tail barbette, and about 17,500 lb (8000 kg) of internal stores or ('Blinder-B') one AS-4 'Kitchen' cruise missile

Operators: Iraq, Libya, USSR

Tupolev Tu-22 Blinder

Tupolev Tu-22 "Blinder-A" of the Libyan Arab air force. Some original Soviet equipment has probably been removed. This sub-type does not carry the AS-4 "Kitchen" stand-off missile, but has front and rear bays for free-fall bombs up to 6,615 lb size, with damage-assessment cameras in the tail of the main-gear wing pods. Like many Tu-22s in Soviet service this example lacks a flight-refuelling probe. In the bulge under the cockpit are the tandem crew hatches, and white "Bee Hind" radar serves the 23 mm guns at the tail.

Tupolev Tu-26 Backfire

History and notes

Few contemporary combat aircraft have been the subject of as much controversy as the Tupolev bureau's swing-wing bomber, codenamed 'Backfire' by NATO and referred to as the Tu-26 by the US Department of Defense. The Soviet Union has quoted the designation Tu-22M, but this is not universally believed to be the actual service designation of the type. Throughout the Strategic Arms Limitation Talks (SALT) negotiations, the Soviet Union has maintained that the 'Backfire' is intended for maritime and European strike missions rather than long-range strike against the USA; US negotiators, on the other hand, have consistently argued that the aircraft has strategic range, and there have been accusations that some estimates of 'Backfire' performance have been deliberately suppressed to suit the political line. However, the aircraft is now regarded as a 'peripheral' system, and unless it is equipped with long-range cruise missiles (allowing it to fly its entire mission to the launch point at subsonic speed, while still threatening a large proportion of the USA) it is not seen as a true strategic system. However, it still presents a very serious threat to Western Europe, the North Atlantic and above all to China, which completely lacks the air-defence capability needed to intercept the 'Backfire' at any altitude. Its potential in the maritime strike role is also significant; in the 1980 US Department of Defence annual report its was suggested that "the Backfire threat . . . will exceed the menace of Soviet attack submarines."

'Backfire' development started in 1964-65, to meet a joint Soviet Naval Aviation (AVMF) and Long-Range Aviation (DA) requirement for a Tu-22/Tu-16 replacement. It is questionable whether or not, by that time, the decision to abandon the bomber as a strategic weapon had been reversed. It was inevitable that any bomber developed with variable sweep and turbofans would have very long subsonic range, and thus some strategic potential, as a corollary of improved low-level and loiter performance.

The first prototype, representative of the aircraft known as 'Backfire-A' to NATO, flew in 1969 and demonstrated a considerable range deficiency as a result of excessive drag, probably affecting low-level performance most severely. It was therefore decided to modify the aircraft radically. The 'Backfire-B' features new outer wings of increased span, with a distinctive double-taper on the trailing edge, and a new landing gear, which retracts inwards into the fuselage. There may have been other changes, but the nose and tail were little altered. The first trials unit started working up in 1975.

Production has been reported to be running at a rate of 35 aircraft af year, but this is hard to square with the US Defence Department's statement that only 100 aircraft were in service in early 1980, suggesting an average production rate of 20 ships/year.

With refuelling, the 'Backfire-B' does sustain a one-way threat to the continental USA, but its main role (particularly in view of the long-range bomber anticipated in early 1979) is in the European and maritime theatres. In Europe, the 'Backfire' remains the only aircraft in the Soviet inventory which can cover the whole of the NATO region at low level from a 'starting line' on the Eastern bloc border, operating on a hi-lo-hi profile from secure bases in the western Soviet Union.

An equally serious threat is posed by AVMF 'Backfires', with their capability to launch long-range strikes from the North Cape area over much of the Atlantic. The 'Backfire' force thus menaces NATO's vital resupply route; NATO's main counter seems to be to close the gap between Scotland and Iceland with AWACS aircraft (BAe Nimrod AEW.3) and long-range interceptors (Panavia Tornado F.2).

Missile armament of the 'Backfire' is an area of uncertainty. The Mach 3 AS-6 'Kingfish anti-shipping missile was reported to be under development for the 'Backfire', and at one stage it was thought that two of these weapons might be carried. However, as seen in late 1977 the weapon appears to be larger than first reported, and is more suited to a single installation like that of the AS-4, on the Tu-22. Armament of the 'Backfire' on long-range missions is likely to comprise a single AS-4 or AS-6 at present, but a new 750-mile (1200-km)-range weapon has been test-fired from a Tu-26; it is believed to exist in surface- and air-launched versions.

Specification

Type: medium-range bomber and maritime strike/reconnaissance aircraft
Powerplant: two 45,000-lb (20500-kg) Kuznetsov NK-144 afterburning turbofans
Performance: maximum speed at 36,000 ft (11000 m) 1,200-1,320 mph (1930-2120 km/h) or Mach 1.8-2.0; cruising speed 560 mph (1900 km/h) at 33,000 ft (11000 m); maximum speed at sea level 650 mph (1050 km/h); cruising speed at sea level 500 mph (800 km/h); service ceiling 55,000 ft (17000 m); range 5,000 miles (8000 km); hi-lo-hi combat radius 1,600 miles (2600 km); sea-level combat radius 850 miles (1400 km)
Weights: empty 110,000 lb (50000 kg); internal fuel 105,000 lb (47500 kg); maximum take-off 245,000 lb (11000 kg)
Dimensions: span (unswept) 113 ft (34.5 m) span (swept) 86 ft (26.2 m); length 132 ft (40.2 m); height 30 ft (9.1 m); wing area 1,785 sq ft (166 m²)
Armament: two 23-mm cannon in radar-directed tail barbette, plus one or two AS-4 'Kitchen', or AS-6 'Kingfish' missiles recessed into fuselage or under wings; other stores may be carried in internal weapons bay, for a total stores capacity estimated at 17,500 lb (8000 kg)
Operators: USSR

Tupolev Tu-26 Backfire

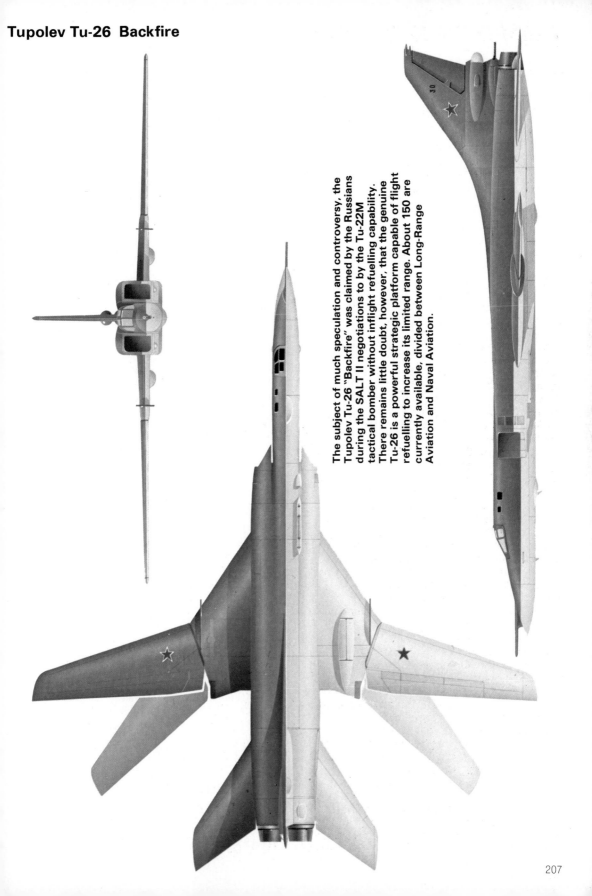

The subject of much speculation and controversy, the Tupolev Tu-26 "Backfire" was claimed by the Russians during the SALT II negotiations to by the Tu-22M tactical bomber without inflight refuelling capability. There remains little doubt, however, that the genuine Tu-26 is a powerful strategic platform capable of flight refuelling to increase its limited range. About 150 are currently available, divided between Long-Range Aviation and Naval Aviation.

Tupolev Tu-28 Fiddler

History and notes

Originally developed as the Soviet Union's counter to missile-carrying subsonic bombers in the late 1950s and early 1960s, the Tupolev Tu-28 'Fiddler' remains the largest fighter in the world. Most of the aircraft of this type appear to be deployed along the northern edge of the Soviet Union; in that sense, their opposite numbers are the fighters of the Canadian Armed Forces, with a vast periphery to protect an inhospitable territory beneath them.

The Tu-28P appears to have entered service rather later than the Tu-22, but the design is earlier in origin and carries the bureau designation Tu-102. It represented a development of one of the most publicised but least used of Soviet aircraft, the Tupolev Tu-98 'Backfin'. It is difficult to work out the characteristics of the Tu-98, because in 1956-60 it was the object of a vast amount of speculation in the West, by intelligence and press sources alike.

In fact the Tu-98 had been flown in 1955, as a light transonic tactical bomber intended as a successor to the Ilyushin Il-28. Like the contemporary Il-54, it was powered by two Lyulka AL-7F afterburning turbojets of 20,000-lb (9000-kg) thrust.

Both the Tu-98 and Il-54 were cancelled in favour of the small Yak-28, but the Tupolev bureau developed the Tu-98 into the refined Tu-102, which was apparently intended to fill the light strike role as well as having potential as an interceptor.

In the event, the Tu-102 was to be adapted as the carrier for a new long-range air-to-air missile and its powerful 'Big Nose' radar. The intended role of the eventual Tu-28P was to intercept Western subsonic bombers before they came close enough to launch long-range missiles such as the North American

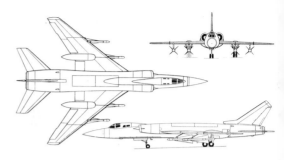

Tupolev Tu-28P "Fiddler".

Hound Dog, Hawker Siddeley Blue Steel or Douglas Skybolt. This demanded considerable endurance at remote patrol points, and the answer was an aircraft of considerable size.

Production deliveries are believed to have started in 1963-64, but it was not until 1967 that the production standard aircraft was observed, at the Domodedovo air display. Production Tu-28Ps carry two AA-5s under each wing, and are reported to be armed with a mix of semi-active radar and infra-red homing weapons.

The Tu-28 continues to fill a niche in the defensive cordon of the Soviet Union which cannot be catered for adequately by any other type, and it is likely to remain in service until the new air-defence system expected in the early 1980s becomes operational. The aircraft referred to by US sources as the 'Super MiG-25', the main air vehicle in the new system, is the only other two-seat Soviet fighter. It is also likely to match the range and loiter capability of the Tu-28P; the present MiG-25 lacks this by a large margin. The effectiveness of the Tu-28P depends on the degree to which it has been updated, but it is likely to fall well short of Western systems such as the AWG-9/Phoenix system carried by the Grumman F-14. Even operating in conjunction with the Tu-126 'Moss', the Tu-28P is unlikely to be effective against low-flying targets.

Specification

Type: two-seat long-range interceptor
Powerplant: two 24,500-lb (11000 kg) Lyulka AL-21F afterburning turbojets
Performance: maximum speed 1,200 mph (1900 km/h) Mach 1.8 at 36,000 ft (11000 m); maximum speed with four missiles 1,000 mph (1600 km/h), or Mach 1.5; service ceiling 60,000 ft (18000 m); range 2,000 miles (3200 km); tactical radius 800 miles (1300 km)
Weights: empty 40,000 lb (18000 kg); maximum take-off 85,000 lb (38500 kg)
Dimensions: span 65 ft (20 m); length 85 ft (26 m); height 23 ft (7 m); wing area 850 sq ft (80 m^2)
Armament: four AA-5 'Ash' air-to-air missiles
Operators: USSR

Three of the world's biggest fighters, Tu-28P "Fiddler" all-weather interceptors of the PVO of the kind still used in remote areas of the Soviet Union. They carry four 'Ash' missiles and almost 40,000 lb (18 145 kg) of internal fuel, enough for eight hours.

Tupolev Tu-95 Bear

Tu-95 Bear-D long-range strategic bomber. About 45 of these aircraft continue in Soviet maritime reconnaissance service.

History and notes
Unquestionably the most spectacular of contemporary warplanes, the vast Tupolev Tu-95 'Bear' remains in service with the DA and the AVMF (Soviet Naval Aviation) by virtue of its unmatched range. The Tupolev giants are the only turboprop combat aircraft in use, and the only swept-wing turboprop aircraft ever to see service. Their mighty propellers still defy conventional design wisdom, which states that the peak in propeller efficiency has been passed long before the speed of the aircraft is high enough to justify a swept wing.

The design of the Tu-95 is directly descended from that of the Boeing B-29, copied by Tupolev as the Tu-4 'Bull'. The refined Tu-80 development of the Tu-4 led to the much larger Tu-85, whose speed was inadequate to evade jet fighters. In view of the progress being made on turbine engines, it was decided to abandon the Tu-85 and develop a more advanced design using a similar fuselage.

Design of the Tu-95 started before 1952, in parallel with the Myasishchev M-4 'Bison'. The massive NK-12 turboprop was bench-tested at 12,000 hp (8952-kW) in 1953 and the first prototype Tu-95 flew in the following year. In flight tests without military equipment the Tu-95 attained a speed of 590 mph (950 km/h), equivalent to nearly Mach 0.9, an achievement matched by scarcely any other propeller aircraft, and certainly by none of its size.

The Tu-95 entered service in 1955 with the DA bomber force, and caused something of a panic in US defence circles; at that time most of the all-weather/night fighters in US service were still straight-winged, and would have had trouble intercepting the Soviet bomber. However, with the advent of the surface-to-air guided missiles and radar-controlled, missile-armed interceptors in the late 1950s, the Tu-95 became largely obsolete as a bomber. To maintain a credible deterrent, the massive AS-3 'Kangaroo' missile was developed, measuring 49 ft (15 m) from nose to tail and weighing nearly 10 tons.

About 50 of the DA's Tu-95s became 'Bear-Bs' with the AS-3 missile and a large nose radar, and the bomber force retains more than 100 Tu-95s. However, a major user of the aircraft is the AUMF, whose aircraft are apparently designated Tu-142. 'Bear-C' is apparently an MR type with the same

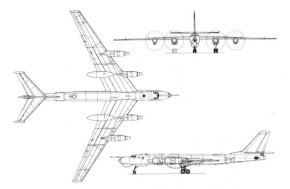

Tupolev Tu-95 "Bear".

radar. The 'Bear-E' is similar to the bomber, but equipped for Elint (electronic intelligence) and other reconnaissance duties. The 'Bear-F' is a more recent MR modification, with extended inner engine nacelles, and conversion of Tu-95s to this standard continues. The 'Bear-D' is a highly interesting variant, with a large ventral radar in a bulged radome. One theory is that the 'Bear-D' is a director for over-the-horizon surface-to-surface missiles such as the SS-N-3 and SS-N-12.

Specification
Type: strategic bomber, missile platform and maritime reconnaissance aircraft
Powerplant: four 15,000-shp (11190-kW) Kuznetsov NK-12MV turboprops
Performance: maximum speed 540 mph (870 km/h); economical cruising 465 mph (750 km/h); service ceiling 41,000 ft (12500 m); maximum range 11,000 miles (17500 km)
Weights: empty about 165,000 lb (about 75,000 kg); normal take-off 330,000 lb (150000 kg); maximum overload, 375,000 lb (170000 kg)
Dimensions: span 167 ft 8 in (51.1 m); length 155 ft 10 in (47.5 m); height 38 ft 8 in (11.78 m)
Armament: (original aircraft) six NR-23 23-mm cannon on dorsal semi-retractable barbette, ventral barbette and manned tail turret, plus a normal bomb load of 22,000 lb (10000 kg); 'Bear-B' converted to carry AS-3 'Kangaroo' stand-off weapon
Operator: USSR

...olev Tu-126 Moss

Moss serves with the IA-PVO Strany in the airborne warning and control system role.

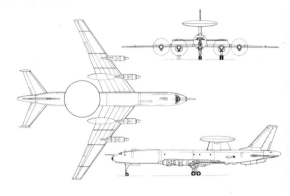

History and notes

The existence of a Soviet equivalent to the Western Boeing E-3A Sentry airborne warning and control system (AWACS) was revealed in late 1969, by which time the type had probably been flying for at least two years. The fact that the type was not among those demonstrated at the 1967 Domodedovo air display may be significant: the Soviet Union would hardly have anything to gain from attempting to conceal so large and distinctive a weapon system while at the same time revealing so many smaller aircraft. It is therefore likely that the first flight of a development aircraft took place in late 1967, with the system becoming operational in 1970. In 1971 a single aircraft was detached with its crew to assist the Indian air force in the war with Pakistan, indicating that the type was operational by that time.

Carrying the designation Tu-126 in Soviet service, and codenamed 'Moss' by NATO, the Soviet AWACS resembles the Boeing aircraft in the location of its main radar in a saucer-shaped rotodome on a fuselage. The location is chosen to reduce the interference generated by the wing and propellers while minimizing the effects of the radome and its pylon on stability.

The Tu-126 is based on the airframe of the Tu-114 airliner, and it is probable that aircraft of this type have been converted from Tu-114s surplus to Aeroflot requirements. The advantages of the Tu-114 for this role include its roomy cabin (the comparable E-3A has a crew of 17, including systems operators) and its impressive endurance, especially at reduced patrol speeds. Less favourable aspects of the design probably include high vibration levels at cruising speed, providing a less-than-perfect environment for delicate electronic systems.

In addition to the main radar, the Tu-126 carries a considerable array of smaller aerials, enabling it to communicate with the fighter aircraft it controls and to interrogate the IFF (identification, friend or foe) systems of radar contacts. Blister fairings around the rear fuselage presumably contain defensive and offensive electronic countermeasures (ECM) equipment.

The Tu-126 programme ran some eight years ahead of the Western AWACS development, and the US Department of Defense has a low opinion of its performance. According to the DoD, the Tu-126 system is 'ineffective' over land and 'only marginally effective' over water. If this unsubstantiated estimate is accurate, it would explain why only a small number of these aircraft have been seen in service: Western estimates are that fewer than 20 are

Tupolev Tu-126 "Moss".

in use.

The ability of the Tu-126 system to look-down on targets in the presence of high sea states or ground clutter depends on the technological standard of its radar and data-processing equipment, and it is thought that the Soviet Union has not progressed as far in these areas as the West. Moreover, the Tu-126 is the first airborne early warning (AEW) aircraft of any sort to enter service with the Soviet air forces. This contrasts with the 35 years of continuous US experience in the field. It would thus be surprising if the Tu-126 did fully match Western standards.

A more capable Soviet AWACS system is expected to be deployed in the early 1980s. It is expected to incorporate important advances in the areas of data processing and radar performance and to have overland look-down capability. A likely carrier aircraft for the new system is the Ilyushin Il-86 wide-body airliner, first flown in December 1976.

Specification

Type: airborne warning and control (AWACS) aircraft

Powerplant: four 15,000-shp (11900-kW) Kuznetsov NK-12MV turboprops

Performance: maximum speed at 33,000 ft (10000 m) 460 mph (740 km/h); long-endurance patrol speed 320 mph (520 km/h); service ceiling 33,000 ft (10000 m); endurance more than 20 hours

Weights: empty 200,000 lb (90000 kg); loaded 365,000 lb (165000 kg)

Dimensions: span 167 ft 8 in (51.1 m); length 188 ft (57.3 m); height 38 ft (11.6 m); wing area 3,350 sq ft (312 m²)

Operator: USSR

Vought A-7 Corsair II

Start of a 'cat shot' of a Vought A-7E Corsair II of 'The Clansmen' — who are not necessarily Scotsmen — from the *JFK*. A big flat-top in action is rather like an American football game; all the crew colours have meanings.

History and notes

In late 1962 the US Navy was considering the procurement of a supplement for the Douglas A-4 Skyhawk, which had first entered service in 1956. Though aware since July 1954 of the potential of the A-4, the US Navy saw the need for an attack aircraft capable of carrying twice the weight of disposable stores over twice the range. Thus in May 1963 the US Navy initiated a design competition to find a supplement for the A-4 Skyhawk. At this stage it was identified as VAL, signifying a heavier-than-air lightweight attack aircraft, and the specification called for subsonic speed, a maximum weapon load exceeding 10,000 lb (4536 kg), and the ability to fly three differing missions with a reduced weapon load.

In fact, the US Navy regarded the requirement as very urgent, and the ability to achieve an in-service target date in 1967 was an important factor. Four years in which to design, develop and start producing hardware is not very long in terms of the highly sophisticated aircraft needed by major powers in modern times, and it was probably this factor which limited to four the number of design proposals received by the US Navy. They came from Douglas, Grumman, North American and LTV Aerospace, and it was the last which, on 11 February 1964, was named as the winner of the competition; little more than a month later, on 19 March, LTV received a contract for seven test aircraft and the first 35 production aircraft, these having the designation A-7A.

LTV bestowed the name Corsair, resurrected from the famous Vought-Sikorsky F4U carrier-based fighter of World War II, adding the Roman II to ensure that historians would not get them confused.

The A-7A Corsair II was derived from the Chance Vought F-8 Crusader, the last US Navy fighter to emanate from that company before organisational changes brought in the name LTV (Ling-Temco-Vought) Aerospace (today Vought). It was, however, a very different aeroplane, with a less-swept, increased-span, fixed-incidence wing of which the outer panels folded upward, a shorter fuselage, and a more robust wing and fuselage structure to cater for the heavy weapons load.

The first A-7A had flown for the first time on 27 September 1965, and the first deliveries to the US Navy's Air Test Center at Patuxent River NAS were made between 13 and 15 September 1966. Deliveries to squadrons began on 14 October 1966, and the first aircraft involved in combat was an A-7A of Navy Squadron VA-147, which was flown into action off the USS *Ranger* in the Gulf of Tonkin on 3 December 1967.

A total of 199 A-7As were built for the US Navy and delivered by the spring of 1968, and these were followed into production by an improved version designated A-7B, the first of which made its first flight on 6 February 1968. These aircraft had the more powerful 12,200-lb (5534-kg) thrust Pratt &

A compact aircraft derived aerodynamically from the F-8 Crusader, the A-7 Corsair II is capable of carrying more than 15,000 lb (6804 kg) of stores on its eight hardpoints. The aircraft illustrated has only ferry tanks.

Whitney TF30-P-8 turbofan engine, and the first of these were used operationally in Vietnam on 4 March 1969. These engines were modified later to TF30-P-408 configuration, providing 13,400-lb (6078-kg) thrust. The A-7C designation was reserved originally for a two-seat trainer version, but was used retrospectively in late 1971 for the first 67 A-7Es which were powered by the TF30-P-408 engines.

In October 1966 the USAF ordered a tactical attack version which was to be powered by a 14,250-lb (6464-kg) thrust Allison/Rolls-Royce TF41-A-1 turbofan, derived from the Spey, and this version has the designation A-7D. The first two were powered by TF30-P-8 engines, but all of the 457 aircraft built subsequently for the US Air Force had the Allison engine. The first flight with this latter engine was made on 26 September 1968 and the first production aircraft was accepted by the USAF three months later. This version had advanced avionics to provide its pilot with continuous-solution navigation, and a weapon delivery system that could ensure all-weather radar bomb delivery. Under a programme initiated in mid-1978, 383 A-7Ds are being modified to carry a Pave Penny laser target designation pod. The A-7D also introduced a 20-mm M-61 gun in the fuselage. The A-7E was a developed version for the US Navy to fulfil a light attack/close air support/interdiction role, the first 67 of which were powered by TF30-P-408 engines and which were designated subsequently A-7C. From the 68th production aircraft onward, the powerplant consisted of the 15,000-lb (6804-kg) thrust Allison/Rolls-Royce TF41-A-2 turbofan. The first flight of an A-7E was made on 25 November 1968, and this version entered US Navy service on 14 July 1969. In early 1977 an A-7E FLIR (forward-looking infra-red) version entered production, this equipment offering improved night capability.

Other versions of the A-7 Corsair II which have been designated to date include the TA-7C, a tandem two-seat trainer with operational capability, of which 60 are being converted from A-7B/C aircraft

(none of which remain active); A-7H, a land-based version of the A-7E of which 60 were built for the Greek air force; TA-7H two-seat trainer for the Greek air force, to be powered by the Allison TF41-A-400 engine, of which five have been ordered for delivery in 1980; and the YA-7E Corsair II$_2$ advanced trainer of which, so far, only a prototype has been built.

During operations in south-east Asia, USAF and USN A-7s flew more than 100,000 sorties, proving that this subsonic aircraft was more than capable of holding its own against supposedly superior aircraft. It seems likely that with improved sensors and equipment it could well be around for some time to come. The Allison/Rolls-Royce TF41 has the remarkable time between overhauls of 1,500 hours.

All US Navy Corsair IIs are currently being fitted with a forward-looking infra-red (FLIR) pod designed by Vought. The FLIR pod is linked to the nav/attack system and the pilot's HUD.

Specification

Type: single-seat subsonic tactical fighter
Powerplant: (A-7E) one 15,000-lb (6804-kg) thrust Allison/Rolls-Royce TF41-A-2 turbofan
Performance: (A-7E) maximum speed at sea level 691 mph (1112 km/h); maximum speed at 5,000 ft (1525 m) clean 685 mph (1102 km/h); ferry range with maximum fuel 2,861 miles (4604 km).
Weights: (A-7E) empty 19,111 lb (8669 kg); maximum take-off 42,000 lb (19051 kg)
Dimensions: span 38 ft 9 in (11.81 m); length 46 ft 1½ in (14.06 m); height 16 ft 0¾ in (4.90 m); wing area 375 sq ft (34.84 m²)
Armament: a wide range of stores totalling more than 15,000 lb (6804 kg) can be carried on two fuselage stations and six underwing pylons, and these can include air-to-air and air-to-surface missiles, TV and laser-guided weapons, general purpose bombs, rockets and gun pods; a 20-mm M61A-1 Vulcan gun is mounted in the fuselage
Operators: Greece, Portugal, US Air Force, US Navy

Vought A-7 Corsair II

defence two early-model AIM-9B Sidewinders are carried on the fuselage, pylons, high on each side. Just visible under the rear fuselage is the retracted sting hook, identical to that for carrier use.

This late-model A-7D is the wing commander's aircraft from the 355th TFW at Davis-Monthan AFB, near Tuscan, Arizona. Internal ALR-46(V) digital radar warning is fitted, but a jammer pod (ALQ-101) would have to displace bombs. For self-

Westland Lynx

History and notes

Produced jointly by Westland in the UK and by Aérospatiale in France under the overall design leadership of the British company, the Lynx is perhaps the most outstanding example of a multi-role helicopter in service during early 1980s. The origins of the design lie in the Westland WG.13, one of the three helicopter designs (Gazelle, Lynx and Puma) subject to the Anglo-French co-production agreement of 2 April 1968. While the other two were largely French, the Lynx was predominantly British. Thirteen prototypes were ordered, the first of these flying on 21 March 1971. As other proto-types joined the test programme, the Lynx was revealed as a truly exceptional design, with excellent performance and handling characteristics.

The Lynx has been developed in two basic forms, the one military and the other naval. The Lynx in its military form really comes into its own in the offensive role, especially as an anti-tank or air-to-surface aircraft. In these roles the armament can consist of a 20-mm cannon with up to 1,500 rounds, or (mounted in or out of the cabin) a 0.30-in (7.62-mm) Minigun with up to 3,000 rounds. On each side of the cabin there is a pylon capable of accepting two Miniguns or 36 68-mm (2.68-in) unguided rockets in two pods. The pylons can also accommodate a variety of air-to-surface missiles, such as six AS.11, or eight HOT or eight TOW, and a further eight missiles can be stored in the cabin for rearming.

The naval Lynx is largely distinguishable from the military version by its wheel rathan than skid under-carriage, which allows the Lynx to operate from ships in very difficult conditions of sea and wind. Anti-submarine operations are possible with the aid of Alcatel DUAV.4 dunking sonar and an armament of two Mk 44 or 46 torpedoes, or two Mk 11 depth charges, carried on the pylons outside the cabin. The naval Lynx can also attack surface vessels with the aid of Ferranti Seaspray rader and an armament of four AS.12 missiles, to be replaced in the mid-1980s by four Sea Skua missiles.

Like the military Lynx, the maritime version has automatic flight control, and has proved itself an excellent machine. The first Royal Navy squadron to operate the Lynx was formed in 1978, and the type has entered service with other navies.

Specification (Westland Lynx (Navy))

Type: twin-engined multi-purpose helicopter
Powerplant: two 750-shp (560-kW) or 900-shp (671-kW) maximum contingency (uprated aircraft 1,050-shp/783-kW) Rolls-Royce BS.360-07-26 Gem turboshafts
Performance: maximum cruising speed 167 mph (269 km/h); maximum cruising speed (single-engine) 130 mph (209 km/h); radius of action, out and return at maximum cruising speed, crew of three, maximum hover weight 9,500 lb (4309 kg), take-off and landing allowances, 15-minute loiter in

The Westland Lynx HAS.2 will soon be the most important helicopter in the navies of NATO, perfectly suited to all-weather multi-role duties on surface vessels. This Lynx, armed with Mk 46 torpedoes, is about to leave HMS *Birmingham* in a gale.

Westland Lynx AH.1 (Army)

search area, 2-minute hover for each of two survivors, reserves for 20-minute loiter at end of mission 157 miles (253 km); maximum forward rate of climb 2,020 ft (616 m) per minute; maximum vertical rate of climb 1,235 ft (376 m) per minute
Weights: empty equipped (anti-submarine strike) 6,836 lb (3101 kg); empty equipped (reconnaissance) 6,794 lb (3082 kg); empty equipped (dunking-sonar search and strike) 7,515 lb (3409 kg); take-off (normal) 9,500 lb (4309 kg); take-off (maximum) 10,500 lb (4763 kg)
Dimensions: main rotor diameter 42 ft 0 in (12.8 m); length (rotors turning) 49 ft 9 in (15.16 m); height (tail rotor turning) 11 ft 9¾ in (36 m); main rotor disc area 1,385 sq ft (128.7 m²)
Armament: two Mk 44 or Mk 46 torpedoes; or two Mk 11 depth charges; dunking sonar; Sea Skua or AS.12 air-to-surface missiles (see text for more details)
Users: Argentina, Brazil, Denmark, Egypt, France, Netherlands, Norway, Qatar, UK, others

Westland Scout

History and notes

Production of this compact five/six-seat general-purpose helicopter ceased in 1970, but the type remains in service. Its main roles are liaison, casualty evacuation, air/sea rescue (although the Wasp is the truly naval variant), air-to-ground attack, reconnaissance, training and light freight work. Equipped as an air ambulance, the Scout carries two internal stretchers, and a further two can be carried on external panniers. Normal seating is for five, with three on a rear bench seat and two in the front.

Early prototypes were powered by a 325-shp (242-kW) Blackburn-Turboméca Turmo, derated from 400 shp (298 kW), but the production prototype flew with a Bristol Siddeley (now Rolls-Royce) Nimbus, which was derived from the Turmo and adopted for all subsequent examples. Originally a Saunders-Roe design, the Scout first flew on 20 July 1958, followed by the Nimbus-powered variant on 9 August 1959. The helicopter entered service with the British army in the spring of 1963, and some 120 examples are still operated by the Army Air Corps. One hundred Westland/Aérospatiale Lynx AH.1 general-purpose helicopters have supplemented and largely replaced them, and these larger, faster aircraft will carry TOW missiles for the anti-tank role. Forming part of the 400-strong Army Air Corps helicopter fleet, the Scouts have seen extensive duty in Northern Ireland on anti-terrorist duties. The AAC has put the Scout's versatility to wide use, the aircraft having filled almost every role except heavy lift: for anti-tank duty the Scout carries a roof-mounted sight and SS.11 missiles. Distinguishing features of the Scout against the maritime Wasp are a skid undercarriage and a low-set horizontal stabilizer under the tail rotor.

A number of Scouts were sold for export, including two to the Royal Australian Navy for operation from survey ships. Three went to the Jordanian air force, one for the personal use of King Hussein.

The Westland Scout AH.1, of which 120 were deployed, has been the British army's chief helicopter but is now being replaced by 100 Lynx. This Scout, XP897, has a new paint job and fin insignia, but lacks the pylons and roof sight for missiles.

The government of Uganda bought two for police work; and a further two went to the Bahrain State Police.

Specification

Type: (AH.1) five/six-seat general-purpose helicopter

Powerplant: one 685-shp (511-kW) Rolls-Royce Nimbus 102 free-turbine turboshaft

Performance: maximum design speed 132 mph (212 km/h); maximum cruising speed 122 mph (196 km/h); range (four passengers, reserves) 315 miles (510 km); maximum rate of climb 1,670 ft (510 m) per minute; vertical rate of climb at sea level 600 ft (183 m) per minute

Weights: empty equipped 3,232 lb (1465 kg); maximum 5,300 lb (2405 kg)

Dimensions: main rotor diameter 32 ft 3 in (9.83 m); length (rotors turning) 40 ft 4 in (12.29 m); fuselage length 30 ft 4 in (9.24 m); height (tail rotor turning) 11 ft 8 in (3.56 m); main-rotor disc area 816.86 sq ft (75.9 m^2)

Armament: manually-controlled guns of up to 20-mm calibre; fixed GPMG or other gun installations; rocket pods or guided missiles such as SS.11 anti-tank

Operators: Australia, Bahrain, Jordan, Uganda, UK

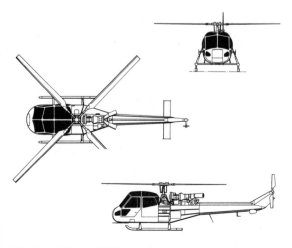

Westland Scout AH.1

and Sea King/Commando
so Sikorsky S-61A/B)

History and notes

The Westland Sea King, of which the first example for the Royal Navy made its initial flight on 7 May 1969, is usually dismissed as a licence-built version of the Sikorsky S-61/SH-3 Sea King. This simple and unvarnished statement has not really been acceptable to Westland Helicopters from the first occasion that it was used, because considerable development work was carried out by the British company to produce an advanced anti-submarine helicopter to meet the Royal Navy's requirements. The central factor was the inclusion of a tactical compartment so that ASW operations could proceed with no assistance from a ship or other platform. In addition to its basic ASW role, this aircraft was required also to fulfil such secondary roles as cargo transport, casualty evacuation, search and rescue, and tactical troop transport. Good ferry range was considered essential.

The original HAS.1 version for the Royal Navy was developed from four imported Sikorsky SH-3D airframes. Westland's licence agreement allowed utilisation of the basic airframe and rotor system, and in addition to the installation of two Rolls-Royce Gnome turboshaft engines and specialized avionics and equipment to satisfy the Royal Navy's requirements, numerous improvements have been made to the airframe and systems during 10 years of development. Production of the Sea King was continuing in 1979, and specialized equipment includes an advanced Newmark automatic flight-control system, Plessey 195 long-range sonar, doppler navigation radar, and AW.391 search radar.

The Commando, designed for tactical transport, assault, close support and rescue operations, has a fixed tailwheel landing gear, with the sponsons of the Sea King replaced by small stub wings. The revised fuselage accomodates a flight crew of two and up to 28 troops, and can be equipped to carry a wide range of guns and missiles in a secondary air-to-surface strike role.

Specification

Type: (Commando) tactical military helicopter
Powerplant: two 1,660-shp (1238-kW) Rolls-Royce Gnome H.1400-1 turboshafts

Westland Commando

Performance: (Commando) cruising speed at sea level 129 mph (208 km/h); range with maximum payload (28 troops), allowance for take-off and 30-minute reserves 276 miles (444 km); ferry range with maximum standard and auxiliary fuel 937 miles (1508 km)
Weights: (Commando) operating empty 12,566 lb (5700 kg); maximum take-off 21,000 lb (9525 kg)
Dimensions: (Commando) main-rotor diameter 62 ft 0 in (18.90 m); tail rotor diameter 10 ft 4 in (3.15 m); length (rotors turning) 72 ft 8 in (22.15 m); height 16 ft 10 in (5.13 m); main-rotor disc area 3,019 sq ft (280.5 m^2)
Armament: (Commando) can include guns, rocket pods, missiles, and avionics to customer's requirements
Operators: (Commando) Egypt, Qatar, UK; (Sea King) Australia, Belgium, Egypt, India, Norway, Pakistan, UK, West Germany

Though the transducer is not visible here the dunking sonar of this Royal Navy Sea king is probably a Plessey Type 195, which is also used by other navies.

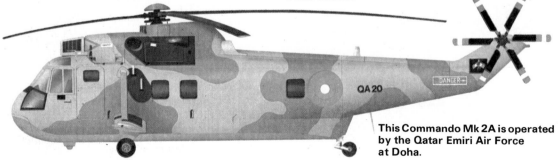

This Commando Mk 2A is operated by the Qatar Emiri Air Force at Doha.

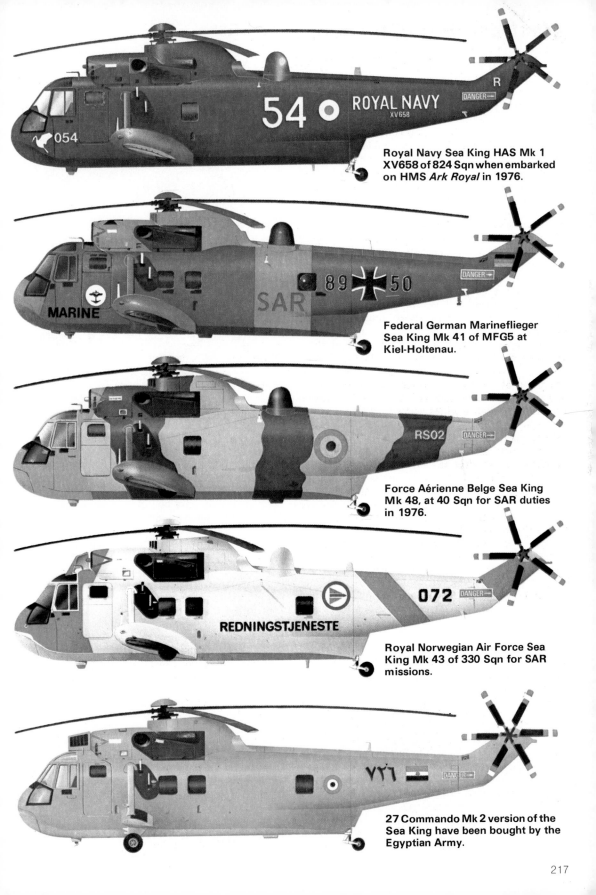

Royal Navy Sea King HAS Mk 1 XV658 of 824 Sqn when embarked on HMS *Ark Royal* in 1976.

Federal German Marineflieger Sea King Mk 41 of MFG5 at Kiel-Holtenau.

Force Aérienne Belge Sea King Mk 48, at 40 Sqn for SAR duties in 1976.

Royal Norwegian Air Force Sea King Mk 43 of 330 Sqn for SAR missions.

27 Commando Mk 2 version of the Sea King have been bought by the Egyptian Army.

Westland Wasp

History and notes

The Westland Wasp general-purpose naval helicopter was developed from the Scout for the Royal Navy. It originated in a Saunders-Roe design and differs from its land-based counterpart in having totally different equipment (for the anti-submarine warfare role), a more powerful engine, folding tail, and special landing gear for deck operations. This last consists of four non-retractable, fully castoring wheels with sprag brakes and special damping. Following an evaluation of three P.531s (the designation of pre-production Scouts), the Royal Navy ordered development and production of the Wasp HAS.1 for shipboard use. The first flew on 28 October 1962, and some 60 were subsequently bought. Their main role is to operate from small platforms on board frigates and destroyers on anti-submarine missions, for which they carry two Mk 44 torpedoes. The aircraft is also used aboard an ice patrol ship for ice reconnaissance and personnel ferrying work, as well as for survey. Deliveries to the Royal Navy began in the second half of 1963, after more than 200 landings had been made in February of that year on board the frigate *Nubian*. They were conducted with the wind coming from all directions, by day and by night, in a rigorous trials programme. Standard equipment fit on the Wasp includes UHF and UHF homing radio, plus a standby set, blind-flying instrumentation, and an autostabilization system/autopilot with radio altimeter. Royal Navy aircraft were later fitted with APX Bézu M.260 gyrostabilized periscopic weapon sights (for AS.11 or AS.12 missiles), licence-built by the Precision Products Group of BAC's Guided Weapons Division. The Wasp has a crew of two, with provision for three passengers or a stretcher across the rear of the cabin. In place of the two Mk 44 torpedoes, a variety of external stores can be carried. Well over 100 Wasps were built, some 40 for export. The South African air force operates 11 of the type. This country is the subject of an arms ban by several nations, and the country is as far as possible extending the useful lives of its current inventory to maintain an effective military posture. The 11 Wasps are deployed aboard a number of South African navy ships, serving with Maritime Command's 22 Flight in the anti-submarine-warfare and communication roles. Seventeen Wasps were ordered originally. The *Forca Aeronaval*, Brazil's naval air arm, has been a helicopter since the early 1950s, using the Westland Widgeon. This type was succeeded by two Wasps, a number augmented in 1977–78 with the delivery of a further six. They fly with a liaison and general-duties squadron alongside three Westland Whirlwind 3s and 18 Bell 206B JetRangers. The anti-submarine role will be filled by the Westland/Aérospatiale Lynx. Despite being surrounded by watér, New Zealand fields a very small truly naval air arm, in the form of two Wasps. When deployed they fly from the frigates HMNZS Canter-

This Westland Wasp HAS.1 probably belongs to No 829 Sqn, which supplies the aircraft for all Royal Navy frigates. Most Wasps can carry Mk 44 or 46 torpedoes and a few have AS.11s.

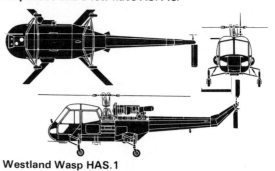

Westland Wasp HAS.1

bury and Waikato, but when shore-based they are operated by No 3 Sqn at Hobsonville. (Maritime patrol work is performed by the air force's five Lockheed P-3B Orions.) After South Africa, the Netherlands' Marine *Luchtvaartdienst* is the largest export operator of the type. Designated AH-12A, 10 are still flown No 860 Sqn, although they will be replaced by the uprated Lynx after 1983.

Specification

Type: five/six-seat general-purpose helicopter
Powerplant: one 710-shp (530-kW) Rolls-Royce Nimbus 503 turboshaft
Performance: maximum design speed 126 mph (203 km/h); maximum level speed at sea level 120 mph (193 km/h); maximum cruising speed 110 mph (177 km/h); range with maximum fuel, 5 minutes for take-off and landing, and four passengers 270 miles (435 km); maximum rate of climb at sea level 1,440 ft (439 m) per minute; maximum vertical rate of climb at sea level 600 ft (183 m) per minute
Weights: empty equipped 3,452 lb (1566 kg); maximum take-off and landing 5,500 lb (2495 kg)
Dimensions: main rotor diameter 32 ft 3 in (9.83 m); length (rotors turning) 40 ft 4 in (12.29 m); height (tail rotor turning) 11 ft 8 in (3.56 m); main rotor disc area 816.86 sq ft (75.9 m^2)
Armament: two Mk 44 torpedoes
Users: Brazil, Netherlands, New Zealand, South Africa, UK

Yakovlev Yak-28 Firebar/Brewer/Maestro

Soviet Air Force Yakovlev Yak-28P "Firebar" two-seat interceptor of the IAP-VO Strany. The type is now obsolete and is being phased out of use.

History and notes

Alexander Yakovlev's Yak-28 family of combat aircraft, similar in concept and performance to the French Sud-Ouest Vautour series, continues to fill an important role in the Soviet air arm, although the numbers in service are declining. The last to be retired will be the 'Brewer-E' ECM aircraft, with some Yak-28P 'Firebar-Es' carrying on in less strategically important areas of the Soviet periphery.

The current Yak-28s are direct descendants of the original Yak-25, developed from 1950 as the Soviet Union's first all-weather jet fighter. The layout of the Yak-25, with engines under the swept wings, was conventional and followed wartime German studies; it was one of the first aircraft to feature a 'zero-track tricycle' undercarriage, with a single twin-wheel main unit on the centre of gravity and single nose and outrigger wheels. Like the Mikoyan-Gurevich MiG-19, the Yak-25 was initially powered by Mikulin AM-5 engines, but most aircraft were fitted with the Tumansky RD-9. Developments of the Yak-25 included the Yak-25RD 'Mandrake', Yak-26 and Yak-27 'Mangrove'.

The Yak-28 series bears little relationship to these earlier aircraft, beyond a general similarity in configurations. Initially, the Yak-28 seems to have been developed as a transonic all-weather fighter using two of the Tumansky R-11 turbojets developed for the MiG-21, designed to carry a more effective radar and missile to turn the SU-9. The Yak-28's wing is more sharply swept than that of its predecessors and is raised from the mid to the shoulder position. The landing gear has a true bicycle layout, leaving space for a large weapons bay between the main units. On the Yak-28P interceptor this space is used for fuel; the strike version carries stores in the internal bay, and drop tanks on underwing stations.

Deliveries of the Yak-28P 'Firebar' started in 1962, and the type is still widely used by the PVO air-defence force. It offers considerably better endurance than the Sukhoi Su-15, which has similar engines but is lighter and much faster. Later Yak-28Ps, seen from 1967, have sharper and much longer nose radomes and provision for AA-2 'Atoll' short-range missiles on additional underwing pylons.

Developed in parallel with the Yak-28P was a glazed-nose strike version with a second crew member seated ahead of the pilot and a bombing-navigation radar aft of the nose landing gear. Originally codenamed 'Firebar' by NATO, the type

Yakovlev Yak-28P

was re-christened 'Brassard' when its bomber role became obvious, and the reporting name was then changed to 'Brewer' to avoid confusion with the French Holste Broussard.

The 'Brewer-C' was used as a replacement for the Ilyushin Il-28 in Soviet Frontal Aviation strike units, but was not supplied to any aligned nations. The presence of an internal weapons bay strongly suggests that its primary role was tactical nuclear strike; the small cross-section of the fuselage limits the load that can be carried internally, but the internal bay may have been necessary for the environmental control and arming of a nuclear weapon.

Specification

Type: Yak-28 'Brewer-C' strike; 'Brewer-D' reconnaissance; 'Brewer-E' electronic countermeasures (ECM); Yak-28P 'Firebar-8' all-weather interceptor; Yak-28U 'Maestro' two-seat conversion trainer

Powerplant: two 13,000-lb (6000-kg) Tumansky R-11 afterburning turbojets

Performance: maximum speed at medium altitude 750 mph (1200 km/h) or Mach 1.13; maximum speed at sea level Mach 0.85; service ceiling 55,000 ft (17000 m)

Weights: empty 30,000 lb (13600 kg); maximum loaded 45,000-50,000 lb (20000-22000 kg)

Dimensions: span 42 ft 6 in (12.95 m); length (except late 'Firebar') 71 ft (21.65 m); length (late 'Firebar') 76 ft (23.17 m); height 13 ft (3.95 m)

Armament: ('Brewer-C') one 30-mm NR-30 cannon plus underwing bombs or rocket pods and 4,500 lb (2000 kg) of internal stores; ('Firebar C') two AA-3 'Anab' air-to-air missiles and, on some aircraft, two AA-2 'Atoll' air-to-air missiles

Operators: USSR

Yakovlev Yak-36 Forger

History and notes

In the late 1960s US reconnaissance satellites revealed that the Nikolayev shipyards on the Black Sea were starting construction of a warship far bigger than the 'Moskva' class ASW helicopter cruisers. As work progressed, it became clear that the new ship was to be a compound of missile cruiser and aircraft-carrier, with an open angled flight-deck over more than half its length. The new ship, *Kiev*, the first of its class, was obviously designed to carry V/STOL aircraft as well as helicopters, and Western observers waited with interest for the *Kiev*'s first voyage in international waters.

Some indication of progress in V/STOL technology in the Soviet Union had already been given. In the late 1950s, a group of Soviet engineers flew a VTOL test rig called the Turbolet, a simple wingless machine intended, like the similar Rolls-Royce Flying Bedstead, to explore the problems of zero-airspeed reaction control systems. Some years later, the Kolesov engine bureau began to study the design of specialized lift engines.

The Yakovlev bureau became involved in the study of V/STOL airframes, and two examples of a small research aircraft of Yakovlev design were demonstrated at the Domodedovo air display in 1967. Codenamed 'Freehand' by NATO, the type appeared to be crude in comparison with Western designs; the third-generation BAe Harrier was at that time undergoing flight tests before entering RAF service, while the 'Freehand' appeared little more advanced than the Bell X-14 of 1957. The basic layout was awkward, with two engines in the forward fuselage feeding rear vectoring nozzles, and the type clearly had little space for operational equipment. At the same time, a number of conventional aircraft fitted with lift-jets were demonstrated, showing that considerable progress had been made in this area.

A considerable number of V/STOL prototypes appears to have been tested in the Soviet Union before the Yakovlev Yak-36 'Forger' design was selected for large-scale evaluation. The configuration is unique, with only two rear vectoring nozzles on the lift-cruise engine and two lift jets forward, and imposes some basic limitations on the design. The most important is that the Yak-36 is apparently unable to make a short take-off. The short take-off is the standard operating mode for the Harrier, and permits a substantial increase in payload: the aircraft rolls forward with nozzles aft for 200 ft (60 m), the nozzles are rotated partially down and the aircraft lifts off with a combination of wing and engine lift (with the 'ski jump' ramp the gains are even greater). The Yak-36 cannot emulate this performance because the thrust of its lift jets has to be balanced by full vectoring of the rear nozzles, and is limited to what can be achieved with a vertical lift-off. Other drawbacks of the layout include a far higher risk of engine failure (more than tripled, because the lift

engines are started twice as often as the cruise engine), this will usually result in loss of the aircraft because the Yak-36 cannot land with one engine out. Neither can the Yak-36 take advantage of an incidental benefit of the Harrier's V/STOL technique: the ability to use vectored thrust for air combat (Viffing).

Theoretical advantages of the 'Forger' layout include a cruise-matched main engine, but the improvement in efficiency is at least partly offset by the higher fuel consumption in transition. The 'Forger' is, however, notably stable in transition, and the smoothness of operational approaches to *Kiev* has led to speculation about precision ship-guidance.

When *Kiev* sailed into the Mediterranean in the summer of 1976, details of the Yak-36 became quickly apparent. She carried a small trials unit of about 12 Yak-36s, including two or three 'Forger-B' trainers with an ungainly lengthened forward fuselage and a balancing 'stretch' aft. The 'Forger-A' single-seaters were apparently pre-production aircraft, some being equipped with blow-in doors around the inlets and others lacking them. At the time of writing it appears that the aircraft embarked on *Minsk*, the second of the 'Kiev' class ships, are not greatly different from the *Kiev*'s aircraft; *Minsk* made her maiden voyage into the Mediterranean in early 1979. *Kharkov,* third of the class, was reported to be nearer commissioning in late 1979, with a fourth carrier under construction.

The avionic systems carried by the Yak-36 limit them to a clear-weather role; the only weapon-aiming system is apparently a small ranging radar in the extreme nose. Although the aircraft on *Kiev* carry AA-8 'Aphid' missiles and gun pods, the unit seems to be concerned mainly with operational trials of VTOL operating techniques and control systems.

In the absence of any consensus on what the Kiev-class ships are intended to do, it is difficult to define the role of the Yak-36. If it is intended for point air defence against, for example, Harpoon-carrying Lockheed P-3s, its present performance may be adequate and the main modification needed would be the addition of air-to-air radar; if it is regarded as a multi-role aircraft in the class of the BAe Sea Harrier, however, it will probably be necessary greatly to increase its payload and offensive capability. The Soviet Union almost certainly intends to develop a completely new aircraft which can exploit the angled flight-decks of the 'Kiev' class by means of a rolling take-off.

Specification

Type: light VTOL shipboard strike fighter
Powerplant: one 16,500-lb (7500-kg) class lift/cruise engine (possibly a relative of the Tumansky R-27/R-29 series) and two 5,500-lb (2500-kg) Kolesov lift jets

Yakovlev Yak-36 Forger

This Yak-36 was seen aboard the carrier *Kiev*, first of her class, on her initial cruise from July 1976. It is probably that of the CO of the embarked jet VTOL unit, which was undoubtedly of an evaluation and indoctrination status. Operationally this aircraft, in either single-seat or dual form, is limited in roles, though it can carry gun pods, rockets and short-range air-to-air missiles.

Performance: maximum speed at 36,000 ft (11000 m) 800 mph (1280 km/h) or Mach 1.2; maximum speed at sea level 650 mph (1050 km/h) or Mach 0.85; service ceiling 46,000 ft (14000 m); combat radius 150 miles (250 km)

Dimensions: span 23 ft (7.0 m); length 49 ft 2 in (15.0 m); height 10 ft 6 in (3.2 m); wing area 170 sq ft (15.8 m²)

Armament: four external pylons for up to 2,200 lb (1000 kg) of stores, including AA-8 'Aphid' air-to-air missiles and gun pods

Operator: USSR

INDEX

INDEX